Unlock the Bible:
Keys to Exploring the Culture and Times

Other Unlock the Bible Titles

Unlock the Bible: Keys to Understanding the Scripture

Unlock the Bible: Keys to Exploring the People and Places

Unlock the Bible

Keys to Exploring
the Culture and Times

General Editor
Ronald F. Youngblood

General Editor of Original Edition
Herbert Lockyer Sr.

Consulting Editors
F. F. Bruce   R. K. Harrison

THOMAS NELSON
Since 1798

NASHVILLE   DALLAS   MEXICO CITY   RIO DE JANEIRO

Published in Nashville, Tennessee, by Thomas Nelson. Thomas Nelson is a registered trademark of Thomas Nelson, Inc.

Book design and composition by Upper Case Textual Services, Lawrence, Massachusetts.

Thomas Nelson, Inc., titles may be purchased in bulk for educational, business, fund-raising, or sales promotional use. For information, please e-mail SpecialMarkets@ThomasNelson.com.

978-1-4185-4726-4

Printed in the United States of America

12 11 10 09 08 RRD 05 04 03 02 01

Contents

Contributors xiii

A

Abib 1
Ablution 1
Acco 2
Acropolis 3
Adriatic 3
Age 3
Alexandria 3
Amalekites 5
Ammonites 6
Amorites 6
Antediluvians 8
Antonia, Tower of 8
Apostolic Age 9
Apostolic Council 9
Aqueduct 9
Arabia 10
Arameans 12
Archaeology of the Bible 13
Areopagus 27
Armageddon 28
Army 28
Asher, Tribe of 30
Assyria 31
Augustan Regiment 34

B

Babylonia 35
Banking 37
Battle 38
Battlement 38
Benjamin, Tribe of 38

C

Calendar 40
Canaanites 46
Captivity 49
Cavalry 52
Census. 53
Chaldeans 53
Chislev 55
Christianity 55
Chronology, New Testament 57
Chronology, Old Testament. 64
Clay Tablets 72
Commerce 72
Creed 73
Crete. 75
Crucifixion of Christ. 75
Cuneiform 76
Cyprus. 77

D

Dan, Tribe of 79
Dead Sea 80
Decapolis 83
Dispensation 83
Dispersion 84
Dispersion of the Nations 87

E

Easter 88

Egypt, History of 88

Elamites 95

Elul 97

Ephraim, Tribe of .97

Exodus, The. 98

F

Famine 101

Farm, Farming 102

Feasts and Festivals 103

Flood, The 110

Future 114

G

Gad, Tribe of 115

Gezer 115

Gnosticism 116

Greece 119

H

Hammurapi, Code of 121

Harvest 123

Hebrew People 123

Hellenism 125

Herodians 125

High Places 126

History 127

Hittites 127

Hivites 129

I

Innocents, Slaughter of 130
Insurrection 130
Israel, History of 130
Issachar, Tribe of 145
Italian Regiment 146

J

Jebusites 147
Jews 148
Jordan 148
Judah, Tribe of 151
Judaizers 152
Judea 152

L

Lachish 154
Lebanon 155
Legion 157
Levites 157
Levitical Cities 160
Lord's Day 162

M

Macedonia 164
Manasseh, Tribe of 165
Marheshvan 166
Media 166
Mediterranean Sea 168
Memphis 169
Metals of the Bible 169
Midianites 171
Millennium, The 173

Millo. 174
Minerals of the Bible. 174
Mithraism. 188
Moabite Stone 188
Money of the Bible. 189
Month 194
Morning. 194
Mystery Religions 194

N

Nabatea 196
Naphtali, Tribe of. 197
Nations 198
Navy. 199
Nebuchadnezzar 199
New Age. 201
New Year 201
Nicolaitans 201
Nile 202
Nineveh 204
No, No Amon. 207

O

Ophel 208

P

Palestine. 209
Parthians 223
Persepolis 223
Persia 224
Petra 227
Pharisees 227
Philistia 231
Philistines. 231

Phoenicia 235
Phoenicians 235
Plagues of Egypt 238
Plants of the Bible 242
Praetorium, Praetorian Guard 263
Preparation Day 264
Purim 265

R

Rameses, Raamses 266
Red Sea 266
Release, Year of 269
Reuben, Tribe of 269
Roman Empire 270
Roman Law 275
Rome, City of 276

S

Sabbath 279
Sabbatical Year 282
Sadducees 282
Samaria, Region of 285
Samaritans 286
Sanhedrin 289
Science 291
Scythians 291
Second Coming 292
Shebat 292
Sidon 292
Siege 294
Siloam 295
Simeon, Tribe of 296
Sivan 297
Stoicism 297
Sumer 298
Synagogue 299

Syria 303
Syrians. 305

T

Tabernacle 308
Tax, Taxes 313
Temple. 315
Tiberias 326
Time. 327
Tishri 329
Tools of the Bible. 329
Trade and Travel 342
Transjordan. 345
Tribulation, The Great. 345
Tyre 345
Tyropoeon Valley 348

U

Ur 349

W

Wadi. 351
War, Warfare 351
Watch 354
Week. 355
Weights and Measures of the Bible. 355
Winter. 362
Winter House. 362

Y

Yarmuk 363
Year 363
YHWH 363

Z

Zealot 365
Zebulun, Tribe of. 366
Ziggurat 367
Ziv 367
Zoroastrianism 367

Contributors

Robert L. Alden
    Conservative Baptist Seminary, Denver, Colorado
Leslie C. Allen
    Fuller Theological Seminary, Pasadena, California
Ronald B. Allen
    Christian Theological Seminary, Indianapolis, Indiana
Timothy R. Ashley
    Acadia Divinity College, Wolfville, Nova Scotia, Canada
David W. Baker
    Ashland Theological Seminary, Ashland, Ohio
John J. Bimson
    Trinity College, Bristol, England
E. M. Blaiklock
    Auckland, New Zealand
Gerald Borchert
    Southern Baptist Theological Seminary, Louisville, Kentucky
Stephen G. Brown
    Shasta Bible College, Redding, California
F. F. Bruce
    University of Manchester, Manchester, England
John A. Burns
    Retired from Criswell Center for Biblical Studies, Dallas, Texas
Newton L. Bush
    Lima, Ohio
G. Lloyd Carr
    Retired from Gordon College, Wenham, Massachusetts
E. Clark Copeland
    Reformed Presbyterian Theological Seminary, Pittsburgh, Pennsylvania

Leonard J. Coppes
  Denver, Colorado

Walter M. Dunnett
  Retired from Northwestern College, St. Paul, Minnesota

Kendell H. Easley
  Mid-America Baptist College, Memphis, Tennessee

Kermit A. Ecklebarger
  Conservative Baptist Seminary, Denver, Colorado

James R. Edwards
  Jamestown College, Jamestown, North Dakota

John M. Elliott
  Aurora, Illinois

Millard J. Erickson
  Bethel Theological Seminary, St. Paul, Minnesota

Harvey E. Finley
  Retired from Nazarene Theological Seminary, Kansas City, Missouri

Royce G. Gruenler
  Gordon-Conwell Theological Seminary, South Hamilton, Massachusetts

Timothy Hadley
  Lubbock Christian University, Lubbock, Texas

Donald A. Hagner
  Fuller Theological Seminary, Pasadena, California

R. K. Harrison
  Wycliffe College, Toronto, Ontario, Canada

Harvey Hartman
  Liberty Baptist College, Lynchburg, Virginia

Robert Hendren
  Donelson, Tennessee

Herschel H. Hobbs
  Oklahoma City, Oklahoma

Harold W. Hoehner
  Dallas Theological Seminary, Dallas, Texas

John J. Hughes
  Whitefish, Montana

Robert Hughes
  Miami Christian College, Miami, Florida

Harry B. Hunt Jr.
  Southwestern Baptist Theological Seminary, Fort Worth, Texas

W. Bingham Hunter
  Trinity Evangelical Divinity School, Deerfield, Illinois

David K. Huttar
    Nyack College, Nyack, New York
William W. Klein
    Conservative Baptist Seminary, Denver, Colorado
Woodrow M. Kroll
    Back to the Bible, Lincoln, Nebraska
Alvin S. Lawhead
    Nazarene Theological Seminary, Kansas City, Missouri
Gordon Lewis
    Conservative Baptist Seminary, Denver, Colorado
Jack P. Lewis
    Harding Graduate School of Religion, Memphis, Tennessee
Walter L. Liefeld
    Trinity Evangelical Divinity School, Deerfield, Illinois
G. Herbert Livingston
    Retired from Asbury Theological Seminary, Wilmore, Kentucky
Tremper Longman, III
    Westminster Theological Seminary, Philadelphia, Pennsylvania
Robert S. MacLennan
    McAlester College, St. Paul, Minnesota
W. Harold Mare
    Covenant Theological Seminary, St. Louis, Missouri
Elmer A. Martens
    Mennonite Brethren Biblical Seminary, Fresno, California
Wayne O. McCready
    University of Calgary, Alberta, Canada
Scot McKnight
    Trinity Evangelical Divinity School, Deerfield, Illinois
Janet McNish
    Nashville, Tennessee
Robert R. Moore
    Asbury College, Wilmore, Kentucky
William Mounce
    Azusa Pacific College, Azusa, California
John Nolland
    Regent College, Vancouver, British Columbia, Canada
Dave O'Brien
    St. Paul Bible College, Bible College, Minnesota
Vernon S. Olson
    St. Bonifacius, Minnesota

Grant R. Osborne
    Trinity Evangelical Divinity School, Deerfield, Illinois

Mildred Ottinger
    Nashville, Tennessee

Arthur G. Patzia
    Fuller Seminary, Pasadena, California

Gary Pratico
    Gordon-Conwell Divinity School, South Hamilton, Massachusetts

Richard A. Purdy
    West Norwalk, Connecticut

Robert V. Rakestraw
    The Criswell College, Dallas, Texas

John Rasko
    Alaska Bible College, Glennallen, Alaska

Richard O. Rigsby
    Talbot Theological Seminary, La Mirada, California

Allen P. Ross
    Dallas Theological Seminary, Dallas, Texas

Glenn E. Schaefer
    Simpson College, San Francisco, California

Stephen R. Schrader
    Liberty Baptist Seminary, Lynchburg, Virginia

Jack B. Scott
    Decatur, Georgia

Martin J. Selman
    Spurgeon's College, London, England

Norman Shepherd
    Minneapolis, Minnesota

Gary V. Smith
    Bethel Theological Seminary, St. Paul, Minnesota

Douglas K. Stuart
    Gordon-Conwell Theological Seminary, South Hamilton, Massachusetts

Robert L. Thomas
    Talbot Theological Seminary, La Mirada, California

Willem A. VanGemeren
    Reformed Theological Seminary, Jackson, Mississippi

Dolores Walker
    Walla Walla, Washington

Larry L. Walker
    Mid-America Baptist Seminary, Memphis, Tennessee

Daniel B. Wallace
>   Mukilteo, Washington

Forest Weddle
>   Fort Wayne Bible College, Fort Wayne, Indiana

Tom Wells
>   Cincinnati, Ohio

Stephen Westerholm
>   Toronto, Ontario, Canada

Frederick E. Young
>   Central Baptist Seminary, Kansas City, Kansas

Ronald F. Youngblood
>   Bethel Theological Seminary, West San Diego, California

ABIB [A bibb] (*sprouting* or *budding*) — one of the months of the Hebrew calendar (corresponding to our March–April). On the 15th of this month, the people of Israel left Egypt. Abib was made the first month of the year in commemoration of the Exodus (Ex. 23:15; Deut. 16:1). The Passover and the Feast of Unleavened Bread were celebrated during the month of Abib. After the captivity, the month was called Nisan (Neh. 2:1; Esth. 3:7).

ABLUTION — the ceremonial washing of one's body, vessels, and clothing for the purpose of religious purification. This word is not found in the NKJV, but it occurs in Hebrews 6:2 and 9:10 in the RSV. In both places the Greek word is *baptismos* (literally, "dipping"), which can be translated "washings" (Heb. 9:10). Ablutions have nothing to do with washing one's body for sanitary or hygienic purposes. Rather, these were performed in order to remove ritual defilement. Some of the causes of ritual uncleanness in Bible times were bloodshed (Lev. 17), childbirth (Lev. 12), sexual intercourse (Lev. 18), leprosy (Lev. 12), menstruation (Lev. 15), and contact with dead bodies (Num. 19). At Mount Sinai, the Israelites were told to wash (literally, "trample") their clothes in preparation for worship (Ex. 19:10,

14). Similarly, the Levites as well as Aaron and his sons were prepared for service by washing their clothes and their bodies (Ex. 12–13). By New Testament times, ceremonial washings became almost an end in themselves. The Pharisees were preoccupied with ritual purifications (Matt. 15:2; Mark 7:4). Jesus exhorted the scribes and Pharisees to "cleanse the inside of the cup and dish"—that is, cleanse their hearts and spirits—and not just wash the outside by religious rituals. Moral filth cannot be washed away with physical cleansing agents (Jer. 2:22; Is. 1:16). Jesus Christ is to be praised, for He "loved us and washed us from our sins in His own blood" (Rev. 1:5; 7:14).

ACCO [ACK coe] — a city of Canaan on the Mediterranean coast about 40 kilometers (25 miles) south of Tyre and about 15 kilometers (9 miles) north of Mount Carmel. Situated on the north shore of a broad bay, Acco was at the entrance to the rich, fertile plain of Jezreel. Although Acco was located in the portion of land assigned to the tribe of Asher, the Hebrews were never able to drive out the original Canaanite inhabitants (Judg. 1:31; Accho, KJV).

Acco was mentioned in the Amarna letters of the 14th century B.C. In the Hellenistic period the name was changed to Ptolemais. It came under Roman domination in 65 B.C. Acco is mentioned only once in the New Testament and then as Ptolemais (Acts 21:7), the name coming from Ptolemy, the king of Egypt who rebuilt the city. Sailing from Tyre to Caesarea at the end of his third missionary journey, the apostle Paul docked at Ptolemais and spent the day with his fellow Christians while his ship was anchored in the harbor.

During the Crusades, Ptolemais recaptured some of its former prominence under the name Acre, by which name it is still known today. Its importance has once again waned, being overshadowed by the city of Haifa, which lies directly across the bay.

The apostle Paul visited Acco after he returned from his third missionary journey (Acts 21:7).

ACROPOLIS [uh CROP oh lis] (*topmost city*) — an elevated, fortified part of an ancient Greek city, such as Athens, Philippi, and Corinth. The Acropolis of Athens, the most famous acropolis of all ancient cities, was located on a hill about 500 feet high. It was adorned with stunning architectural works. Among these works was the Parthenon, a magnificent temple with 8 Doric columns in front and rear and 17 along each side.

ADRIATIC [a drih AT ick] — a name for the central part of the Mediterranean Sea south of Italy. It is mentioned in Luke's account of Paul's voyage to Rome (Acts 27:27). Paul's courage in the midst of this terrible storm is an inspiration: "Do not be afraid ... for I believe God" (Acts 27:24–25). The Greek geographer Strabo (63 B.C.?–A.D. 24?) identified the Adriatic as the Gulf of Adria, pointing out that the name comes from the old Etruscan city of Atria. The KJV translates as Adria.

AGE — an aeon; a specified period of time during which certain related events come to pass. As used in the New Testament, age generally refers to the present era, as opposed to the future age. According to the apostle Paul, Satan is "the god of this age" (2 Cor. 4:4). But the age to come will belong to Jesus Christ and His rule of justice and righteousness (Heb. 6:5).

ALEXANDRIA [eh leg ZAN drih uh] — the capital of Egypt during the Greek and Roman periods. Situated on the Mediterranean Sea at the western edge of the Nile delta, the city was established by Alexander the Great when he conquered Egypt in 331 B.C. After Alexander's death, the capital of Egypt was moved from Memphis to Alexandria, and it became one of the most significant cities of the Greek Empire. The population of Alexandria included native Egyptians, learned Greeks, and many Jews. The commercial strength of the city was aided by the famous towering lighthouse (one of the Seven Wonders of the ancient world) that guided ships into port. Paul himself sailed in an Alexandrian ship on his way to Rome (Acts 27:6; 28:11).

As a cultural center, Alexandria had a large museum and a library that attracted many scholars and writers. These learned people carried out research to establish accurate versions of the important Greek myths and epics as well as scientific investigations in astronomy, botany, and mathematics. One of the results of these interests was the commissioning of 70 (or 72) Jewish scholars to translate the Old Testament from Hebrew to Greek. The translation they produced is known as the Septuagint.

Philo and other learned Jews in Alexandria wrote many books in defense of the Jewish faith to show that their beliefs were consistent with Greek philosophical thinking. This sometimes resulted in unusual methods of interpretation because the literal understanding of Scripture often was mixed with fanciful explanations—a type of interpretation known as allegory. A Christian school of thought that used the allegorical method grew up in Alexandria, led by such great church fathers as Clement and Origen.

Apollos, a believer from Alexandria, who worked with the church at Corinth after it was founded by the apostle Paul, may have attended one of these early schools. The book of Acts describes Apollos as one who was well versed in the Scriptures (Acts 18:24). Because the book of Hebrews reflects thinking that is similar to writings from Alexandria, some scholars believe Apollos may have written the book.

The early church father Eusebius recorded the tradition that John Mark was one of the first missionaries who brought the message of Christ to the people of Alexandria. Years earlier, prominent Jews from Alexandria who gathered in Jerusalem strongly opposed Stephen's preaching about Christ (Acts 6:9).

Of the many Alexandrias that Alexander the Great founded and named after himself, the one in Egypt outshines them all. It remains a thriving city to this day.

A MALEKITES [AM uh leck ites] — an ancient wandering tribe descended from Esau's grandson Amalek (Gen. 36:12, 16; 1 Chr. 1:36). The main territory of the Amalekites was in the Sinai peninsula and in the Negev, the southern part of present-day Israel. But they roamed widely throughout the territory later settled by the people of Israel. Throughout the Old Testament period the Amalekites were bitter foes of the Israelites.

The Amalekites are first mentioned in the time of Abraham, when a group of kings under the leadership of Chedorlaomer defeated Amalek (Gen. 14:7). At the time of Israel's journey through the wilderness, the Amalekites lived in the southern part of the land promised to Israel. The Amalekites attacked the Israelites, but Joshua later defeated them in a battle at Rephidim (Ex. 17:8–16). Because of their treacherous attacks, Moses declared that God would continually wage war against them (Ex. 17:14–16).

During the period of the judges, the Amalekites joined forces with the Ammonites and Eglon, king of Moab, to attack and capture Jericho (Judg. 3:13). Along with the Midianites and the people of the East, they were defeated in the Valley of Jezreel by Gideon's army (Judg. 6:3, 33; 7:12–22). Eventually the Amalekites gained a mountain in the land of Ephraim. King Saul of Israel won this area back and then chased the Amalekites from the land (1 Sam. 14:48; 15:1–9). But Saul did not destroy the rich booty of livestock as God commanded, and so he was rebuked by the prophet Samuel (1 Sam. 15:10–33).

The Amalekites continued to raid Israel. David attacked and defeated them (1 Sam. 27:8–10), but they countered by raiding Ziklag and carrying off two of David's wives. He pursued and defeated them (1 Sam. 30:1–31), executing one of them for claiming to have killed Saul in battle (2 Sam. 1:1–16).

In the days of Hezekiah, 500 men of the tribe of Simeon defeated the Amalekites. Consequently, the Simeonites took their land and the Amalekites became a dispossessed people (1 Chr. 4:39–43).

AMMONITES [AM **muhn ites**] — a nomadic race descended from Ben–Ammi, Lot's son, who became enemies of the people of Israel during their later history. During the days of the Exodus, the Israelites were instructed by God not to associate with the Ammonites (Deut. 23:3). No reason is given in the Bible for such hostility, but the rift between the two peoples continued across several centuries.

In the days of the judges, Eglon, king of Moab, enlisted the aid of the Ammonites in taking Jericho from the Hebrew people (Judg. 3:13). In Saul's time, Nahash, the Ammonite king, attacked Jabesh Gilead. Saul responded to the call for help and saved the people of Jabesh Gilead from being captured by Nahash (1 Sam. 11:1–11).

Later in the history of the Israelites, Ammonites were among the armies allied against King Jehoshaphat; God caused confusion among them, and they destroyed themselves (2 Chr. 20:1–23). The prophets of the Old Testament often pronounced God's judgment against the Ammonites (Jer. 9:26; Amos 1:13–15). Archaeological evidence suggests that Ammonite civilization continued from about 1200 B.C. to 600 B.C.

AMORITES [AM **oh rites**] (*Westerners*) — the inhabitants of the land west of the Euphrates River, which included Canaan, Phoenicia, and Syria. The Amorites were one of the major tribes, or national groups, living in Canaan. The Old Testament frequently uses "Amorites" as a synonym for Canaanites in general. The book of Genesis cites Canaan as the ancestor of the Amorites (Gen. 10:16).

Shortly before 2000 B.C., the Amorites lived in the wilderness regions of what today is western Saudi Arabia and southern Syria. In the court records of Accad and Sumer they were known as barbarians, or uncivilized people. Beginning about 2000 B.C., Amorites migrated eastward to Babylonia in large numbers. There they captured major cities and regions from the native Mesopotamians. "Abram" is an Amorite name, and Abraham himself may have been an Amorite.

Throughout Old Testament times, other Amorites remained in Syria, Phoenicia, and the desert regions to the south (Josh. 13:4). A significant number, however, settled in the land of Canaan itself, eventually occupying large areas both east and west of the Jordan River (Judg. 11:19–22). These Amorites spoke a dialect that was closely related to Canaanite and Hebrew. Occasionally, the Amorites were identified as a Canaanite tribe (Gen. 10:16). At other times they were called the people of Canaan (Deut. 1:27).

When Israel invaded Canaan under Joshua, the first Israelite victories came against the Amorite kings Sihon and Og, who ruled much of the promised land east of the Jordan River (Josh. 12:1–6). Various cities west of the Jordan—Jerusalem, Hebron, Jarmuth, Lachish, and Eglon—also were called "Amorite" cities (Josh. 10:5), even though Jerusalem was also known as a Jebusite city.

While conquering Canaan, the Israelites frequently fought with the Amorites. After the Israelites prevailed, the Amorites who had not been killed remained in Canaan and became servants to the Israelites (1 Kin. 9:20–21).

Much of our knowledge about the Amorites and their culture comes from clay tablets discovered at Mari, a major Amorite city situated on the Euphrates River in western Mesopotamia.

ANTEDILUVIANS — the people who lived before the Flood. They possessed some skills that compare with modern technology. For example, Cain built cities (Gen. 4:17), Jubal was a musician (Gen. 4:21), and Tubal-Cain was an "instructor of every craftsman in bronze and iron" (Gen. 4:22). Such crafts imply the skills to mine, smelt, and purify copper and iron. That Noah could construct his huge ark is witness to the engineering skills and tools that were available. The antediluvians also lived long lives (Gen. 5:5–31).

Before the Flood, sin was rampant. Life was marked by disobedience, murder, and immorality: "The earth also was corrupt before God, and the earth was filled with violence" (Gen. 6:11). Humanity's spiritual condition was appalling.

Both Noah and Enoch preached to the antediluvians (2 Pet. 2:5; Jude 14–15). Their preaching, however, was not heeded, and the sinful world was destroyed by the Flood. Noah was the only righteous man whom God could find on the entire earth at the time: "Noah was a just man, perfect in his generations. Noah walked with God" (Gen. 6:9).

In the New Testament, Jesus compared the antediluvians—who were "eating and drinking, marrying and giving in marriage"—to the people who will be living in the end times (Matt. 24:37–41). His words point to the need for watchfulness, for "as it was in the days of Noah, so it will be in the days of the Son of Man" (Luke 17:26).

ANTONIA, TOWER OF [an TONE ih ah] — a fortress-palace rebuilt by Herod the Great and situated at the northwest corner of the temple area. Herod named the rebuilt tower after his friend, Mark Antony. The fortress was rectangular in shape, measuring about 165 meters (490 feet) by 87 meters (260 feet), with walls about 19 meters (60 feet) high. Each corner had a high tower, three of which were 24 meters (75 feet) high. The tower in the northwest corner, which overlooked the temple area, however, was about 32 meters (100 feet) high. Stairs connected the Antonia with the temple area (see Acts 21:35, 40). Soldiers from the Antonia ("the barracks") rescued the apostle Paul from enraged crowds on several occasions (Acts 21:27–36; 22:24; 23:10). Paul was held in the fortress in protective custody until a military escort took him to Caesarea (Acts 23:12–24, 31–35).

APOSTOLIC AGE — that period of church history when the apostles were alive, beginning with the Day of Pentecost (about A.D. 30) and ending near the conclusion of the first century (about A.D. 100) with the death of the apostle John. During the apostolic age, all the books of the New Testament were written, including the four Gospels, the book of Acts, the letters of Paul, the general letters, and the book of Revelation.

APOSTOLIC COUNCIL — the assembly of apostles and elders of the New Testament church in Jerusalem (A.D. 50). This council considered the question of whether Gentiles had to be circumcised and keep certain other laws of the Jewish faith in order to be members of the church (Acts 15). This assembly decided that a Gentile does not first have to become a Jew in order to be a Christian.

AQUEDUCT — a channel for transporting water from a remote source to a city. Israel's climate provides abundant rainfall in the winter months, but there is seldom any rain from May to October. This, along with the scarcity of good water supplies, made it necessary to build artificial storage areas to catch the winter rains. Elaborate systems of stone and masonry aqueducts and storage pools were sometimes constructed to bring water from the hill country to the cities and larger towns.

The best-known biblical accounts of the building of an aqueduct occur in 2 Kings 20:20 and 2 Chronicles 32:30. King Hezekiah of Judah had a tunnel dug under the city of Jerusalem to bring water from the spring outside the city to the Siloam reservoir inside the city wall. Across part of the course the workmen cut a tunnel through solid rock to complete the aqueduct. "Hezekiah's Tunnel" is still a major tourist attraction in Jerusalem.

"Solomon's Pools" near Bethlehem are part of an ancient aqueduct system that brought water from the hills south of Jerusalem into the temple area. During his administration, Pontius Pilate, Roman prefect of Judea, built an aqueduct to bring water to Jerusalem. Some scholars suggest that the Tower of Siloam (Luke 13:4) that fell and killed 18 people may have been part of that building project.

ARABIA [uh RAY bih uh] — the large peninsula east of Egypt, between the Red Sea and the Persian Gulf. About 1,300 kilometers (800 miles) wide and 2,300 kilometers (1,400 miles) long, Arabia is nearly one-third the size of the United States. It has almost no rainfall except along the coast, where it measures about 51 centimeters (20 inches) per year. There is only one river and one lake in the entire peninsula. Although a sudden shower may create a short-lived stream, most of the water in Arabia comes from deep wells or desert oases. Consequently, there is little agricultural activity on the peninsula.

The Arabian peninsula is a sandy, rocky desert with high mountain ranges on the western and southern coasts. The western mountains reach a height of 3,660 meters (12,000 feet) and show some evidence of past volcanic activity. Because of this volcanic activity, a few scholars have suggested that Mount Sinai was located in the western region of this mountain range.

However, the traditional site at the southern end of the Sinai Peninsula is much more likely. Much of the sandy interior of Arabia is uninhabited, although there is barely enough grass on the lower mountain slopes to support its nomadic population. In addition to its lack of water, the desert was known for its sandstorms driven by violent winds (Job 1:19; 27:20–21).

The queen of Sheba came from Arabia, bringing gold, spices, and precious stones to Solomon (1 Kin. 10:2, 10, 14; 2 Chr. 9:1, 9, 14). Solomon and other kings sent their ships to Ophir in Arabia to bring back gold (1 Kin. 9:28; 2 Chr. 9:10). Ophir, Raamah, and Sheba were famous for their gold, silver, and precious stones (Job 22:24; Is. 13:12; Ezek. 27:22).

The people who lived in Arabia included the children of Joktan (Gen. 10:26–30), Cush (Gen. 10:7), the sons of Abraham and Keturah (Gen. 25:1–6), and Esau (Gen. 36). The "country of the east" (Gen. 25:6) is probably a reference to Arabia. The early history of many of these peoples is unknown. Israel's earliest contacts with the inhabitants of Arabia probably came through their camel caravans. Some of them oppressed the Israelites during the time of the judges, but God delivered Israel from them by raising up the judge Gideon (Judg. 6:11).

David subdued some of the Arabian tribes that were close to Israel (2 Sam. 8:3–14), and Solomon established extensive trade relations with more distant tribes in Arabia to obtain their gold for his building projects (1 Kin. 9:28; 10:2, 11). Jehoshaphat, king of Judah, received rams and goats from the Arabians as tribute (2 Chr. 17:10–12), but after his death they revolted and refused to pay tribute to his son Jehoram. Instead, they invaded Jerusalem and carried away Jehoram's wealth, his wives, and all but his youngest son (2 Chr. 21:16–17).

Most of the tribes of southern and eastern Arabia were not well known to Israel. Joel referred to the slave-trading Sabeans [Shebaites] as a people who lived far away (Joel 3:8). Isaiah pictured the Arabians wandering as far east as Babylon (Is. 13:19,

20. Tribes that lived closer—those at Tema, Dedan, and Kedar—were included in Isaiah's prophecies of judgment against the foreign nations (Is. 21:13-17). Jeremiah also announced God's judgment upon Dedan, Tema, Buz, Kedar, Hazor, and all the kings of Arabia (Jer. 25:23-24; 49:28-33).

Although most of Israel's knowledge of the Arabians and their habits (Jer. 3:2) was due to a passing association with their caravan traders (Ezek. 27:21), some Arabians eventually settled in Palestine. While attempting to rebuild the walls of Jerusalem, Nehemiah struggled against Geshem the Arab, who scorned and despised the Jews (Neh. 2:19). When this tactic failed to discourage the work on Jerusalem's walls, the Arabs, Ammonites, Ashdodites, and others planned to attack the city by force (Neh. 4:7-13). When this strategy also failed, Sanballat, Tobiah, and Geshem the Arab set a trap to lure Nehemiah out of the city and kill him (Neh. 6:1-7). Nehemiah prayed for guidance, and God delivered him from this plot.

It is likely that Job was from Arabia. Uz, the home of Job (Job 1:1), appears to be named after a descendant of Esau and the Edomites (Gen. 36:28; Lam. 4:21). Eliphaz, one of Job's comforters, was from Teman, a city in Arabia (Job 2:11). Bands of Sabeans [Shebaites] and Chaldeans were close enough to attack Job's cattle (Job 1:15, 17). A great desert wind destroyed the house of Job's children (Job 1:19). The dialogue between Job and his comforters is filled with desert imagery and animals (Job 39).

ARAMEANS [AIR ah mee unz] — an ancient desert people who flourished along with the Israelites during much of their history, sometimes as enemies and sometimes as friends. The region of the Arameans, the land of Aram, extended from the Lebanon Mountains on the west eastward to the Euphrates River and from the Taurus Mountains on the north southward to Damascus. Arameans were among the ancient peoples who settled the Near East as early as 2250 B.C. They were fully established as a separate kingdom by the 12th century B.C., which made their history parallel with Israel's.

The Arameans made their presence felt internationally during the time of the judges, when they existed in large numbers in the region east of the Jordan River. An Aramean ruler, Cushan-Rishathaim, overran the land of Israel and oppressed it for eight years (Judg. 3:8–10).

In later years, David extended the boundary of Israel to the Euphrates River by subduing the Aramean rulers Hadadezer of Zobah and Toi of Hamath (2 Sam. 8:1–13). But a third Aramean official, Rezon, fled to Damascus and founded a strong Aramean city-state there (1 Kin. 11:23–24). This city-state was Israel's bitter foe for many generations.

Between quarrels and hostilities, there were times when either the nation of Judah or the nation of Israel was allied with Aram against a common foe. Judah and Aram were allied with each other against Israel (1 Kin. 15:18–20); Israel and Aram were allies against Judah (2 Kin. 16:5). Judah also joined with Assyria against Israel and Aram.

The result of this strong alliance was the downfall of Damascus and the end of the Aramean power, about 732 B.C. (2 Kin. 16:7–18). Many Arameans were taken as hostages to other lands, in keeping with the foreign policy of the conquering Assyrians.

ARCHAEOLOGY OF THE BIBLE — The word *archaeology* comes from two Greek words meaning "a study of ancient things." But the term usually applies today to a study of excavated materials belonging to a former era. Biblical archaeology is the scientific study, by excavation, examination, and publication, of the evidences of cultures and civilizations from the biblical period. Archaeological findings help scholars, as well as Bible students, in understanding the Bible better. They reveal what life was like in biblical times, throw light on obscure passages of Scripture, and help us appreciate the historical context of the Bible.

Archaeology is a complex science, calling on the assistance of other sciences, such as chemistry, anthropology, and zoology. Many talented professionals—including engineers, historians, chemists, paleontologists, photographers, artists, and surveyors—are involved in the discovery, interpretation, and publication of archaeological knowledge.

Every object an archaeologist discovers—whether a piece of bone, pottery, metal, stone, or wood—is studied in detail. The archaeologist's work often requires translating ancient writings and studying an ancient city's art and architecture. These detailed studies are carried out in museums and laboratories, but the archaeologist must first recover the material by carefully excavating an ancient city.

For the New Testament period, biblical archaeology has concentrated upon a geographical area that parallels the reaches of the old Roman Empire. The area is somewhat smaller for Old Testament times, and the focus shifts eastward to include the Mesopotamian Valley and Persia (modern Iran).

The hub for Old Testament research is Palestine, or Israel (ancient Canaan), but it fans out to include the great empires in the Nile and Mesopotamian valleys. The culture of Phoenicia (modern Lebanon) was very similar to that of Canaan to the south. Syria to the east is also studied because its history often was tied to Israel's. Still farther north, Asia Minor was the homeland of the Hittites and several Greek cultures.

Until the early 1800s, little was known of biblical times and customs, except what was written in the Old Testament. Although the Greek historians preserved considerable background material on New Testament times, little documentation was found for the Old Testament period. The reason for this is that Alexander the Great forced the Greek language and customs upon all the lands his armies conquered. This policy almost destroyed the languages and culture of Egypt, Persia, Canaan, and Babylon. Before the rise of modern archaeology, scarcely any historical evidence was available to illustrate or confirm the history and literature of the Old Testament.

Modern Near Eastern archaeology began during the 18th century. Before that, some research had been done by collectors of antiquities, usually museums or wealthy individuals. Biblical archaeology probably began with the discovery of the Rosetta Stone during Napoleon's invasion of Egypt in 1799. Discovered by an officer in the expedition, the stone was inscribed in three columns consisting of Greek, Egyptian hieroglyphics, and later Egyptian script. With Napoleon's encouragement, the stone was studied and recorded with scientific accuracy, then displayed in the British Museum. This discovery opened the door to the study of the remains of ancient Egypt, a rich resource for biblical researchers.

How Ancient Ruins (Tells) Were Formed. In ancient times, cities were usually built on sites that were easy to defend and were located near a source of water and on a good trade route. The homes were constructed primarily of sun-baked bricks, which could be destroyed quite easily by flood, earthquakes, or enemy attack. In rebuilding the town, the inhabitants would usually level the rubble and debris and build new buildings on the same location. Cities continued to be destroyed by windstorm, enemy attack, or other catastrophes until gradually a mound of earth containing remnants of buildings, tools, vases, and pottery rose on the site. Eventually many layers of habitation lay upon one another.

The sites of these mounds in the ancient Near East are called *tells*, the Arabic word for mounds. These mounds do not look like natural hills, appearing instead as unnatural rounded humps on the landscape. They often rise from their surroundings by as much as 15 to 23 meters (50 to 75 feet).

If a city was destroyed by famine, disease, earthquake, or some other natural catastrophe, the townspeople might conclude that the gods had cursed their city and that it would be unwise to rebuild on the same site. The area might lie unused for hundreds of years until a new group decided to build again on this strategically located site.

When a site is occupied continuously by the same group of people, one layer or stratum of the mound is very similar to the next. Some slight changes in artifacts and ways of doing things, such as the method of baking pottery or the shape of certain tools, will occur in an orderly fashion from generation to generation. If a long period with no habitation has taken place between layers, the new people who inhabit the mound may have discovered new techniques. Also peoples with new skills—perhaps the conquerors of the former dwellers—may inhabit the site. A sharp change in the pattern of living or in types of artifacts discovered may indicate a gap in habitation of the site.

As he excavates these ancient sites, an archaeologist will first find large stationary objects such as houses, monuments, tombs, and fortresses. Also there will be smaller artifacts such as jewelry, tools, weapons, and cooking utensils. Archaeology provides the Bible researcher with the rich remains of material culture over the course of centuries to supplement what is recorded in the Bible, as well as in art and literature.

How Archaeologists Do Their Work. In organizing his work (called a dig), the archaeologist first will divide the site, or area, by a "grid system," using lines parallel to the longitude and latitude of the area. A "field," 5.8 meters (19 feet) square, is then divided into four squares or quadrants, leaving room for a catwalk (baulk) among them to observe the work. Each area has an area supervisor, who in turn works under the supervision of the excavation director. The area supervisor is responsible for directing the actual digging in his area and recording everything as it comes from the ground. It is more important to excavate small areas in detail than to excavate a large area carelessly.

Those who actually work the site are of three categories: Pickmen carefully break up the soil, noticing every difference in the hardness of the earth and how it is compacted. It takes skill to distinguish a clay wall from ordinary packed clay or to develop the delicate touch that can bring forth a vase or a human bone unharmed. Hoemen work over the loosened soil, saving anything of potential interest. Basketmen carry off the excavated dirt, perhaps using a sieve to sift the soil—to be sure nothing of value is discarded. Often archaeology students serve as laborers on expeditions.

Everything found in a quadrant of the site is collected in an individual basket and tagged with all pertinent information, including the date and location of discovery. The baskets are then photographed and evaluated by experts who record all the data. The materials and information then go to laboratories and museums where they are studied in detail. Conclusions are then published by the excavation director and are circulated to other archaeologists and scholars.

In 1832, while a Danish archaeologist, C. J. Thomsen, was classifying some implements for display in a Copenhagen museum, he wondered about the age of the various tools made of iron, bronze, and stone. Returning to the peat bog where the implements had been found, he discovered that artifacts made of stone were found in the bottom layer. Higher levels contained many tools made of copper and bronze. At the top of the bog were instruments of iron, indicating they were made last. (We now speak of the Stone Age, the Bronze Age, and the Iron Age.)

Thomsen had made a very simple application of the principle of stratigraphy, or keeping track of the layers of soil in which artifacts were found, to establish a sequence of events. Archaeologists base many of their conclusions on their study and evaluation of the various strata of the mound.

An archaeologist can determine how many times a town has been destroyed and rebuilt, but he will want to know the date of each occupation, how long it lasted, and why it was destroyed. Each level of occupation will contain the foundations of walls and buildings and often a layer of debris from the destruction. Also the articles of everyday living such as weapons, tools, pottery, and ornaments will be revealed. Sometimes the different strata are separated by thick layers of ash from a great fire. At other times, only a difference in soil color or compactness distinguishes the levels.

Furthermore, during centuries when the mound was not inhabited, erosion and random digging at the site can disrupt a stratum. A new group of settlers may have dug foundations, garbage pits, or trenches deep into an earlier layer, making the job of the archaeologist more difficult.

Pottery is one of the most important keys to dating the strata of a tell. Pottery typology, or the study of various types of pottery, is now refined to almost an exact science. The scientist can call upon the detailed knowledge of the characteristics of pottery of each period to identify and date the pottery, usually within a half century of the exact time when it was made. The scientific method of carbon-14 dating is also used to establish the age of some archaeological materials.

Earlier pottery designs were simple and functional; later vessels became more delicate and elaborate, often showing Persian and Greek influences. The method of baking the clay can also indicate the approximate time when it was made. Changes in everyday objects such as lamps, tools, weapons, and jewelry help scientists identify broader periods of history. Ancient coins found on a site can also help to establish the dates when the site was inhabited.

How Archaeology Helps Us Understand the Bible. During the early years of exploring Bible lands, archaeologists hoped to make discoveries that would confirm the main events of Bible history. Today's archaeologists realize that many things about the Bible cannot be proved in a direct way. Instead of providing proof of specific events, archaeology is used to increase our knowledge of the everyday life, the history, and the customs of the people who appear in the Bible's long story—the Egyptians, Phoenicians, Philistines, Moabites, Assyrians, Babylonians, and others, as well as the Hebrews. For example, discoveries of ancient texts on clay tablets—in many languages—show us what the various peoples of the ancient Near East thought about the gods they worshiped, as well as the types of laws by which they lived. Ancient texts also tell us of alliances, trade agreements, and wars between the great cities and nations of the past.

Archaeological discoveries paint in the background of the Bible, helping to explain many of its events. Thanks to archaeology, we now know that in the time of Abraham (about 2000 B.C.) many thriving cities existed in the ancient Near East. Civilization was already over a thousand years old in Egypt and in the region of the Tigris and Euphrates rivers. It was from a city on the Euphrates River, called Ur, that Abraham (then called Abram) began the journey that eventually brought him to the land of Canaan (Gen. 11:31). The excavation of Ur early in this century (1922–1934) by Sir Charles Leonard Woolley revealed that Abraham was surrounded by idolatry on all sides when God called him to begin a new people through which God could do His redemptive work.

The discovery of large bodies of cuneiform literature in Babylon and other places also has proved most revealing. For example, the Amarna letters from Egypt give an inside glance into conditions in Canaan just after the conquest by Joshua and the Israelites.

In 1890 the famed archaeologist Flinders Petrie began an excavation at Tell el-Hesi in southwestern Palestine. He carefully recorded the pieces and types of broken pottery found at each level of occupation. This exploration helped refine the method known as "ceramic chronology," which is one of the methods still used to date ancient finds.

Inscriptions and ancient manuscripts also have made an important contribution to biblical study. In fact, today's archaeological work is increasingly concerned with the text of the Bible. Intensive study of more than 3,000 New Testament Greek manuscripts dating from the 2nd century A.D. and subsequent years has shown that the New Testament text has been preserved remarkably from that time. Not one doctrine has been perverted due to major errors in transmission.

The science of papyrology developed after large quantities of papyri, or ancient writing materials, were discovered in Egypt around the turn of the century. The papyri, written on paper made from the papyrus reed of Egypt, included a wide variety of topics presented in several languages. More than 70 papyri containing portions of the New Testament have been found. These fragments help to confirm the texts of the longer manuscripts dating to the 4th century A.D. and following. Since many of the papyri date to the first three centuries after Christ, the impact of papyrology upon biblical studies has been significant. These discoveries make it possible to establish the grammar of the period and, thus, to date the composition of New Testament books to the 1st century A.D.

The mass of papyri also demonstrated that New Testament Greek was not invented by New Testament writers. Instead, it was the common language generally used during the first century of the Christian era. Moreover, the papyri have shown that the New Testament contained good grammar, judged by first-century standards.

The search for buildings and places associated with the ministry of Jesus has taken place for centuries. A synagogue was unearthed in Capernaum, although it hardly can be the one in which Jesus taught (Mark 1:21). It may well be the successor of the synagogue Jesus knew, however. Archaeologists think they may have discovered Peter's house at the same site (Matt. 8:14). Graffiti on the plastered wall of this second-century house clearly links it with Peter. Atop Mount Gerizim, excavations have uncovered the foundations of the Samaritan temple. Although tradition has assigned sites for the birth and the crucifixion of Jesus, archaeologists disagree on the authenticity of these locations.

Significant Archaeological Digs and Their Contributions. Many important archaeological discoveries of this century have contributed to Bible knowledge. Following are descriptions of five of these projects, with an analysis of their contribution.

The Law Code of Hammurapi — In 1901 a slab of black marble over 7 feet tall and 6 feet wide, containing over 300 paragraphs of legal inscriptions, was discovered at Susa (Shushan) in ancient Elam. Engraved on the large rock were legal provisions dealing with the social, domestic, and moral life of the ancient Babylonian people of King Hammurapi's time (about 1792–1750 B.C.). The code furnishes important background material for comparison with other ancient bodies of law, particularly the laws of the Pentateuch.

The fact that Hammurapi's Code is older by three centuries than the laws of Moses has ruined some of the theories of critics and has given rise to others. A discovery of this sort illustrates how archaeology roots out views that earlier placed the origin of many of the laws attributed to Moses at a much later time. The discovery of Hammurapi's laws indicates that the law of Moses is neither borrowed from, nor dependent upon, the Babylonian.

The resemblances between the Mosaic laws and the code of Hammurapi are clearly due to the similarity of the general intellectual and cultural heritage of the Hebrews and the Babylonians at that ancient time. The striking differences, however, demonstrate that there is no direct borrowing and that the

Mosaic law—although later by three centuries—is in no way dependent upon the Babylonian.

The two laws are radically different in their origins and morality. The Babylonian laws are alleged to have been received by Hammurapi from the sun god, Shamash. Moses received his laws directly from the Lord. Hammurapi's laws list at least ten varieties of bodily mutilation prescribed for various offenses. For example, if a physician performed an operation that was unsuccessful, his hand was to be cut off.

By contrast, in the Mosaic legislation, only one instance of mutilation occurs, where a wife's hand is to be severed (Deut. 25:11–12). Also in the Hebrew laws a greater value is placed upon human life. A stricter regard for the honor of womanhood is evident and masters are ordered to treat their slaves more humanely.

The City of Ur — Ur was an important city of ancient Babylonia situated on the Euphrates River in lower Mesopotamia, or present-day Iraq. But the glory of the city was suddenly destroyed about 1960 B.C. Foreigners stormed down from the surrounding hills, captured the reigning king, Ibbi-Sin, and reduced the city to ruins. So complete was its destruction that the city lay buried in oblivion until it was excavated in modern times by archaeologists.

Abraham lived in the city of Ur at the height of its splendor. The city was a center of religion and industry. The Babylonians worshiped many gods, but the moon god Sin was supreme. Accordingly, Ur was a theocracy centered in worship of the moon deity. Abraham's father, Terah, probably worshiped at the altar of Sin.

God's sovereign grace called Abraham out of this polluted atmosphere to begin a new line of people, the Hebrews, who were to be separated from idolatry and to become a blessing to all mankind. The archaeological findings of ancient Ur have greatly illuminated the biblical references to the patriarch

Abraham and have given a much wider view of the ancient world before 2000 B.C.

The Ras Shamra Tablets — Recovered in another significant excavation were hundreds of clay tablets that had been housed in a library located between two pagan temples in Ugarit, modern Ras Shamra in Syria. These tablets date from about the 15th century B.C. They were inscribed in the earliest known alphabet written in wedge-shaped signs. The strange writing was recognized as ancient Canaanite in origin, and it turned out to be religious and cultic (related to worship) in nature. The tablets were inscribed in a dialect closely akin to biblical Hebrew and Phoenician.

So important were the initial discoveries that archaeologist Claude F. Schaeffer continued excavations in the area from 1929 to 1937. Aside from the knowledge gained about the ancient city of Ugarit, the Ras Shamra texts have great literary importance. The translation of the texts showed the important parallels between the Ugaritic and Hebrew literary style and vocabulary. These texts have been invaluable to scholars studying Hebrew poetry and the general literary style and vocabulary of Old Testament Hebrew. The most important contribution of the religious texts from Ras Shamra consists of the background material they provide for careful study of the pagan religions mentioned repeatedly in the Old Testament. As a result of archaeological work, an independent witness to the degenerate nature of Canaanite cults is now available. No longer can critics accuse the Old Testament of projecting a bloodthirsty mentality because Joshua ordered that all Canaanites be destroyed. This order was given to purge the immoral worship of the Canaanites from the land.

The Lachish Letters — In the excavations of Lachish, a city in southwestern Canaan, the most astonishing finds consisted of letters imbedded in a layer of burned charcoal and ashes. Written in Hebrew of the ancient Phoenician script, the documents throw additional light on the life and times of the prophet Jeremiah. The letters were inscribed on pieces of broken pottery called ostraca. Most of the letters were written by a citizen named Hoshayahu, who was stationed at a military outpost. He sent these letters to Yaosh, evidently a high-ranking officer in the garrison at Lachish.

The Babylonians had attacked and partly burned Lachish some ten years earlier during the reign of King Jehoiakim of Judah. These letters were found in the layers of ashes that represent the final destruction of the city. This dates them from 588–586 B.C., when Nebuchadnezzar of Babylon made his final siege of the Hebrew cities of Jerusalem, Lachish, and Azekah.

One letter lists names, the majority of which are found in the Old Testament; two letters consist largely of greetings; another letter describes movements of troops and makes an interesting reference to an unnamed prophet and his word of warning. The Lachish Letters give an independent view of conditions in Judah during the last days before the fall of Jerusalem.

The prophet Jeremiah conducted his ministry in these times. His reference to Azekah and Lachish says, "When the king of Babylon's army fought against Jerusalem and all the cities of Judah that were left, against Lachish, and Azekah: for only these fortified cities remained of the cities of Judah" (Jer. 34:7).

Tell ez-Zakariyeh has been identified as the ancient city of Azekah. It had a strong inner fortress buttressed with eight large towers. The Lachish Letters concern the time just prior to the fall of the city and present the same conditions of turmoil and confusion that are revealed in the book of Jeremiah. This information is of immense value in explaining historical backgrounds and illuminating Old Testament Scripture.

The Dead Sea Scrolls — The greatest manuscript discovery of modern times began with the uncovering of the Dead Sea Scrolls in 1947. A young shepherd boy stumbled upon a cave south of Jericho containing numerous leather scrolls of Hebrew and Aramaic writing and some 600 fragmentary inscriptions. Great excitement quickly spread throughout the archaeological world. In 1952, new caves containing fragments of later scrolls in Hebrew, Greek, and Aramaic were found enclosed in jars. These startling discoveries have been followed by the uncovering of other manuscripts around the Dead Sea area, particularly at Qumran.

After intensive study, scholars dated the manuscripts from as early as 250 B.C. to as late as A.D. 68. Although attacks have been made against the age and authenticity of the manuscripts, two lines of evidence establish their integrity. Radiocarbon count, a scientific method of dating, places the linen in which some of the scrolls were wrapped in the general period of 175 B.C. to A.D. 225. Scholars of ancient writing (paleographers) date documents by the form of the letters and the method of writing. This line of evidence also places the Dead Sea Scrolls during the period of time about three centuries before A.D. 70.

The scrolls contain ancient texts of parts of the Old Testament, as well as writing that originated between the Old and New Testament periods. The biblical section contains two scrolls of Isaiah, one complete, and fragments of several Old Testament books. Coins found at the site at Qumran reveal that the settlement was founded about 135 B.C. It was abandoned during the Jewish war with the Romans in A.D. 66–73.

The scrolls discovered near the Dead Sea were part of the library of the people who lived at Qumran, possibly the Essenes, a religious group mentioned by ancient writers. The sect was even stricter in its interpretation of the religious laws than the Pharisees of the New Testament. Some scholars believe that John the Baptist may have lived among these people before beginning his work of announcing the ministry of Jesus.

The Essenes expected the coming of a new age, ushered in by a ruler who would serve as a prophet and a priest. Although the finds at Qumran do not relate directly to any events described in the Bible, they throw useful light on the way certain people thought during the period between the Old and New Testaments.

A full text of the book of Isaiah is the best known of the discoveries at Qumran, although other texts discovered are also significant. As a group, the documents make up the oldest existing manuscripts of the Bible in any language. One of the caves yielded 18 scraps of papyri written entirely in Greek. Some have identified them as fragments of the earliest New Testament version yet discovered, claiming that one of them, a fragment of Mark's Gospel, dates from about 15 years after the events recorded. Although this dating is disputed by many, the Dead Sea material in general has had a stabilizing effect upon New Testament criticism.

The thrilling story of biblical archaeology is not completed. Scholars are now studying thousands of clay tablets found at Ebla in northern Syria—a task that will require a generation of careful study and analysis. Dialogue between the biblical text and archaeological finds must continue because each can help us understand and interpret the other. The Bible helps us appreciate the archaeologist's discoveries, while biblical archaeology helps us understand and interpret the message of God's inspired Word.

In spite of its great contribution to biblical studies, there are certain things that archaeology cannot do. In general, it cannot prove that a particular Bible event happened or that a specific person mentioned in the Bible actually existed. This is true because of the small amount of evidence archaeology can really recover. Many objects do not survive long enough for a modern archaeologist to discover.

Paper, wood, and clothing will rot away quickly unless they are buried in extremely dry conditions. Also, archaeology discovers only a small portion of the things that do survive. For example, the careful and detailed exploration at Hazor, an ancient city in Israel, between 1956 and 1970 uncovered only a small fraction of the whole mound. It has been estimated that to excavate every area of Hazor's 21 strata would take 800 years.

The truth of the Bible is not only a matter of facts, but of their interpretation. Even if we could prove the accuracy of the entire Bible, its redemptive significance would not be proven. Because the Christian faith is based on historical events, Christians should welcome any supportive evidence that archaeology can provide—but they do not anchor their faith to it.

Neither lack of evidence nor critical skepticism can disprove God's Word. It is better to emphasize how archaeology helps us understand the Bible than to believe that it proves the Bible true. It is heartening, however, to note that so far there has been no instance of an archaeological discovery conclusively proving the Bible to be in error.

AREOPAGUS [air ee OP ah gus] (*hill of the god Ares*) — a limestone hill in Athens situated between the Acropolis and the Agora; by association, also the council which often met on or near the hill. The apostle Paul addressed the Areopagus in his "philosophical sermon" that attempted to meet the objections of the Epicurean and Stoic philosophers to the gospel (Acts 17:16–34).

Paul's speech before the Areopagus (Acts 17:22–31) is a good example of the council meeting to discuss and evaluate a philosophical issue. Paul argued about the nature of God and the way God relates to human beings, especially through Jesus Christ. Paul's argument must have made an impact in the council. "Dionysius the Areopagite" was among those who joined Paul and believed in Christ (Acts 17:34).

Paul's argument on the Areopagus is extremely important. It identifies the decisive difference between Greek philosophy and the Christian faith. Apparently the philosophers were not greatly troubled by Paul's talking about God or God's relationship to people. But when he spoke of the resurrection of Jesus, they mocked him, although some apparently gave his words careful thought (Acts 17:32). The resurrection of Jesus was, and continues to be, a decisive element in Christian theology. It always provokes controversy among unbelievers.

Today Paul's speech is affixed in Greek on a tablet at the entrance to the Areopagus. With the benches carved into the rock and the worn steps to the summit, it stands as a monument to a time when the Athenians deliberated before the gods and missed the significance of the One whom Paul identified with the "unknown God" (Acts 17:23).

ARMAGEDDON [ar mah GED un] (*mountain of Megiddo*) — the site of the final battle of this age in which God intervenes to destroy the armies of Satan and to cast Satan into the bottomless pit (Rev. 16:16). Scholars disagree about the exact location of this place, but the most likely possibility is the valley between Mount Carmel and the city of Jezreel. This valley (known as the Valley of Jezreel and sometimes referred to as the Plain of Esdraelon) was the crossroads of two ancient trade routes and thus was a strategic military site and the scene of many ancient battles. Because of this history, Megiddo became a symbol of the final conflict between God and the forces of evil. According to the book of Revelation, at Armageddon "the cup of the wine of the fierceness of His [God's] wrath" (Rev. 16:19) will be poured out, and the forces of evil will be overthrown and destroyed.

ARMY — a large body of warriors organized and trained for warfare. The nation of Israel developed a regular standing army at a relatively late time in its history. One reason for this is that the nation lacked political unity until the time of the United Kingdom under David and Solomon. The sense that God was the Divine Warrior and would protect His people regardless of their military strength may have been another reason why they were slow to develop an army.

Thus, from the time of Abraham to the beginning of Saul's reign there was no regular army continually prepared to respond to foreign attacks. Instead, the call would go out at the moment of crisis, and able-bodied, nonexempt males would gather in response. The first example comes from Genesis 14, when Abraham's nephew Lot was kidnapped by Chedorlaomer, king of Elam, and his allies. Abraham rallied to Lot's aid by gathering 318 trained men of his household and defeating the foreign forces.

During the years of the Exodus, wilderness wanderings, and conquest of the land of Canaan, the whole nation was temporarily changed into an army. All the men from every tribe participated in the warfare. Numbers 2 pictures the nation of Israel camped as an army in battle, with their Heavenly Commander in the center and the various divisions (individual tribes) dwelling under their battle banners. The same chapter describes the position of each tribe marching behind the Ark of the Covenant as they traveled toward Canaan and holy war. At this time the army was under the command of Moses, and later of Joshua; but each tribal division had its own leader as well.

The period of the judges that followed was characterized by lack of unity and purpose. This was true militarily as well as politically and religiously. At times of military crisis, God would raise up a military leader, called a judge, who would then seek the aid of the tribes in order to gather an army. Judges 5 (particularly vv. 15–18) shows that Deborah, one of these judges, met with reluctance or indifference from some of the tribes.

The development of a regular standing army in Israel came only after a strong, centralized political system had developed. This came with kings Saul, David, and Solomon. Although Saul began his reign as a type of gifted leader, as were the earlier judges, he soon began to form a permanent army (1 Sam.

13:2; 24:2; 26:2). Nevertheless, the army had to be supported by food and other supplies from the homes of individual soldiers (1 Sam. 17:17–19). What Saul began, David continued. He increased the army, brought in hired troops from other regions who were loyal to him alone (2 Sam. 15:19–22), and turned over the direct leadership of his armies to a commander-in-chief (Joab). Under David Israel also became more aggressive in its offensive military policies, absorbing neighboring states like Ammon (2 Sam. 11:1; 1 Chr. 20:1–3). David established a system of rotating troops with 12 groups of 24,000 men serving one month of the year (1 Chronicles 27). Although Solomon's reign was peaceful, he further expanded the army, adding chariots and horsemen (1 Kin. 10:26).

The standing army came into existence with these three kings. It continued (though divided along with the kingdom after the death of Solomon) until 586 B.C., when Israel ceased to exist as a political entity.

The most important army to the faithful Israelite was not a human army; it was God's holy army. The human army could not succeed unless the Lord of hosts led his troops into battle. Thus Joshua conferred with the "commander of the army of the Lord" before the battle of Jericho (Josh. 5:13). David awaited the movement of God's army in the balsam trees before attacking the Philistines (2 Sam. 5:24). The prophet Elisha prayed that God would open the eyes of Gehazi so he might be comforted by seeing the power of God's army (2 Kin. 6:8–23).

ASHER, TRIBE OF — a tribe descended from Asher and that part of Canaan where the tribe of Asher lived (Josh. 19:24, 31–34). The territory of Asher extended to the northern boundary of Canaan; its southern border was the tribe of Manasseh and the mountains of Mount Carmel. Asher was bounded on the west by the Mediterranean Sea and on the east by the tribe of Naphtali. The Asherites never succeeded in expelling the inhabitants of the Phoenician strongholds—such as Tyre, Sidon, and Acco (Judg. 1:31–32)—which were in their territory.

ASSYRIA [as SIHR ih ah] — a kingdom between the Tigris and Euphrates rivers that often dominated the ancient world. After defeating the northern kingdom of Israel in 722 B.C., the Assyrians carried away thousands of Israelites and resettled them in other parts of the Assyrian Empire. This was a blow from which the nation of Israel never recovered.

The early inhabitants of Assyria were ancient tribesmen (Gen. 10:22) who probably migrated from Babylonia. They grew powerful enough around 1300 B.C. to conquer Babylonia. For the next 700 years they were the leading power in the ancient world, with their leading rival nation, Babylonia, constantly challenging them for this position.

Tiglath-Pileser I (1120–1100 B.C.) built the Assyrian kingdom to the most extensive empire of the age. But under his successors, it declined in power and influence. This decline offered the united kingdom of Judah, under the leadership of David and Solomon, the opportunity to reach its greatest limits. If the Assyrians had been more powerful at that time, they probably would have interfered with the internal affairs of Israel, even at that early date.

After the Assyrians had languished in weakness for an extended period, Ashurnasirpal (844–860 B.C.) restored much of the prestige of the empire. His son, Shalmaneser III, succeeded him, and reigned from about 860 to 825 B.C. Shalmaneser was the first Assyrian king to come into conflict with the northern kingdom of Israel.

In an effort to halt the Assyrian expansion, a group of surrounding nations formed a coalition, of which Israel was a part. Ahab was king of Israel during this time. But the coalition eventually split up, allowing the Assyrians to continue their relentless conquest of surrounding territories.

During the period from 833 to 745 B.C., Assyria was engaged in internal struggles as well as war with Syria. This allowed Israel to operate without threat from the Assyrian army. During this time, Jeroboam II, king of Israel, was able to raise the Northern Kingdom to the status of a major nation among the countries of the ancient Near East.

The rise of Tiglath-Pileser III (745–727 B.C.) marked the beginning of a renewed period of Assyrian oppression for the nation of Israel. Tiglath-Pileser, known also in the Bible as Pul (2 Kin. 15:19), set out to regain territories previously occupied by the Assyrians. He was resisted by a coalition led by Rezin of Damascus and Pekah of Israel. These rulers tried to force Ahaz, king of Judah, to join them. When Ahaz refused, Rezin and Pekah marched on Jerusalem, intent on destroying the city. Against the counsel of the prophet Isaiah, Ahaz enlisted the aid of Tiglath-Pileser for protection. This protection cost dearly. From that day forth, Israel was required to pay tribute to Assyria. Israel also was forced to adopt some of the religious practices of the Assyrians (2 Kings 16).

Tiglath-Pileser was succeeded by his son, Shalmaneser V (727–722 B.C.). When Hoshea, king of Israel, who had been placed on the throne by Tiglath-Pileser, refused to pay the required tribute, Shalmaneser attacked Samaria, the capital of Israel. After a long siege, Israel fell to Assyria in 722 B.C., perhaps to Sargon II; and 27,000 inhabitants of Israel were deported to Assyrian territories. This event marked the end of the northern kingdom of Israel. Most of the deported Israelites never returned to their homeland.

Israel's sister nation, the southern kingdom of Judah, also felt the power of the Assyrian Empire. In 701 B.C., Sennacherib, king of Assyria (705–681 B.C.), planned an attack on Jerusalem. However, the Assyrian army was struck by a plague, which the Bible referred to as "the angel of the Lord" (2 Kin. 19:35). Sennacherib was forced to retreat from his invasion when 185,000 Assyrian soldiers died. Thus, Jerusalem was saved from Assyrian oppression by divine intervention.

The religion of the Assyrians, much like that of the Babylonians, emphasized worship of nature. They believed every object of nature was possessed by a spirit. The chief god was Asshur. All other primary gods whom they worshiped were related to the objects of nature. These included Anu, god of the heavens; Bel, god of the region inhabited by people, animals, and birds; Ea, god of the waters; Sin, the moon-god; Shamash, the sun-god; and Ramman, god of the storms. These gods were followed by five gods of the planets. In addition to these primary gods, lesser gods also were worshiped. In some cases, various cities had their own patron gods. The pagan worship of the Assyrians was soundly condemned by several prophets of the Old Testament (Is. 10:5; Ezek. 16:28; Hos. 8:9).

The favorite pursuits of the Assyrian kings were war and hunting. Archaeologists have discovered that the Assyrians were merciless and savage people. The Assyrian army was ruthless and effective. Its cruelty included burning cities, burning children, impaling victims on stakes, beheading, and chopping off hands. But, like Babylonia, which God used as an instrument of judgment against Judah, Assyria became God's channel of punishment and judgment against Israel because of their sin and idolatry.

Because of the cruelty and paganism of the Assyrians, Israel harbored deep-seated hostility against this nation. This attitude is revealed clearly in the book of Jonah. When God instructed Jonah to preach to Nineveh, the capital of Assyria, Jonah refused and went in the opposite direction. After he finally went to Nineveh, the prophet was disappointed with God because He spared the city.

AUGUSTAN REGIMENT — one of five cohorts, or regiments, of the Roman army stationed at or near Caesarea. While the apostle Paul was being transported to Rome as a prisoner, he was put in the charge of "one named Julius, a centurion of the Augustan Regiment" (Acts 27:1). A regiment, or cohort, was made up of about 600 infantrymen.

BABYLONIA [bab i LOW nih uh] — ancient pagan empire between the Tigris and Euphrates rivers in southern Mesopotamia. The Babylonians struggled with the neighboring Assyrians for domination of the ancient world during much of their history. At the height of their power, the Babylonians overpowered the nation of Judah, destroyed Jerusalem, and carried God's Covenant People into captivity in 586 B.C. The fortunes of the Babylonians rose and fell during the long sweep of Old Testament history—from about 2000 B.C. to about 500 B.C. References to these people—their culture, religion, and military power—occur throughout the Old Testament.

Babylonia was a long, narrow country about 65 kilometers (40 miles) wide at its widest point and had an area of about 8,000 square miles. It was bordered on the north by Assyria, on the east by Elam, on the south and west by the Arabian desert, and on the southeast by the Persian Gulf. Among the earliest inhabitants of this region were the Sumerians, whom the Bible refers to as the people of the "land of Shinar" (Gen. 10:10). Sargon I (the Great), from one of the Sumerian cities, united the people of Babylonia under his rule about 2300 B.C. Many scholars believe Sargon was the same person as Nimrod (Gen. 10:8).

In 1792 B.C. Hammurapi emerged as the ruler of Babylonia. He expanded the borders of the empire and organized its laws into a written system, referred to by scholars as the Code of Hammurapi. Abraham had earlier left Ur, one of the ancient cities in lower Babylonia, and moved to Haran, a city in the north. Abraham eventually left Haran and migrated into the land of Canaan under God's promise that he would become the father of a great nation (Gen. 12:1–20).

Any account of Babylonia must also mention Assyria, which bordered Babylonia on the north. Assyria's development was often intertwined with the course of Babylonian history. About 1270 B.C., the Assyrians overpowered Babylonia. For the next 700 years, Babylonia was a second-rate power as the Assyrians dominated the ancient world.

In 626 B.C., Babylonian independence was finally won from Assyria by a leader named Nabopolassar. Under his leadership, Babylonia again became a great empire. In 605 B.C., Nebuchadnezzar, the son of Nabopolassar, became ruler and reigned for 44 years. Under him the Babylonian Empire reached its greatest strength. Using the treasures he took from other nations, Nebuchadnezzar built Babylon, the capital city of Babylonia, into one of the leading cities of the world. The famous "hanging gardens" of Babylon were known as one of the Seven Wonders of the Ancient World.

In 586 B.C., the Babylonians destroyed Jerusalem and carried the leading citizens of the nation of Judah as captives to Babylon. During this period of captivity, the Persians conquered Babylonia, and the Babylonians passed from the scene as a world power.

During its long history, Babylonia attained a high level of civilization that was influential beyond its borders. Sumerian culture was its basis, which later Babylonians regarded as traditional. In the realm of religion, the Sumerians already had a system of gods, each with a main temple in a particular city.

The chief gods were Anu, god of heaven; Enlil, god of the air; and Enki or Ea, god of the subterranean ocean. Others were Shamash, the sun-god; Sin, the moon-god; Ishtar, goddess of love and war; and Adad, the storm-god. The Amorites promoted the god Marduk at the city of Babylon, so that he became the chief god of the Babylonian religion, beginning about 1100 B.C. Babylonian religion was temple-centered, with elaborate festivals and many different types of priests, especially the exorcist and the diviner, whose function was to drive away evil spirits. Babylonian literature was dominated by mythology and legends. Among these was a "creation" myth called Enuma Elish, written to glorify a god known as Marduk. According to this myth, Marduk created heaven and earth from the corpse of the goddess Tiamat. Another work was the Gilgamesh Epic, which includes a flood story and was written about 2000 B.C. Scientific literature of the Babylonians included treatises on astronomy, mathematics, medicine, chemistry, botany, and zoology.

An important aspect of Babylonian culture was a codified system of law. Hammurapi's code was the successor of earlier collections of laws going back several centuries. The Babylonians used art for the celebration of great events and glorification of the gods. It was marked by stylized and symbolic representations, but it expressed realism and spontaneity in the depiction of animals. The Old Testament contains many references to Babylonia. Genesis 10:10 mentions four Babylonian cities: Babel (Babylon), Erech (Uruk), Accad (Agade), and Calneh. These, along with Assyria, were ruled by Nimrod.

BANKING — the business of a bank; the occupation of a banker. Institutional banking was not known in ancient Israel until the time of the captivity (586 B.C.). The lending of money at interest, a traditional function of banks, was forbidden in Old Testament law, at least among native Israelites (Ex.

22:25; Deut. 23:19–20). People protected their valuable possessions by burying them (Matt. 13:44; Luke 19:20) or depositing them in temples or palaces. During the captivity the Israelites became familiar with Babylonian banking institutions. Some Jews even joined the banking industry and became prominent officers. By New Testament times banking was an established institution. Jesus' parable of the talents (or minas) shows that bankers received money for safekeeping and also paid interest (Matt. 25:27; Luke 19:23). They were also involved in money changing (Matt. 21:12).

BATTLE — armed combat between two enemy forces. Canaan was the scene of numerous battles. Conflict was so frequent in Old Testament times that the spring of the year was known as "the time when kings go out to battle" (2 Sam. 11:1; 1 Chr. 20:1), probably because the ground had dried out after the winter rains and therefore chariots and troops would not be slowed down by mud. The first battle mentioned in the Bible is the one in which Chedorlaomer and three other kings attacked the five kings who ruled over the cities of the plain (Gen. 14:8). The last mentioned is the battle of Armageddon, also called "the battle of that great day of God Almighty" (Rev. 16:14; also Rev. 20:8).

BATTLEMENT — a protective wall surrounding the flat roofs of houses in Bible times. This wall was required by law (Deut. 22:8, KJV) to prevent accidental injuries by falling. "Battlements" (Jer. 5:10, KJV) on a city wall protected soldiers from enemy attack (Song 8:9, NKJV, NRSV).

BENJAMIN, TRIBE OF — the tribe descended from Benjamin (Num. 1:36–37; Judg. 1:21). Its northern boundary ran westward from the Jordan River through Bethel and just south of Lower Beth Horon; its western boundary picked up at this point to Kirjath Jearim; its southern border ran eastward to the northern point of the Dead Sea; and its easternmost limit was the Jordan River (Josh. 18:11–20). The chief towns in this hilly, fertile region were Jerusalem, Jericho, Bethel, Gibeon, Gibeah, and Mizpah (Josh. 18:21–28).

Saul, Israel's first king, was a Benjamite, and the Benjamites supported Saul over David (2 Sam. 2:9, 15; 1 Chr. 12:29). Although the Benjamites continued to show some unrest throughout David's reign (2 Sam. 20:1; Ps. 7), most of the tribe remained loyal to the house of David and became part of the southern kingdom of Judah when Israel divided into two nations (1 Kin. 12:21; Ezra 4:1). Saul of Tarsus, who later became known as the apostle Paul, was a Benjamite (Phil. 3:5).

C

CALENDAR — a system of reckoning time, usually based on a recurrent natural cycle (such as the sun through the seasons or the moon through its phases); a table, or tabular register, of days according to a system usually covering one year and referring the days of each month to the days of the week. From the beginning of recorded history, the calendar has been used to keep records and predict the time for the changing of the seasons. The calendar provided a framework in which people could plan their work. It was an effective timetable for marking various religious festivals that were to be celebrated at regular intervals.

Calendar Units

The day — In calendar terms, the day is the smallest and most consistent unit of time. In the ancient world, the term "day" was used in at least two senses. It described a 24-hour period, as well as daylight in contrast to the night (Gen. 1:5). The beginning point of the 24-hour day varied. The Bible contains references to the day beginning in the morning (Gen. 19:34; Acts 23:32) as well as in the evening (Neh. 13:19). In the time of the Roman Empire, the day may have begun at midnight, as indicated by the Gospel of John (4:6; 19:14). The dawn was the twilight before sunrise (1 Sam. 30:17; Matt. 28:1).

The evening was the late afternoon (Deut. 16:6) between the day and the night (Prov. 7:9; Jer. 6:4), or it could mean literally "late" in the day (Mark 11:19) just before the stars came out (Neh. 4:21). Noon was the end of the morning (1 Kin. 18:26) and marked mealtime (Gen. 43:16). Noon was also referred to as "midday" (Neh. 8:3), "broad daylight" (Amos 8:9), and "heat of the day" (2 Sam. 4:5). The day was divided into three parts: evening, morning, and noon (Ps. 55:17). Midnight was the midpoint of the night (Matt. 25:6; Acts 20:7). In the Old Testament the night was divided into three watches (Ex. 14:24; Judg. 7:19), while it was divided into four watches in the New Testament (Matt. 14:25; Mark 13:35). The term "hour" was used to mean "immediately" (Dan 3:6, 15), or it could express the idea of one-twelfth of daylight (John 11:9).

The week — The week was a seven-day unit begun at the time of creation (Gen. 1:31–2:2). The word *week* means "seven" (Gen. 29:27; Luke 18:12). In the Bible the days of the week were called the "first day," "third day," and so forth (Gen. 1:8–31; Matt. 28:1), although the seventh day was known as "sabbath" (Ex. 16:23; Matt. 12:1). The day before the Sabbath was called "the Preparation Day" (Mark 15:42), and Christians referred to the first day of the week as "the Lord's Day" (Rev. 1:10).

The month — The month was a unit of time closely tied to the moon. The Hebrew word for "month" also meant "moon" (Deut. 33:14, NIV, NASB). The reason for the connection between the month and the moon is that the beginning of a month was marked by a new moon. The moon was carefully observed by the people of Bible times. When it appeared as a thin crescent, it marked the beginning of a new month. The lunar month was about 29 days long. Therefore, the first crescent of the new moon would appear 29 or 30 days after the previous new moon. At times the crescent was not visible because of clouds. But this was allowed for with a rule that the new moon would never be reckoned as more than 30 days after the last new moon. This prevented too much variation in the calendar.

The year — The Hebrew word for year comes from the idea of change or repeated action. Thus the year expresses the concept of "a complete cycle of change." Due to the repeated seasons, people set up a calendar to account for yearly events and to alert them of the coming seasons. The calendar revolved around the agricultural cycles. People observed the climatic changes and the length of days in their planting and harvesting. Religious festivals were also established to parallel the agricultural year. No major religious festival, for example, was celebrated during the busy harvest season. People observed that there were four seasons and that the year was about 365 days long. Although the calendars were not always precise, adjustments were made periodically to account for the lack of precision.

Calendar Systems in the Old Testament — The marking of time in Old Testament days revolved primarily around the months, seasonal religious festivals, and the year. The month was marked by the first appearance of the crescent of the new moon at sunset. The first day of each month was considered a holy day marked by special sacrifices (Num. 28:11–15), and it was to be announced with the blowing of trumpets (Num. 10:10; Ps. 81:3). Normally the months were designated numerically: first (Ex. 12:2), second (Ex. 16:1), third (Ex. 19:1), fourth (2 Kin. 25:3), fifth (Jer. 28:1), sixth (1 Chr. 27:9), seventh (Gen. 8:4), eighth (Zech. 1:1), ninth (Ezra 10:9), tenth (Gen. 8:5), eleventh (Deut. 1:3), and twelfth (Esth. 3:7).

The first month of the Hebrew calendar was in the spring, around March/April. In their early history the Israelites adopted Canaanite names for the months, which were connected with agriculture and climate. Only four of these names are mentioned in the Old Testament. The month Abib (Ex. 13:4; 23:15) was the first month (around March/April), which was at the time of barley harvest. The word *Abib* means "ripening of grain" (Lev. 2:14). The month Ziv (1 Kin. 6:1, 37; Zif, KJV) was the second month (April/May). Ethanim (1 Kin. 8:2) was the seventh month (September/October), which occurred during the rainy season. Bul (1 Kin. 6:38) was the eighth month (October/November), which was between the early and latter rains. These four names for the months were associated with the most important agricultural times of the year.

In its later history the nation of Israel adopted all 12 months of the Babylonian calendar as their civil calendar. But not all of the names of these months are listed in the Bible. The seven that occur are Nisan, the first month (Neh. 2:1); Sivan, the third month (Esth. 8:9); Elul, the sixth month (Neh. 6:15); Chislev, the ninth month (Zech. 7:1); Tebeth, the tenth month (Esth. 2:16); Shebat, the eleventh month (Zech. 1:7); and Adar, the twelfth month (Ezra 6:15). The first month of this calendar also fell during the springtime.

Since Israel was an agricultural society, its calendar worked well for the people and their religious festivals. In the first month (coinciding with our March/April), the fourteenth day was Passover (Ex. 12:18); the fifteenth day through the twenty-first day was Unleavened Bread (Lev. 23:6); the sixteenth day was First Fruits (Lev. 23:10–14), dedicating the first-ripe barley sprigs. The second month (April/May) marked the celebration of a later Passover, in case some had missed the first celebration (Num. 9:10–11). On the sixth day of the third month (May/June), the people celebrated Pentecost, which was also called the Feast of Weeks (Lev. 23:15–22), in commemoration of the completion of the barley and wheat harvests. In the seventh month (September/October), the first day was the Feast of Trumpets (Lev. 23:23–25; Num. 29:1), celebrating the New Year; the tenth day was the Day of Atonement (Lev. 16:29–34; 23:26–32); the fifteenth to the twenty-second days were the Feast of Tabernacles or Ingathering (Lev. 23:33–43) in commemoration of all the harvests of the year. Thus, the feasts revolved around the harvests.

With regard to the year, the Jewish historian Josephus stated that Israel had two New Years—the commercial New Year, which began in the fall (seventh month), and the religious New Year, which began in the spring (first month). Since the months were based on the lunar system and since each month averaged 29½ days, the year would be 354 days long, or 11 days short of the solar year. In just three years the calendar would be off more than a month. To reconcile the lunar month with the solar year, Babylonia had a sophisticated system where seven months would be added to the calendar over a 19-year cycle, resulting in an error of only two hours and four minutes by the end of the cycle. This is remarkable accuracy for that day. Israel must have adjusted her calendar in a similar fashion by adding a "Second Adar" month whenever necessary.

Between the Testaments — During the period when the Greeks ruled the ancient world, the Seleucid calendar system was most widely used. Two basic systems were used for reckoning time in the Seleucid era—the Macedonian calendar and the Babylonian calendar. It is difficult to be dogmatic as to which system was used, but the Jewish people seem to have used the Macedonian calendar. This means the Seleucid era in Jewish history began on the first day of their seventh month, Tishri, about 312/311 B.C.

In the New Testament — The New Testament contains no references to the Roman or Gentile calendar or to the Jewish calendar, except in speaking of the days of the week. There is also one reference to the "new moon" (Col. 2:16). The Sabbath, Saturday, is mentioned about 60 times (for instance, Matt. 12:1–12). The New Testament also mentions the "first day," Sunday (Mark 16:2; Luke 24:1; Acts 20:7; 1 Cor. 16:2), "the Lord's Day," Sunday (Rev. 1:10), and the "Day of Preparation" or "Preparation Day," Friday (Matt. 27:62; Mark 15:42; Luke 23:54; John 19:14, 31,

42). However, these are references to the cultic aspects of the Jewish calendar. Frequent mention is made, especially in the Gospel of John, of the Passover (John 2:13, 23; 6:4; 11:55; 12:1; 13:1; 18:39). Other festivals mentioned in the New Testament are Unleavened Bread (Matt. 26:17; Mark 14:1, 12), Pentecost (Acts 2:1; 20:16; 1 Cor. 16:8), Feast of Tabernacles (John 7:2), and the Feast of Dedication (John 10:22). Although the New Testament makes no references to the Roman or Gentile calendar, it does refer to the reigns of rulers. The most specific example is Luke 3:1, which speaks of "the fifteenth year of the reign of Tiberius Caesar." This refers to the time of the rulers then in office in Judea and the surrounding territories and to the beginning of the ministry of John the Baptist. This must have been in A.D. 28–29, assuming that Luke used either the Julian calendar, which began in January, or the regnal calendar, which began in August. The most general references speak not of the year but of the reigns of emperors Caesar Augustus (Luke 2:1) and Claudius Caesar (Acts 11:28), of provincial governors Quirinius (Luke 2:1–2) and Gallio (Acts 18:12), of King Herod (Matt. 2:1; Luke 1:5), and of the ethnarch Aretas (2 Cor. 11:32). One New Testament calendar problem is that the Gospels of Matthew, Mark, and Luke portray Jesus as having celebrated the Passover with His disciples on the eve of His betrayal (Matt. 26:19–20; Mark 14:16–17; Luke 22:13–15), whereas the Gospel of John pictures the Jews as not having celebrated the Passover at this time (John 18:28). Many attempts have been made to reconcile this problem. Possibly, the solution is that the first three Gospels reckoned their timetable of the crucifixion events according to the Galilean method (beginning the day at sunrise), which was used by Jesus, the disciples, and the Pharisees. But John may have reckoned according to the Judean method (beginning the day at sunset), a system used by the Sadducees. If this is true, different calendar systems may have been in use at the same time within the nation of Israel.

CANAANITES [KANE un ites] — an ancient tribe that lived in the land of Canaan before they were displaced by the nation of Israel. The Canaanites, along with the Amorites, settled the land well before 2000 B.C. Archaeological exploration of their native land and adjacent territories has provided information on many aspects of their culture. Among the numerous sites excavated in ancient Canaan, or the present-day Holy Land, are Hazor, Megiddo, Beth Shan, Jericho, Jebus (Jerusalem), Debir, Lachish, and Arad. Sites in the northern part of ancient Canaan include Byblos and Ras Shamra (Ugarit) along the coast of the Mediterranean Sea and Hamath on the Orontes River.

Although both Canaanites and Amorites were established in Canaan before 2000 B.C., the Canaanites established their civilization as dominant during the Middle Bronze Age (about 2100 to 1550 B.C.). Their society had several classes, ranging from the ruling nobility to the peasants. The northern Canaanites used a particular cuneiform script, featuring a wedge-shaped alphabet. Their land was also dotted with walled cities. Several of these served as the centers of city-states, each having its own king, or mayor, and army.

The Canaanites, therefore, were a highly civilized people in many ways when Joshua led the Israelites across the Jordan River to conquer the people and settle the land. Canaanite history ended with the Israelite conquest. But certain segments of Canaanite culture remained to make both positive and negative impacts on the life of God's Covenant People.

Canaanite Language and Literature. Knowledge of Canaanite language and literature was enhanced by the discovery of the Ugaritic texts at Ras Shamra (ancient Ugarit), a site on the Mediterranean coast in modern Syria. Accidental discovery of a vaulted room by a farmer while plowing his field on the top of Ras Shamra led to several full-scale excavations by Claude F. A. Schaeffer, the first in 1929. These excavations resulted in the recovery of a store of religious texts and other documents on clay tablets. These writings have yielded a great deal of knowledge about Canaanite life, particularly their form of religion.

The Canaanite language in written form, as revealed by the Ugaritic texts of Ras Shamra, is an alphabetic cuneiform (wedge-shaped) type of writing. This form contrasts markedly with the syllabic cuneiform of the ancient Babylonian and Assyrian languages. It does have many similarities to other ancient languages of the Middle Eastern world during this period, but it also has many significant differences. These differences are so significant that archaeologists can say with certainty that the Canaanites developed a language all their own. The Ugaritic texts from Ras Shamra are by far the most significant literary sources of the Canaanite language in the alphabetic cuneiform script. These texts go back to the 14th century B.C. or earlier. Most of them are of a religious nature, providing valuable details on both the literature and the religion of the Canaanites. These texts have also given Bible scholars a better understanding of Old Testament writings and background.

The texts of greatest importance for giving details on Canaanite religion are three mythologies: (1) the Baal Epic, an account of the activities of Baal, including his building of a temple; (2) the Legend of Aqhat, the only son of an ancient Canaanite king; and (3) the Legend of King Keret of Hubur, who suffered the loss of his family and who later obtained another wife by conquest. In doing so, however, he displeased the gods. Comparative studies between these texts and Old Testament writings, particularly early Hebrew poems and the Psalms, show how the Old Testament has been influenced by its ancient setting. But they also show that the Israelites' faith in their one Redeemer God was a dramatic contrast to the pagan religion of the Canaanites.

Canaanite Religion. The Canaanite religion featured many gods. These gods were worshiped with elaborate ritual. Various kinds of cultic personnel, or priests, officiated at these pagan ceremonies. Their religious system also featured many different places of worship, varying from simple outdoor altars to massive stone temples.

The Old Testament refers frequently to Baal (Num. 22:41), Baals (Hos. 2:13, 17), or a Baal of a particular place, such as Baal of Peor (Num. 25:3, 5). The Old Testament also refers to Asherah (1 Kin. 18:19), Ashtoreth (1 Kin. 11:5, 33), and the Ashtoreths (Judg. 2:13). References to these Canaanite gods and goddesses always carry strong denunciations by the biblical writers. But these names mentioned in the Old Testament are only a few of the many additional names for Canaanite gods that appear in the Ugaritic texts.

The highest of all the Canaanite gods was El, as shown clearly by the Ugaritic texts. But El chose to remain in the background, conferring power and authority upon his brood of gods and goddesses. The main goddess by whom El fathered children was Asherah. She and El were the parents of more than 70 other deities. The Baal mentioned frequently in the Old Testament was lord among the gods because of authority granted by El. Baal was known chiefly as the god of fertility and as god of the storm. Temples were built in his name at a number of sites, including one at Ugarit. Three Canaanite goddesses mentioned frequently in the Ugaritic texts are Anath (Judg. 3:31), Asherah, and Astarte (Ashtoreth of the Old Testament). Among the many other deities of the Canaanites were Resheph, god of pestilence, and Mot, god of drought and death.

Canaanite religion had a number of features that were similar to certain practices of the religious system of the Israelites. Like the Israelites, the Canaanites offered various kinds of offerings to their gods. Animals offered included sheep, cattle, and certain wild animals. A high priest among the Canaanites served as the head of 12 priestly families. Other important worship leaders who served in the Canaanite temples included singers, who used liturgy or a form of psalmody; consecrated persons—in effect, male and female prostitutes; vestment makers and sculptors; and priest-scribes, who were responsible for preserving important literary traditions. Like the Hebrew feasts and festivals, the celebrations of the Canaanites also paralleled the seasons or cycles of the agricultural year. But in other important ways, Canaanite and Hebrew religion were poles apart. The religion of these pagan people was basically a fertility cult. At temples scattered throughout their land, Canaanite worshipers actually participated in lewd, immoral acts with "sacred" prostitutes. Theirs was a depraved form of worship that appealed to the base instincts of sinful human nature. They also practiced human sacrifice, and their religion sanctioned unbelievable cruelty in warfare. In contrast, the Hebrews worshiped a holy God who insisted on purity and righteousness among His people. Although the Israelites were called to a high ethical plane in their worship, at times the sensual appeal of the Canaanite cults enticed them into sin and idolatry. This explains the strong appeal Joshua made to the people of Israel in his farewell speech. Joshua had led them to take the land, but many of the Canaanites still remained. The aging warrior knew their form of pagan worship would be a strong temptation to the people. Thus he declared, "Put away the foreign gods which are among you, and incline your heart to the Lord God of Israel" (Josh. 24:23).

CAPTIVITY — the state or condition of being in bondage to one's enemies, especially if this involves deportation to a foreign land. The term "captivity" is commonly used to describe two periods when the nations of Israel (722 B.C.) and Judah (605 B.C. and later) were taken away from their native lands and into exile.

The Captivity of Israel, the Ten Northern Tribes. The first captivity was partly the result of Assyria's march toward Palestine in an attempt to reduce the power of the Syrian Empire. Since about 950 B.C., the Syrians had extended their borders eastward to Assyria. On the south and west they had attacked the kingdom of Israel.

Syria and Israel quickly forgot their quarrel in the face of Assyria's threat. They formed an alliance and fought a great battle against the Assyrians in 853 B.C. at Qarqar in Syria. The Assyrians were fought to a draw, effectively checking their threat for several years. Soon the old hostility between Syria and Israel flared anew.

In 841 B.C. the Assyrians began another campaign. This time King Jehu of Israel (about 841–814 B.C.) chose to pay tribute to Assyria and not join with Syria. For four years the Assyrians attacked the Syrians without success. For a short period Syria was dominant in the Near East, but its power ended when a new Assyrian king, Tiglath-Pileser III, ascended to the throne.

The new king was determined to crush the power of Syria and its allies. Accordingly, he attacked King Menahem of Israel (who reigned from about 752–742 B.C.), who quickly paid tribute to Assyria. The Syrians tried to persuade Judah to ally with them against Assyria; they even marched through Judah and occupied the port of Elath on the Gulf of Aqaba to show their strength. Instead, King Ahaz of Judah (who ruled from about 732–716 B.C.) urgently appealed to the Assyrians for help. Tiglath-Pileser responded by attacking the Syrians and besieging their capital, Damascus.

When Damascus fell in 732 B.C., Tiglath-Pileser then attacked Israel, preventing it from further aiding the Syrians. He took the tribes of Gad and Reuben and the half-tribe of Manasseh to Mesopotamia as captives (2 Kin. 15:29). He also made the remaining tribes pay tribute. However, when Tiglath-Pileser died (727 B.C.), the Israelites stopped sending tribute to Assyria. Instead, they allied themselves secretly with Egypt. Assyria reacted quickly and attacked Samaria; in 722 B.C., the city finally fell. The rest of the Israelite tribes were taken captive to Assyria, and the Northern Kingdom came to an end. The Hebrew prophets interpreted this event as God's punishment for Israel's idolatry (2 Kin. 17:7–23) and rejection of covenant spirituality (Amos 5:1–15). There is no record of the people of the northern tribes of Israel ever returning to the land in large numbers.

The Captivity of Judah, the Southern Kingdom. Israel's collapse ought to have served as a warning to rebellious Judah, which now had no protection against attack by the Assyrians. Assyria was determined to reduce Egypt's influence in Judah and Syria. Since Judah already had political contact with Egypt, the slightest move toward Egypt would bring the wrath of the Assyrians. In an astute move, King Hezekiah of Judah (about 716–686 B.C.) took advantage of the tension between Egypt and Syria and made Judah independent of both. He also regained control of the Philistine cities in the land.

When Sennacherib succeeded Sargon II in 705 B.C. as king of Assyria, he continued Assyria's westward expansion. Assyria, however, was under increasing pressure from the east. The Babylonian Empire was reviving, and its king sought to draw Judah and Egypt into an alliance against Assyria. In 701 B.C. the Assyrian armies got as far as the Mediterranean, but failed to conquer Jerusalem (2 Kin. 19:20–36). About 650 B.C. Judah and Egypt revolted against Assyrian domination, but Assyria quickly crushed that attempt. Assyria's power, however, was on the decline, and its end occurred when Babylon gained its independence about 626 B.C. The battles of the next 16 years resulted in the complete collapse of the Assyrian Empire.

Pharaoh Necho of Egypt allied with the faltering Assyrian armies in order to protect his own interests, but his action could not prevent disaster. Instead, he attracted the attention of the Babylonians, who defeated the Egyptian armies at Carchemish in 605 B.C., placed Judah under tribute, and deported a number of Judah's nobles (Dan. 1:1–5). Three years later King Jehoiakim of Judah rebelled, and in 597 B.C. powerful Babylonian armies conquered Jerusalem and took "three thousand and twenty-three Jews" captive to Mesopotamia (Jer. 52:28). A third (586 B.C.) and fourth (581 B.C.) deportation involved 832 and 745 captives, respectively (Jer. 52:29–30), and ended the kingdom of Judah.

Little is known about Israel and Judah's life during the captivity. Captivity meant a shameful and humiliating punishment for this disobedient, idolatrous people. The royal court of Judah was taken into captivity, along with the priests, skilled workers, and anyone else who might ever lead a revolt against Babylon. The captives realized that God had finally brought the long-standing covenant curses (Deut. 28:15–68) to bear upon them. Torn from their homes and familiar surroundings, they were forced to travel across a hot desert to a strange land. Many of them had to work for their conquerors.

The punishment of captivity lasted 70 years for Judah (Jer. 25:11–12; Dan. 9:2), after which the penitent were allowed to return to their homeland under the leadership of Zerubbabel and others (Ezra 2:1–2). Israel's tribes, however, never returned and became lost to history.

CAVALRY — warriors or soldiers on horseback, assigned to battles that require great mobility. The Bible mentions the cavalry units of Solomon (1 Kin. 9:19, 22; 2 Chr. 8:6, 9), Ben-Hadad the king of Syria (1 Kin. 20:20), and the Chaldeans (Hab. 1:8; horsemen, KJV, NRSV, NIV). Both the Egyptians and the Canaanites had cavalries that threatened the Israelites at various times (Ex. 14:9; 15:19; Judg. 4:15). Most of the references to "cavalry" in the Old Testament probably intend "charioteers," since the use of soldiers on horseback was a relatively late development.

CENSUS — an official counting and registration of citizens; a property evaluation for tax purposes in early Rome.

The first numbering of the people in the Old Testament occurred at the time of the exodus. All men 20 years of age or older who were able to go to war were counted (Num. 1:2–46). One purpose of this census was to help in the distribution of the land (Num. 26:52–56). After the captivity, there was another census (Ezra 2) of men to show how many had returned from Babylonian captivity and also as an aid for the distribution of the land.

In New Testament times the Roman government conducted periodic countings of the people to assess the amount of tax their country should pay to the treasury of the Roman Empire. The New Testament mentions two censuses. At the time of Jesus' birth, Joseph and Mary went to Bethlehem to be registered (Luke 2:1–5). This was probably a census required of all nations under the rule of Rome. All citizens were required to return to their places of birth for an official registration of their property for tax purposes.

The second Roman census was conducted to make an assessment of the property of Judea in A.D. 6. At this time Judea came under direct Roman rule. Because of this, Judas of Galilee incited a revolt, stating that the Jews should be ruled by God rather than by a foreign power (Acts 5:37). The Roman system of taking census began in 10–9 B.C. Such a registration took place every 14 years.

CHALDEANS [kal DEE unz] (*conquerors*) — one of the ancient peoples that formed the dominant population in Babylonia, especially beginning with the empire of Nebuchadnezzar II (king of Babylonia from 605 to 562 B.C.).

The Chaldeans are first mentioned in secular literature in the annals of the Assyrian king Ashurnasirpal II (who reigned from 884/883 to 859 B.C.). Earlier documents refer to the same area as the "sea lands." In 850 B.C. Shalmaneser III, king of Assyria (reigned from 859 to 824 B.C.), raided Chaldea and reached the Persian Gulf, which he called the "Sea of Kaldu." On the accession of Sargon II (reigned from 721 to 705 B.C.) to the Assyrian throne, the Chaldean Marduk-apla-iddina II—in the Bible called Merodach-Baladan (Is. 39:1) or Berodach-Baladan (2 Kin. 20:12)—a ruler of Bit-Yakin (a district of Chaldea), rebelled against the Assyrians and became king of Babylonia.

In spite of Assyrian opposition, Merodach-Baladan held power from 721 to 710 B.C. In 712 B.C. (2 Kin. 20:12–19; Is. 39:1–8) he sent an embassy to Hezekiah, king of Judah, inviting him to join a confederacy with Babylonia, Phoenicia, Moab, Edom, Philistia, and Egypt against Assyria. After Merodach-Baladan seized power, the Chaldeans became the dominant power in Babylon (Is. 13:19; 47:1, 5; 48:14, 20). He finally fled, however, and Bit-Yakin was placed under Assyrian control.

When Assyrian power declined, a Chaldean governor, Nabopolassar (the father of Nebuchadnezzar) led a revolt. In 626 B.C., he became king of Babylonia and founded a Chaldean (Neo-Babylonian) dynasty that lasted until the Persian invasion of 539 B.C., led by Cyrus the Great (king of Persia from 550 to 529 B.C.). The prestige of Nabopolassar's successors, Nabu-kudurri-usur (Nebuchadnezzar; king of Babylonia from 605 to 562 B.C.) and Nabonidus (king of Babylonia from 556 to 539 B.C.), was such that the term "Chaldean" became synonymous with the term "Babylonian."

Nebuchadnezzar was the king involved in the capture of Jerusalem and the deportation of its inhabitants into Babylonian captivity (2 Kin. 24:1–2; Jer. 25:1; 26:9–11; 52:30). The son of Nebuchadnezzar, Awel-Marduk (called Evil-Merodach in 2 Kin. 25:27 and Jer. 52:31), freed Jehoiachin, king of Judah, from prison after he had been there for 37 years. He gave Jehoiachin a daily allowance of food for the rest of his life.

In the Bible the term "Chaldeans" is first mentioned in connection with Haran—the son of Terah and brother of Abram—who "died before his father Terah in his native land, in Ur of the Chaldeans" (Gen. 11:28). The book of Genesis tells us that "Terah took his son Abram [Abraham] and his grandson Lot, the son of Haran, and his daughter-in-law Sarai [Sarah], his son Abram's wife, and they went out ... from Ur of the Chaldeans to go to the land of Canaan" (Gen. 11:31). Abraham lived in Ur of the Chaldeans before the Chaldeans dominated Babylonia.

The term "Chaldean" also was used by several ancient authors to denote the priests and other persons educated in the classical Babylonian literature, especially in traditions of astronomy and astrology (Dan. 2:2, 4–5, 10). Some scholars believe the "wise men [magoi] from the East" (Matt. 2:1) who came to Jerusalem at the time of Jesus' birth may have been Chaldean astrologers.

In the Bible most of the references to Chaldeans appear in the book of Jeremiah (21:4, 9; 35:11; 51:4, 54). Jeremiah identified the Chaldeans with the Babylonians, who besieged the city of Jerusalem during the reign of Nebuchadnezzar, looted the temple, and carried the Israelites into captivity.

CHISLEV [KIZZ lehv] — the ninth month in the Hebrew calendar (Neh. 1:1; Zech. 7:1; Chisleu, KJV; Kislev, NIV).

CHRISTIANITY — the Christian religion, based on Jesus Christ, the only Savior and Mediator between God the Father and sinful humankind. Christianity is unique among all the religions of the world. Most of them emphasize the life of the founder, but Christianity is based on the death of Jesus Christ. The death of Jesus is unique for it was prophesied in the opening pages of the Bible (Gen. 5) and came to pass in the New Testament age thousands of years later. Not only is the death of Christ absolutely essential to Christianity, so is His resurrection. His death and resurrection are so important that all four Gospels—Matthew, Mark, Luke, and John—devote at least one-fifth of their teachings to this combined subject. Mark 10:45 summarizes this unique mission of Christ's: "For even the Son of Man did not come to be served, but to serve, and to give His life a ransom for many." The world already had plenty of religions and gods at the time of Jesus' birth. The Romans had combined their gods with those of the Greeks, and thousands of deities were worshiped. None of these gods had ever lived; most were based on imagination or heroic stories. But Jesus had actually lived in Palestine, had been crucified under Pontius Pilate (the Roman governor of Judea), and had been raised from the dead by the power of God the Father. People who worshiped the mythical gods actually chose to ignore the visible signs of truth that pointed them toward God and eventually to salvation through grace (Rom. 1:20–21). This plan of salvation came to full maturity on the cross. In the apostle Paul's time there was a grave danger that Jewish converts to Christianity would make the new religion nothing more than an extension of Judaism. Paul fought to keep salvation-by-grace-plus-nothing the essence of Christianity (Eph. 2:8–9). Paul's conflict was with a group of converts called Judaizers (Acts 15; Galatians 2), who thought a Gentile convert had to be circumcised before he could become a Christian. Paul, Barnabas, and others traveled to Jerusalem, the center of Judaism, to settle the issue with the church leaders. In effect, Christianity was declared to be a full-grown, independent religion, not simply an extension of the Jewish faith. Today, Paul's battle cry still rings forth as the banner of the Christian faith: "A man is not justified by the works of the law but by faith in Jesus Christ" (Gal. 2:16). Salvation is available only through Christ (Acts 4:12), made possible by His death, burial, and resurrection. Christianity is more than a creed, more than a religion; it is a way of life for all who accept Jesus Christ as Lord and Savior.

CHRONOLOGY, NEW TESTAMENT — the chronology of the New Testament has been debated over the centuries. This is due partly to the limited data given in the biblical record. The biblical writers were more interested in the events that occurred than in the exact dates when they took place. Many times specific chronological facts are given as incidental remarks in the Bible. From these facts scholars attempt to reconstruct a chronological framework.

The Chronology of the Life of Jesus. The first task the student of the New Testament faces is to construct a chronology of the life of Jesus. The following high points in His life and ministry, with approximate dates, are accepted by most New Testament scholars.

His birth — According to Matthew 2:1 and Luke 1:5, Jesus' birth happened before Herod the Great's death, which was no later than March or April in 4 B.C. Luke 2:1–5 states that just before Jesus' birth, Quirinius took a census of Israel while he was governor of Syria. The date of Quirinius's governorship is debated. Some scholars believe Quirinius was governor of Syria twice: once around the time of Herod's death and then a decade later in A.D. 6–7.

Another chronological note is that when Herod was tricked by the Wise Men who visited the baby Jesus, he ordered all children two years of age and younger to be killed. Some think this would indicate that Jesus was born two years before Herod's order. This is not necessarily true, for Herod was more likely just making sure that he would not miss Jesus in this senseless slaughter. Furthermore, some try to make the star in the east a conjunction of several stars. Again, the text talks about one star that seemed special to the wise men. A conjunction of stars would not have signified the birth of a king, according to the astrology of that day.

In conclusion, it seems that Jesus was born sometime around 6 to 4 B.C., with the probability that it was the winter of 5/4 B.C. just before Herod's death.

The beginning of His ministry — Luke 3:1–3 states that John the Baptist's ministry began in the 15th year of Tiberius Caesar. Tiberius began reigning in August in A.D. 14. So this would mean that John the Baptist's ministry began sometime in A.D. 29. From the Gospel narratives about Jesus, it seems that He was baptized and began His ministry shortly after John began preaching. Luke 3:23 states that Jesus was "about" 30 years of age when He began His ministry. If Jesus was born in the winter of 5/4 B.C. and began His ministry in the summer or fall of A.D. 29, He would have been 32.

The duration of His ministry — Although a few scholars hold to a one- or two-year ministry of Jesus, most think He had at least a three-year ministry. The Gospel of John records three specific Passover celebrations during Jesus' ministry (John 2:13; 6:4; 11:55), which would account for at least two years of His ministry. However, it is thought that an additional year must be added between the Passovers of John 2:13 and 6:4. The reasons for this additional year come from two notes about time in John.

In John 4:35 Jesus speaks of four months before harvest, which would mean that He was in Samaria around January or February after the Passover celebration of John 2:13. John 5:1 also mentions a "feast." Although scholars disagree on the identification of this feast, it probably refers to Passover or the Feast of Tabernacles.

Thus, after the Passover of John 2:13 there is the reference to January or February of John 4:35 and a "feast" of John 5:1. This most likely refers to the Passover or Feast of Tabernacles before the Passover of John 6:4. Thus, there is a two-year interval between the Passovers of John 2:13 and 6:4 and a one-year interval between the Passovers of John 6:4 and 11:55. Therefore, if Jesus began His ministry in the summer or autumn of A.D. 29 and His first Passover is to be identified as the one mentioned in A.D. 30 and the last one in A.D. 33, the duration of His ministry would be about three and a half years.

Jesus' ministry before the first Passover in A.D. 30 would include the temptation (Matt. 4:1–11; Mark 1:12–13; Luke 4:1–13), the call of His first disciples (Matt. 4:18–22; Mark 1:16–20; John 1:35–51), the wedding at Cana (John 2:1–11), and His journey to Capernaum (John 2:12) just before He went to Jerusalem for His first Passover (John 2:13).

After this Passover Jesus' ministry was primarily in Jerusalem and Judea (John 3:1–26). Following John the Baptist's imprisonment, Jesus moved to Galilee (Matt. 4:12–17; Mark 1:14–15; Luke 4:14–15; John 4:3–36). He continued His ministry in Galilee until John the Baptist was executed. Although the date of the beheading is not specified, it occurred at about the same time as the feeding of the 5,000 (Matt. 14:13–21; Mark 6:30–44; Luke 9:10–17), which happened sometime around the Passover of A.D. 32 (John 6:4).

After this Passover Jesus withdrew from public ministry to be with His disciples. Other events during the final year of His ministry included His journey to Phoenicia (Matt. 15:21–28; Mark 7:24–30), the feeding of the 4,000 (Matt. 15:32–39; Mark 8:1–10), Peter's confession at Caesarea Philippi (Matt. 16:13–23; Mark 8:27–33; Luke 9:18–22), and the Transfiguration (Matt. 17:1–8; Mark 9:2–8; Luke 9:28–36). Finally, Jesus went to Jerusalem to be crucified during the Passover celebration of A.D. 33 (John 11:55).

The date of His death — Since Jesus was tried by Pilate, His death occurred during Pilate's governorship, which lasted from A.D. 26 to A.D. 36. Astronomically, Jesus' death fits best with either A.D. 30 or 33. Because of the political situation and other facts surrounding Jesus' life, it seems that A.D. 33 is the best date for the crucifixion. The day of the week of His crucifixion has been debated. But it seems best to consider it as Friday, since His body was laid in the tomb on the evening of the "Day of Preparation" (technical term for Friday), the day before the Sabbath (Matt. 27:62; 28:1; Mark 15:42; Luke 23:54, 56; John 19:31, 42). Thus Jesus was crucified on Friday, April 3, in A.D. 33.

The Chronology of the Apostolic Age. Another important task in New Testament studies is to construct a chronology of the important events that occurred during the lives of the apostles and the early years of the Christian church.

The book of Acts and the New Testament epistles serve as the basis of the chronology of the apostolic period. References to the political leaders during this time help pinpoint the dates.

From Pentecost to Paul's second Jerusalem visit — Pentecost, which would have occurred on May 24, A.D. 33, is the starting point of the apostolic age. To establish the date of Paul's conversion, scholars have determined the time of Paul's first two visits to Jerusalem. The first visit occurred three years after his conversion (Acts 9:26–29; Gal. 1:18) when he escaped from Damascus while it was under Aretas's control (2 Cor. 11:32–33). The Romans let Aretas control Damascus from A.D. 37 until his death in A.D. 39. Thus Paul's conversion would have occurred sometime between A.D. 33 and A.D. 36.

Paul's second visit to Jerusalem was 14 years after his conversion (Gal. 2:1–10) when he brought relief to the Christians suffering a famine (Acts 11:28–30; 12:25). According to the Jewish historian Josephus, Helena, queen of Adiabene, shipped figs from Cyprus and grain from Egypt, probably at the height of the famine (A.D. 47–48), or shortly thereafter. Paul brought contributions after the shipment from Helena and would have come to Jerusalem a second time around A.D. 47–48. Counting 14 years between his conversion and this visit would mean that Paul's conversion occurred in A.D. 33 or 34, although it could have been later, since the ancients counted parts of years as whole years. Most likely Paul's conversion was sometime in A.D. 35, probably in the summer of that year.

The events in the first part of Acts may be summarized as follows: Peter's ministry in Jerusalem, A.D. 33–35 (Acts 2–5); Stephen's martyrdom in the spring of A.D. 35 (Acts 6–7); Paul's conversion in the summer of A.D. 35 (Acts 9:1–7); Paul in Damascus and Arabia, A.D. 35–37 (Acts 9:8–25; Gal. 1:16–17); Paul's first visit to Jerusalem and ministry in Tarsus and Syria-Cilicia, A.D. 37 (Acts 9:26–30; Gal. 1:18–21); Peter's ministry to the Gentiles, A.D. 40–41 (Acts 10:1–11:18); Barnabas and Paul's journey to Antioch, A.D. 41–43 (Acts 19:19–26); Agabus's prediction of famine, A.D. 44 (Acts 11:27–28); James's martyrdom during Agrippa I's persecution, A.D. 44 (Acts 12); and Paul's second visit to Jerusalem and his return to Antioch, A.D. 47–48 (Acts 11:30; 12:25; Gal. 2:1–10).

Paul's first missionary journey — On his first missionary journey (Acts 13–14) Paul went from Antioch to Cyprus when Sergius Paulus ruled as proconsul before A.D. 51 and most likely in A.D. 46–48. Paul next went to the Galatian churches in Asia Minor and then returned to Antioch. This journey lasted from the spring of A.D. 48 to the fall of A.D. 49. Upon his return to Antioch, he saw Peter (Gal. 2:11–16) and wrote the book of Galatians. Paul's third visit to Jerusalem in the autumn of A.D. 49 was to attend the Jerusalem Council (Acts 15), after which he returned and wintered at Antioch in A.D. 49/50.

Paul's second missionary journey — Paul's second missionary journey began in the spring of A.D. 50 and ended in the fall of A.D. 52 (Acts 15:36–18:22). He revisited the Galatian churches and went on to Troas. Crossing over into Europe, he founded churches at Philippi, Thessalonica, and Berea. He waited in Athens for Silas and Timothy and then went to Corinth and stayed there a year and a half (Acts 18:11), from the spring of A.D. 51 to the fall of A.D. 52. Paul wrote 1 and 2 Thessalonians in

A.D. 51 while he was in Corinth. Two chronological notes need to be considered.

First, while at Corinth he met Priscilla and Aquila, who had fled Italy because of the persecution of the Jews in A.D. 49 (Acts 18:2). Hence, Paul could not have come to Corinth before A.D. 49. Second, Paul was tried before Gallio (Acts 18:12–16), who was the proconsul of Achaia from the summer of A.D. 51 to the summer of A.D. 52. Thus, Paul must have been in Corinth sometime during Gallio's rule. After his long stay in Corinth, Paul brought Priscilla and Aquila to Ephesus and then moved on to Jerusalem (fourth visit) and returned to Antioch for the winter in A.D. 52/53.

Paul's third missionary journey — Paul's third missionary journey was from the spring of A.D. 53 to the spring of A.D. 57 (Acts 18:23–21:16). Leaving Antioch, he revisited the Galatian churches, arriving in Ephesus around the fall of A.D. 53 and staying there until the spring of A.D. 56. Just before his departure from Ephesus, he wrote 1 Corinthians. Because of the riot at Ephesus, he left for Macedonia. From Macedonia he wrote 2 Corinthians (fall of A.D. 56). He traveled to Corinth, wintered there in A.D. 56/57, and wrote Romans. In the spring of A.D. 57 he revisited the churches in Macedonia, went to Miletus to meet the Ephesian elders, and then went on to Jerusalem (fifth visit) for the Feast of Pentecost in A.D. 57.

Paul's imprisonments — While in Jerusalem, Paul was arrested and taken to Caesarea, where he was tried by Felix and imprisoned for two years in A.D. 57–59 (Acts 21:26–27). Although there is debate concerning the time that Festus succeeded Felix, it is likely that this succession occurred in the summer of A.D. 59. Paul was heard first by Festus (Acts 25:7–12) and shortly afterward by Agrippa II (Acts 26). Then he appealed to Caesar.

Paul went to Rome on a hazardous journey from August of A.D. 59 to February of A.D. 60 and was imprisoned from the spring of A.D. 60 to the spring of A.D. 62 (Acts 27–28). While in prison Paul wrote Ephesians, Colossians, Philemon, and Philippians.

Chronology from this point on is drawn from inferences in the epistles in the New Testament and other evidence from the early church. It seems likely that Paul was released after a two-year imprisonment in Rome and went to Ephesus and Colossae and then left for Macedonia. In the fall of A.D. 62 Paul wrote to Timothy at Ephesus. Also in A.D. 62, James, the brother of Jesus, was martyred during the time of anarchy between the death of Festus and Albinus's arrival. Peter probably went to Rome that year and remained there until his martyrdom in the persecution of the Roman emperor Nero in A.D. 64. While Peter was in Rome, the Gospel of Mark may have been written under Peter's guidance. Also, Peter would have written his two epistles.

Paul moved to Asia Minor in the spring of A.D. 63 and remained there until the spring of A.D. 64. He then went to Spain from the spring of A.D. 64 to the spring of A.D. 66. Leaving Spain, he went to Crete with Titus and left Titus there while he went on to Asia Minor in the summer/autumn of A.D. 66. While there he wrote the epistle to Titus. Paul spent the winter of A.D. 66/67 at Nicopolis (Titus 3:12), after which he went to Macedonia and Greece. But he was arrested and brought to Rome in the fall of A.D. 67 for his second Roman imprisonment. While there he wrote 2 Timothy. Paul was executed around the spring of A.D. 68.

About two years after Paul's death, Jerusalem was destroyed. At that time only a few remaining books of the New Testament had not been written. It is possible that the Gospel of John was written around A.D. 70. Jude may have been written about A.D. 75, the three epistles of John about A.D. 85–95, and the book of Revelation about A.D. 95–96. This marked the end of the age of the apostles.

CHRONOLOGY, OLD TESTAMENT — the scientific identification of the time when the events recorded in the Old Testament took place. With all the information the Old Testament contains, some of it detailed and lengthy, drawing up a settled list of dates for the events it reports might appear to be a simple task. Actually it is very difficult. Not only do we not have a sufficiently continuous record of events, much of the information we do have can be interpreted in different ways.

It is hard to relate specific events in Hebrew history to what was taking place in neighboring nations until about the 8th century B.C. In turn, dating the events of each of these nations presents its own problems. Finally, the systems by which Israel and its neighbors kept track of time and events are not clear.

Problems in Establishing a Chronology. The first of these obstacles can be illustrated from the work of the 17th-century archbishop James Ussher, who treated the biblical genealogies as though they were modern records of generation-by-generation descent. Basing his work on that assumption, he calculated back to the time of creation, which he set at 4004 B.C. More recent information about ancient lists of descendants, however, indicates that unimportant family members often were omitted. This led to compressed lists that did not precisely conform to the period of time that they were supposed to cover.

Ussher also took the ages of the people who lived before the Flood at face value. Later research has shown that they appear to be based upon an ancient Sumerian system of reckoning—such as that used for the Sumerian king lists—which we do not yet fully understand. As a result, Ussher's chronology is totally inaccurate until the time of Moses—a period that itself is also a matter of considerable debate among scholars.

If it were possible to link the period of the biblical Flood with what was happening in the rest of the world, as described in Sumerian or Babylonian literature, Old Testament chronology would be a simple matter. But there are a number of reasons why this is impossible.

The first problem is that there was no uniform basis in the ancient world on which dates were reckoned. When attempts at dating were made, they were often expressed in phrases such as "after the earthquake," or "in the fourth year of the king." While these statements were perfectly clear to everyone who read them at the time of their writing, they are completely meaningless for comparing the events that took place in that culture with events that happened at the same time somewhere else. Consequently, the problems involved in trying to establish dates from the ancient Near East in general also apply to the attempt to establish dates for Old Testament events.

Scholars who have tried to establish dating sequences for Babylonian history have found themselves embarrassed by two dating sequences for one of the earlier periods. There is a "high" chronology for the First Babylonian Dynasty; it is arrived at by connecting Amraphel, king of Shinar (Gen. 14:1), with Hammurapi of Babylon and dating him around 2100 B.C. By contrast, the "low" chronology places Hammurapi between about 1728 and 1686 B.C. Even this late date, however, is regarded as too high by some scholars, who interpret the data differently.

A similar situation is true for Egyptian history. Information provided by lists and annals of kings generally is notably unreliable for purposes of chronology, and just as much caution is needed when dealing with Egyptian sources as with their counterparts in Mesopotamia (the region between the Tigris and Euphrates rivers).

Historians have discovered that Egyptian records are not so much factual history as propaganda; they present the "official" view of events for the instruction of future Egyptian generations. Historians have grouped the lists of Egyptian rulers into 31 dynasties. While this is a convenient way of looking at Egyptian history for the historian, the dates for events are not reliable until about the Saitic period (about 663–525 B.C.). Furthermore, both the First and Second Dynasties have "high" and "low" chronologies, the former supported by scholars who date the period between 3867 and 3100 B.C., and the latter supported by scholars who date the period between 2900 and 2760 B.C. Other difficulties in Egyptian dating include the Eighteenth Dynasty, which introduced the New Kingdom period (about 1570–1150 B.C.). This was the period of time during which pharaohs such as Amunhotep II, Akhenaten, Tutankhamun and others ruled.

In spite of these confusions, some dates in Near Eastern history can be established reasonably well. So skillful were the ancient Egyptians in determining the length of the solar year that the earliest precise year-date in human history can now be set as 1991 B.C., the beginning of the magnificent Twelfth Dynasty. Hammurapi of Babylon's 42-year reign was almost certainly 1792–1750 B.C. The fall of Samaria in 722 B.C. (2 Kin. 17:6) is confirmed by a statement in the annals of Sargon of Assyria for that year. Again, the first Babylonian attack on Jerusalem, resulting in the captivity of 597 B.C., occurred on March 15–16 of that year, as recorded in the Babylonian Chronicle, a contemporary cuneiform text. Unfortunately, such points of contact are few. It was unusual in ancient times for a defeated nation to record its losses.

First of all, if the war resulted in the extinction of one nation—as happened when the Sea Peoples brought the Hittite Empire to an end about 1200 B.C.—the conquered nation usually was unwilling, or unable, to record its defeat. Furthermore, it was the common practice among ancient Near Eastern nations—with the exception of the Hebrews—to exaggerate victories and to ignore defeats. In those instances where both sides fought to a standstill, each usually counted the battle as a victory.

Another practice that seems very strange to the modern reader was the practice in some Near Eastern countries of including an accession year as part of a king's reign. This period was not necessarily a full calendar year; often it consisted only of the interval between the accession of the new king and the beginning of the next calendar year. This is why it is so difficult to compare and make sense of the list of kings in the books of 1 and 2 Kings and 1 and 2 Chronicles.

Another device that complicates the chronology of the Old Testament was the system of co-regencies. A king would begin his reign while his predecessor was still alive, governing with him several years before he died. This system is the reason for some of the obvious difficulties in harmonizing dates of kings in the Old Testament. Thus, in the history of Judah, Jehoshaphat (about 870–848 B.C.) actually was co-regent from 873 B.C., while Jehoram (Joram), who reigned from about 848 to 841 B.C., had been co-regent from 853 B.C.

But even after recognizing all these dating problems, the Bible student can rest assured that the ancient Near Eastern scribes worked with great care and precision in passing on the Old Testament. They furnish the patient modern interpreter with the information needed to gain a reliable picture of Old Testament history.

Time of the Patriarchs. Because of the problems involved, archaeological periods might be used to date the earliest history of the Old Testament. But these periods are general rather than precise, and archaeologists disagree about the length of each period. Therefore these archaeological descriptions may be used for the periods up to, and including, the Hebrew Patriarchs. These dates should be regarded as approximate.

A late period of the Old Stone Age known as Natufian (8000 B.C.) corresponds with the introduction of agriculture into the Near East. This period was followed by the pre-pottery Neolithic phase (8000–5000 B.C.) at Jericho and elsewhere.

The Chalcolithic period (4500–3000 B.C.) was marked by the increasing use of metals in Mesopotamia and Egypt, and by weaving and pottery making in Mesopotamia. The Sumerians began draining the southern Mesopotamian marshes during this period. This led to the beginning of a culture that has left its mark on the rest of humanity. This civilization reached its height in the Early Bronze Age (3000–2100 B.C.), when the first Semitic kingdom was established in Babylonia.

The Sumerian words and phrases in the early chapters of Genesis show there was an important cultural connection between Sumer and Israel. The Flood may well have occurred about the middle of this period, but actual data is lacking. According to some scholars, Abraham, Isaac, and Jacob lived at this time; but others place them in the Middle Bronze Age (2100–1550 B.C.). A few writers even think that they flourished toward the end of the Late Bronze Age (1550–1200 B.C.).

Four dates have been suggested for the Hebrew patriarchs. These are based upon two different dates for the Exodus. The first and most likely date is 2166–1805 B.C., assuming a 15th-century B.C. date for the Exodus and a 430-year Hebrew settlement in Egypt. The archaeological background material used to support this date comes from Mesopotamia and Syria. The second, also assuming a 15th-century B.C. Exodus but reckoning a 215-year Egyptian settlement by the Hebrews, is 1952–1589 B.C. Once more, Mesopotamian archaeological materials are claimed as evidence.

The third date, assuming a 13th-century B.C. period for the Exodus, is 1950–1650 B.C. Advocates of this theory argue from archaeological evidence from the Middle Bronze Age. The fourth date, also assuming a 13th-century B.C. Exodus, is 1500–1300 B.C. Advocates of this date support their position with evidence from the Amarna Age culture of the 14th century B.C.

The Time of the Exodus. The two suggested dates for the Exodus must now be considered. The first is 1446 B.C., indicated by 1 Kings 6:1 and suggested by Judges 11:26. Mycenaean pottery from the Judges period at Jericho and Hazor appears to support this date. The second is 1280 B.C., relying upon archaeological evidence indicating that the Egyptian cities of Pithom and Raamses (Ex. 1:11) were rebuilt in the 13th century B.C., probably with Israelite labor. Furthermore, the Merneptah stele, which describes that pharaoh's campaign in Palestine about 1220 B.C., regarded Israel as an already settled nation. This suggests an exodus from Egypt some 60 years earlier. On the basis of these two dates there obviously will be two corresponding dates for the wilderness wanderings, namely 1446–1406 B.C. and 1280–1240 B.C. The date of the Exodus is one of the most difficult problems in Old Testament history. It is made worse by the fact that solid evidence can be produced to support both positions, although that favoring the earlier date is somewhat more convincing.

This situation not only affects the dating of the Exodus and the wandering of Israel in the wilderness, it also affects the dates for the conquest and the period of the Judges. Alternate dates have been suggested for both these events. The first alternative is 1406–1050 B.C., to accommodate all the judges (assuming that the works of the judges follow one another historically); the second is a shorter interval of 1230–1025 B.C. (assuming that their work overlapped). The earlier date is supported partly by the Mycenaean pottery at Hazor, which suggests a date for the conquest shortly after 1400 B.C. The second date claims a great deal of evidence from archaeological studies at Bethel, Hazor, and several Philistine sites. In both instances the archaeological data are open to various interpretations.

The United Kingdom. Few problems are associated with the date of the United Kingdom. Saul probably was made king in 1050 B.C. He ruled for 40 years (compare Acts 13:21), being succeeded by David in 1010 B.C. David was king for roughly the same length of time, as was Solomon his successor (970–931

B.C.). The year of the death of Solomon and the division of his kingdom, 931 B.C., is the earliest precise year-date in biblical history. Following Solomon's death, it again becomes difficult to set precise dates, due to the different methods the scribes used in their work.

The Divided Kingdom. When the kingdom divided, Israel followed the Egyptian system of not counting accession years until the 9th century B.C. Then it changed to the Babylonian system, which did count accession years.

Under Rehoboam, Judah began by using the accession-year method, but in the 9th century B.C. it adopted the Egyptian system that Israel had abandoned. After a short interval, Judah returned to the accession-year method and continued to use it until the captivity. It also appears that the scribes also included co-regencies in their reckonings; in addition, two different calendars were involved. Israel's new year began in the spring (Nisan), and Judah's began in the autumn (Tishri).

In any event, Israel and Judah both kept careful records of the lengths of reign of their rulers. The books of 1 and 2 Kings synchronized the records by cross-referencing them to each other.

Many of the kings in the separate nations of Judah and Israel also were mentioned in the annals or records of foreign nations. This proves their historicity and lays a foundation for an integrated system of Near Eastern dates.

The nation of Israel crumbled in 722 B.C. with their defeat by the Assyrians. Her sister nation, Judah, suffered the same fate about 150 years later, in 586 B.C., when Jerusalem fell to Babylonia. The leading citizens of Judah were carried into captivity by the Babylonians, beginning their period of exile in a foreign land.

Return from Captivity. The 70-year Babylonian captivity (605–538 B.C.) ended with Babylon's fall to Cyrus, founder of the Persian Empire, and his proclamation of freedom to the captive peoples in Mesopotamia. The captives returned to Judea beginning in 538 B.C., and the prophets Haggai and Zechariah (520 B.C.) encouraged the rebuilding of the temple, which was accomplished four years later (516/515 B.C.). The period of Xerxes (Ahasuerus) and Esther (486–465 B.C.) was followed in Judah by the work of Ezra and Nehemiah (458–445 B.C.). Together they rehabilitated the faithful community and established its life on the basis of the law. Some scholars have tried to reverse the historical order of Ezra and Nehemiah by placing Ezra in the reign of Artaxerxes II (404–359 B.C.), but this requires an unnecessary alteration of the Hebrew text of Ezra 7:7.

From the Persians to the End of the Old Testament. The Persian period (539–331 B.C.) ended abruptly with the conquests of Alexander the Great, and was replaced by the Greek period (331–65 B.C.). Alexander died in 323 B.C., and his empire was divided among his generals. Judah was controlled by the Egyptian Ptolemies until 192 B.C., when it was taken over by the Seleucids of Syria, who were led by Antiochus III the Great. He died in 190 B.C. while resisting the Romans and was later succeeded by his younger son Antiochus IV Epiphanes (175–163 B.C.).

The cruelty of Antiochus IV Epiphanes quickly caused a revolt by a Jewish family known as the Maccabees (167–163 B.C.). This revolt ultimately secured Jewish independence from Syria. (The Dead Sea community at Qumran was probably founded about the time that Antiochus III died, although this is uncertain.) The Maccabees (or Hasmoneans) governed Judea for a century, from 142 B.C. Their rule was ended by the Roman occupation of Syria under Pompey in 63 B.C. This meant the beginning of the Roman period in Palestine. For the next century Roman soldiers were stationed in Jerusalem. Under the watchful eye of Rome, Herod the Great (37–4 B.C.) became governor of Galilee and controlled political life in Judea; the religious affairs of the nation were governed by the Pharisees and Sadducees.

With the defeat of Antony and Cleopatra in 31 B.C., Octavian became the head of the Roman Empire. Under the title of Augustus, he brought a period of peace and prosperity to the empire until his death in A.D. 14. During the reign of Augustus, and just before the death of Herod the Great, Jesus Christ was born (about 6 B.C.). With this event the chronology of the Old Testament formally comes to an end.

CLAY TABLETS — one of the world's oldest known writing materials, perhaps originating in Mesopotamia. Made of clean, smooth clay, the tablets were imprinted with cuneiform signs or symbols (by means of a stylus) while still wet, then allowed to dry slowly. When baked in an oven, they hardened into a strong, durable material. Such tablets were used by the Sumerians, Akkadians, Elamites, Hittites, Hurrians, and Canaanites of Ugarit. These writing materials are a major source of our knowledge about these civilizations.

COMMERCE — the buying, selling, and trading of goods, especially on a large scale (as between nations) involving transportation from place to place. Trade began well before recorded history in the ancient world. By the time of Abraham (about 2000 B.C.), trade was highly developed in such places as ancient Babylon and other cultures between the Tigris and Euphrates rivers. Canaan was the crossroads for important trade routes that connected Mesopotamia and Egypt; armies also made these trips as Egyptian and Mesopotamian rulers fought one another. Israel did not have many suitable harbors; so most of the sea trade went by way of the more northern ports like Tyre and Ugarit. Israel did, however, export agricultural products such as wheat and olive oil (1 Kin. 5:11). Solomon was the most successful Israelite king in developing international trade relations (1 Kin. 5:10; 9:26–28), although later Ahab and Jehoshaphat also were apparently involved in trade (1 Kin. 20:34; 22:48). Ezekiel 27 (Tyre) and Revelation 18 ("Babylon") give the most complete picture of commerce to be found in the Bible.

CREED — a brief, authoritative, formal statement of religious beliefs. The word *creed* comes from the Latin word *credo* ("I believe"), the first word of both the Nicene Creed and the Apostles' Creed.

The following are the three classic, or most historically important, creeds of the church (see sidebar on the following page for the text of each creed):

The Nicene Creed. A creed adopted by the First Council of Nicaea (A.D. 325) and revised by the First Council of Constantinople (A.D. 381). The First Council of Nicaea, convened by the Roman emperor Constantine the Great (ruled A.D. 306–337), rejected a heresy known as Arianism, which denied the divinity of Jesus. The Nicene Creed formally proclaimed the deity of Christ and His equality among the persons of the Trinity.

The Athanasian Creed. A Christian creed originating in Europe in the 4th century and relating especially to the doctrines of the Trinity and the bodily incarnation of Christ. This creed was originally ascribed to Saint Athanasius (A.D. 293?–373), but it is now believed to be the work of an unknown writer of the time.

The Apostles' Creed. This well-known creed lies at the basis of most other religious statements of belief. Although it bears the name of the apostles, it did not originate with them. It was written after the close of the New Testament, and it held an important place in the early church. This creed has been appealed to by all branches of the church as a test of authentic faith.

Apostles' Creed: I believe in God the Father Almighty, Maker of heaven and earth, And in Jesus Christ His only Son our Lord; who was conceived by the Holy Ghost, born of the Virgin Mary, suffered under Pontius Pilate, was crucified, died, and was buried. He descended into hell. The third day He rose again from the dead. He ascended into heaven, and sitteth on the right hand of God the Father Almighty; from thence He shall come to judge the quick and the dead. I believe in the Holy Ghost, the holy Catholic Church, the communion of saints, the forgiveness of sins, the resurrection of the body, and the life everlasting.

Nicene Creed: I believe in one God the Father Almighty, Maker of heaven and earth, and of all things visible and invisible. And I believe in one Lord, Jesus Christ, the only-begotten Son of God, born of the Father before all ages, God of God, Light of Light, true God of true God; begotten, not made, of one substance with the Father, by whom all things were made, who for us and for our salvation came down from heaven. And He became flesh by the Holy Spirit of the Virgin Mary and was made man. He was also crucified for us, suffered under Pontius Pilate, and was buried. And on the third day He rose again, according to the Scriptures. He ascended into heaven and sits at the right hand of the Father. He will come again in glory to judge the living and the dead. And of His kingdom there will be no end. And I believe in the Holy Spirit, the Lord and Giver of life, who proceeds from the Father and the Son, who together with the Father and the Son is adored and glorified, and who spoke through the prophets, and one holy, Catholic, and Apostolic Church. I confess one baptism for the forgiveness of sins. And I await the resurrection of the dead. And the life of the world to come. Amen.

Athanasian Creed: We believe and confess that our Lord Jesus Christ, the Son of God, is at once both God and Man. He is God of the substance of the Father, begotten before the worlds, and He is man, of the substance of his Mother, born in the world; perfect God; perfect man, of reasoning soul and human flesh consisting; equal to the Father as touching His Godhead; less than the Father as touching His manhood, who, although He be God and man, yet He is not two, but is one Christ; one, however, not by change of Godhead into flesh but by taking of manhood into God; one altogether, not by confusion of substance, but by unity of person. For as reasoning soul and flesh is one man, so God and man is one Christ; who suffered for our salvation, descended to the world below, rose again from the dead, ascended into heaven, and sat down at the right hand of the Father to come from thence to judge the quick and the dead, at whose coming all men shall rise again with their bodies, and shall give account for their own deeds. And they that have done good will go into life eternal; they that have done evil into eternal fire.

CRETE [kreet] — an island in the Mediterranean Sea where a ship on which the apostle Paul was sailing was struck by a storm. Crete is about 258 kilometers (160 miles) long and varies between 11 and 49 kilometers (7 and 30 miles) wide (Acts 27:7, 12–13, 21). It is probably to be identified with Caphtor (Deut. 2:23; Amos 9:7), the place from which the Philistines (Caphtorim) originated. A number of legends are associated with Crete, particularly those involving King Minos and the Minotaur (the half-bull, half-man monster). The island was captured by the Romans in 68–66 B.C. and made a Roman province.

During his voyage to Rome, Paul's ship touched at Fair Havens, a harbor on the south coast of Crete (Acts 27:8). Not heeding Paul's advice about the weather, the Roman soldier who held Paul in custody agreed with the captain and set sail for Crete's large harbor at Phoenix. The result was a shipwreck at Malta (Acts 27:9–28:1).

CRUCIFIXION OF CHRIST — the method of torture and execution used by the Romans to put Christ to death. At a crucifixion the victim usually was nailed or tied to a wooden stake and left to die.

Crucifixion was used by many nations of the ancient world, including Assyria, Media, and Persia. Alexander the Great of Greece crucified 2,000 inhabitants of Tyre when he captured the city. The Romans later adopted this method and used it often throughout their empire. Crucifixion was the Romans' most severe form of execution, so it was reserved only for slaves and criminals. No Roman citizen could be crucified.

Crucifixion involved attaching the victim with nails through the wrists or with leather thongs to a crossbeam attached to a vertical stake. Sometimes blocks or pins were put on the stake to give victims some support as they hung suspended from the crossbeam. At times the feet were also nailed to the vertical stake. As the victim hung dangling by the arms, the blood could no longer circulate to the vital organs. Only by supporting themselves on the seat or pin could victims gain relief.

But gradually exhaustion set in, and death followed, although usually not for several days. If victims had been severely beaten, they would not live this long. To hasten death, the executioners sometimes broke the victims' legs with a club. Then they could no longer support their bodies to keep blood circulating, and death quickly followed. Usually bodies were left to rot or to be eaten by scavengers.

To the Israelites, impalement was the most disgusting form of death: "He who is hanged is accursed of God" (Deut. 21:23). Yet the Jewish Sanhedrin sought and obtained Roman authorization to have Jesus crucified (Mark 15:13–15). As was the custom, the charge against Jesus was attached to the cross; He was offered a brew to deaden His senses, but He refused (Mark 15:23). There was no need for the soldiers to break His legs to hasten death. By the ninth hour (Mark 15:25, 34, 37), probably 3:00 P.M.—in only six hours—Jesus was already dead (John 19:31–33). Jesus' body was not left to rot; the disciples were able to secure Pilate's permission to give Him a proper burial.

The cross has been a major stumbling block in the way of the Jews, preventing the majority of them from accepting Jesus as the Messiah. The apostle Paul summed up the importance of the crucifixion best: "We preach Christ crucified, to the Jews a stumbling block and to the Greeks foolishness, but to those who are called, both Jews and Greeks, Christ the power of God and the wisdom of God" (1 Cor. 1:23–24). Out of the ugliness and agony of crucifixion, God accomplished the greatest good of all—the redemption of sinners.

CUNEIFORM [kyu NAY uh form] (*wedge-shaped*) — a system of writing developed before 3000 B.C. in Mesopotamia (the lower Tigris and Euphrates Valley) probably by the

Sumerians and then adopted and modified by the Akkadians, Hurrians, Hittites, Elamites, Persians, and Canaanites from Ugarit.

The wedge-shaped signs of cuneiform writing were carved on stone and metal or inscribed with a stylus on clay tablets. These clay tablets received the wedge marks while soft and moist, but they became as hard as stone after they were dried in the sun or baked in a kiln. Thousands of such tablets were discovered by archaeologists at the site of Ras Shamra (ancient Ugarit, a Canaanite settlement).

Cuneiform was originally a pictographic form of writing, but it soon was used to signify syllables and consonants. Variations of cuneiform scripts were developed for Ugaritic and Old Persian writing.

CYPRUS [SIGH prus] — a large island in the northeastern corner of the Mediterranean Sea, about 97 kilometers (60 miles) off the coast of Syria and about 66 kilometers (41 miles) off the coast of Cilicia (modern Turkey). Although Cyprus is a rocky island, many nations sought its rich copper deposits and timber reserves (especially the cypress tree). Consequently, in the course of its history, Cyprus frequently was conquered by many powerful nations, including the Mycenaeans, Phoenicians, Assyrians, and Persians.

After Alexander the Great, the Egyptian Ptolemies controlled Cyprus until the Romans took it in 58 B.C. During the Roman period it was joined to the province of Cilicia, then made an independent imperial province; and in 22 B.C. it became a senatorial province, with a proconsul in charge at the capital city of Paphos.

The name Cyprus is not found in the Old Testament, but because extra-biblical texts refer to Alashiya as a primary source of copper, many believe that Elishah (Gen. 10:4; 1 Chr. 1:7; Ezek. 27:7) is Cyprus. Kittim is another Old Testament name that may refer to Cyprus (Gen. 10:4; 1 Chr. 1:7). Another spelling is Chittim (Num. 24:24; Is. 23:1; Jer. 2:10, KJV).

The New Testament contains several references to Cyprus— all in the book of Acts. Barnabas was a native "of the country of Cyprus" (Acts 4:36). The first Christians fled to Cyprus because of the persecution of the early church after the death of Stephen (Acts 8:1–4; 11:19–20). Barnabas, Mark, and Paul began their first missionary journey by stopping at Salamis, the largest city of Cyprus on the east coast of the island (Acts 13:4–5). After the split between Paul and Barnabas, Barnabas took John Mark and returned to Cyprus to do missionary work there (Acts 15:39). Mnason, an early Christian, was from Cyprus (Acts 21:16). Later Paul sailed past the island (Acts 21:3; 27:4).

DAN, TRIBE OF — the tribe of Dan, descended from
the son of Jacob. This tribe never lived up to its promise. The area allotted to Dan included the towns of Aijalon,
Ekron, Eltekeh, and Zorah in the west-central part of Canaan
(Josh. 19:40–46; 21:5, 23–24) and stretched to Joppa on the
Mediterranean Sea. The Danites, however, were unable to
conquer much of the territory assigned to them. The original
inhabitants, the Amorites, kept the Danites confined to the hill
country of Ephraim and Benjamin. Unable to conquer their
allotted territory, some members of the tribe of Dan migrated
far to the northernmost area of the promised land and conquered the isolated city of Laish, which they renamed Dan. The
tribe's one glorious moment occurred when the mighty Danite
Samson judged Israel (Judg. 13–16).

Apparently, Dan was among the tribes that were the least
supportive of the Israelite tribes. The Song of Deborah, which
celebrates the Israelite victory over the Canaanite king Jabin
and his mighty general Sisera, reproves the tribes of Gilead,
Dan, and Asher. Of Dan, Deborah asked: "And why did Dan
remain on ships?" (Judg. 5:17). Dan's apparent lack of interest in
assisting the other tribes suggests that Dan, situated on Israel's

northernmost border, had more in common with its foreign neighbors to the north than with Israel's other tribes.

The exclusion of the tribe of Dan from the sealing of the twelve tribes (Rev. 7:5–8) should not be overlooked. It appears that Dan had been cut off from the other tribes of Israel. However, Ezekiel prophesied a "portion for Dan" (Ezek. 48:1).

DEAD SEA — a large lake in southern Israel at the lowest point on earth. In the Old Testament it is called the Salt Sea (Gen. 14:3; Josh. 3:16); the Sea of the Arabah (Deut. 3:17); and the Eastern Sea (Ezek. 47:18; Joel 2:20). Josephus, the Jewish historian, referred to this buoyant body as Lake Asphaltitis. The Arabic name is Bahr Lut, meaning "Sea of Lot." But from the second Christian century onward, Dead Sea has been the most common name for this unusual body of water.

The topography of the Middle East is dominated by a geologic fault that extends from Syria south through Palestine, all the way to Nyasa Lake in east-central Africa. The Dead Sea is located at the southern end of the Jordan valley at the deepest depression of this geologic fault. With a water level approximately 390 meters (1,300 feet) below sea level, the surface of the Dead Sea is the lowest point on earth. At the deepest point of the sea, on the northeast corner at the foot of the Moab mountains, the bottom is 390 meters (1,300 feet) deeper still.

The dimensions of the sea change from year to year. Many factors, such as rainfall and irrigation, contribute to this. In general, however, the Dead Sea measures approximately 80 kilometers (50 miles) in length and averages 15 to 16 kilometers (9 to 10 miles) in breadth, yielding a surface area of from 600 to 640 square kilometers (350 to 400 square miles).

A large peninsula known as el-Lisan ("the Tongue") protrudes into the sea from the southeast shore. It extends to within 3 kilometers (2 miles) of the western shore and is located some 24 kilometers (15 miles) from the southern tip. Throughout the centuries this tongue separated the sea into two parts with a channel of water flowing between them on the west. From the depths of the northeast corner, the bottom of the sea quickly shelves and rises southward. Thus the area of the sea south of el-Lisan is extremely shallow. It is at the entrance to el-Lisan that the destroyed cities of Sodom and Gomorrah most probably lie (Gen. 19:24–29).

Except on the north where the Jordan River enters, the Dead Sea is nearly surrounded by hills and cliffs. From these hills, streams feed fresh water to the Salt Sea. In addition to these year-round streams and the Jordan River, waters flow into the sea from the winter torrents of several seasonal streams.

These water sources pour millions of gallons of water each day into the Dead Sea. However, the extreme hot temperatures and sparse rainfall (about two inches a year) cause an enormous evaporation rate that has kept the water level constant over the years. Due to increased irrigation by the Israeli government, the volume of water flowing into the Dead Sea from the Jordan River is decreasing each year. Thus the level of the sea goes down proportionately. As a result, "the Tongue" often stretches all the way across the sea, completely separating the northern portion from the southern portion. Evidence of a Roman road across the peninsula has been discovered, indicating that at other periods in its history the Dead Sea was shallow enough for traffic to cross its southern tip.

Because the Dead Sea has several watercourse entrances but no exits, it is indeed a "dead" sea. Although lush vegetation can be found at the mouths of these tributaries, the water itself is very salty. This is because it flows through nitrous soil and is fed by sulphurous springs. With the absence of an outlet, the water from the Dead Sea is left to evaporate, leaving behind most of its minerals. Thus it contains a very large supply of potash, bromine, magnesium chloride, salt, and other minerals. Although the value of these chemicals is enormous, making the Dead

Sea the richest mineral deposit on earth, the cost of retrieving these minerals is also high. Potash extraction has been one of the most successful operations. But as technology increases, the interest in "mining" the Dead Sea will also increase.

The salt and mineral content of the Dead Sea constitutes more than 25 percent of the water. This compares with about 6 percent mineral content in the ocean. The specific gravity of the water is greater than that of the human body, making it next to impossible for any person to sink in the Dead Sea.

The Dead Sea formed part of Israel's eastern border (Num. 34:12; Ezek. 47:18). In addition to the destruction of Sodom and Gomorrah, many other historical and biblical events occurred along its shores. The springs of En Gedi provided a refuge for David in his flight from King Saul (1 Sam. 24:1). In the Valley of Salt south of the sea, David and Amaziah won victories over the Edomites (2 Kin. 14:7; 1 Chr. 18:12). Here, too, Jehoshaphat encountered the Edomites (2 Kin. 3:8–9; 2 Chr. 20:1–2). The last days of Herod the Great were spent on the eastern shore of the Dead Sea at the hot sulphur springs of Callirhoe. At Machaerus, just to the southeast, his son Herod Antipas imprisoned John the Baptist.

The prophet Ezekiel (Ezek. 47:1–12) saw a vision of a river issuing from the temple sanctuary in Jerusalem and flowing to the desert sea, the Dead Sea. And the prophet Zechariah wrote: "And in that day it shall be that living waters shall flow from Jerusalem, half of them toward the eastern sea [the Dead Sea] and half of them toward the western sea [the Mediterranean Sea]" (Zech. 14:8). Prophetically this is apparently a reference to the "pure river of water of life" said to flow from the throne of God in John's vision (Rev. 22:1–2).

The great fortress of Masada guarded the southern approaches toward Palestine, perhaps the road crossing from Moab to Judea at el-Lisan. Herod refortified this strong fortress, which finally fell in A.D. 73 to the Romans under Flavius Silva.

He also refortified the Maccabean stronghold at Machaerus on the eastern shore.

The discovery of the Dead Sea Scrolls in caves on the northwest shore of the Dead Sea near Qumran has mustered renewed historical interest in this area. The remains of the Essene community at Qumran and the search for scrolls in the more than 250 surrounding caves focused the eyes of the world on a tiny sea devoid of marine life but bristling with mineral potential and archaeological promise.

DECAPOLIS [dih CAP oh liss] (*ten cities*) — a district of northern Palestine, with a large Greek population, mostly on the east side of the Jordan River and embracing ten cities. Early in his ministry, Jesus was followed by "great multitudes," including people from Decapolis (Matt. 4:25). When Jesus healed the demon-possessed man from Gadara, he "began to proclaim in Decapolis all that Jesus had done for him" (Mark 5:20). Later, Jesus traveled through the midst of the region (Mark 7:31).

Pliny, the Greek historian, identified the ten cities of the Decapolis as Canatha (or Kanatha), Damascus, Dion, Gadara, Gerasa (or Galasa), Hippos (or Hippo), Pella, Philadelphia (the Old Testament Rabbah or Rabbath Ammon and present-day Amman, the capital of Jordan), Raphana (or Rephana), and Scythopolis (Beth Shan). Later, other towns, such as Abila and Edrei, were added to this district.

DISPENSATION — a period of time under which mankind is answerable to God for how it has obeyed the revelation of God that it has received. The term "dispensation" is found twice in the NKJV: "The dispensation of the fullness of the times" (Eph. 1:10) and "the dispensation of the grace of God" (Eph. 3:2; administration, NIV). The KJV uses the term four times (1 Cor. 9:17; Eph. 1:10; 3:2; Col. 1:25).

Many Bible students believe all of history can be divided into several dispensations. According to this view, all of history has been pointing toward the Second Coming of Christ, when salvation will be made complete. Others reject this view, insisting that God has had faithful, loyal followers in all times who have lived according to His covenant with them.

Seven dispensations are commonly identified by traditional dispensationalists: *Innocence*, from Creation to the Fall of Adam and Eve and God's sending them out of the Garden of Eden (Gen. 3:24); *Conscience*, the covenant with Adam, ending with the judgment of the Flood (Genesis 9); *Human government*, the covenant with Noah, extending to the time of Abraham; *Promise*, from Abraham's call (Gen. 12:1) to Moses; *Law*, from the giving of the law to Moses (Ex. 19:8, 20–31) to the death of Jesus Christ; *Grace*, from the death and resurrection of Christ to His Second Coming; *Kingdom*, the establishment of God's kingdom on earth and the thousand-year reign of Christ over the nations.

DISPERSION — a scattering of the Jewish people among other nations. Throughout their history, the Hebrew people have experienced many dispersions—a term which comes from a Greek word meaning "to scatter." Some of these dispersions have been voluntary, while others have been forced upon them.

Voluntary movements were sometimes made by God's people to escape the threat of destruction, as with those who moved to Egypt in the time of the prophet Jeremiah. Others left their homeland on various occasions with the expectation of pursuing an easier and more profitable way of life, as with the brothers of Joseph. Some migrants were most probably traveling merchants who chose to settle in a new homeland for business reasons, whereas others found themselves on foreign territory in a military capacity (2 Sam. 8:14).

While all Israelites regarded the land promised to them by God through Abraham as their natural home, none of them were ever compelled to live in it for an entire lifetime. In periods of economic hardship or political upheaval many took advantage of the opportunity to leave and begin life afresh in another country.

But forced dispersion was another matter. Periods of captivity for Israel may have begun as early as the invasion by Shishak of Egypt, about 926 B.C. (1 Kin. 14:25–26). But most significant were the fall of Israel to the Assyrians in 722 B.C. and the collapse of Judah before Babylonian attacks in 597–581 B.C. Already in 732 B.C. Tiglath-Pileser III had carried Reuben, Gad, and the half-tribe of Manasseh captive to Mesopotamia when Damascus fell. A decade later the capture of Samaria resulted in the remaining Israelite tribes being carried away as captives to Assyria.

The end of national life in Judah began with the first attack on Jerusalem by the Babylonians in 597 B.C. The final attack in 581 B.C. marked the end completely. By the end of this period, a total of some 4,600 prominent persons had been deported from Judah (Jer. 52:28–30). This number probably did not include family members or servants. The total may well have been many times the number recorded by Jeremiah. The dispersion actually began earlier in Judah, for early in his ministry Jeremiah reported that a significant number of Jewish emigrants lived in such Egyptian cities as Migdol, Tahpanhes, and Noph (Memphis). The prophet ministered to these people even before Jerusalem fell (Jer. 43:8; 44:1).

But the settlement in Egypt was small compared to that in Assyria, Babylonia, and Persia as a result of the deportation from Israel and Judah. Captives from the Northern Kingdom were apparently absorbed completely into their foreign surroundings. But a small group of Jews ultimately returned from Persia to Judah as a result of the decree of Cyrus (538 B.C.).

Those who remained behind in Babylonia formed the basis of the Dispersion that was well known in New Testament times (John 7:35; Acts 2:9–11).

This dispersed Jewish community in Mesopotamia flourished into the medieval Christian period, maintaining its distinctive religious practices. Earlier, it was here that the Babylonian Talmud, a work that formed the basis for law and faith in the community, was compiled. The Dispersion had been supported by conditions in the Persian Empire and in the later Greek Empire, as the character of the crowd at Pentecost illustrates (Acts 2:9–11).

Interesting light has been shed on a 5th-century B.C. Jewish colony in Egypt by the discovery of the Elephantine papyri. These documents disclosed the existence of a Jewish trading community near Aswan that had its own temple worship. This community was also an important center for commerce in southern Egypt. With the rise of the Greek Empire, further Jewish settlements occurred in Egypt, along with a significant increase in the use of the Greek language across the Near East. One result of this was the translation of the Hebrew Scriptures into Greek at Alexandria, Egypt. This version (called the Septuagint) became so popular that the New Testament writers often quoted the Old Testament from it instead of using the traditional Hebrew text.

By 139 B.C. Jews who had migrated to Italy and settled in Rome were being expelled from the capital city. Even so, they had gained a foothold in Italy. By the beginning of the Christian period, colonies of Jews were scattered across the Near East and southeastern Europe. Although they were often disliked and sometimes persecuted, they managed to survive and prosper. By the time of Philo (20 B.C.–A.D. 50), a Jewish philosopher of Alexandria, an estimated one million Jews lived in Alexandria. An equal number had settled in both Persia and Asia Minor, and about 100,000 lived in Cyrenaica and Italy. The Jews who were dispersed throughout the world in this manner outnumbered the Jews who remained in their native land.

These colonies provided useful bases for evangelistic efforts by the apostle Paul and later Christian preachers. Eventually Christian communities were established in those cities that had a large Jewish population. Thus, the Dispersion helped to prepare the world for the reception and growth of the gospel.

DISPERSION OF THE NATIONS — the dividing and scattering of the people of the earth after the Flood and the Tower of Babel through the three sons of Noah (Gen. 10:32; 11:9). Japheth's descendants were scattered to the north, Ham's to the south, and Shem's to the central regions between his two brothers.

EASTER — a feast or festival of the Christian church that commemorates the resurrection of Christ. It is celebrated on the first Sunday following the full moon that occurs on or after March 21—or one week later if the full moon falls on Sunday. In other words, Easter falls between March 22 and April 25. Easter was originally a pagan festival honoring Eostre, a Teutonic goddess of light and spring. At the time of the vernal equinox (the day in the spring when the sun crosses the equator and day and night are of equal length), sacrifices were offered in her honor. As early as the 8th century, the word was used to designate the annual Christian celebration of the resurrection of Christ. The only appearance of the word *Easter* (KJV) is a mistranslation of *pascha,* the Greek word for "Passover" (Acts 12:4).

EGYPT, HISTORY OF — Information about Egyptian history is found in the Bible, Egyptian and Greek historical books, various Egyptian papyrus documents and stone writings, and facts from archaeological investigations of ancient Egyptian cities, temples, and graves. One of the most helpful chronological surveys of the Egyptian kings was provided by the Egyptian priest Manetho. He divided the kings of Egypt into 31 different dynastic families who ruled from about 3100 to 250 B.C. Some of these dynasties were strong, while others were comparatively weak.

The history of Egypt can be simplified by ordering the dynasties into three main periods of strength: the Old Kingdom (2700–2200 B.C.); the Middle Kingdom (2000–1800 B.C.); and the New Kingdom (1570–1100 B.C.). Each of these kingdoms was followed by a period of weakness.

After the New Kingdom, Egypt was dominated by Libyan, Ethiopian, Persian, Greek, and finally Roman powers during New Testament times. The dates for these periods and the length of the reigns of each king are not securely fixed. But Egyptologists have been able to reconstruct a fairly accurate chronology by using evidence from many different sources.

Archaeologists have found a number of small villages that date prior to the beginning of the Old Kingdom period of Egyptian history. These primitive hunting and farming communities were the descendants of Mizraim (Gen. 10:6). Metal objects, tools, pottery, jewelry, and religious objects were found in these early graves. Trade with Mesopotamia may have been an important factor in the development of a written Egyptian language, which used pictures in a system known as hieroglyphics.

Around 3100 B.C., some 1,000 years before Abraham, all of Egypt was joined together under one king at Memphis. The land was divided into districts called "nomes." Irrigation and the plow were introduced to increase the nation's agricultural productivity. Shortly thereafter, the Old Kingdom period of Egypt's history began. During this era, the famous pyramids of Egypt were built. Djoser's step pyramid at Saqqara and the three great pyramids at Giza are a testimony to the power and prosperity of the nation, as well as evidence of the people's belief in the divine character of the pharaoh, the Egyptian ruler.

Several pyramids have long series of curses, magical spells, and ritual formulas written on the walls of the burial chambers.

These were to be used by the dead pharaoh for protection on his journey to the afterlife. Large open-air temples where various rituals in honor of the king were performed were built beside the pyramids. The arts of painting, sculpting, and architecture excelled in Egypt. One group of texts known as the "Memphite Theology" probably dates back to this era. It describes how the god Ptah spoke and created all things, indicating that the pharaoh was considered divine. Wisdom writings from Imhotep and Ptahhotep reveal something of the moral values and ideals of the nation and the high literary achievements of the educated classes.

As the government of Egypt expanded, noblemen from various parts of the nation began to gain greater power. This led to a decentralization of power and ultimately to the First Intermediate Period of weakness around 2200 B.C. The time was described as an epic of chaos, instability, poverty, and despair.

Two texts from this period describe man's disillusionment with life. Another expresses a strong desire for social stability and justice. These events led to a rethinking of human ideals. As a result, the highly structured social order was reevaluated and social justice for even the peasant was proclaimed as important. The possibility of life after death, which had been limited to the kings, became the goal of noblemen as they rose to higher power. Ultimately even the common person pursued this hope.

The Middle Kingdom era of Egypt's history (2000–1800 B.C.) parallels the time of Abraham's journey into Egypt (Gen. 12:10–20). Wisdom texts, one supposed prophecy, and stories about fishing and hunting depict life at this time. During this era, the new kings centralized the government, expanded agricultural production through new irrigation projects, established the security of the nation by defeating the Nubians from Cush, and set up a series of defensive fortresses on the southern and western borders.

Trade with Phoenicia, mining in the Sinai desert, and at least one military raid into Palestine to Shechem indicate that Egypt had close relationships with Palestine when the patriarchs such as Abraham and his descendants first came to the land. The "Story of Sinuhe" describes an Egyptian's trip to Palestine and the fertility of the land. A painting in a tomb from the time of Sesostris III (1890 B.C.) shows 37 people from Canaan who traveled to Egypt. Texts containing magical curses (the Execration Texts) on Egypt's enemies contain the names of the kings of Tyre, Beth-Shemesh, and Jerusalem. These indicate that Egypt's stability was weakening and that the Second Intermediate Period of weakness (1750–1570 B.C.) was about to begin.

During this time of weakness, many non-Egyptians entered the country. A group called the Hyksos ("rulers from a foreign land") took control of the nation. Joseph's rise to an important position in the house of Potiphar (Genesis 39) and his appointment to the task of collecting grain during the years of plenty (Genesis 41) may have been made possible because other foreigners had significant places in the Hyksos government.

Some scholars once thought the Hyksos were the people of Israel, but few accept this view today. The Hyksos used the bow, body armor, the horse and chariot, and a new defensive wall system for Egyptian cities. But in spite of their military power, they were driven out of Egypt when the New Kingdom began.

The New Kingdom period (1570–1100 B.C.) parallels the biblical period before the birth of Moses until the time of Samuel. The New Kingdom began when the Egyptians managed to drive out the Hyksos and reunite Egypt. This new dynasty was made of kings "who did not know Joseph" (Ex. 1:8). They began to persecute the Hebrews, forcing them to build the stone cities of Pithom and Rameses (Ex. 1:11). The Hebrews were seen as foreigners who were a threat to the security of the nation (Ex. 1:10), so they were enslaved.

Queen Hatshepsut carried out many building and reconstruction projects and expanded trade relations with several
foreign countries. The next king, Thutmose III, was an aggressive warrior and he conducted several campaigns into Palestine.
Many believe his son, Amenhotep II, was the pharaoh of the
Exodus. Egyptian texts do not mention the ten plagues, the
Exodus of Israel from Egypt, or the defeat of Pharaoh and his
army in the Red Sea (Exodus 7–15). But this would hardly be
expected since the Egyptians seldom recorded any of their
defeats. Before the Exodus, Egypt was at the height of its power,
but God humbled the nation and taught its people that He was
God—not pharaoh or any of the other gods of Egypt (Ex. 7:5;
8:10, 22; 9:14, 29; 10:2; 12:12).

Many interesting stories come from this period of Egyptian
history. "The Tale of Two Brothers" describes how the wife of
one brother lied about the sexual advances of the other brother.
This story is similar to the false accusation of Potiphar's wife
against Joseph. Myths about the struggles between the gods
Horus and Seth and the "Wisdom of Amenemopet," which are
similar to Proverbs 22:17–24:22, are a few of the important literary compositions from Egypt during these years.

No one knows how the Exodus affected Egypt's religious
beliefs. However, several years later King Akhenaten rejected
the worship of Amon at Thebes and proclaimed that Aten, the
solar disk of the sun, was the only god. A beautiful hymn of
praise to Aten has been discovered. This shows clearly that
Akhenaten was pushing the Egyptians to adopt belief in one
god. Religious tension was very high because Akhenaten dis-
missed the priests at the other temples and moved his capital
to El-Amarna.

About 350 letters from Babylon, the Hittites, and many cities in Palestine were found at this capital. These letters reveal
that Palestine was under a great deal of political unrest during
the time of Joshua and the judges. A few years later the famous

King Tut (Tutankhamen), whose burial chambers were found near Thebes by Howard Carter in 1922, ruled for a few years. He brought the nation back to the worship of its traditional gods at Thebes, relieving much of the tension within the nation.

During the final 200 years of the New Kingdom, the capital of Egypt was moved from Thebes to the city of Rameses in the delta area. Large construction projects at Thebes, Abydos, Abu Simbel, and in the delta stand as a memorial to the greatness and power of these kings. Some believe the Exodus took place during the reign of Rameses (1304–1238 B.C.), but this contradicts the statement of the Bible that the Exodus took place 480 years before Solomon began to build the temple in 966 B.C. (966 plus 480 equals 1446 B.C. for the Exodus). One king, Merneptah, described his defeat of several Canaanite countries and actually mentions his defeat of Israel.

There is a wealth of historical, literary, and religious writings from the New Kingdom period of Egyptian history. Papyri, ostraca, and tomb and temple accounts give a graphic picture of Egyptian life. A primitive alphabetic script was discovered on the rocks in the Egyptian mines in the Sinai desert. The New Kingdom ended because of government corruption, strikes, inflation, and the increasing power of the temple priests, who constantly contended for greater advantage.

After the New Kingdom came the Late Period of Egyptian history (1100–330 B.C.). The fragmentation of Egyptian power allowed David and Solomon to establish Israel as a strong nation. The Egyptian story of Wen-Amon's trip to Byblos to secure cedar for the construction of a ship for the pharaoh tells how he was robbed and then refused the needed lumber until proper payment could be made. Such incidents clearly indicate the low status of Egypt during this time. The nation was not a strong military power, so more emphasis was placed on trying to form peaceful trade relations with neighboring states.

Solomon married the daughter of an Egyptian pharaoh (1 Kin. 3:1), another sign of Egypt's weakness. But later in his reign a new king (probably Shishak) provided refuge for two of Solomon's enemies (1 Kin. 11:17, 40). A few years after Solomon's death (930 B.C.), Shishak, a Libyan who had become pharaoh, attacked Rehoboam and plundered the gold from the king's palace and the temple in Jerusalem (1 Kin. 14:25–28). A monument of Shishak was discovered during excavations of Megiddo. His record of his battles on the walls of a temple at Thebes indicates that he defeated 150 towns in Judah and Israel. Later Zerah, an Ethiopian general or pharaoh (2 Chr. 14:9–15; 16:8), led an Egyptian army against Asa, king of Judah, but God miraculously gave victory to Asa.

Ethiopian and Saite dynasties controlled Egypt for several hundred years until the destruction of Israel by the Babylonian king Nebuchadnezzar in 587 B.C. These pharaohs were not particularly powerful because of the political supremacy of the Assyrians and the Babylonians. The Israelite king Hoshea sought the help of Pharaoh So around 725 B.C. (2 Kin. 17:4) to fight against the Assyrians, but the Egyptians were of little help.

Around 701 B.C. Hezekiah was attacked by the Assyrian king Sennacherib. Tirhakah, the Ethiopian king of Egypt, came to Hezekiah's aid (2 Kin. 19:9; Is. 37:9). The Assyrians marched into Egypt in 671 and 664 B.C., destroying the Egyptian forces as far south as Thebes. To strengthen the Egyptian army, the nation hired Greek mercenaries to fight in their army, but this still did not give them any great strength. Josiah, king of Judah, was killed by the Egyptian pharaoh Necho in 609 B.C. because Josiah tried to interfere with the Egyptian efforts to help the Assyrians who were under attack by the Babylonians (2 Kin. 23:29). After Josiah's death, Judah came under the control of Egypt, but in 605 B.C. the Egyptians were crushed by the Babylonians at Carchemish on the Euphrates. Many Jews fled to Egypt after the destruction of Jerusalem, although the prophet

Jeremiah warned against it (Jeremiah 39–44). Nebuchadnezzar later defeated Egypt (Jer. 46:13); he was followed by the Persians (525 B.C.) and the Greeks (330 B.C.). After 330 B.C. a group of Ptolemaic kings ruled Egypt, developing the great city of Alexandria as a center of culture and learning.

Many Jews lived in Alexandria during this period. The Greek translation of the Old Testament from Hebrew to Greek was completed during this time so the Greek-speaking Jews would have a Bible in their language. The Romans took control of Egypt around 30 B.C. From the 2nd century A.D. until the Muslim conquest of Egypt in 642 A.D., Egypt was primarily a Christian nation.

ELAMITES [EE lum ites] — descendants of Elam, an ancient people who lived in the area east of the Tigris and Euphrates rivers. During their history, the Elamites struggled with the Babylonians, Assyrians, and Persians for domination of the Mesopotamian region of the ancient world.

The great Babylonian dynasty of Ur was brought to an end about 1950 B.C. by the Elamites, who destroyed the city and took its king prisoner. The capital of Elam during its entire history was Shushan (Susa). To it the Persian king, Darius I, transferred the Persian capital about 520 B.C. The city is therefore mentioned several times in the books of Nehemiah, Esther, and Daniel, since these books deal with events during the time of the Persian Empire (Neh. 1:1; Esth. 1:2; Dan. 8:2).

From about 2000 to 1800 B.C., the Elamites expanded their kingdom at the expense of the Mesopotamian states, until Hammurapi (about 1792–1750 B.C.) put an end to Elamite expansion. Elam was a virtual province of Babylon until about 1200 B.C. Then from about 1200–1130 B.C. Babylon was ruled by Elam. Under the leadership of a succession of strong kings, the Elamites raided and defeated Babylon. In 1130 B.C., however, Nebuchadnezzar I of Babylon captured Elam. For almost three centuries thereafter the Elamites were again under Babylonian domination.

From about 740 B.C. onward, Assyria's power created a more serious threat to the Elamites. Finally, Ashurbanipal, king of Assyria, conquered Elam about 645 B.C. The Persians had already taken the part of Elam called Anshan; after the Assyrian Empire was destroyed (609 B.C.), the Medes annexed most of Elam. When the Persians, in turn, began to control Media, all of Elam became a Persian administrative district. After the 6th century B.C., Elam was never again an independent nation.

Genesis 10:22 identifies Elam, the ancestor of the Elamites, as a son of Shem. Chedorlaomer, who led a group of eastern kings on raids to Palestine about 2000 B.C., also was an Elamite. These kings defeated several cities in the Jordan River plain, including Sodom and Gomorrah. Abraham and his allies finally defeated Chedorlaomer and his fellow kings and rescued Lot, regaining the wealth the easterners had captured (Genesis 14). Chedorlaomer himself was driven back to Elam.

After the Assyrians captured the northern kingdom of Israel in 722 B.C., they followed their usual practice of deporting the population as a means of strengthening their control over them. Elamites were among the national groups deported to Samaria. Some Samaritan Israelites were in turn deported to Elam (Ezra 4:9). Some of the Israelites returned from Elam when the Persians allowed the Jews to go back to Palestine after the captivity.

Isaiah prophesied that Elam would be involved in the defeat of Babylon (Is. 21:2). By its connection with the Persians during their conquest of the Babylonian Empire, they fulfilled Isaiah's prophecy (Dan. 8:1–4). Elamites serving in the Assyrian army also took part in the siege of Jerusalem (Is. 22:6) in 701 B.C. The prophets Jeremiah and Ezekiel prophesied that Elam itself would eventually be destroyed (Jer. 49:34–39; Ezek. 32:24–25).

Elamites were among the pilgrims at Jerusalem on the Day of Pentecost (Acts 2:9). They probably were Jews from Elam or descendants of those who had been exiled there in 722 B.C. This group may also have included native Elamites who had converted to Judaism.

ELUL [ee LOOL] — the sixth month of the Hebrew year, corresponding roughly to a lunar month during our August-September (Neh. 6:15).

EPHRAIM, TRIBE OF — descendants of Ephraim, who settled the land of Canaan as one of the twelve tribes of Israel. Their territory was bounded on the north by Manasseh (west of the river Jordan) and on the south by Dan and Benjamin (Josh. 16:5–10).

From the early days, the tribe of Ephraim was an influential force in Israel, being highly commended by Gideon (Judg. 8:2), and including such key religious and political centers as Bethel and Shechem. At the time of the first census in their new land, the tribe contained 40,500 men eligible for military service (Num. 1:33).

Following the revolt of the ten tribes after Solomon's rule, Ephraim became a leader in the northern kingdom of Israel (1 Kin. 12:25–33). Often the name Ephraim was used for Israel because of its size and its leadership role. The Hebrew prophets, especially Hosea, chastised Ephraim for idolatry (Hos. 4:17), spiritual unfaithfulness (8:9–10), and relationships with heathen nations (12:1). Ephraim was involved in an alliance with Syria against Judah and King Ahaz (2 Chr. 28:5–8; Is. 7:3–9).

In 722 B.C., the northern kingdom of Israel was taken into captivity in Assyria. This seemed to be the end of the tribe of Ephraim, but the Lord would not forget them. Through the prophet Jeremiah, He declared that these people were still His "dear son" and He would have mercy on them (Jer. 31:20). Years later, after God's people returned to their homeland following a long period of captivity in Babylon, "children of Ephraim" settled in Jerusalem (1 Chr. 9:3).

EXODUS, THE — the departure of the Israelites from captivity in Egypt under the leadership of Moses. The actual Exodus was the final event in a series of miracles by which God revealed Himself to His people in bondage, humbled the pride of the pharaoh who opposed the Israelites, and enabled Jacob's descendants to live in freedom once again.

The precise date of the Exodus from Egypt is uncertain, because the information in the Bible can be interpreted to support more than one date. Archaeological discoveries also present a confused picture. The result is that some scholars date the Exodus as early as 1446 B.C., while others place it later, about 1290 B.C.

The circumstances of Egyptian history are not very helpful either, because surviving Egyptian records do not mention either Joseph or Moses in any historical period. Neither does the Bible name the pharaoh who ruled Egypt in Moses' day. The Exodus occurred after the rise of a new king who "did not know Joseph," or who refused to recognize Joseph's achievements (Ex. 1:8).

The promise of the Exodus began with God's revelation of Himself to Moses at the burning bush (Ex. 3:2). This was followed by the commissioning of Moses and Aaron to stand before Pharaoh and demand the release of the Israelites. When he refused, a series of ten plagues began. Nine of these involved partially natural occurrences that were miraculously concentrated within a short time, affecting the Egyptians only and leaving the Israelites untouched. Each plague involved an Egyptian god in some manner, showing how powerless such deities were in comparison to Israel's God.

The final, tenth, plague resulted in the death of all the Egyptian firstborn male children and animals. Only then did Pharaoh agree to release the Hebrew people. They were spared from death by remaining in their houses and putting sacrificial blood on the doorposts before they ate the newly instituted Passover meal (Ex. 12:6–13). The Egyptians were so glad to be relieved of what had become a great burden to them that they gave the departing Israelites gifts of gold, silver, and clothing (Ex. 12:35).

Then the Exodus from Egypt began, with the whole company under Moses being directed away from the northerly road (Ex. 13:17) leading from Egypt to Gaza in Canaan. From Rameses, probably near Qantir, they moved to Succoth, perhaps the ancient Tell el-Maskhuta situated in the Wadi Tumilat in the southeastern region of the Nile delta. Then the Hebrews camped at Etham, on the edge of the Wilderness of Shur (Ex. 13:20), at a site still unknown but probably north of Lake Timsah close to the fortifications guarding Egypt's northeastern frontier. They were directed by a pillar of cloud during the day. At night they were guided by a pillar of fire, which led them away from Etham, probably in a northwesterly direction, to a site opposite Baal Zephon and Pi Hahiroth.

At this site a body of water stood in the way (Ex. 14:2). To the Egyptians this spelled the doom of a group of runaway slaves that had become thoroughly confused about their location as they struggled to get out of the Goshen area. This misunderstanding was part of God's plan to destroy the Egyptian armies (Ex. 14:3–4). They closed in on the Israelite camp, eager to recapture their escaped slaves. While the Hebrews assembled and rushed to the edge of the water, the pillar of cloud moved to the rear of the fleeing Hebrews, preventing the movement of the Egyptian armies.

A strong east wind from the desert began to blow on the surface of the water, which is also described more fully as a "reed sea" (Ex. 15:22) or lake of papyrus reeds. Earlier versions of the Bible mistakenly translated the phrase as "Red Sea," but this name describes a large oceanic gulf far to the southeast in which papyrus reeds do not grow. The concentrated, hot winds miraculously parted the marsh waters and dried the bottom so the Israelites could flee across it.

As the Egyptians followed, the winds stopped and the waters drowned the pursuers. The miracles of the Exodus were thus completed by the destruction of the Egyptian armies. The jubilant Israelites sang a victory song with Moses to celebrate the event (Ex. 15:1–18). The women, led by Miriam the sister of Aaron, also danced and sang (Ex. 15:20–21) as they praised God for His deliverance.

Then the Israelites began to journey into the wilderness (Ex. 15:22), known in Numbers 33:8 as the wilderness. They had traveled in a circular manner, except that now they were east of the body of water. Being free from the threat of capture, they traveled east and south into the Sinai peninsula in order to meet with God at Mount Sinai (Horeb). Here they would establish a covenant that would make them God's chosen nation. Etham contained very little water. But after God enabled Moses to locate a supply, the Hebrews arrived at an oasis named Elim.

The Exodus became for the Israelites the supreme occasion when God acted to deliver His people from harsh captivity, binding them to Himself by a solemn covenant. Even today when the Jews celebrate the Passover, they are reminded of God's mighty deliverance in that long-ago time.

FAMINE — the lack of a supply of food or water. This word occurs often in the Bible in both literal and figurative senses. Since the line between famine and plenty in Palestine depends mainly on the rains coming at the right time and in the proper supply, famine was an ever-present threat. In the face of famine, Abraham migrated to Egypt (Gen. 12:10), Isaac went to Gerar in Philistine territory (Gen. 26:1), and Jacob moved to Egypt (Genesis 41–47).

The most famous famine recorded in the Bible is the seven-year famine in Egypt foretold by Joseph in interpreting Pharaoh's dream. Extending even into Canaan, it eventually brought the rest of Joseph's family to Egypt (Genesis 41–47; Ps. 105:16). During another famine Elijah was kept alive by the widow of Zarephath (1 Kin. 17:8; Luke 4:25-26).

Drought and conditions of war brought famine to besieged cities (1 Kin. 18:2; Ezek. 6:12). Pathetic descriptions of famine conditions include people's resorting to cannibalism (2 Kin. 6:28-29), cries of hungry children (Lam. 4:4), and the fainting of people in the streets (Is. 51:20).

Famine was also one of the punishments sent by the Lord upon His people because of their sins (Is. 51:20; Ezek. 14:21). A famine in the time of David was caused by Saul's mistreatment of the Gibeonites (2 Sam. 21:1). A striking description of famine conditions was given by the prophet Amos in his phrase, "cleanness of teeth" (Amos 4:6)—clean because there was no food to foul them.

A famine is one of the signs of the approaching fall of Jerusalem (Matt. 24:7), and one of the plagues coming upon "Babylon," as recorded in Revelation 18:8.

Using figurative language, the prophet Amos described a famine of an entirely different sort—not one of lack of food or water, but a famine of hearing the word of the Lord (Amos 8:11). Those who had refused to hear the prophets would have no prophets to guide them in the perilous days when God's judgment would fall upon His people.

FARM, FARMING — the practice of growing livestock and crops for food or commercial purposes. Although the word *farm* occurs only in Matthew 22:5, farming was an important occupation in Bible times. Practically every family owned a piece of land in Israel, and many families farmed a small area of their own.

Outside the cities, most Israelites lived in villages rather than on farms. Cultivated land usually was outside the village, situated near the water supply or on western or northern slopes where rainfall was greatest. Crops grown included wheat, barley, grapes, olives, and figs.

Farm animals lived in the houses with the families. All but the poorest owned at least one ox or donkey as a work animal. Cattle, sheep, and goats were common, providing milk products as well as skins for clothes. Richer families and royal estates employed farm managers and workers (1 Chr. 27:25-31) and hired laborers for special tasks, particularly at harvest time (Matt. 20:1-16).

Frequent difficulties, such as hilly ground, stony soil, and unpredictable rainfall, did not make farming easy. But there were certain rewards, such as the joys of shearing animals and gathering the crops at harvest time (1 Sam. 25:2-8; Is. 9:3).

FEASTS AND FESTIVALS — the holy convocations, the regular assemblies of the people of Israel for worship of the Lord.

The feasts and festivals of the nation were scheduled at specific times in the annual calendar and they were both civil and religious in nature. Some feasts and festivals marked the beginning or the end of the agricultural year, while others commemorated historic events in the life of the nation. All of the feasts were marked by thanksgiving and joyous feasting.

Meat, a scarce item in the daily fare of the people, was eaten at these affairs, and wine was also consumed. The fat and the blood of the animals were reserved for sacrifice to God. The libation (or offering) of wine may have been drunk by the worshipers as part of the meal ceremony. First the blood and the fat were offered to God; then sometimes the worshipers ate.

The feasts and festivals of Israel were community observances. The poor, the widow, the orphan, the Levite, and the sojourner or foreigner were invited to most of the feasts. The accounts of these feasts suggest a potluck type of meal, with some parts of the meal reserved for the priests and the rest given to those who gathered at the temple or the altar for worship. One of the feasts, Passover, originated in the home and later was transferred to the temple. The rest were apparently observed at specific times during the year and in designated places.

The Hebrew word for "pilgrimage" seems to be reserved mostly for the three great annual feasts: the Feast of Unleavened Bread, the Feast of Weeks, and the Feast of Tabernacles. These feasts are discussed in Leviticus 23. Every Israelite male was expected to observe them.

The religious pilgrimage from the various towns and cities to the temple or to the Levitical cities scattered throughout the land became annual events. This yearly event may also have progressed from an annual "pilgrimage" early in Israel 's history to a "processional" at the temple or at the Levitical center in later times. In all the feasts and festivals the nation of Israel remembered its past and renewed its faith in the Lord who created and sustained His people.

Following is a complete list of all the feasts and festivals observed by the people of Israel. Some were annual events, while others occurred weekly or once every several years.

Atonement, Day of. The tenth day of the seventh month was set aside as a day of public fasting and humiliation. On this day the nation of Israel sought atonement for its sins (Lev. 16:29; 23:27; Num. 29:7). This day fell in the month equivalent to our August, and it was preceded by special Sabbaths (Lev. 23:24). The only fasting period required by the Law (Lev. 16:29; 23:31), the Day of Atonement was a recognition of people's inability to make any atonement for their sins. It was a solemn, holy day accompanied by elaborate ritual (Lev. 16; Heb. 10:1-10).

The high priest who officiated on this day first sanctified himself by taking a ceremonial bath and putting on white garments (Lev. 16:4). Then he had to make atonement for himself and other priests by sacrificing a bullock (Num. 29:8). God was enthroned on the Mercy Seat in the sanctuary, but no person could approach it except through the mediation of the high priest, who offered the blood of sacrifice.

After sacrificing a bullock, the high priest chose a goat for a sin-offering and sacrificed it. Then he sprinkled its blood on and about the mercy seat (Lev. 16:12, 14, 15). Finally the scapegoat bearing the sins of the people was sent into the wilderness (Lev. 16:20-22). This scapegoat symbolized the pardon for sin brought through the sacrifice (2 Cor. 5:21; Gal. 3:12).

Dedication, Feast of. This feast, also known as Hanukkah and the Feast of Lights, is mentioned only once in the Bible (John 10:22). It developed in the era of the Maccabees and celebrated the cleansing of the temple after its desecration by Antiochus IV Epiphanes. The Feast of Dedication is observed on the 25th day of the ninth month.

Jubilee, Year of. The references to the Year of Jubilee in the Bible include Leviticus 23:15-16; 25:8-55; 27:14-24; Isaiah 61:1-2; and Jeremiah 34:8, 14-17. The Jubilee Year began with the blowing of the ram's horn. It took place after seven sabbatical years, or every 49 years; and the 50th year was thereby set aside as the Year of Jubilee. Once the Israelites entered and possessed the promised land, it became their obligation to observe this year.

The Year of Jubilee was a special year in family renewal. A man who was bound to another as a slave or indentured servant was set free and returned to his own family. If any members of his family were also bound, the entire family was set free. Houses and lands could also be redeemed in the Year of Jubilee. If they were not redeemed within a year, however, they became the permanent possession of the previous owner. The land owned by Levites was exempted from this law; they could redeem their land at any time.

The rights and privileges extended by the Israelites to other Israelites did not extend to non-Israelites. Servants obtained by Israelites from the non-Israelite world were permanent slaves. And property purchased from nonIsraelites was not redeemable. The law of the Year of Jubilee favored the Israelites.

Jeremiah 34:8, 14-17 warned Judah for first practicing the Jubilee and then taking away people's liberty. Apparently, those who gained wealth and power in Israel did not observe this festival willingly. The inscription on the Liberty Bell in Philadelphia—"Proclaim liberty throughout the land to all the inhabitants thereof" (Lev. 25:10)—is a modern application of the Year of Jubilee.

New Moon. The references in the Bible to the New Moon celebration include Exodus 40:2, 17; Numbers 10:10; 28:1-10, 11-15; and Psalm 104:19. The law specified that two bullocks, one ram, seven lambs, and one kid were to be offered in connection with this celebration. Grain mixed with oil accompanied the offerings; a trumpet blast introduced this feast. The sins committed and not expiated during the previous month were covered by the offerings of the New Moon.

Passover and the Feast of Unleavened Bread. References to the Passover and the Feast of Unleavened Bread include Exodus 12:1–13:16; 23:15; 34:18-20, 25; Leviticus 23:4-14; Numbers 28:16-25; Deuteronomy 16:1-8; Joshua 4:19-23; 5:10-12; and 2 Chronicles 30:2, 3, 13, 15.

The Passover was the first of the three great festivals of the Israelite people. It referred to the sacrifice of a lamb in Egypt when the people of Israel were slaves. They smeared the blood of the lamb on their doorposts as a signal to God that He should "pass over" their houses when He destroyed all the firstborn of Egypt (Ex. 12:13).

Passover was observed on the 14th day of the first month, Abib, with the service beginning in the evening (Lev. 23:6). It was on the evening of this day that Israel left Egypt. Passover commemorated this departure from Egypt in haste. Unleavened bread was used in the celebration because this showed that the people had no time to put leaven in their bread as they ate their final meal as slaves in Egypt.

Several regulations were given concerning the observance of Passover. Passover was to be observed "in the place which the LORD your God will choose." This implied the sanctuary of the tabernacle or the temple in Jerusalem.

Joshua 5:10-12 refers to the observing of Passover in the plains of Jericho near Gilgal. Second Chronicles 30:1, 3, 13, 15 describes a Passover during the reign of Hezekiah. Messengers were sent throughout the land to invite the people to come to Jerusalem to observe the Passover.

Many refused; some even scorned the one who carried the invitation. Because the people were not ready to observe the Passover, a delay of one month was recommended. That year the Passover was on the 14th day of the second month. Even after the delay many still were not ready to observe the Passover.

In New Testament times, large numbers gathered in Jerusalem to observe the annual Passover. Jesus was crucified in the city during one of these Passover celebrations. He and His disciples ate a Passover meal together on the eve of His death. Like the blood of the lamb that saved the Hebrew people from destruction in Egypt, His blood, as the ultimate Passover sacrifice, redeems us from the power of sin and death (1 Cor. 5:7).

Purim, Feast of. References to Purim include Esther 3:7; 9:24, 26, 28-29, 31-32. This feast commemorates the deliverance of the Jewish people from destruction by an evil schemer named Haman during the days of their captivity by the Persians. It took its name from the Babylonian word *put*, meaning "lot," because Haman cast lots to determine when he would carry out his plot against the Jews. The Feast of Purim took place on the 14th and 15th of Adar, and during its celebration the book of Esther is read as a reminder of their deliverance. A happy ceremony, Purim is accompanied with the giving of gifts and much celebration.

Sabbath. The Sabbath is taught in many places, including Exodus 16:22-30; 20:8-11; 23:12; 31:12-16; 34:21; 35:2-3; Leviticus 23:3; 26:2; Numbers 15:32-36; 28:9-10; Deuteronomy 5:12-15. The Hebrew word for Sabbath means "to cease or abstain." Two reasons are given for observing the Sabbath: Creation and Exodus.

Exodus 20:8-11 reminded the nation of Israel to remember that God rested on the seventh day (Gen. 2:2). This grounds the observance of the Sabbath in the creation of the world. Deuteronomy 5:12-15 reminded Israel to remember its bondage years when there was no rest. This passage fixed the origin of the Sabbath in the bondage of the Hebrews in Egypt.

The Israelites were instructed to include the family, the hired servants, the stranger, and even their domestic animals in observance of this holy day. All were commanded to cease from normal labor. This included the command not to gather firewood (Num. 15:32-36) or to kindle a fire (Ex. 35:2-3). Stoning to death was apparently the penalty for gathering firewood on the Sabbath. Those who violated the Sabbath would be excommunicated from the community or could be put to death (Ex. 31:12-16).

The Sabbath became not only a day of rest, but a convocation to the Lord as well. A specific sacrifice on the Sabbath is required in Numbers 28:9-10. It included a lamb, a grain offering mixed with oil, and a drink offering. This was to be offered as a burnt offering. In later periods, prayer and other rituals became the procedure for observing the Sabbath.

The purpose of the Sabbath was twofold. It symbolized that the nation of Israel had been set apart by the Lord as His special people. The Sabbath was also a celebration of the fact that the land belonged to God. This is seen in His provision of a Sabbatical Year—one year out of every seven when the land should rest from cultivation in order to renew and replenish itself.

The observance of the Sabbath set the Israelites apart from their neighbors. Unfortunately, burdensome restrictions and heavy requirements eventually grew up around its observance. The day that was set apart for rest, renewal, and worship became a day filled with rules of many things that must not be done.

Jesus attempted to restore the purpose of the Sabbath (Matt. 12:1-14; Mark 2:23–3:6; Luke 6:1-11). He declared God's intention for the Sabbath by pointing out that "the Sabbath was made for man, and not man for the Sabbath" (Mark 2:27).

Sabbatical Year. The concept of the sabbatical year was that the land was to be given a rest every seventh year. This law included grain fields and vineyards. Even that which grew from the planting and pruning of the sixth year was not to be consumed by the owner.

Eventually, the cancellation of debts was added to the land rest as a part of the sabbatical year. Debts to fellow Israelites were to be forgiven during this year, although debts of non-Israelites might be collected. But the spirit of generosity was encouraged even toward non-Israelites. Indentured servants were to be granted their freedom. They were also to be provided with grain, meat, and drink in generous portions.

The purpose of the sabbatical year was renewal—renewal of the land, renewal of hope in the canceling of debts, and renewal of life in a new start.

Seventh Month Festival. This festival is mentioned in Leviticus 23:24-25, 27-32 and Numbers 29:1-40. It was introduced with the blowing of trumpets, the halt of labor, sacrifices, and a testing (Lev. 23:24-32; Num. 29:1-40). The exact reason for its observance is not clear. Some scholars believe it originated during the Babylonian captivity as a way of counteracting the influence of the Babylonian New Year Festival. This feast is also known as the Feast of Trumpets.

Tabernacles, Feast of. References to the Feast of Tabernacles in the Bible include Exodus 23:16; 34:22; Leviticus 23:33-36, 39-43; Numbers 29:12-32; Deuteronomy 16:13-16; Ezra 3:4; and Zechariah 14:16, 18-19.

This festival was observed on the 15th day of the seventh month to celebrate the completion of the autumn harvest. Features of the celebration included a holy convocation on the first and eighth days, and the offering of many animal sacrifices. The Israelites were also commanded to live in booths made of palm and willow trees during the festival to commemorate their period of wilderness wandering when they lived in temporary shelters. This feast is also known as the Feast of Booths.

Unleavened Bread, Feast of. This feast began on the 15th day of the first month as a part of the larger celebration of Passover (Ex. 13:3-10; Lev. 23:6-8). Manual labor was strictly forbidden. Strangers and native-born people alike were punished if they failed to keep this holy day. A convocation began the feast.

Only unleavened bread was to be eaten during this feast. Bread without leaven commemorated the haste with which Israel left Egypt. As the blood was drained from the sacrificial animal, so the life or the power of leaven was removed from the bread offered to God during this annual celebration.

Weeks, Feast of. Biblical references to the Feast of Weeks include Exodus 23:16; 34:22; Leviticus 23:15-21; Numbers 28:26-31; Deuteronomy 16:9-12; and 2 Chronicles 8:13. This feast was observed early in the third month on the 50th day after the offering of the barley sheaf at the Feast of Unleavened Bread. It included a holy convocation with the usual restriction on manual labor.

Numbers 28:26-31 describes the number and nature of offerings and Deuteronomy 16:9-12 describes those who were to be invited to this feast. They include servants, sons and daughters, Levites, the fatherless, the widow, and the stranger.

This feast was also known as the Feast of Harvest as well as Pentecost (a Greek word meaning "fifty"). The early Christian believers, who were gathered in Jerusalem for observance of this feast, experienced the outpouring of God's Holy Spirit in a miraculous way (Acts 2:1-4).

FLOOD, THE — the divinely-sent deluge that destroyed all sinful humankind by water during the time of Noah.

The inspired writer of Genesis took two chapters to tell of the creation of the world and one chapter to portray the Fall, but he devoted four chapters to the Flood. Since the concern

of the writer was to reveal the nature of God and His dealings
with humankind, he evidently saw this story as a good vehicle
for this truth. The Flood reveals both the judgment and the
mercy of God.

Archaeologists have discovered a number of flood stories
among pagan nations in the ancient world. One Sumerian and
two Babylonian stories have survived. A comparison of these
stories with the Flood account in Genesis is both interesting
and significant.

In one of the Babylonian stories, the gods became irritated
with the people because they grew too numerous and became
too noisy, so they considered several different ways to get rid of
these bothersome people. Finally, they decided on a flood. But
the flood apparently got out of hand. For a while the gods were
afraid they would be destroyed. They began to quarrel among
themselves, shrinking in fear from the rising waters and crowd-
ing around a sacrifice like flies.

In stark contrast to such pagan stories, the book of Genesis
presents the holy and sovereign God who acted in judgment
against sin and yet mercifully saved Noah and his family
because of their righteousness.

The Flood was not simply a downpour of ordinary rain. The
text indicates a cosmic upheaval. "The fountains of the great
deep" were broken up (Gen. 7:11). Perhaps there were earthquakes and the ocean floors may have been raised up until
the waters covered the earth. By a supernatural upheaval, God
returned the earth to the primitive chaos described in Genesis
1:2.

A Degenerate Humanity. The Flood was a drastic judgment,
but the condition that brought it to pass was also serious. Society
degenerated to the point that "every intent" of the thoughts of
man's heart "was only evil continually" (Gen. 6:5). Violence
raged upon earth. Instead of living responsibly as persons created in the image and likeness of God, people existed as beasts.

Because the situation was hopeless, God chose to destroy that generation and make a new start with the family of righteous Noah.

The Divine Grief. While the minds of people were filled with every evil, the heart of God was filled with grief and sorrow. Like a parent whose children have gone bad, God mourned for his wayward children. The Lord was sorry He had created them and "was grieved in his heart" (Gen. 6:6).

Since God knows the end from the beginning, how could He be sorry for what He had done? This was the biblical writer's way of showing the extreme disappointment of the Lord and the radical change in His attitude and action toward humanity. He had blessed the race, but now He would turn against the wicked people who refused to repent. Their failure to repent caused God to repent, or turn around, in his approach to humanity.

Righteous Noah. In stark contrast to the degenerate people among whom he lived, "Noah was a just man" who "walked with God" (Gen. 6:9). God's righteous judgment is seen in the destruction of the wicked, but His mercy and care are seen in His saving of Noah and, through him, the human race. God's judgment was accompanied by grief, but His grace was freely given to Noah and his family.

The Ark. The Lord revealed to Noah that His judgment was coming by way of a terrible flood. Noah could save himself and his family by building an ark of wood. The ark was to be large enough to hold Noah, his wife, his three sons, and their wives. In addition, it must provide room for two of every kind of animal and bird. Plenty of time was allowed for this massive building project by Noah and his sons.

The dimensions of the ark were 140 meters (450 feet) long, 23 meters (75 feet) wide, and 14 meters (45 feet) high. There were three levels—lower, middle, and upper decks. The displacement or capacity of a vessel of these dimensions has been estimated as 43,300 tons.

The Long Voyage. The raging waters kept rising for 40 days, and the ark floated high above the hills and mountains. When the waters finally stopped rising, Noah and his passengers faced a long wait for the waters to go down. The total time spent in the ark was about one year and ten days. The ark came to rest on "the mountains of Ararat" (Gen. 8:4) in what is now Turkey. Numerous attempts across the centuries to find traces of the ark have proved futile.

Noah released a raven and a dove to determine whether the waters were low enough to allow them to leave the ark. When the dove returned to the ark, he knew it had been unable to survive outside the ark. After seven days, he again released the dove. This time it came back with an olive leaf. This was good news, indicating that the waters had dropped further and the time when the people and animals could leave the ark was near. Finally the earth dried, and they left the ark (Gen. 8:7-19).

Worship and Covenant. The first act of the grateful Noah was to build an altar and worship God, thanking Him for deliverance from the Flood. Then the Lord made a covenant with Noah. Never again would He destroy the world by water. The rainbow was given as a covenant sign. The bow was an instrument of war, but the rainbow represents a bow with the string on the ground—a symbol of peace.

The Flood came upon the earth as a severe judgment of God against wickedness. But God's grace and mercy were also revealed in the preservation of Noah and, through him, the human race. The covenant was granted to reassure humanity about God's care.

New Testament References to the Flood. References to the Flood are found in Matthew 24:38; Luke 17:26, 27; Hebrews 11:7; 1 Peter 3:20; and 2 Peter 2:5. The Flood was used to illustrate the holy God's wrath against human wickedness and the salvation of His people.

FUTURE — the time that is yet to come (Ps. 37:37-38). After the archangel Gabriel interpreted Daniel's vision, he said to Daniel, "Seal up the vision, for it refers to many days in the future" (Dan. 8:17-26). The Christian believer is confident of the future because he belongs to Jesus Christ.

GAD, TRIBE OF — the tribe that sprang from Gad and the territory this tribe inhabited, often referred to as Gilead (Num. 1:14). The territory of Gad lay east of the Jordan River between the half-tribe of Manasseh to the north and the tribe of Reuben to the south. Its western boundary was the Jordan River; on the east it faced the territory of the Ammonites. Gad had few major towns.

When Moses assigned the territory east of the Jordan River to the Gadites, he stipulated that they must cross over the river to help the other tribes in the conquest of Canaan (Num. 32:20–32). They did not always do this, however, most likely because the tribe experienced a great deal of trouble holding its own territory.

GEZER [GEZ ur] (*portion, division*) — an ancient Canaanite city 17 kilometers (20 miles) west of Jerusalem that was conquered by Joshua (Josh. 10:33; 12:12). Because the Israelites never fully obeyed God's command to destroy the Canaanites in this city (Josh. 21:21; 1 Chr. 6:67), they eventually lost it to the Philistines (2 Sam. 5:25; 1 Chr. 20:4).

During the reign of Solomon, an Egyptian pharaoh conquered Gezer, burned the city, and killed its inhabitants.

Pharaoh gave the city and his daughter to Solomon to establish peace between Egypt and Israel. Solomon rebuilt Gezer and turned it into a strategic military and economic center (1 Kin. 9:15, 17–19). Many years later, Gezer was destroyed by the Assyrian king Tilgath-Pileser (2 Kin. 16:5–7) when he came to rescue Ahaz, king of Judah, from the attack of the Syrians and Israelites.

In the Jewish wars just before the time of Christ, Gezer was an important military fortress (1 Macc. 9:52; 13:53). The city is not mentioned in the New Testament because it was destroyed earlier by the Romans.

Major archaeological excavations at Gezer were conducted by R. A. S. Macalister from 1902–1909 and by G. E. Wright, W. G. Dever, and J. D. Seger from 1964–1973. The city covered an area of about 30 acres and was first established before the time of Abraham. Some of the most significant discoveries at Gezer were (1) a Palestinian calendar based on the agricultural seasons. This inscription in the ancient Hebrew script is one of the oldest Hebrew documents (from the time of Solomon); (2) a four-entryway gate that was characteristic of the construction methods of Solomon at Hazor and Megiddo; (3) an impressive sloping tunnel about 50 meters (150 feet) long that leads down to a large cistern under the city. This water supply was important to ancient walled cities if the people hoped to withstand an extended enemy siege; and (4) a row of ten huge stones standing on end. These stones may be a part of a High Place where heathen gods were worshiped.

GNOSTICISM [NOS tuh siz em] — a system of false teachings that existed during the early centuries of Christianity. Its name came from *gnosis*, the Greek word for knowledge. The Gnostics believed that knowledge was the way to salvation. For this reason, Gnosticism was condemned as false and heretical by several writers of the New Testament.

Sources. Our knowledge of Gnosticism comes from several sources. First, there are the Gnostic texts, which are among the New Testament Apocrypha. These texts are not recognized as Scripture because they contain teachings that differ from those in the Bible. Then there are the refutations of the Gnostics by the early church fathers. Some of the more important ones are Irenaeus, *Against Heresies*; Hippolytus, *Refutations of All Heresies*; Epiphanius, *Panarion*; and Tertullian, *Against Marcion*.

Still a third source about Gnosticism is the New Testament itself. Many Gnostic teachings were condemned by the writers of the New Testament. Paul emphasized a wisdom and knowledge that comes from God and does not concern itself with idle speculations, fables, and moral laxity (Col. 2:8–23; 1 Tim. 1:4; 2 Tim. 2:16–19; Titus 1:10–16). John, both in his Gospel and in the epistles, countered heretical teaching that, in a broad sense, can be considered Gnostic.

Teachings of the Gnostics. The Gnostics accepted the Greek idea of a radical dualism between God (spirit) and the world (matter). According to their worldview, the created order was evil, inferior, and opposed to the good. God may have created the first order, but each successive order was the work of anti-gods, archons, or a demiurge (a subordinate deity).

The Gnostics believed that the earth is surrounded by a number of cosmic spheres (usually seven) that separate human beings from God. These spheres are ruled by archons (spiritual principalities and powers) who guard their spheres by barring the souls who are seeking to ascend from the realm of darkness and captivity that is below to the realm of light that is above.

The Gnostics also taught that every human being is composed of body, soul, and spirit. Since the body and the soul are part of people's earthly existence, they are evil. Enclosed in the soul, however, is the spirit, the only divine part of this triad. This "spirit" is asleep and ignorant; it needs to be awakened and liberated by knowledge.

According to the Gnostics, the aim of salvation is for the spirit to be awakened by knowledge so the inner person can be released from the earthly dungeon and return to the realm of light where the soul becomes reunited with God. As the soul ascends, however, it needs to penetrate the cosmic spheres that separate it from its heavenly destiny. This, too, is accomplished by knowledge. One must understand certain formulas that are revealed only to the initiated.

Ethical behavior among the Gnostics varied considerably. Some sought to separate themselves from all evil matter in order to avoid contamination. Paul may be opposing such a view in 1 Timothy 4:1–5. For other Gnostics, ethical life took the form of libertinism. For them knowledge meant freedom to participate in all sorts of activities. Many reasoned that since they had received divine knowledge and were truly informed as to their divine nature, it did not matter how they lived.

Such an attitude is a misunderstanding of the gospel. Paul, on a number of occasions, reminded his readers that they were saved from sin to holiness. They were not to have an attitude of indifference toward the law. They had died to sin in their baptism into Christ (Rom. 6:1–11) and so were to walk "in newness of life." John reminded the Christians that once they had been saved they were not to continue living in sin (1 John 3:4–10).

These Gnostic teachings also had a disruptive effect on fellowship in the church. Those who were "enlightened" thought of themselves as being superior to those who did not have such knowledge. Divisions arose between the spiritual and the fleshly. This attitude of superiority is severely condemned in the New Testament. Christians are "one body" (1 Cor. 12) who should love one another (1 Cor. 13; 1 John). Spiritual gifts are for the Christian community rather than individual use; they should promote humility rather than pride (1 Cor. 12–14; Eph. 4:11–16).

GREECE — a region or country of city-states in southeastern Europe between Italy and Asia Minor. Greece was bounded on the east by the Aegean Sea, on the south by the Mediterranean Sea, on the west by the Adriatic Sea and Ionian Sea, and on the north by Mount Olympus and adjacent mountains. The Old Testament name for Greece was Javan (Gen. 10:2, 4; Is. 66:19).

In the early years of its history, Greece was a country of self-governing city-states. Politically and militarily, the Greek city-states were weak. Their varied backgrounds led to frictions and rivalries that kept them from becoming one unified nation.

In 338 B.C., Philip II, king of Macedon, conquered the southern peninsula of Greece. Under Philip's son, Alexander the Great (336–323 B.C.), the Greek Empire was extended from Greece through Asia Minor to Egypt and the borders of India. Alexander's military conquests and his passion to spread Greek culture contributed to the advancement of Greek ideas throughout the ancient world. This adoption of Greek ideas by the rest of the ancient world was known as Hellenism. So thoroughly did Greek ideas penetrate the other nations that the Greek language became the dominant language of the known world.

Greek learning and culture eventually conquered the ancient Near East and continued as dominant forces throughout the New Testament era. Even after the rise of the Romans, about 146 B.C., the influence of Greek language, culture, and philosophy remained strong, even influencing the Jewish religion.

Greek religion included many gods. The religions of Egypt, Asia Minor, and Persia were more appealing than the old Greek gods because they promised immortality. However, the Greeks did not abandon their former gods; they simply adopted new gods and gave them old names. A renewed interest in astrology among the Greeks also led to widespread belief that the planets governed the lives and fates of human beings. The Greeks sought to control any turn of fate through worship. They even erected an altar inscribed "to the unknown god" in their capital city of Athens (Acts 17:23).

The peninsula of Greece fell to the Romans in 146 B.C. and later became the senatorial province of Achaia with Corinth as its capital. The apostle Paul visited this area on his second missionary journey, delivering his famous sermon to the Athenian philosophers (Acts 17:22–34). Later he appeared before the proconsul Gallio at Corinth (Acts 18:12–17). On his third missionary journey, he visited Greece for three months (Acts 20:2–3).

Greece is important to Christianity because of its language. In New Testament times Greek was the language spoken by the common people of the ancient world, as far west as Rome and the Rhone Valley in southeastern France. Most of the New Testament was written originally in Greek, a precise and expressive language.

HAMMURAPI, CODE OF [hah muhr RAH pee] — an ancient law code named after a king who ruled Babylonia from about 1792 to 1750 B.C. These laws from the ancient world are valuable to Bible students because they are so similar to the law as revealed to Moses in the first five books of the Old Testament.

The Code of Hammurapi was discovered in 1901–1902 by the archaeologist V. Scheil at Susa, an early city of the ancient Babylonians. It was written on a seven-foot-high stone monument (called a stele) with the upper part picturing Hammurapi receiving a scepter and a ring, symbols of justice and order, from Shamash, the Babylonian sun-god and divine lawgiver. The rest of the monument contains the code; the direction of writing is from top to bottom. Hammurapi's law dates from about 300 years after Abraham and some 300 years before the events described in the books of Exodus, Leviticus, and Deuteronomy. This law code was written for a complex urban culture, in contrast to the simple agricultural culture of Palestine.

The contents of Hammurapi's Code are listed as follows:

1. Various offenses and crimes, including false witness, sorcery, corrupt judgment, theft, and kidnapping.

2. Property, with special reference to crown tenants, tenant farmers, and loans of money or seed. The king of Babylon owned crownland in the Old Babylonian period, as did the God of Israel. According to the code, land owned by the king could not be sold.

3. Commercial law, related to partnerships and agencies.

4. Marriage law, including dowry settlements, bridal gifts, divorce, and matrimonial offenses.

5. The firstborn, who had special rights and privileges (compare Deut. 15:19).

6. Special cases involving women and priestesses, whose support was weakened by an increase in state and private ownership of land.

7. Adoption, as it relates to Genesis 17:17–18.

8. Assault and damage to persons and property, including pregnant women, a surgeon's liability in an eye operation, and the hire of boats.

9. Agricultural work and offenses, including goring by an ox (compare Ex. 21:28–32).

10. Rates and wages for seasonal workers, hire of beasts, carts and boats, and so forth.

11. An appendix concerning slaves, including their purchase and sale.

The contents of the Code of Hammurapi and the law of Moses are similar in many ways. This may be a result of the common cultural background the Babylonians and Israelites shared. Both were ancient peoples of the Near East who inherited their customs and laws from common ancestors. Yet it should be noted that much is different in the Old Testament revelation. For example, the Law given at Mount Sinai reflects a unique and high view of the nature of God, and the Old Testament law is presented as an expression of His holy nature, as Leviticus 19:2 clearly shows. Also, when compared with the Code of Hammurapi, the Old Testament law is usually less harsh.

HARVEST — the period at the end of the growing season when crops were gathered. Harvest was one of the happiest times of the year in Palestine (Ps. 126:5–6; Is. 9:3), marked with celebrations and religious festivals (Ex. 23:16). There were two grain harvests. Barley was gathered from mid-April onwards and wheat from mid-May. The harvest of fruit from trees and vines took place in the fall.

Cutting with a sickle began the process of harvesting grain (Deut. 16:9; Mark 4:29). Then it was gathered into sheaves (Deut. 24:5). Next the grain was taken to the threshing floor, an important local site with a hard surface and often situated on higher ground. Various tools, such as metal-toothed sledges drawn by oxen, were used for threshing (Is. 28:28; 41:15). Then the grain was winnowed, or tossed into the air, with a pitchfork. The wind carried off the chaff, but the heavier kernels and straw fell to the ground (Matt. 3:12).

Finally, the kernels were shaken in a sieve, made of a wooden hoop with leather thongs (Is. 30:28; Amos 9:9). Then the grain was stored.

Harvest became a picture of God's judgment (Jer. 51:33; Joel 3:13), and Jesus compared the Last Judgment with the harvest (Matt. 13:30, 39; Rev. 14:14–20). However, Jesus used the same metaphor for the gathering together of those who believed in Him (Matt. 9:37–38; Luke 10:2), indicating that the final harvest has already begun with His first coming (John 4:35).

HEBREW PEOPLE — an ethnic term designating the lineage of the nation of Israel and the Jewish people.

Abram was the first person in the Bible to be called a Hebrew (Gen. 14:13). Thereafter, his descendants through Isaac and Jacob were known as Hebrews (Gen. 40:15; 43:32). The term is used five times in the story of Joseph (Gen. 39:14–43:32), including a reference to Joseph by Potiphar's wife as "the Hebrew servant"

(Gen. 39:17). Joseph told Potiphar's chief butler, "For indeed I was stolen away from the land of the Hebrews" (Gen. 40:15).

The origin of the term "Hebrew" is a mystery to scholars. Some believe the word came from Eber, a descendant of Noah through Shem and an ancestor of Abraham (Gen. 10:21, 25; 11:16–26). Eber, literally meaning "on the other side of," may allude to Abraham's departure from a region east of the Euphrates River.

This possibility harmonizes with the statement made by God to the Israelites in Joshua's time: "Then I took your father Abraham from the other side of the River, led him throughout all the land of Canaan, and multiplied his descendants and gave him Isaac. To Isaac I gave Jacob and Esau" (Josh. 24:3–4). Of Eber's descendants, Abraham, Nahor, and Lot stand out. The genealogical list in Genesis 10 and other passages indicate that Abraham was the ancestor of the Hebrews; Nahor was the ancestor of the Arameans; and Lot was the ancestor of the Moabites and the Ammonites (Gen. 10:21, 24, 25; 11:14–27).

Still other scholars believe the Hebrew people are related to a people known as the Habiru. These people are mentioned in clay tablets dating to the 18th and 19th centuries B.C. They are also featured in the Nuzi, Hittite, and Amarna documents of the 14th and 15th centuries B.C. "Habiru," however, is a sociological term, while "Hebrew" is ethnic.

There is considerable evidence in the Old Testament that the Hebrews regarded themselves as a composite race, "My father was a Syrian, about to perish, and he went down to Egypt and dwelt there few in number; and there he became a nation" (Deut. 26:5). In their wandering tribal days and during their early years in Canaan, the Hebrews experienced a mixture of blood through marriage with surrounding peoples. When Abraham sought a suitable wife for Isaac, he sent to northwest Mesopotamia, near Haran, for Rebekah, daughter of the Syrian

Bethuel (Gen. 24:10; 25:20). Jacob found Rachel in the same location (Genesis 28–29).

Strains of Egyptian blood also appeared in the family of Joseph through Asenath's two sons, Ephraim and Manasseh (Gen. 41:50–52). Moses had a Midianite wife, Zipporah (Ex. 18:1–7), and an unnamed Ethiopian (Cushite) wife (Num. 12:1).

Although several unanswered questions about the origin of the Hebrews remain, no culture has equaled their contribution to mankind. In a pagan world with many gods, the Hebrews worshiped one supreme, holy God who demanded righteousness in His people. From the Hebrews also sprang Jesus Christ, who gave His life to set us free from the curse of sin.

HELLENISM [HELL un is em] — a style of Greek civilization associated with the spread of Greek language and culture to the Mediterranean world after the conquests of Alexander the Great.

On the advice of Aristotle, his teacher, Alexander sought to instill a love for the Greek way of life within those whom he conquered. His generals adopted the same pattern of operation. Conflict soon arose between the Jews and his successors in Israel, the Seleucids. The history of this conflict is detailed in the books of the Maccabees.

In the Hellenistic period, Greek became the common language throughout the ancient world. So many Jews spoke Greek that an authorized Greek translation of the Old Testament, the Septuagint, was made at Alexandria, Egypt. In the Bible, the word *Hellenists* (NKJV) or *Grecians* (KJV) in Acts 6:1 and 9:29 (*Grecian Jews*, NIV) refers to Greek-speaking Jews.

HERODIANS [heh ROW dee uns] — Jews of influence and standing who were favorable toward Greek customs and Roman law in New Testament times. Although the Herodians should not be equated with the Sadducees, they sided with the

Sadducees in their pro-Roman sympathies and opposed the Pharisees, who were anti-Roman. The Herodians joined forces with the Pharisees, however, in their opposition to Jesus.

In Galilee, the Herodians and the Pharisees plotted against Jesus' life (Mark 3:6). At Jerusalem, the Herodians and the Pharisees again joined forces, seeking to trap Jesus on the issue of paying tribute to Caesar (Matt. 22:16; Mark 12:13). Jesus warned his disciples, "Take heed, beware of the leaven [evil influence] of the Pharisees and ... of Herod" (Mark 8:15).

HIGH PLACES — elevated or hilltop sites dedicated to worship of pagan gods. Ancient peoples often built their shrines on hilltops. In Mesopotamia, where the land is flat, they built artificial mountains in the shape of step pyramids called ziggurats. The Tower of Babel (Gen. 11:1–9) was probably such a ziggurat.

Most of the Old Testament references to high places imply a form of pagan worship forbidden to the Israelites. But sometimes the Lord's people, with His approval, worshiped Him at elevated altars. This happened between the time Shiloh was destroyed and before the ark of the covenant was installed in Solomon's temple. For instance, Samuel blessed the offerings made at a high place that perhaps was Ramah, a word that itself means "high place" (1 Sam. 9:12–14). At nearby Gibeon there was a high place. During the reign of David the tabernacle was there (1 Chr. 16:39; 21:29; 2 Chr. 1:3–4). At this high place Solomon made many sacrifices, had his dream, and asked God for wisdom (1 Kin. 3:4–15).

After this early period in Israel's history, all high places mentioned in the Bible were off limits to God's people. In Leviticus 26:30 God promised to destroy the high places, which He knew His people would later build. They probably got the idea for such shrines of worship from the native Canaanites.

In his waning years, Solomon established high places for his pagan wives (1 Kin. 11:7–8). After Solomon's death, the rebellious Northern Kingdom had its high places. The two major ones, containing golden calves, were at Dan and Bethel (1 Kin. 12:28–33). Then as evil kings came to the throne in Judah they inaugurated high places, and successive good kings abolished them. During Rehoboam's reign high places appeared (1 Kin. 14:23), but Hezekiah broke them down (2 Kin. 18:4). Wicked Manasseh built them again (2 Kin. 21:3), but righteous Josiah dismantled them (2 Kin. 23:8). Eventually, "high place" became a general term for a pagan shrine, whether or not it was established in an elevated site.

The prophets condemned the high places (Jer. 17:1–3; 32:35; Ezek. 6:3; Amos 7:9). God is not found on a mountaintop or at a hilltop shrine. He is everywhere, always ready to listen to the prayers of those who call on him (John 4:21–24).

HISTORY — a narrative or chronological record of significant events (Gen. 2:4; story, REB; account, NASB, NIV; generations, KJV, NRSV). The Hebrew word translated as "history" literally means "genealogy."

HITTITES [HIT tights] — a people of the ancient world who flourished in Asia Minor between about 1900 and 1200 B.C. The name Hittite comes from Hatti, another name for Anatolia, the capital of which was Hattusha. Later the Hittites spread into northern Syria and populated such cities as Aleppo, Carchemish, and Hamath. The Old Testament contains many references to the Hittites (Gen. 15:20; Num. 13:29; 1 Kin. 10:29; Ezra 9:1; Ezek. 16:3, 45).

Hittites in the Bible. When Sarah died, Abraham purchased the field of Machpelah with a burial cave from Ephron the Hittite (Gen. 23:10–20). This incident between a patriarch and a Hittite was followed later by Esau's act of taking two Hittite women as wives (Gen. 26:34).

Hittites were included among the peoples dwelling from the river of Egypt to the river Euphrates—the region promised to Abraham. Hittites also occupied the land of Canaan while the Israelites were in Egypt. They were among the people who had to be driven out when Israel conquered Canaan under Joshua (Ex. 3:8, 17; Deut. 7:1; Judg. 3:5).

After the dissolution of the Hittite Empire, remnants of the Hittites were particularly visible in Palestine during the reign of David. Ahimelech the Hittite was among the close associates and trusted companions of David during his flight from Saul (1 Sam. 26:6). The most famous of these later Hittites was Uriah, Bathsheba's husband, whom David sent to his death to conceal his adultery with Uriah's wife (2 Sam. 11:15). The northern border of Israel during David's time was extended to the river Euphrates (2 Sam. 8:3) to include Syrian city-states. It is highly possible that "Hittites" of the Syrian region served in David's administration (2 Sam. 8:17; 1 Kin. 4:3).

Solomon had a Hittite wife (1 Kin. 11:1), apparently from a royal marriage to seal an alliance with a foreign power. After Solomon's time, the "kings of the Hittites" were powerful rulers in Syria during the time when Judah and Israel existed as separate kingdoms (2 Kin. 7:6; 2 Chr. 1:17).

Hittite Religion. The Hittites themselves described their array of pagan gods as "the thousand gods." Among this diversity of deities, there were many names that were Hattic, Hurrian, Sumerian, and Canaanite in origin. The names of many gods occur in treaties of the Hittite people as guardian deities over the parties bound by treaty commitments. Each god was worshiped in its own native language. A storm god was the chief male god, and a solar goddess was his mistress.

The Hittites may have been one of the pagan influences that pulled the nation of Israel away from worship of the one true God during its long history. Students of the Old Testament point out that the Hittites formed treaties with other countries long before the Hebrew people developed the consciousness of being a nation governed directly by God. Some scholars believe these treaties were used as a model for the covenant that God established with the Hebrews at Mount Sinai.

HIVITES [HIGH vights] — a people descended from Canaan (Gen. 10:17) who lived in the land before and after Israel's conquest of the land of Canaan (Ex. 13:5; Deut. 7:1; Josh. 11:3; Judg. 3:5; 1 Kin. 9:20). No reference to the Hivites exists outside the Bible. Many scholars think the name "Hivite" is an early scribal error for "Horite" (Hurrian). Other scholars suggest that the Hivites were a smaller group within the Horites.

The Bible indicates that the Hivites lived near Tyre and Sidon (2 Sam. 24:7), in the hill country of Lebanon (Judg. 3:3), in Mizpah near Mount Hermon (Josh. 11:3), in central Palestine at Shechem (Gen. 34:2), and in the town of Gibeon north of Jerusalem (Josh. 9:7; 11:19).

Many Hivites were murdered by Simeon and Levi, sons of Jacob, after a member of a Hivite clan assaulted their sister Dinah (Genesis 34). Later, the Israelites were commanded to take Canaan from various groups of Canaanites, including Hivites (Ex. 13:5; 23:23, 28).

Hivites from Gibeon tricked Joshua and the Israelites into making a covenant with them (Joshua 9). Joshua spared the Hivites and made them servants (Josh. 9:27). Hivites were also among those Canaanites whom Solomon used as slave laborers for his building projects (1 Kin. 9:20–21; 2 Chr. 8:7–8).

I

INNOCENTS, SLAUGHTER OF — Herod the Great's attempt to dispose of the infant Jesus by having all the male children of the region who were two years old and under put to death (Matt. 2:16–18). Such an act is in keeping with the cruelty that marked Herod's reign. He thought the security of his throne was threatened when he received news of one "born King of the Jews" (Matt. 2:2). But God protected His Son by directing Joseph in a dream to flee with his family to Egypt (Matt. 2:13–15). Matthew compared this event with Pharaoh's slaughter of male Israelite babies at the time of Moses' birth (Ex. 1:15–22), and the tragedy of the Babylonian captivity (Jer. 31:15). Such tragedy comes, even on the innocent, when leaders and people do not obey God (Matt. 27:25).

INSURRECTION — an act of rebellion against the established government (Ezra 4:19; Ps. 64:2; Acts 21:38). Barabbas, the criminal who was released by Pilate before Jesus' crucifixion, was guilty of insurrection against the Roman government (Mark 15:7).

ISRAEL, HISTORY OF — The ancient Hebrews were just one of a number of nations living in the ancient Near East. This region of the world included ancient Persia, Mesopotamia (the area between the Tigris and Euphrates rivers), Syria, Anatolia, Palestine, and Egypt. Each of the nations in the area experienced at least one period in its history when it was more powerful or influential than its neighbors. But the nature of empires is such that each of them was destined to fall and to be replaced by a society that was more aggressive than those it overthrew.

The first of these great empires was that of the Sumerians. It consisted of about a dozen small city-states located in southern Mesopotamia in an area about 245 kilometers (150 miles) northwest of the Persian Gulf. The Sumerians established the first high culture in human society in the 4th millennium B.C. They made fundamental discoveries in many important areas of life. They were at their height when a person named Sargon founded an aggressive culture at Agade, some 128 kilometers (80 miles) northwest in central Mesopotamia, adopting much of the Sumerian culture.

Sargon's dynasty was overthrown ultimately by a nation that was itself conquered after a century of rule by a powerful Babylonian king named Hammurapi (about 1792–1750 B.C.). During Hammurapi's reign, the Sumerian cities were conquered and the First Dynasty of Babylon was established in Mesopotamia.

Abraham and the Patriarchs. It is difficult to assign an exact beginning to Hebrew history. But if we regard Abraham as the forefather of the Israelites, it is clear that they had their roots in ancient Sumer. Abraham came from Ur, a Sumerian city (Gen. 11:31). Abraham became prosperous in Haran in northwestern Mesopotamia, then later moved to the land of Canaan (Gen. 12:5), where he received God's assurance that he would be the ancestor of a mighty people.

Abraham's promised son Isaac had two sons of his own, Esau and Jacob. God chose Jacob for the renewal of His promise to Abraham (Gen. 28:13–15). Jacob later moved from Haran, where he had married Leah and Rachel, daughters of Laban, and settled in Canaan. Jacob, whose name was changed to Israel after an encounter with God (Gen. 32:24–30), had 12 sons. Eleven of these sons plotted to sell their youngest brother Joseph into slavery in Egypt.

Years in Egypt. When God prospered Joseph and made him a high official in Egypt, the brothers were forgiven, after being humiliated. They were instructed to bring their father and other family members to Egypt, where they settled in the fertile Goshen area for over two centuries. Then a pharaoh who did not acknowledge Joseph's achievements came to power. The descendants of Israel, now known as Hebrews or Israelites, were uprooted from their land and forced to work on the rebuilding of great Egyptian cities.

After the Israelites experienced considerable suffering, God appointed Moses to liberate His people from bondage. Moses had been born to Hebrew slaves. He was set adrift in a basket on the Nile River in an attempt to prevent him from being killed by Pharaoh's troops. An Egyptian princess rescued him and brought him up as her own son.

Fleeing later from Egypt because of a crime that he had committed (Ex. 2:12), Moses experienced a divine revelation in the wilderness. He was ordered by God to return to Egypt where, with Aaron his brother, he would confront Pharaoh and demand the release of the captive Israelites. Pharaoh's stubborn refusal resulted in the death of the Egyptian firstborn, after which Moses led the Israelites across the Red Sea to safety in the Sinai region.

The Covenant at Sinai. God appeared to Moses on Mount Sinai (Horeb) and entered into a relationship with the twelve tribes, which bound them to Himself and made them, in effect, the nation of Israel. The relationship was in the form of a covenant, or a written contract.

This covenant is fundamentally important for Israelite history. Through it a number of independent tribes were bonded together into one nation and given a specific destiny as the people chosen by God as a channel for divine revelation. The Israelites, however, were not to behave just like any nation of the ancient world. All of these were pagan, following depraved and corrupt moral practices as part of their worship.

The Israelites were to live as a religious community in which each member cared for the others. The exploitation of such helpless persons as strangers, widows, and fatherless children was strictly forbidden under the Mosaic law (Deut. 24:17), since God Himself was their champion (Deut. 10:18).

God promised to provide a land for the Israelites in which they could settle in obedience to covenant law as a holy nation (Ex. 19:6) and be witnesses of His existence and power to all the neighboring nations.

Throughout their history, God's covenant people were meant to be an example of spirituality to the world. This, rather than political activity or territorial conquest, was to be their true destiny. Unfortunately, much of Israelite history was marked by periodic disobedience of the covenant laws.

Israelite history began badly with an idolatrous act. The people made and worshiped a golden calf while Moses was still on Mount Sinai (Ex. 32:1–6). After their punishment, the covenant was renewed and work began on the building of the tabernacle. The structure was portable, and it moved with the Israelites whenever they wandered in the wilderness. Subsequent Hebrew temples were to reflect something of its structure.

The Wilderness Years. Because the Israelites disobeyed God by refusing to enter Canaan (Num. 14:30–35), they were compelled to wander for a generation in the wilderness. These aimless wanderings are summarized in Numbers 33. The people apparently moved between various oases in the Sinai wilderness. After Aaron's death (Num. 20:22–29), the Israelites moved steadily toward Moab in Transjordan and prepared to conquer Canaan. The tribes of Reuben, Gad, and half of the tribe of Manasseh, who owned large herds, were allowed to settle in the conquered Transjordan lands and to raise their cattle. The remainder of the Israelites prepared to cross the Jordan River at Jericho and occupy the promised land. Moses was not permitted to lead the Israelites to victory because he had not carried out God's will properly (Deut. 32:51). Instead he was allowed to view Canaan from the summit of Mount Nebo. After this, he died and was buried in Moab (Deut. 34:6).

Conquest of Canaan. Jericho was like a town under siege when Joshua, who had been commissioned as leader shortly before Moses died (Deut. 34:9), advanced to overthrow it. He obeyed God's instructions regarding the attack upon the fortress-like city that guarded the entrance to Canaan. The Israelite people marched around it daily for six days, and it collapsed dramatically on the seventh day (Josh. 6:12–20).

The next assault was on nearby Ai. This offensive, however, met with disaster because an Israelite named Achan had defied God's instructions about not taking plunder from Jericho. When his sin was discovered, he and his family were stoned to death (Josh. 7:25), after which Ai was overthrown.

Shortly afterward, Joshua was tricked into establishing a covenant with the neighboring Gibeonites. This was followed by a defense of the royal city of Gibeon against the attack of five Canaanite kings who resented the pact made with Joshua. The kings were captured and executed (Josh. 10:16–27). Then Joshua proceeded to conquer the southland, where Lachish and Hebron were important cities. Jerusalem, however, was not captured at this time, nor was Megiddo.

The final phase of occupation involved northern Canaan, where Joshua was confronted by a military group led by Jabin, king of Hazor. Perhaps because the Israelites were anxious to keep the cities intact, none were destroyed except Hazor, the chief city of the north. This policy proved costly in later years. Although the Israelites had occupied the promised land, they had not conquered the people completely. Once the Canaanites were able to reestablish themselves, they presented serious problems for the Israelites.

Period of the Judges. After Joshua died, individual charismatic leaders known as judges provided leadership for the Israelites. This event coincided with increasingly independent activity by the Israelite tribes, caused partly because of Canaanite resistance to the conquerors. This lack of centralized leadership meant that covenant law was not being observed, and it was being replaced by idolatry.

Although the judges tried hard to correct local problems, they were no match for the increasingly militant Canaanites, or for Eglon, a Moabite ruler who oppressed some of the Israelites for 18 years before being killed by a left-handed judge named Ehud (Judg. 3:15–30). By this time Hazor had been reoccupied by Canaanites under Jabin, their king, who made several northern tribes his subjects for 20 years (Judg. 4:2–3).

Jabin's forces were superior because they had iron-fitted, horse-drawn chariots. These chariots were effective on level ground, but they proved less threatening in the hill country. Jabin's general Sisera was defeated by Barak and slain by Jael, the wife of an ally named Heber (Judg. 4:21).

The book of Judges shows clearly that Israel's troubles were the result of rejecting covenant law and adopting various forms of Canaanite idolatry. Canaanite religion was one of the most sensuous and morally depraved that the world has ever known; it contrasted dramatically with the holiness and moral purity demanded of the Israelites by the Sinai covenant.

Because of their persistent idolatry, the Israelites were punished further by Midianite and Ammonite attacks. The most serious threat, however, came from the Philistines. These warlike people had migrated to Canaan in small numbers in the time of Abraham. But they came in a body about 1175 B.C. and settled on the southwestern coast of Canaan. The Philistines established a group of five cities—Gaza, Gath, Ashkelon, Ashdod, and Ekron—and began to push the Israelites into the hill country.

The Philistines were superior in military power because they monopolized the manufacture and sale of iron implements and weapons. Samson had delivered the Israelites periodically from Philistine oppression, but after his death (Judg. 16:27–30) they were at the mercy of the enemy once more.

The United Kingdom Years. The social chaos described in the closing chapters of the book of Judges came to a head in the religious corruption in Israel at the time of Samuel 's childhood (1 Sam. 2:12–18, 22). Although Samuel himself exercised a wholesome ministry, the Israelites were more intent on being ruled by a king than in living as a holy nation in covenant with their God (1 Sam. 8:19–20). Saul, son of Kish, was duly anointed by Samuel as a charismatic leader over the nation (1 Sam. 10:1).

But Saul had an unbalanced personality, which soon showed signs of paranoia. He disobeyed God's commands (1 Sam. 13:13), and a successor was chosen and anointed in the person of David, son of Jesse. David gained popular favor by his defeat of the Philistine champion Goliath. Thereafter David was seen as Israel's savior, much to the dislike of Saul, who felt his own position threatened. Saul fought at intervals against both David and the Philistines, but was ultimately killed along with five sons at Mount Gilboa. The northern tribes then looked to Ishbosheth, the surviving son of Saul, who was made king at Mahanaim in Transjordan by Abner, his father's commander (2 Sam. 2:8–10).

David settled in Hebron (2 Sam. 2:11), and Abner tried to gain favor with him. But Abner was murdered by Joab, David's commander, at Hebron (2 Sam. 3:27). When Ishbosheth was also murdered (2 Sam. 4:5–6), the way was clear for David to assume sole rule of Israel and unify the kingdom. He established his capital at Jerusalem, which he captured from the Jebusites. He also brought the ark of the covenant to the city, making it a religious as well as a political center.

For the remainder of his reign, David fought against the Ammonites and Syrians as well as the Philistines. His later years were clouded by family dissension and by a revolt among some of his subjects. In spite of his troubles, he behaved with great courage and managed to overcome all his enemies. Before his death, he proclaimed his son Solomon as his successor. Solomon was duly anointed at Gihon by Zadok the priest (1 Kin. 1:39).

Solomon became renowned for his wisdom. He brought the kingdom of Israel to great prominence at a time when other Near Eastern nations were weak politically. He renewed the alliance that David had made with Hiram, king of Tyre, engaging Hiram's workmen to construct a temple complex in Jerusalem. Although the finished building had some of the characteristics of the wilderness tabernacle, it also included some pagan features. These included the freestanding columns found in Syrian shrines, while certain aspects of the internal decoration reflected Canaanite religious symbolism.

The cost of Solomon's ambitious building projects in and around Jerusalem was high. Much of the agricultural productivity of the land was sent to Phoenicia to pay for materials and workmen's wages. Although Solomon levied tolls on the caravan trade that passed through his kingdom, he could not meet the rising costs that an increasingly lavish way of life involved. He attempted to replenish his depleted resources by building a fleet of ships near Elath for trading purposes (1 Kin. 9:26).

In desperation, Solomon finally began a program of forced labor that involved 30,000 men working by rotation (10,000 working every third month), laboring in the forests, mines, and cities under harsh conditions.

Rebellion of the Northern Tribes. As he grew older, Solomon entered into political marriages with non-Israelites. These women brought with them the gods of their native lands (1 Kin. 11:7–8), adding to the problem of idolatry in Israel. Before Solomon died, he managed to antagonize almost all his subjects. When he was succeeded by his son Rehoboam, the ten northern tribes led by Jeroboam, a former head of the forced labor units, met with him and sought relief from the burdens of work and taxation.

Rehoboam followed bad advice and refused. The northern tribes declared independence and formed a separate kingdom with Jeroboam as head. They named their kingdom "Israel" (this sometimes causes confusion because the name is also used for the remnant of the Covenant People at a later time). The southern section of the divided kingdom was known as Judah. It soon attracted the attention of Shishak, pharaoh of Egypt (about 945–924 B.C.), who moved into Judah, robbed the temple of its golden objects, and destroyed a number of Judah's fortresses. This event weakened still further an already vulnerable people.

Threat from Syria. Israel's troubles had also begun. The Arameans of Damascus were becoming powerful in Syria and were beginning to put pressure on Israel's northern borders. There was internal instability in the kingdom as well, indicated by the murder of King Nadab (about 908 B.C.), two years after his father Jeroboam's death. His murderer, Baasha, fortified a site close to Jerusalem (1 Kin. 15:17). Asa, the king of Judah (about 911–870 B.C.), appealed to the Syrians for help against Baasha. Baasha's son Elah reigned for two years (about 886–884 B.C.); Elah was murdered by Zimri, who committed suicide after seven days and plunged the nation into civil war.

Four years later the army general Omri gained control of Israel and began his own dynasty. Omri moved Israel's capital from Tirzah to Samaria, which he fortified strongly. He allied with Phoenicia, and arranged a marriage between his son Ahab and Jezebel, a princess of Tyre. When Ahab (about 874–853 B.C.)

became king, he continued Omri's policy of resistance to Syria. But his support of pagan Tyrian religion in Israel drew strong criticism from the prophet Elijah (1 Kin. 18:18). The nation was punished by famine, but this did little to halt the widespread spiritual and social corruption.

About 855 B.C. the Syrian Ben-Hadad attacked Samaria (1 Kin. 20:1) but suffered heavy losses, as he also did the following year at Aphek. Israel was saved by the appearance of the powerful Assyrian forces who, under Shalmaneser III (about 859–824 B.C.), attacked allied Syrian and Israelite forces in 853 B.C. at Qarqar on the Orontes River. Ahab died while trying to recover Ramoth Gilead from Syrian control. Meanwhile Mesha, king of Moab, had refused to pay further tribute to Israel; consequently, he was attacked by Ahaziah (about 853–852 B.C.), Ahab's successor.

Jehoram (about 852–841 B.C.) of Israel enlisted Jehoshaphat of Judah (about 873–848 B.C.) in the struggle against Moab, which proved successful (2 Kings 3) as Elisha the prophet had predicted. About 843 B.C. Ben-Hadad was murdered by Hazael (2 Kin. 8:7–13), and two years later Jehu seized the throne of Israel, carrying out a vicious purge of Ahab's house and suppressing pagan religions.

At the same time, Athaliah, queen of Judah, exterminated the royal house except for Jehoash, who was proclaimed king six years later. Jehoash first banned idolatry, but then became attracted to it and subsequently killed the son of the high priest who had protected him earlier. In 841 B.C. Shalmaneser III again attacked a Syrian coalition. But Jehu wished to avoid fighting the Assyrians, so he paid heavy tribute to this powerful nation instead.

Prosperity and the Prophets. For both Israel and Judah the 8th century B.C. was marked by a period of prosperity. Jeroboam II (about 782–752 B.C.) was able to develop agriculture, trade, and commerce because the westward advance of Assyria compelled the Syrian armies to defend their eastern territories. In Judah, Uzziah (790–740 B.C.) raised the prosperity of the country to levels unknown since the time of David. In both nations there was a sense that the true "golden age" had arrived.

Unfortunately, however, idolatry and the rejection of covenant spirituality were prominent, especially in Israel. Prophets such as Amos, Hosea, Micah, and Isaiah spoke out against these abuses. They condemned the exploitation of the poor. They also rebuked the rich for accumulating land and wealth illegally, and for forsaking the simple Hebrew way of life for the luxurious living of pagan nations.

Fall of the Northern Kingdom. The end of all this for Israel occurred shortly after Jeroboam's death. The kingship was left to political opportunists. But they were dwarfed by the powerful Assyrian monarch Tiglath-Pileser III. About 745 B.C. he placed Menahem of Israel (752–741 B.C.) under tribute. But when Menahem died, Israel joined an alliance against Assyria.

Ahaz of Judah, alarmed by this move, appealed to Tiglath-Pileser for help. Tiglath-Pileser overthrew Damascus in 732 B.C. (Is. 8:4; 17:1; Amos 1:4). He then carried people from the territory of Naphtali captive to Assyria (2 Kin. 15:29). But he still had to reckon with the resistance from Samaria under Pekah, whose murderer, Hoshea, was later made an Assyrian vassal.

On Tiglath-Pileser's death (727 B.C.), Hoshea of Israel rebelled. This brought the Assyrians to Samaria in a siege that ended three years later with the fall of Israel and the deportation of more northern tribesmen in 722 B.C. Isaiah's prediction that God would use Assyria as the rod of His anger upon Israel (Is. 10:5–6) had been fulfilled.

Fall of the Southern Kingdom. The Southern Kingdom under the godly Hezekiah (716–686 B.C.), son and successor of Ahaz, prospered for a time. This was possible because Hezekiah took advantage of a developing power struggle between Assyria and Egypt to fortify Judah and build up its resources. Some 20 years after Samaria fell, Sennacherib, who succeeded Sargon, invaded Palestine and reduced the cities of Joppa, Ashkelon, and Ekron in quick succession. An Egyptian army sent to relieve Ekron was defeated about 701 B.C., and the frontier fortress of Lachish came under heavy assault.

The Assyrians also threatened Jerusalem. To gain relief, Hezekiah offered to pay tribute to Sennacherib. In the end the Assyrians withdrew as the result of being devastated by a plague (2 Kin. 19:35). Hezekiah's successor, Manasseh (about 687–641 B.C.), encouraged idolatry and depravity in Judah, but he reformed toward the end of his life (2 Chr. 33:10–17).

Manasseh's grandson Josiah reigned until 609 B.C. He finally died at Megiddo while trying to prevent the Egyptians from helping the tottering Assyrian Empire. Assyria collapsed with the fall of Nineveh (612 B.C.) and Haran (610 B.C.) to Babylonian and Median forces. Later the Babylonians turned against Jerusalem. In the days of the prophet Jeremiah, they devastated the city in three assaults between 597 and 581 B.C.

The Captivity Years. With the removal of prisoners to Babylonia (Jer. 52:28–30), the Southern Kingdom collapsed and the shock of captivity began for the Hebrew people. The prophets Ezekiel and Daniel ministered in various ways to the distraught captives. For almost seven decades the Jewish people were occupied in building the Babylonian Empire under Nebuchadnezzar II (605–562 B.C.) and Nabonidus (556–539 B.C.). In this alien environment some captives lost all hope for the future. But through a ministry of prayer, study of the law, memorial observances, worship, and personal testimony to God's power, Ezekiel was able to promote trust in divine mercy. He kept alive the hope that someday a faithful remnant would return to the ancestral homeland.

Return from Captivity. Magnificent as the Babylonian Empire appeared, it was fundamentally weak. It collapsed under the attack of the Persian ruler Cyrus II. Babylon fell in

539 B.C., and the same year Cyrus proclaimed liberty to all captives in Babylonia. The Hebrew remnant that longed to return home was able to do so between 538 and 525 B.C.

The returnees, however, found a desolate land claimed by Arab tribes and the Samaritans. They had to be urged by Haggai and Zechariah to reconstruct the ruined temple before they could expect divine blessing (Hag. 1:9–11). Even after this had been done, life was still insecure because Jerusalem lacked a defensive wall.

In 458 B.C. Ezra came from Persia as a royal commissioner to survey the situation and report to King Artaxerxes I (465–423 B.C.). Twelve years passed before action was taken, due to the initiative of Nehemiah, a high court official, who in 445 B.C. was appointed governor of Judah. As a preliminary step toward restoring regional security and prosperity, he supervised the reconstruction of Jerusalem's wall in the short period of 52 days, after which it was dedicated (Neh. 12:27).

Then Ezra led a ceremony of national confession and commitment to covenant ideals. He also instituted religious reforms that made the law central in community life, as well as reviving tithe-offerings and stressing Sabbath worship. He expelled non-Israelites from the community, regulated the priesthood carefully, and in general laid the foundations of later Judaism.

The Period of Greek Dominance. The restoration of the national life of the Jewish people was achieved quickly because of the peaceful conditions in the Persian Empire. But this phase ended with revolts under Artaxerxes II (404–359 B.C.) and the defeat of Darius III in 331 B.C. by Alexander the Great of Greece. Thereafter Greek culture became firmly established in the ancient world, in spite of the premature death of Alexander in 323 B.C.

The small Judahite community, which had faced extinction before because of Canaanite paganism, now reacted with fear lest it should become engulfed by the idolatry of Greek religion.

The adoption of Greek traditions transformed the old Persian Empire. When Egypt became Hellenized, the culture of Greece was represented strongly in cities such as Alexandria.

The chief threat to the Jewish community was not so much military or political as religious. Greek religion was coarse and superstitious, and its sensuous nature encouraged a wide following. The philosophy of Stoicism attracted some adherents because of its fatalism and the view that God was in everything, while a less rigorous view of life was taught by Epicurus (341–270 B.C.). He stressed the values of friendship, advising his followers to avoid sensual excesses if they wished to enjoy true pleasure.

By contrast, emphasis upon the teachings of the Jewish law became the hallmark of the scribes, who had replaced the wise men as guardians of Jewish religious tradition. About the 2nd century B.C., they were aided by the rise of a separatist or Pharisee group, which taught scrupulous observance of the Mosaic law, advocated synagogue worship, and professed belief in angels, demons, and the resurrection of the dead.

Another influential religious group during this period of Jewish history was the Sadducees, an aristocratic priestly minority that exercised close control over temple ritual. The Sadducees accepted only the Law as Scripture. They would not allow any doctrine that could not be proved directly from the Law. This brought them into conflict with the Pharisees.

Revolt of the Maccabees. The political conflict in Palestine became critical under the Syrian ruler Antiochus IV Epiphanes (175–163 B.C.), who was determined to force Greek culture upon the Jewish community. Greek fashions were imposed upon Jerusalem. This provoked such unrest that Antiochus deliberately polluted the temple in 168 B.C. and forbade traditional Jewish worship. A Jewish family near Jerusalem rebelled against Greek authority. Its leader, Mattathias, began what is known as the Maccabean revolt. This continued under his son,

Judas Maccabeus, who finally won concessions from the Syrian regent Lysias.

Even after the Maccabean war ended, Greek culture exerted a considerable influence in Judea. The province came under Roman rule after 64 B.C. with the rise of the Roman Empire, but this did little to stop the threat presented by Greek religion. In spite of all adversity, the faithful remnant of God's people, Israel, struggled on in hope, looking for the long-promised Messiah who would deliver them from their enemies and bring God's kingdom upon earth.

Jesus and His Ministry. More than 700 years after the prophet Micah had foretold the birthplace of the Messiah (Mic. 5:2), the birth of a baby was announced by an angel to astonished shepherds in Bethlehem. The child was Jesus, God's Messiah (Anointed One), who would ultimately die for the sin of the world.

Jesus carried out a ministry of teaching, preaching, and healing for about three years. He came increasingly under suspicion by the Jewish authorities in Jerusalem. His work won for Him widespread acceptance, but He refused to allow His mission of salvation to be set aside in favor of following popular messianic expectations.

When Jesus condemned Jewish legalism (Mark 7:1–23), the Sadducees and Pharisees rose up in anger. The local Roman ruler Herod Antipas was also becoming concerned about Christ's activities (Luke 13:31). Matters came to a head when He was betrayed to the priests by one of His disciples. The Roman authorities took part in His trial and death, but even His disciples were unprepared for His dramatic resurrection on the first Easter morning.

After 40 days Jesus returned to heaven, leaving His disciples with an evangelistic commission (Matt. 28:18–20), which received a powerful impetus at the feast of Pentecost (Acts 2:1–4). The Christian church that came into being on this day spread across Palestine into Europe and ultimately throughout the world. At the forefront of evangelistic activity was a converted Jew, Paul of Tarsus, whose writings form a large part of the New Testament.

In Palestine, Pontius Pilate was removed from office just before Tiberius died in A.D. 37. Seven years later, Herod Agrippa died. In the Roman Empire, Caligula followed Tiberius. Four years later, he was succeeded by Claudius. During Paul's missionary journeys, Jews were expelled from Rome (about A.D. 49). About A.D. 52 Felix was made procurator of Judea. Seven years later he was succeeded by Porcius Festus, before whom Paul appeared (Acts 25:1–12).

There were threats of persecution of Christians in the Roman Empire, and these became a reality under Nero. He blamed a disastrous fire in Rome (A.D. 64) upon them to divert suspicion from himself. In A.D. 66 the first revolt against Roman power occurred in Judea. Four years later, the Roman emperor Titus marched into Jerusalem, destroyed it, and brought the Jewish state to an end. Thereafter the Jews became a religious group that was scattered across Europe and Asia, while God's message of redemption and salvation was committed to the Christian church.

ISSACHAR, TRIBE OF — the tribe made up of Issachar's descendants. It consisted of four clans, the descendants of Issachar's four sons (Gen. 46:13; Num. 26:23–24; 1 Chr. 7:1). The territory allotted to this tribe was bounded on the north by Zebulun and Naphtali, on the south and west by Manasseh, and on the east by the Jordan River (Josh. 19:17–23). Most of the fertile Valley of Jezreel, or Esdraelon, fell within Issachar's territory. Its fertile, flat plains were well suited for the raising of cattle. In spite of its reputation for seeking comfort, the tribe did fight bravely against Sisera (Judg. 5:15).

Moses prophesied a quiet and happy life for Issachar (Deut. 33:18). At the first census, the tribe numbered 54,400 fighting men (Num. 1:28–29); at the second census 64,300 (Num. 26:25). By David's time it numbered 87,000 (1 Chr. 7:5). Its leaders mentioned in the Bible were Nethaneel (Num. 1:8; 2:8; 7:18; 10:15), and Paltiel (Num. 34:26), the judge Tola (Judg. 10:1), King Baasha (1 Kin. 15:27), and Omri (1 Chr. 27:18).

In accordance with Jacob's blessing, the tribe of Issachar showed an unusual insight into political situations. The tribe switched allegiance from Saul to David (1 Chr. 12:32). Although the tribe was a member of the Northern Kingdom, its members attended Hezekiah of Judah's Passover feast (2 Chr. 30:18).

ITALIAN REGIMENT — a unit of the Roman army stationed in Caesarea (Acts 10:1), to which Cornelius was attached as a centurion. The Greek word translated as "regiment" refers to a cohort, consisting of about 600 men under the command of a tribune.

J

JEBUSITES [JEBB you sites] — the name of the original inhabitants of the city of Jebus, their name for ancient Jerusalem (Judg. 19:10–11; 1 Chr. 11:4–6). When the Israelites invaded Palestine under the leadership of Joshua, the Jebusites were ruled by Adoni-Zedek (Josh. 10:1, 3), one of five Amorite kings who resisted the Hebrew conquest. These five kings were defeated and slain by Joshua (Josh. 10:16–27). But the Jebusites were not driven out of Jebus (Jerusalem).

After David was anointed king, he led his army against the Jebusites. His military commander, Joab, apparently entered the city through an underground water shaft and led the conquest (2 Sam. 5:6–9; 1 Chr. 11:4–8). David then made this former Jebusite stronghold, now called the "City of David," the capital of his kingdom.

The site on which Solomon's temple was built in Jerusalem was previously a threshing floor that belonged to a Jebusite by the name of Araunah (2 Sam. 24:16–24), or Ornan (1 Chr. 21:24–25). David refused to accept this property as a gift from Araunah and paid him 50 shekels of silver for the land. Apparently David treated the defeated Jebusites humanely, but his son Solomon "raised forced labor" (1 Kin. 9:21) from their ranks.

JEWS — a name applied first to the people living in Judah (when the Israelites were divided into the two kingdoms of Israel and Judah); after the Babylonian captivity, all the descendants of Abraham were called "Jews." The term is used in the New Testament for all Israelites as opposed to the "Gentiles," or those of non-Jewish blood. Since a number of Jews (especially the Jewish leaders) were hostile toward Jesus' ministry, the New Testament sometimes speaks simply of "the Jews" (John 6:41), when it really means "those Jews who did not believe in Jesus." This is especially true in John's Gospel (John 5:16, 18; 6:41, 52; 7:1).

Because the Jews were God's Chosen People, Paul could speak of the true "Jew" as being the person who pleases God, whatever his race (Rom. 2:28–29). In the Christian church, distinctions between "Jews" and "Greeks" (or Jewish people and foreigners) are wiped away (Gal. 3:28; Col. 3:11).

JORDAN [JORE dun] (*descending, flowing*) — the name of the longest and most important river in Palestine. The river is part of the great rift valley that runs north to south into Africa. This rift valley is one of the lowest depressions on earth.

The headwaters of the Jordan River, which has three main sources, begin north of Lake Huleh. After the Jordan flows through Lake Huleh, it descends into the Sea of Galilee. It is possible to ford the river just below the lake where the waters are low. In the ancient world, trade caravans going from Damascus to Egypt probably crossed at this point.

At Lake Huleh the headwaters of the Jordan are about 70 meters (230 feet) above sea level. Some 16 kilometers (10 miles) south of the Sea of Galilee the river is about 213 meters (700 feet) below sea level. At the northern end of the Dead Sea (the end of the Jordan), the river has dropped to about 393 meters (1,290 feet) below sea level. This drastic drop is reflected in the name of the river, which means "the descender." The Jordan made a natural boundary as a serious obstacle in any east-to-west movement in the land of Palestine. A number of shallow spots, or fords, occur in the Jordan. Possession of these fords was an important military factor.

The distance that the Jordan covers from the southern tip of the Sea of Galilee to the northern end of the Dead Sea is only about 113 kilometers (70 miles). But the winding, zigzag pattern of the river is such that it curves for about 323 kilometers (200 miles) as it weaves its way north to south. The river varies from 27 to 30 meters (90 to 100 feet) in width and between 1 and 3 meters (3 and 10 feet) in depth. The water is not really navigable. With great difficulty, flat-bottom boats are able to move along parts of the waterway; they must be towed, however, through sandbars and must survive swift currents because of the descending nature of the valley. There are some 27 series of rapids in the Jordan.

At one time the Jordan valley may have been a large lake. Earthquakes and tremors over the centuries have dumped loose soil and gravel into the river, forcing new courses for the water that produced the switchback design of the Jordan. The northern part of the Jordan has numerous tributaries that flood their banks in winter and spring, allowing for good irrigation of the farmlands nearby. It was probably this fertile area that caught Lot's attention (Gen. 13:10). The middle and southern areas of Palestine that parallel the Jordan are the badlands with scarcely any rainfall. This type of land is only interrupted by an occasional oasis, such as those at Jericho.

The lower Jordan valley can be divided into three distinct regions. The first region is the Zor, or thickets of underbrush, that because of seasonal flooding has produced a jungle of vines, dense brush, shrubs, willows, and poplar trees. This area is sometimes referred to in the Bible as "Jordan's dense thickets" (Jer. 12:5; 49:19; Zech. 11:3, REB; the thickets of the Jordan, NRSV; the lush thicket of the Jordan, NIV). The sons of the prophets were cutting down trees in the thickets of the Jordan when Elisha made an iron ax head float on the river, after it had been lost (2 Kin. 6:1–7).

The second area is called the Gattara, or badlands, on the outside of the Zor. This area is covered with sediment, probably from the period when the whole valley was flooded. Until the modern period, the soil was too salty for crops. But modern Israeli scientists have reclaimed the soil by washing it with river water.

The third region of the lower Jordan is the Ghor, or higher region. This area is steep but fertile. It has supported farming especially in the first 40 kilometers (25 miles) of the northern end of the river. The last 8 kilometers (5 miles) at the southern end are too barren for farming.

When the Hebrew tribes approached the promised land, they did so from the eastern side of the Jordan. To some degree the Jordan River served as the boundary for the tribes (Num. 34:12). Ancient Israel occupied territory on both sides of the river. The tribes of Reuben, Gad, and half of the tribe of Manasseh settled on the eastern side of the Jordan.

Weak parties often went east of the Jordan to escape from the pressures from their opponents. For instance, Abner took Ishbosheth, the son of Saul, to the eastern side of the Jordan in opposition to David (2 Sam. 2:8). David fled to the eastern side after Absalom's initial success (2 Sam. 17:22–24; 19:15–18). However, the crossing of the Jordan from east to west was symbolic of the arrival of the Hebrews in the promised land. The west side of the Jordan was the area generally thought to have been promised to Abraham.

It was probably at the south end of the river, near Jericho, that ancient Israel entered the region of Canaan (Joshua 3–4). At Gilgal, near the Dead Sea, on the western side of the river about a mile from Jericho, an important shrine area was set up to commemorate the entrance of the Israelites into the land (Josh. 4:19; 1 Sam. 7:16; 10:8).

In the period between the Old Testament and the New Testament, the Jordan River formed the main eastern boundary of the Persian and Greek province of Judea. The Decapolis, a federation of ten Greek cities, was formed on the eastern side of the Jordan in the Greek period. John the Baptist carried out his ministry in the Jordan River region (Matt. 3:5–6; Mark 1:5; Luke 3:3; John 1:28; 3:26). Jesus' ministry was initiated by his baptism in the waters of the Jordan (Matt. 3:13; Mark 1:9; Luke 4:1). Jesus carried out His ministry on both sides of the Jordan (Matt. 4:15, 25; Mark 3:8; John 10:40).

JUDAH, TRIBE OF — the tribe founded by Judah. Its five tribal families sprang from Judah's three sons—Shelah, Perez, and Zerah—and two grandsons, Hezron and Hamul (Num. 26:19–21). In the first census, the tribe of Judah numbered 74,600 men (Num. 1:26–27). In the second census, the tribe numbered 76,500 (Num. 26:22).

Except for Simeon, Judah was the southernmost tribe of the Israelites. However, Simeon seems to have been absorbed into Judah at an early date. Judah's eastern border was the Dead Sea, and its western border was the Mediterranean Sea, although the Philistines usually controlled the plain along the sea. Originally, Judah's northern boundary ran from just south of Jerusalem northwest to Kirjath Jearim and Jabneel. To the south Judah's border ran south to the Ascent of Akrabbim, to the Wilderness of Zin, and south from Kadesh Barnea to the Mediterranean. During the period of the divided kingdom, its northern boundary ran north of Jerusalem.

At its longest point Judah was about 153 kilometers (95 miles) in length. At its widest point it was about 73 kilometers (45 miles) wide, excluding the area controlled by the Philistines.

The tribe of Judah, along with Benjamin, remained true to David's line when the tribes split after Solomon's death. Together they formed the southern kingdom of Judah, which at one time included Edom to the southeast.

JUDAIZERS [JOO dee eye zurs] — early converts to Christianity who tried to force believers from non-Jewish backgrounds to adopt Jewish customs as a condition of salvation. Evidence of this movement within the early church first emerged about A.D. 49, when "certain men came down from Judea and taught the brethren, 'Unless you are circumcised according to the custom of Moses, you cannot be saved '" (Acts 15:1).

The apostle Paul denounced this idea, insisting that only one thing is necessary for salvation: faith in the Lord Jesus Christ (Acts 15:1–29). In the letter to the Galatians, Paul continued this same argument, insisting that the believer is justified by faith alone. To become a new person in Christ is to be set free from the requirements of the Jewish law: "For in Christ Jesus neither circumcision nor uncircumcision avails anything, but a new creation" (Gal. 6:15).

JUDEA [joo DEE uh] — the Greco-Roman name for the land of Judah. Judea is first mentioned in Ezra 5:8 (Judaea, KJV; Judah, NIV), where it is used to designate a province of the Persian Empire. The word *Judea* comes from the adjective "Jewish," a term that was used of the Babylonian captives who returned to the promised land, most of whom were from the tribe of Judah.

Under the rule of the Persians, Judea was a district administered by a governor; usually this governor was a Jew (Hag. 1:14; 2:2). When Herod Archelaus was banished in A.D. 6, Judea ceased to exist as a separate district and was annexed to the Roman province of Syria. The governors of Judea, called prefects or procurators, were appointed by the emperor; their official residence was at Caesarea. However, they were supervised by the proconsul of Syria, who ruled from Antioch (Luke 3:1). It was under this political arrangement that Jesus lived and ministered.

Judea extended from the Mediterranean Sea on the west to the Dead Sea on the east, and from a few miles south of Gaza and the southern tip of the Dead Sea north to about Joppa. Thus, Judea measured about 90 kilometers (56 miles) from north to south and from east to west. The region contained four distinctive types of land: the coastal plains along the Mediterranean Sea, the lowlands in the south, the hill country, and the desert.

L

LACHISH [LAY kish] — an ancient walled city in the lowlands of Judah captured by Joshua and the Israelites. Lachish was situated about 49 kilometers (30 miles) southwest of Jerusalem and about 9.5 kilometers (15 miles) west of Hebron. The city covered about 18 acres and was inhabited for many years before the invasion by Joshua and the Israelites. The city is mentioned in early Egyptian sources as an important military stronghold.

After the Israelites overran the cities of Jericho and Ai, King Japhia of Lachish and four other kings formed an alliance against Israel (Josh. 10:1–4). God aided Israel against these five armies by causing the sun to stand still (Josh. 10:5–14). After a two-day siege, Lachish itself was captured (Josh. 10:31–33). It then was included in the allotment of the tribe of Judah (Josh. 15:39).

Little is known of the city until the time of Solomon, when Solomon's son Rehoboam rebuilt Lachish to protect Judah from Egypt (2 Chr. 11:5–12). Many years later Amaziah, king of Judah, fled from an uprising in Jerusalem to Lachish. Because Amaziah had turned away from following God, judgment was imposed upon him; he was killed while hiding in the city (2 Kin. 14:19; 2 Chr. 25:27).

During the time of Hezekiah (701 B.C.), Sennacherib, king of Assyria, attacked Lachish (2 Kin. 18:13–17; 2 Chr. 32:9). Its capture was so important to Sennacherib that he memorialized it in a magnificent relief on the wall of his palace at Nineveh. He also sent a letter to Hezekiah, demanding his surrender (2 Kin. 18:14, 17; 19:8).

About 100 years later, Lachish was again a stronghold in the nation of Judah. Nebuchadnezzar, king of Babylon, attacked and defeated the city when he took Judah into captivity in 586 B.C. (Jer. 34:7). When the Jews returned from their years of captivity in Babylon, the city of Lachish was inhabited again (Neh. 11:30).

Archaeologists have excavated Lachish (modern Tell ed-Duweir), and it has become one of the most significant sites in the Holy Land. A small temple with an altar for burnt offerings was discovered here; and the bones of many animals also were found—perhaps representing portions of the animals that the priests ate during sacrificial observances (Lev. 7:32–34). Also discovered was a deep well that probably provided water for the city when it was under siege.

Other important finds consisted of early Hebrew writings on bowls, seals, and a stone altar. Twenty-one pottery sherds, on which were written letters about the attack on Lachish and Jerusalem by Babylon in 586 B.C., were also found. One of the letters states that signals from Azekah could no longer be seen. It was written shortly after the events noted in Jeremiah 34:7, which observe that Lachish and Azekah were the only fortified cities left in Judah.

LEBANON [LEB uh none] (*white*) — a nation of the Middle East that includes much of what was ancient Phoenicia in Bible times. This territory has been an important trade center linking Europe and Asia for more than 4,000 years.

In ancient times the Phoenicians used the city-states of Byblos, Sidon, and Tyre as the base of a great sea-trading empire in what is now Lebanon. Over the years, these city-states were conquered by Egyptians, Assyrians, Persians, and the Greeks under Alexander the Great. Later still, Lebanon became part of the Roman Empire, and many inhabitants became Christians. But when the Arabs conquered Lebanon in the 7th century A.D., many turned to the Muslim religion.

Early in the 16th century, the Arabs were overthrown by the Turks. Then in 1918 the British and French forces broke up the Turkish or Ottoman Empire and placed Lebanon under French rule. In 1943, Lebanon achieved independence. The country has continued to be the scene of strife and turmoil involving Israelis, Syrians, and Palestinian guerrillas. Civil war at times between Muslims and Christians has also added to the strife of this war-torn country.

Lebanon takes its name from the Lebanon Mountains, which run parallel to the coast of the Mediterranean Sea for almost the length of the country. The range consists of snow-capped limestone peaks that rise sharply from the shoreline, leaving just enough space for a coastal road. The 160-kilometer-long (100-mile-long) mountains are made up of two parallel ranges, the Lebanons and the Anti-Lebanons. Between the two is the fertile plain of el-Bekaa, measuring about 48 kilometers (30 miles) by 16 kilometers (10 miles), which was also called the Valley of Lebanon (Josh. 11:17).

The scenic beauty of the country has inspired many symbolic references in the Bible (Ps. 92:12; Song 4:15; 5:15). The rich vegetation of Lebanon became a symbol of fruitfulness and fertility (Pss. 72:16; 92:12).

Originally, the famed Cedars of Lebanon covered the region. But bands of marauding conquerors from Mesopotamia, Egypt, Israel, and Tyre destroyed the forests by using the wood for palaces, furniture, ships, coffins, and musical instruments.

By the 6th century A.D., the beautiful groves were almost gone. Egyptian texts from many different periods refer to trade with the Phoenician cities that supplied them with lumber from Lebanon. Ugaritic and Mesopotamian texts mention that cedars from Lebanon were used in building their important temples and palaces.

In recent years a program of reforestation has been conducted in national parks. The prophets of the Old Testament used the destruction of these magnificent trees by aggressors as a symbol of Israel's destruction (Jer. 22:7; Ezek. 27:5; Zech. 11:2).

The climate of Lebanon ranges from the almost tropical heat and vegetation of the plain of Dan to heavy snow in the plain of el-Bekaa. Mainly it has a Mediterranean climate with cool, wet winters and hot, dry summers. In the spring or summer, a searing desert wind sometimes blows in from Syria.

The Lebanon Mountains formed the northwest boundary of the land of Palestine, the "promised land" to the Hebrew people (Deut. 1:7; 11:24). The original inhabitants of Lebanon were independent, warlike tribes of Phoenician stock. Further north were the Hivites and the Gebalites. It is occupied today by various sects of Christians and Muslims.

LEGION — the principal unit of the Roman army, consisting of 3,000 to 6,000 infantry troops and 100 to 200 cavalrymen. The New Testament does not use the word *legion* in its strict military sense, but in a general sense to express a large number. When Jesus healed a man possessed by unclean spirits or demons, He asked the man his name. He replied, "My name is Legion; for we are many" (Mark 5:9). The man was inhabited by many demons.

LEVITES [LEE vytes] — descendants of Levi who served as assistants to the priests in the worship system of the nation of Israel. As Levites, Aaron and his sons and their descendants were charged with the responsibility of the priesthood—offering burnt offerings and leading the people in worship and confession. But all the other Levites who were not descended directly from Aaron were to serve as priestly assistants, taking care of the tabernacle and the temple and performing other menial duties (Num. 8:6).

The choice of the Levites as a people who would perform special service for God goes back to the days of the Exodus when the children of Israel were camped at Mount Sinai.

The people grew restless while they waited for Moses to return from talking with the Lord on the mountain. Breaking their covenant with God, they made a golden calf and began to worship it. The Levites were no less guilty than the other tribes. But when Moses returned and called for those on the Lord's side to come forward, the descendants of Levi were the only ones who voluntarily rallied to his side, showing zeal for God's honor (Ex. 32:26–28).

Even before this event, Aaron and his sons had been set apart for the priesthood. But many helpers were needed to attend to the needs of the tabernacle, which was built later at God's command in the Wilderness of Sinai. The Levites were chosen for this honor.

The designation of a tribe for special service to God grew out of an unusual concept of the Hebrew people known as the first fruits. According to this principle, the first part of a crop to be harvested was dedicated to God. This principle even extended to the first children to be born in a family. Just before the Exodus from Egypt, when God sent the death angel to kill the firstborn of every Egyptian family, He instructed the Israelites to put blood on their doorposts, that their firstborn might be spared the same fate. Thus, the firstborn of every Israelite family became God's special property, dedicated to Him as a memorial. But because the Levites were the ones who voluntarily returned to their Lord after worshiping the golden image, they were chosen for service to the sanctuary, thus replacing the firstborn as God's representatives of the holiness of His people (Num. 3:12–13, 41).

A Levite's special service to God began with his consecration at about age 25. First he was sprinkled with the "water of purification" (Num. 8:7). Next, the hair was shaved from his entire body, his clothes were washed, and sacrifice was made of two young bulls, and a grain offering of fine flour mixed with oil (Num. 8:7–8). After this purification, he was brought before the door of the tabernacle and set apart for service by the laying on of the hands of the elders (Num. 8:9–15).

Young Levites began as assistants to the priests and chief Levites, then progressed through the higher duties and offices such as doorkeeper, member of the temple orchestra, or administrator. In the days before the temple was built and the people worshiped in the tabernacle, the Levites always transported the tabernacle and its furniture when the camp was moved. Then they erected and cared for the tent in its new location. They guarded it, cleaned it, and cleaned the furniture (Num. 1:50–53; 3:6–9; 4:1–33).

Since the Levites served under the priests, they were forbidden to touch any sacred furniture or the altar until it had been covered by the priests (Num. 4:15). Temple slaves often assisted the Levites in the heavier, more menial duties such as cutting wood and carrying water (Josh. 9:21; Ezra 8:20).

The Levites also prepared the showbread and did whatever baking was needed in connection with the sacrifices. They helped the priests slaughter and skin the animals for sacrifices, examined the lepers according to the law, and led music during worship. Retiring from active service at age 50, the Levites were free to remain in the temple as overseers or to give assistance to their young successors (Num. 8:25–26).

Unlike the other tribes of Israel, the Levites received no territorial inheritance in the promised land of Canaan. Their portion was to be God Himself (Num. 18:20), who commanded that 48 cities be set apart for them, along with enough pasture for their cattle (Num. 35:1–8). They were to receive the tithes due God from the fruits of the fields, the flocks and herds, the fruits of the firstborn, and certain portions of the people's sacrificial offerings (Num. 18:24). Of these tithes, the Levites had to turn over a tithe (a tenth part) to the priests (Num. 18:26).

The Levites were not required to devote all their time to the sanctuary. During most of the year, they lived in their own cities. Then at fixed periods they came to the tabernacle to take their turn at work. For example, during David's reign, the Levites were divided into four classes: (1) assistants to priests in the work of the sanctuary, (2) judges and scribes, (3) gatekeepers, and (4) musicians. Each of these classes, with the possible exception of the second, was subdivided into 24 courses or families who served in rotation (1 Chr. 24–25; Ezra 6:18).

During the long period of Old Testament history, the Levites waxed hot and cold in their devotion to God, just like the rest of the nation of Israel. During the period of the judges, for example, a Levite agreed to hire his services to a man who was known as a worshiper of false gods (Judg. 17:8–13). By New Testament times, both Levites and priests presided over a form of worship that had lost its warmth and human concern (John 1:19).

In His parable of the good Samaritan, Jesus insisted that true worship consisted of doing good to others. This is demonstrated by the lowly Samaritan traveler, who stopped to help a wounded man. His compassion is a contrast to the hands-off approach of a priest and a Levite, both of whom "passed by on the other side" (Luke 10:31–32).

LEVITICAL CITIES [luh VIT uh cull] — 48 cities assigned to the tribe of Levi. When the land of Canaan was divided among the tribes of Israel, each tribe, except Levi, received a specific region or territory for its inheritance. The tribe of Levi, however, was made up of priests who were to serve the religious and spiritual needs of the other tribes. Thus, instead of receiving a territory of their own, they were scattered throughout the entire land.

Numbers 35:1–8 sets forth a plan whereby the tribe of Levi was to live in 48 cities scattered throughout Palestine. (This plan was fulfilled according to assignments described in Josh. 20–21 and 1 Chr. 6:54–81.) The 48 cities were apportioned in this way: the Aaronites, one of the families of the Kohathites, received 13 cities (Josh. 21:4, 9–19; 1 Chr. 6:54–60); the rest of the Kohathites received 10 cities (Josh. 21:5, 20–26; 1 Chr. 6:61). The Gershonites received 13 cities (Josh. 21:6, 27–33; 1 Chr. 6:62), and the Merarites received 12 cities (Josh. 21:7, 34–40; 1 Chr. 6:63). These 48 cities and their surrounding common lands—pastures, fields, and vineyards—were to be used exclusively by the Levites.

Six of these Levitical cities were to be Cities of Refuge (Num. 35:6, 9–34; Josh. 20–21). A person who caused the death of another could flee to one of these cities for protection from anyone who wanted to avenge the life of the person killed. The "refugee" thus was protected until he received a fair trial, or until the high priest of that particular city of refuge died (after which he was free to return home and claim the protection of the authorities).

Three of the cities of refuge were east of the Jordan River: Bezer (in the tribe of Reuben), Ramoth in Gilead (in Gad), and Golan (in Manasseh; Josh. 20:8). The other three cities of refuge were west of the Jordan: Kedesh (in the tribe of Naphtali), Shechem (in Ephraim), and Kirjath Arba, also known as Hebron (in Judah; Josh. 20:7). According to this plan, the Levites were situated throughout the land and could assist the other Israelites in spiritual matters. As a practical matter, since six of the Levitical cities were cities of refuge, citizens living in every part of Palestine had a refuge that was relatively near their homes. A look at a map will demonstrate how carefully the cities were spaced out to facilitate ease of access. Some of the ancient Levitical cities, such as Gibeon, Beth Aven, Gilead, Bethel, and Gilgal, became an important part of the religious system of Israel (1 Kin. 3:4; Hos. 4:15; 12:11; Amos 4:4–5).

LORD'S DAY — the first day of the week, or Sunday; the day especially associated with the Lord Jesus Christ.

A special honor was reserved for Sunday, the first day of the week. This was the day on which Jesus was raised from the dead; every Lord's Day, therefore, is a weekly memorial of Christ's resurrection. Clearly the early church assembled for worship and religious instruction on Sunday, the Lord's Day (1 Cor. 16:2).

The Lord's Day is not to be confused with the Sabbath, the Jewish day of rest. The Jewish Sabbath corresponds with our Saturday, the seventh or last day of the week. This special day to the Jews commemorated the day on which God rested after the creation of the world. The Lord's Day is our Sunday, the first day of the week; it celebrates the resurrection of Jesus from the dead.

Under the new dispensation of grace, Christians are not to be trapped by the old legalism of observing days and seasons. The Council of Jerusalem did not include a demand for Sabbath observance in its rules for Gentile Christians (Acts 15:20, 28–29). Some members of the early church "esteemed every day alike"; they made no distinction between days, including Jewish festivals and Sabbaths and possibly also Sunday. The apostle Paul said they were not to be judged if they were acting in good conscience out of the fear of God.

Some Jewish Christians continued to observe the Sabbath and Jewish festivals. Neither should they be judged for "esteeming one day above another," Paul declared, for their behavior was guided by conscience in the fear of God. Paul believed such observance was a matter of Christian liberty, so long as the convert did not regard the observance as necessary for salvation (Rom. 14:5–6; Gal. 4:10; Col. 2:16–17).

Paul's principle of Christian liberty about holy places and holy days comes from the Lord Jesus Christ Himself. Jesus described Himself as one who is greater than the temple (Matt. 12:6) and said, "The Son of Man is Lord even of the Sabbath" (Matt. 12:8; Luke 6:5). When accused by the Pharisees of breaking the Sabbath, Jesus replied, "The Sabbath was made for man, and not man for the Sabbath. Therefore the Son of Man is also Lord of the Sabbath" (Mark 2:27–28).

The phrase "the Lord's Day" occurs only once in the New Testament, in Revelation 1:10, where John declared, "I was in the Spirit on the Lord's Day." In Asia Minor, where the churches to which John wrote were situated, the pagans celebrated the first day of each month as the Emperor's Day. Some scholars also believe that a day of the week was also called by this name.

When the early Christians called the first day of the week the Lord's Day, this was a direct challenge to the emperor worship to which John refers so often in the book of Revelation. Such a bold and fearless testimony by the early Christians proclaimed that the Lord's Day belonged to the Lord Jesus Christ and not the emperor Caesar.

M

MACEDONIA [mass uh DOH neh uh] — a mountainous country north of Greece (Achaia) in the Balkan Peninsula. This area was visited twice, and perhaps three times, by the apostle Paul.

Macedonia was of little international significance until Philip II of Macedon (ruled 359–336 B.C.) established his capital at Philippi. He defeated the Greek city-states and united them into one kingdom. His son Alexander III of Macedon (ruled 336–323 B.C.), later known as Alexander the Great, built an empire from Greece to the Nile River in Egypt and southeast to the Indus River.

After Alexander's death the generals divided the empire, and Macedonia declined in importance. But Macedonia regained its leading position and was made a colony after the Battle of Philippi (42 B.C.), at which Octavian (Augustus) and Antony defeated Brutus and Cassius on the plains near the city.

The first mention of Macedonia in the Bible is in Acts 16: the description of Paul's "Macedonian call." In a vision, a man appeared to Paul "and pleaded with him, saying, 'Come over to Macedonia and help us '" (Acts 16:9). Paul immediately set sail at Troas for Neapolis (Acts 16:11), a seaport of Philippi in the extreme eastern part of Macedonia.

Luke gives a detailed account of Paul's journey through Macedonia (Acts 16:11–17:14). At Neapolis Paul picked up the Egnatian Way—the major road of Macedonia—and came to Philippi, "the foremost city of that part of Macedonia, a colony" (Acts 16:12). At Philippi Paul made his first convert in Europe, "a certain woman named Lydia ... [who] was a seller of purple" (Acts 16:14).

After Lydia's baptism and the healing of "a certain slave girl possessed with a spirit of divination" (Acts 16:16), and his imprisonment (Acts 16:23–24), Paul set out again on the Egnatian Way through Amphipolis and Apollonia to Thessalonica (Acts 17:1)—the capital where the proconsul (governor) resided.

The final city Paul visited before leaving Macedonia for Athens was Berea (Acts 17:10–14), where he left Silas and Timothy for a short time to assist in the work (Acts 17:15; 18:5).

At the close of this, his second missionary journey, Paul went on to Athens and Corinth and then back to Antioch of Syria (Acts 17:15–18:23). He revisited Macedonia at least once again (Acts 20:1–6), and perhaps twice (2 Cor. 2:13; 7:5; Phil. 2:24; 1 Tim. 1:3).

Several of Paul's travel companions and fellow workers were Macedonians: Gaius (Acts 19:29), Aristarchus (Acts 19:29; 27:2), Secundus (Acts 20:4), and Sopater (Acts 20:4). The Macedonian Christians' support of the needs of Paul and others is mentioned several times in Paul's letters (Rom. 15:26; 2 Cor. 8:1–5; Phil. 4:15–18).

MANASSEH, TRIBE OF [muh NASS uh] — the tribe that traced its origin to Manasseh No. 1. The tribe of Manasseh descended through Manasseh's son, Machir; Machir's son, Gilead; and Gilead's six sons (Num. 26:28–34). During their first 430 years in Egypt, the tribe of Manasseh increased to 32,200 men of war (Num. 1:34–35). By the second census, 39 years later, it numbered 52,700 (Num. 26:34).

In the settlement of Canaan, land was provided for Manasseh on both sides of the Jordan River. Eastern Manasseh was able to occupy its land only after it had aided the other tribes in conquering their territories (Num. 32:1–33).

Because of the Canaanite fortresses and strong cities in the land (for example, Megiddo, Taanach, Dor, Ibleam, and Beth Shean), western Manasseh had difficulty settling its territory. When it became strong, however, it did not expel the Canaanites but subjected them to tribute (Josh. 17:11–13).

The tribe of Manasseh was known for its valor, and it claimed two famous judges: Gideon (Judg. 6:11–8:35) and Jephthah (Judg. 11:1–12:7). During Saul's reign men from Manasseh joined David at Ziklag (1 Chr. 12:19–20). Later, many people from both western and eastern Manasseh rallied to make David king at Hebron (1 Chr. 12:31, 37).

MARHESHVAN [mar HESH van] — the eighth month of the sacred Hebrew year, also called Bul (1 Kin. 6:38).

MEDIA [MEE dih uh] — an ancient country of Asia situated west of Parthia, north of the Persian Gulf, east of Assyria and Armenia, and south of the Caspian Sea. The country is now included in parts of Iran, Iraq, and Turkey.

A mountainous country, Media contained some fertile sections, but much of it was cold, barren, and swampy. In the southern area lush plains were used as pastureland for the large herds of horses used in the Median cavalry. The history of the Medes is complex, because it involves many entangling alliances and the rise and fall of several nations. The Medes were an Indo-European people who invaded the rough mountain terrain south of the Caspian Sea. In the 9th and 8th centuries B.C., Assyrian kings conducted campaigns against these people, forcing them to pay tribute. The mighty Tiglath–Pileser (745–727 B.C.) invaded Media and added part of it to the Assyrian

Empire. By 700 B.C., the era of the prophet Isaiah, a prosperous realm had been established.

Media is first mentioned in the Old Testament as the destination to which Shalmaneser, king of Assyria, deported the Israelites from Samaria around 721 B.C. (2 Kin. 17:6; 18:11). Medes are mentioned in Ezra in connection with Darius's search for the scroll containing the famous decree of Cyrus that allowed the Jews to return to Jerusalem (Ezra 6:2). Laws of the Medes are mentioned in the book of Esther (1:19) and in Daniel (6:8, 15).

The prophet Daniel prophesied that King Belshazzar's Babylonian kingdom would fall to "the Medes and Persians" (Dan. 5:28). Medes were also among the people from many different nations in Jerusalem on the day of Pentecost (Acts 2:9).

About 710 B.C. Sargon II of Assyria defeated the Medes and forced them to pay a tribute consisting of the thoroughbred horses for which Media was famous. The Medes, however, increased in strength and joined forces with Babylon. The Medes under Cyaxares and the Babylonians under Nabopolassar captured Asshur, the ancient capital of Assyria, in 614 B.C. In 612 B.C. this alliance overthrew Nineveh, the proud capital of Assyria, causing the crash of the Assyrian Empire. The seventh century Hebrew prophet Nahum expressed the great relief felt by neighboring nations at Nineveh's fall (Nah. 2:3; 3:19). Nabopolassar's son, Nebuchadnezzar, married Cyaxares' daughter, strengthening the bond between the two countries. During the era of Nebuchadnezzar and the time of Jeremiah (about 605–552 B.C.), the Median kingdom reached the height of its power.

Persia was dominated by Media until the time of Cyrus II who was founder of the Persian Empire. In 549 B.C. Cyrus defeated Media. Yet under the Persians, Media remained the most important province of Persia. As a consequence, the dual name "Medes and Persians" remained for a long time (Esth.

1:19; Dan. 5:28). The expression "The laws of the Medes and the Persians" depicted the unchangeable nature of Median law, which even the king was powerless to change (Esth. 1:19).

The Medes and Persians were Indo-European peoples known as Aryans. Their religion was Zoroastrianism. Its adherents believed that spiritual reality was divided between Ahura Mazda, the god of light and goodness, and Angra Mainja, the god of darkness and evil. Influenced by the moral teachings of his religion, Cyrus II of Persia was known for his humane attitude toward conquered peoples. He treated the vanquished Medes with respect. Medo-Persia, a dual nation, became a great empire that ruled Asia until it was conquered by Alexander the Great (330 B.C.). After Alexander's death, Medo-Persia became part of Syria and later a part of the Persian Empire.

MEDITERRANEAN SEA [med ih ter RAIN ih un] — a large sea bordered by many important nations of the ancient world, including Palestine. The Hebrews referred to it by several different names. It was called "the Great Sea" (Num. 34:6), "the Western Sea" (Deut. 34:2), "the Sea of the Philistines" (Ex. 23:31), and simply "the sea" (Josh. 16:8; Jon. 1:4).

The Mediterranean Sea extends about 3,550 kilometers (2,200 miles) westward from the coast of Palestine to the Straits of Gibraltar. At its narrowest point, between Sicily and the coast of Africa, the sea is about 130 kilometers (80 miles) wide. Archaeologists believe that an open channel once existed, connecting the Mediterranean to the Red Sea, and that this channel was closed off by drifting desert sand and silt from the Nile River, providing a land connection between Asia and Africa. Many ancient civilizations grew up around this sea and used it for trade and commerce. The Hebrews were afraid of the Mediterranean and usually hired others, often Phoenicians (1 Kin. 9:27), to conduct their seafaring business for them. Palestine itself had few good harbors.

The apostle Paul crossed the Mediterranean Sea during his missionary journeys. He tried to avoid sailing during the winter months, but was shipwrecked on his way to Rome while sailing in late autumn (Acts 27).

MEMPHIS [MEM fis] — an ancient royal city during the Old Kingdom period of Egypt's history (about 3000 B.C. to 2200 B.C.). It was situated on the west bank of the Nile River about 21 kilometers (13 miles) south of Cairo. Today there is little left to mark the glorious past of the city.

In 670 B.C. Memphis was captured by the Assyrians, followed by a period of Persian dominance. After the Muslim conquest of the city, its ruins were used in the Middle Ages to build Cairo, Egypt's modern capital. The importance of Memphis is demonstrated by the multitude of pyramids and the celebrated Sphinx that are located near the site of the ancient city.

Memphis is found only once in the Bible—a translation of the Hebrew word *noph* (Hos. 9:6). In this passage the prophet Hosea condemned the Israelites for their sinfulness and predicted that some of them would be buried by Egyptians from Memphis. In seven other locations the word *noph* refers to Memphis (Is. 19:13; Jer. 2:16; 44:1; 46:14, 19; Ezek. 30:13, 16). In each passage the NIV has Memphis.

"The princes of Noph [Memphis] are deceived," wrote the prophet Isaiah (Is. 19:13). He prophesied that God would bring judgment on these deluded rulers. The prophet Jeremiah also warned the Jews to trust God and not flee to Memphis, because God was going to send destruction upon the land of Egypt (Jer. 2:16; 44:1; 46:14, 19).

METALS OF THE BIBLE. The metals used in Bible times were gold (Gen. 2:11–12), silver (Gen. 13:2), bronze (Gen. 4:22; Ex. 25:3), copper (Deut. 8:9; Job 28:2), iron (Gen. 4:22; Lev. 26:19), tin (Num. 31:22), and lead (Ezek. 22:18, 20; 27:12).

Gold was almost certainly the first metal known and used by human beings. But it was too soft to be used for tools or weapons. It was used mainly for jewelry and decorative purposes. The same was true of silver.

Copper was especially famous and widely used in ancient times. Until the dawn of the Iron Age (about 1200 B.C.), copper was the most practical metal in the Old Testament era. Like gold, native copper is also soft. But the metalworkers of the ancient world discovered it hardened appreciably when hammered, and especially when alloyed with tin to produce bronze. Various copper alloys were used for making weapons such as daggers, tools such as sickles, and all kinds of utensils (Ex. 38:3; Num. 16:39; Jer. 52:18).

When the Israelites stood on the threshold of the promised land, Moses addressed them with these words: "The Lord your God is bringing you into a good land ... a land whose stones are iron and out of whose hills you can dig copper" (Deut. 8:7, 9). In the nation's later history, King Solomon established a copper-smelting industry at Ezion Geber, a city on the Red Sea at the northern end of the Gulf of Aqaba (1 Kin. 9:26; 22:48; 2 Chr. 8:17; 20:36).

Solomon's copper-smelting refineries at Ezion Geber were built strategically between the hills of Edom (to the east) and the hills of Palestine (to the west). They were ideally situated to take advantage of the draft caused by the strong winds sweeping down from the north.

Not until the time of King David, who broke the Philistine stranglehold over the land of Israel, was iron available to any great degree among the Israelites. During the reign of King Saul, the Philistines still held a monopoly in iron smelting.

The story is told in 1 Samuel 13:19–22: "Now there was no blacksmith to be found throughout all the land of Israel, for the Philistines said, 'Lest the Hebrews make swords or spears.' But the Israelites would go down to the Philistines to sharpen each man's plowshare, his mattock, his ax, and his sickle. ... So it came about, on the day of battle, that there was neither sword nor spear found in the hand of any of the people who were with Saul and Jonathan."

According to archaeological findings, the first substantial smelting of iron occurred about 1400 B.C., probably among the Hittites of Asia Minor. Before the Philistines, the Hittites held the iron monopoly; apparently the Phoenicians (including the Philistines) learned the secret of iron smelting from them.

Archaeological excavations have established that iron ores were occasionally smelted in Mesopotamia, near the Tigris and Euphrates rivers, perhaps as early as 2700 B.C. For some unknown reason, however, the use of iron was not pursued. This metal did not come into general use, at least on a wide scale, until about 1200 B.C., at the beginning of the Early Iron Age.

The primitive method of smelting iron ore involved the use of charcoal and forced air in pits or furnaces. By this method, iron ore was reduced to metallic iron. Then the glowing ball of iron was pulled out of the furnace and hammered vigorously to expel the impurities and give the metal its intended shape (Deut. 4:20; 1 Kin. 8:51; Jer. 6:29; 11:4).

MIDIANITES [MID ee un ites] — a nomadic people who were enemies of the Israelites in Old Testament times. The Midianites were distantly related to the Israelites, since they sprang from Midian, one of the sons of Abraham. But they usually were foes rather than friends of the Hebrew people. Abraham sent the children of Midian "to the country of the east" (Gen. 25:6), which probably included the desert fringes of Moab, Edom, and perhaps parts of the Sinai Peninsula. They are known thereafter in the Old Testament as one of the "people of the East" (Judg. 6:3, 33), or inhabitants of the desert regions of southern Syria and western Arabia.

The Midianites were at least loosely associated with others of this group, including the Ishmaelites (Gen. 37:28; Judg. 8:24). Midianite travelers bought Joseph from his brothers and resold him in Egypt (Gen. 37:25–36). Moses married into a Midianite family (specifically an associated group known as the Kenites) in "the land of Midian" (Ex. 2:15). His wife Zipporah and his father-in-law Jethro were Midianites. "Then Moses was content to live with the man, and he gave Zipporah his daughter to Moses" (Ex. 2:21; 3:1). But this was the last friendly connection the Israelites had with the Midianites.

After the time of Moses, the Midianites consistently opposed the Israelites. They joined with the Moabites, in whose territory they had partly settled, in hiring the prophet-magician Balaam to curse Israel (Num. 22:4, 7). At Moab, just before the conquest of Canaan, the Midianites were among those who practiced sexual immorality as part of the ritual of their idolatrous religion. They involved some of the Israelites in this idolatry, causing God's judgment to come upon His people (Num. 25:1–9). Because of this the Midianites were singled out for destruction (Num. 25:16–18).

Perhaps the most serious Midianite threat to Israel came during the days of the judges when Midianite warriors invaded Palestine. They came on camels, an innovation in combat. The Israelites were driven into the hill country as the Midianites and other easterners raided their territory, plundering crops and cattle for seven years (Judg. 6:1–6).

Then God raised up Gideon to deliver Israel from the Midianites. He and the Ephraimites drove off the Midianites, capturing Oreb and Zeeb, two of their princes (Judg. 7:24–25), and pursuing escapees across the Jordan River to the desert fringes where their kings Zebah and Zalmunna were captured (Judg. 8:10–12). Gideon's great victory was mentioned in several later Old Testament passages as an example of God's deliverance of his people from oppression (Ps. 83:9, 11; Is. 9:4; 10:26).

MILLENNIUM, THE — the thousand-year period mentioned in connection with the description of Christ's coming to reign with His saints over the earth (Rev. 20:1-9). Many Old Testament passages are reputed to refer to the millennium (Is. 11:4; Jer. 3:17; Zech. 14:9).

These and many other Old Testament passages are often taken to refer only to the thousand-year period itself. However, it is often difficult in these passages to see a clear dividing line between the earthly period of the millennium and the eternal state of new heavens and earth. Therefore, it is best to let one's teaching about the millennium be drawn specifically from the words in Revelation 20. The other great promises to Israel, while they may have a temporary fulfillment in the thousand years, still await the fullness of the new heavens and new earth and the unhindered presence of Israel's king and the church's husband—Jesus Christ our Lord.

During that thousand-year period, Satan will be bound in the bottomless pit so he will not deceive the nations until his short period of release (Rev. 20:3, 7-8). The faithful martyrs who have died for the cause of Christ will be resurrected before the millennium. They will rule with Christ and will be priests of God and Christ (Rev. 20:4). The unbelieving dead will wait for the second resurrection (Rev. 20:5). After the thousand years, Satan will be released and will again resume his work of deceit (Rev. 20:7-8).

The most important aspect of the millennium is the reign of Christ. Peter taught that Christ now rules from the right hand of God (Acts 2:33-36). That rule will last until His enemies are made His footstool "The LORD said to my Lord, 'sit at My right hand, till I make Your enemies Your footstool.'" (Ps. 110:1). The apostle Paul also understood Christ to be presently reigning in a period designed to bring all of God's enemies underfoot (1 Cor. 15:25-27). Thus the impact of Christ's present rule over the earth from God's right hand must not be seen as unrelated to His future reign during the millennium.

The millennium is viewed by interpreters in several different ways. One position holds that the millennium only refers to Christ's spiritual rule today from heaven. This symbolic view is known as the amillennial interpretation. Another position views Christ's spiritual rule as working through preaching and teaching to bring gradual world improvement leading up to Christ's return. This is the postmillennial view.

The position that holds to an actual thousand-year period in the future is known as the premillennial view. This interpretation does not diminish the power of Christ's present rule from heaven or limit that rule to the church only. That position sees the need for a thousand-year place in history for an earthly fulfillment of Israel's promises of land and blessing. It stresses that the 1,000 years in Revelation 20 are actual years and are not symbolic.

MILLO [MILL oh] (*fill*) — a fortification or citadel near Jerusalem. The Millo of Jerusalem was probably part of the fortification of the Jebusite city that David captured. It may have been either a solid tower full of earth or a bastion strengthening a weak point in the wall. It was already in existence when David's army captured the Jebusite city (2 Sam. 5:9).

The Millo was one of the building projects included in King Solomon's expansion program in Jerusalem in later years. He strengthened the Millo by using conscripted labor (1 Kin. 9:15). Centuries later, King Hezekiah had the Millo repaired in preparation for an invasion and siege by the Assyrians (2 Chr. 32:5). King Joash was killed "in the house of the Millo" (2 Kin. 12:20)—the victim of a conspiracy.

MINERALS OF THE BIBLE. Minerals are inorganic substances found in the earth's crust. The Bible mentions many of these minerals, which include metallic and nonmetallic rock, sand, clay, soils, salt, and most gemstones. Minerals existed in a variety of colors and degrees of hardness. They were often valued for these characteristics by the people of Bible lands. No one knows exactly how many minerals exist in the earth today, but estimates range between 1,500 and 3,000. Only a small percentage of these were known in the ancient world, and only a few are mentioned in the Bible.

The land of Palestine and surrounding areas were rich in minerals. These minerals provided the people of the Bible with the material for houses, farming implements, household utensils, weapons, art, personal ornaments, medical supplies, and objects for religious purposes. The discovery and use of these minerals helped shape the cultural life of the ancient world.

The Bible mentions six metals known and used by the ancient Hebrews: gold, silver, bronze, iron, tin, and lead (Num. 31:22). Job's reference to metals "taken from the earth" (Job 28:2) seems to indicate a firsthand knowledge of mine operations. The smelting of ores was known apparently in very ancient times. Copper was the first metal smelted by the Egyptians.

Palestine acquired much of its mineral resources through spoils of war (Josh. 22:8) and through trade with foreign countries. This trade reached its greatest height during Solomon's time (1 Kin. 10:10–11, 22, 27). These minerals proved to be a valuable asset to the physical, material, and spiritual welfare of the people of Bible lands.

The following minerals are mentioned in the Bible. This list is keyed to the New King James translation, with cross references from five additional popular versions: KJV, NASB, REB, NIV, and NRSV.

Alabaster. The most common form of alabaster is a fine-textured variety of massive gypsum (sulfate of lime). It is very soft and therefore excellent for carving. The color is usually white, but it may be gray, yellow, or red.

Large quantities of gypsum were quarried in the Jordan Valley in the days before the Hebrew people occupied this territory. Many articles were fashioned from this stone, including vases, jars, saucers, bowls, lamps, and statues. Mary of Bethany anointed Jesus with costly oil from an alabaster flask (Matt. 26:7; Mark 14:3; Luke 7:37). Her willingness to express her love unselfishly won Christ's approval, just as He honors sacrificial expressions of love today.

The ancient variety of alabaster is known as "oriental alabaster" (carbonate of lime), a form of marble. It is much harder than the gypsum variety but is used for the same purpose. Ancient alabaster was found only in Egypt.

Antimony. A hard mineral, metallic gray in color, usually classed as a metal. In Bible times antimony was ground into a fine black powder, moistened with oil or water, and used as eye-paint to accent the eyelashes and make them appear larger (Jer. 4:30). This was an accepted custom in Egypt and Mesopotamia, but it was rejected by the Hebrew people, although Jezebel and other women of ill repute used it (2 Kin. 9:30).

The prophets Jeremiah and Ezekiel compared Israel to unfaithful women who adorned themselves with paint for their lovers (Jer. 4:30; Ezek. 23:40). The material that David furnished for the temple included antimony. This was mixed with resin and used as a setting for gems (1 Chr. 29:2, NRSV).

Asphalt. A black mineral substance, a form of bitumen, derived from crude petroleum (Gen. 11:3; Ex. 2:3). It was found in Mesopotamia and Palestine, especially in the Dead Sea region. Because of the abundance of asphalt around the Dead Sea, the Greeks and Romans referred to it as Lake Asphaltitis (Gen. 14:10). Other versions translate the word for asphalt as bitumen, slime, tar, or clay.

Bitumen. A mineral substance consisting chiefly of hydrogen and carbon. Mineral pitch and asphalt are forms of bitumen. Highly flammable, its consistency varies from solids to semi-liquids (Is. 34:9). Large deposits of bitumen have been known to exist around the Dead Sea, and in Egypt and Mesopotamia since ancient times.

Bitumen was used as caulking to waterproof Noah's ark (Gen. 6:14) and the basket in which Moses was hidden (Ex. 2:3). It was also used as mortar (Gen. 11:3). The pits into which the kings of Sodom and Gomorrah fell were bitumen pits (Gen. 14:10, NRSV). Various English versions of the Bible translate the word for bitumen as asphalt, slime, tar, or pitch.

Brass. True brass is an alloy of copper and zinc. However, when "brass" is mentioned in the Bible, it refers to either copper or bronze (1 Cor. 13:1; Rev. 1:15; 2:18; 9:20). The three words *brass, bronze,* and *copper* are often used interchangeably in various English translations of the Bible.

Copper was in general use relatively early in human history. Numerous refineries have been discovered in Sinai, Armenia, Syria, and many other places in the ancient world.

Many articles in the ancient world were fashioned from bronze or brass. These included cooking utensils, shovels, spoons, musical instruments, weapons, and tools. Solomon used copper and bronze in many of the items in the temple (1 Kin. 7:14).

Brimstone. A bright yellow mineral usually found near active volcanoes. Large deposits of this substance are found in the Dead Sea region. Highly combustible, it burns with a very disagreeable odor.

The Hebrew and Greek words for "brimstone" denote divine fire (Gen. 19:24; Ezek. 38:22; Luke 17:29). Brimstone (burning stone) is often associated with fire (Rev. 9:17–18; 20:10; 21:8), and with barrenness and devastation (Deut. 29:23; Job 18:15). Brimstone was considered an agent of God's judgment (Gen. 19:24). In the New Testament it is used symbolically to represent God's wrath and the future punishment of the wicked

(Rev. 9:17–18; 14:10; 20:10). Another word for brimstone used in various translations of the Bible is sulphur or sulfur.

Chalkstone. A variety of fine-grained limestone rock, chalkstone (or chalk) is a soft porous material consisting largely of calcite. It is usually white, but it can be yellow or gray. Limestone is the dominant stone in Palestine and other Bible lands. The Hebrews burned limestone in kilns to make lime (Is. 33:12).

The prophet Isaiah spoke of chalkstone in a figurative sense to illustrate God's readiness to remove Israel's guilt if they would make their altars "like chalkstone beaten to dust" (Is. 27:9).

Clay. Soil that consists of extremely fine particles of sand, flint, or quartz. Some clays were formed of soft limestone with much grit and flint, while others included quartz, which formed a much harder clay.

Clay was used widely in the ancient world. Among its many uses, clay was an important building material. The Tower of Babel was constructed of clay bricks (Gen. 11:3). The poorest-quality clay was used in making bricks. Both sun-baked and kiln-fired bricks were known (2 Sam. 12:31). Mortar was also usually made of clay. The Hebrew word for "clay" is translated by some English versions as asphalt.

Impressions were made into wet clay with signet rings or cylinder seals to prove ownership (Job 38:14; Dan. 6:17). Clay seals were placed on houses, vessels of various kinds, and perhaps on Christ's tomb (Matt. 27:66).

Clay tablets were used in Mesopotamia for cuneiform writing. Letters were inscribed in soft clay with a stylus. The tablet was then sun-baked or kiln-fired to increase its strength. Various kinds of pottery were made of clay. These included lamps, cooking utensils, pots, vases, jars, dishes, and idols.

Coal. A black, porous form of carbon (Lam. 4:8) or live embers of any kind (2 Sam. 22:9, 13). The Hebrew people learned to form charcoal by burning wood that had been covered with earth and leaves. The lack of air caused the wood to char. According to the prophet Isaiah, cedars, cypress, and oak were some of the trees used for fuel (Is. 44:14–16). Broom or juniper bushes were also used for charcoal (Ps. 120:4).

The intense heat of charcoal made it a valuable form of fuel in smelting furnaces (Song 8:6). The wealthy used charcoal to heat their homes (Jer. 36:22). It was also used for cooking (1 Kin. 19:6), by blacksmiths (Is. 44:12), and for heating (John 18:18).

Copper. A reddish-brown metal derived from many kinds of ores. One of the oldest metals known to humankind, copper was the first to be used for making tools. Gold and meteoric iron were probably used before copper. Pure copper was used until it was alloyed with tin to form bronze sometime between 4500–3000 B.C.

Ancient copper refineries were located in Sinai, Egypt, Syria, Persia, the Phoenician coast, and Palestine. During Solomon's reign (about 970–931 B.C.), enormous amounts of bronze were used in the temple furnishings (1 Kin. 7:13–47).

Many useful articles were made from copper and its alloys, including tools of all kinds, utensils (Lev. 6:28), weapons (2 Sam. 21:16; 22:35; 2 Chr. 12:10), idols, and musical instruments.

Flint. A very hard variety of quartz. Dark gray or brown in color, it is usually found in chalk or limestone rock. A form of silica, it sparks when struck by steel or another flint (2 Macc. 10:3). Because flint has a sharp edge when broken, tools such as knives, weapons, saws, sickles, and many other implements were made from flint by prehistoric people throughout the Stone Age.

Archaeologists have found many flint objects, especially knives, in Palestine. These were dated from the Neolithic or Late Stone Age (about 7000–4500 B.C.). Zipporah used a "sharp stone" to circumcise her children (Ex. 4:25). The Bible refers to "rocks of flint" (Deut. 8:15) or "flinty rock" (Deut. 32:13).

Flint is also spoken of in a figurative manner in the Bible, denoting strength and determination (Is. 5:28; 50:7; Ezek. 3:9).

This mineral is still abundant in the limestone rock of Syria, Palestine, and Egypt.

Gold. A soft, bright yellow metal, gold was one of the first metals known to humankind. It could be used in its pure state without smelting. It never tarnishes—a property that makes it ideal for jewelry. This metal was extremely malleable; it could be hammered into thin strips and delicate objects. "And they beat the gold into thin sheets and cut it into threads, to work it in with the blue and purple and scarlet and fine linen thread, into artistic designs" (Ex. 39:3).

Gold is mentioned over 500 times in the Bible, more than any other metal. Rich deposits of gold were in Havilah (Gen. 2:11), Ophir (1 Kin. 22:48; 2 Chr. 8:18), Sheba (1 Kin. 10:1–2), Egypt, Armenia, Asia Minor, and Persia.

Gold was at first hammered into desired shapes and sizes. In later periods it was refined and cast. Some scholars believe gold was not refined in Palestine until about 1000 B.C.

Many objects were made of gold, including the high priest's vest (Ex. 28:5), crowns (Ps. 21:3), chains (Gen. 41:42), rods (Song 5:14; rings, KJV), and coins (1 Chr. 21:25; Acts 3:6). Hiram brought gold to Israel for Solomon's palace (1 Kin. 10:16–21) and for furnishings for the temple (1 Kin. 6:20; 10:2, 10). Gold was also taken as plunder in war (2 Kin. 24:13).

Iron. This mineral is actually a metal obtained from certain rocks or ores. Iron occurs in a great variety of minerals. Much of the color of other minerals is due to the presence of iron, which has a steel-gray color with a metallic luster.

Meteoric iron is one of the oldest metals known. It existed in Egypt before 3100 B.C. The presence of nickel in meteoric iron distinguishes it from common iron ore. The ancient Egyptian word for this material meant "metal from heaven." Before the knowledge of smelting ores was known, people fashioned small objects from this ore (Gen. 4:22; Deut. 8:9).

The Hittites in Asia Minor were the first to develop skills in the smelting of iron (about 1400 B.C.). Charcoal-fired furnaces were used for this purpose. Since much higher temperatures were required to cast iron, only wrought iron could be made at this time.

When the Philistines learned the secret of smelting iron (about 1200 B.C.), iron became widely used throughout the ancient world. Iron had definitely been in use during the Israelite conquest of the land of Canaan (Josh. 6:24; Judg. 1:19; 4:3). The Philistines became skilled ironsmiths, eventually controlling most of Canaan and later conquering Israel, prohibiting their use of iron (1 Sam. 13:19, 22). After the Israelites' victory over the Philistines, iron became widespread in Palestine.

Iron ore was plentiful in Palestine, Syria, Cyprus, and Asia Minor. Iron gradually replaced copper and bronze for farming implements, weapons, armor, and tools.

The reference to steel in Psalm 18 (KJV) means copper or bronze, because steel was not known at that time. "He teacheth my hands to war, so that a bow of steel is broken by mine arms" (v. 34).

Jacinth. An orange or reddish gemstone. A variety of zircon, this mineral is widely distributed in crystal form in volcanic rocks and in fine granules in sand. Jacinth was the first stone in the third row of Aaron's breastplate (Ex. 28:19; ligure, KJV; turquoise, REB). Jacinth was used to describe one of the colors in the breastplates of the riders in John's vision (Rev. 9:17; sapphire, NRSV; sulfur, NIV; hyacinth, NKJV). Jacinth is also the 11th foundation stone in the heavenly Jerusalem (Rev. 21:20).

Lead. A soft, bluish-gray metal. Next to gold, lead is the heaviest of the common metals. Lead is easily worked, but it tarnishes very quickly. The ancient Roman name for lead was plumbum. The English word *plumber* (worker in lead) comes from this Latin word.

Lead is found in limestone and dolomite rock, usually deposited with other metals. Thus, it is sometimes mentioned in the Bible along with other metals (Num. 31:22; Ezek. 22:18, 20). Lead was never used extensively in Palestine, but it was mined in Egypt and the Sinai Peninsula. This metal was also imported from Tarshish (Ezek. 27:12). Lead was used to purify silver (Jer. 6:29–30; Ezek. 22:18–20), as sinkers for fishing nets (Ex. 15:10), and as weights (Zech. 5:7–8). Job refers to his words being preserved permanently in lead (Job 19:24). Plumb lines may also have been made of lead (Amos 7:7–8).

Lime. A calcium oxide derived from limestone rock or chalk. Limestone was burned in limekilns and reduced to powder. Then it was used mainly for plastering floors and walls. The earliest mention of lime in the Bible is when God instructed Moses to whitewash stones with lime for a memorial of His covenant with Israel (Deut. 27:2, 4; plaster, KJV, REB, NIV, NRSV).

The Hebrew word for lime is also translated by various English versions as plaster, whitewash, or ash (Deut. 27:2, 4; Is. 27:9; 33:12; Dan 5:5; Amos 2:1). Lime was used by the Israelites for mortar and as plaster for floors (Dan. 5:5). The walls of cisterns were also waterproofed with plaster.

Lime may have been used in dyeing to give colors a permanent set in the fabric. Archaeologists have found stone jars containing lime and potash next to dyeing vats.

Lye. An alkaline material used as a cleansing agent. Both Egypt and Palestine produced some form of soap for washing the body as well as clothes. This may have been natron (niter), a sodium carbonate (soda) available in its natural state in southern Egypt. This substance could have been imported into Palestine.

Palestine produced potassium carbonate, an alkaline material made from the ashes of many scrubby plants and mixed with oil to form a soft soap. These plants grew in the Dead Sea region.

The prophet Jeremiah's first sermon declared that the people of Judah were so full of iniquity that it could not be removed. "'For though you wash yourself with lye, and use much soap, yet your iniquity is marked before Me,' says the Lord God" (Jer. 2:22; nitre, KJV; soda, NIV).

Marble. A crystallized form of limestone, marble is extremely hard and capable of a high polish. It is usually white, but is sometimes red or yellow.

The Hebrew and Greek words translated "marble" mean "brightness" or "glistening." Marble was obtained from most Bible lands in some form, but the choicest variety came from Arabia.

David supplied an abundance of marble for the temple (1 Chr. 29:2). Solomon alluded poetically to the strength and beauty of marble (Song 5:15; alabaster, NASB, NRSV). It was used in the palace of Shushan, or Susa (Esth. 1:6).

In the Greek and Roman periods many public buildings and homes of the wealthy contained marble. Archaeologists have found many marble beads and statues in Palestine. Marble is included in the merchandise of symbolic Babylon which will be destroyed (Rev. 18:12). Egyptian alabaster was also a form of marble.

One distinct type of marble mentioned by several English translations is porphyry (Esth. 1:6; NASB, NRSV; malachite, REB). This was a purple rock with imbedded crystals of various sizes, used in the pavement of King Ahasuerus's palace at Susa.

Mercury. A silvery-white liquid metal, popularly called quicksilver. It is obtained from the ores of cinnabar. The Greek word for mercury means "water silver." It is used to extract gold and silver from their ores. This process, called amalgamation, was probably used in the ancient world. Pliny (A.D. 23–79) refers to mercury in this manner.

Mercury is not mentioned in the Bible by name, but it may be implied (Prov. 26:23; Is. 1:22; Ezek. 22:18–20) by the phrase "silver dross."

Mortar. A mixture of clay, sand, lime, and water used for building material. Mortar was sometimes made of clay alone or with chopped straw, sand, or crushed stone added for strength. The Hebrews in Egypt tempered their bricks and mortar with straw (Ex. 1:14; 5:7).

Lime mixed with sand or small stones was used in Palestine for mortar. This was used especially for more expensive houses. Mortar was spread on the walls, floors, and roofs of houses for more durability. The prophet Nahum suggested that the usual method of mixing mortar was treading it (Nah. 3:14).

Oil. In the Bible, the word *oil* usually refers to olive oil, although oil from myrrh, spikenard, and other varieties of trees was often used. Olive oil was one of the most important products in the economy of Palestine and in the daily life of the people. It became a symbol of peace and prosperity (Jer. 31:12), and was looked upon as a blessing from God.

Olives were harvested in the fall of the year, from September through the middle of November. Olives were gathered by shaking the trees (Is. 17:6) or by beating the trees with long sticks (Deut. 24:20). The oil harvested from them was stored in vats for later use. In homes it was stored in jars or flasks for domestic purposes (1 Kin. 17:12).

Every household was dependent upon a good supply of oil for their lamps (Ex. 25:6; Matt. 25:3–4, 8) and as an ingredient for bread (1 Kin. 17:12). Olive oil was also used as a medicine to treat wounds (Is. 1:6; Luke 10:34).

Ceremonial anointing was a common practice, especially for consecrating the high priest (Ex. 29:2) and anointing the king (1 Sam. 10:1). It was also used for personal cleanliness (Ruth 3:3; 2 Sam. 12:20). The early church practiced anointing with oil for healing (Mark 6:13; James 5:14). Oil was an article of trade especially during Solomon's time. Hiram, king of Tyre, received oil each year (1 Kin. 5:11), and it was also traded to Egypt.

Probably the most significant use of oil was in religious ceremonies. The best grade of oil was used for cereal offerings (Ex. 29:2; Deut. 12:17), sacrificial offerings (Ex. 29:40), and for the sanctuary lamp (Lev. 24:2).

Plaster. A mixture of clay, lime, and water used to coat various surfaces. The Hebrew word for plaster means "to coat or overlay." At first plaster was probably made from clay and was used to coat floors, walls, and roofs of houses (Lev. 14:42, 45; Dan. 5:5). In later periods lime was mixed with clay or sand to waterproof cisterns and basins.

Quartz. A hard, glass-like mineral composed of oxygen and silicon. A common mineral, quartz is found in pure crystalline form in such other minerals as agate, flint, sand, and sandstone. Job indicated that wisdom was superior to all the precious gems and minerals of the earth, including quartz (Job 28:18; pearls, KJV; glass, NASB; alabaster, REB; jasper, NIV; crystal, NRSV).

Salt. This mineral is sodium chloride, a white crystalline substance used mainly for seasoning and as a preservative (Job 6:6). Salt is not only one of the most important substances mentioned in the Bible, but it is a necessity of life. The Hebrew people were well aware of the importance of salt to health (Job 6:6).

High concentrations of salt exist in the Dead Sea, a body of water that is 9 times saltier than the ocean and is sometimes called the Salt Sea (Gen. 14:3). The ancient cities of Sodom and Gomorrah may have been located near the south end of the Dead Sea. Here Lot's wife was turned into a pillar of salt (Gen. 19:26).

An ancient method of extracting salt from sea water was to collect salt water in salt pits—holes dug in the sand; the water evaporated, leaving the salt behind (Zeph. 2:9). Salt pans were later used for this purpose.

Salt had a significant place in Hebrew worship. It was included in the grain offering (Lev. 2:13), the burnt offering

(Ezek. 43:24), and the incense (Ex. 30:35). Part of the temple offering included salt (Ezra 6:9). It was also used to ratify covenants (Num. 18:19; 2 Chr. 13:5). Newborn babies were rubbed with salt in the belief that this promoted good health (Ezek. 16:4).

During times of war, the enemies' lands were sown with salt to render them barren (Judg. 9:45). In Roman times salt was an important item of trade and was even used for money. Roman soldiers received part of their salary in salt.

Jesus described His disciples as the salt of the earth, urging them to imitate the usefulness of salt (Matt. 5:13; Col. 4:6).

Sand. Sand is made up of fine grains of rock that are worn away by wind and rain. Numerous minerals such as quartz, calcite, and mica are found in sand.

Sand was plentiful on the Mediterranean shores, along river banks, and in desert regions. It is usually mentioned in the Bible in a figurative manner, to symbolize a multitude (Gen. 22:17; Is. 10:22; Rev. 20:8), weight (Job 6:3), and weakness (Matt. 7:26). Sand was also used in mortar and in the manufacture of glass, which began in ancient Egypt or Phoenicia (Deut. 33:19).

Silver. This mineral is actually a silvery-white metal capable of a high polish. In ancient times it was valued next to gold. Silver was harder than gold, but not as hard as copper. It was usually extracted from lead ore, although it was also found in its native state. Silver never tarnishes when exposed to air, unless sulphur is present. The main sources of silver were Asia Minor, Arabia, Mesopotamia, Armenia, and Persia. Palestine imported most of its silver from these countries, especially during Solomon's time (about 970–931 B.C.), when "the king made silver as common in Jerusalem as stones" (1 Kin. 10:27; 2 Chr. 9:27). Silver was refined and then cast into molds (Judg. 17:4; Ps. 12:6) by silversmiths (Jer. 10:9; Acts 19:24).

Abraham's wealth included silver (Gen. 13:2), which he used as a medium of exchange (Gen. 23:15). Other uses for silver were cups (Gen. 44:2), idols (Ps. 115:4; Is. 40:19; Acts 19:24), various kinds of jewelry (Gen. 24:53; Ex. 3:22), and containers (Num. 7:13; 1 Chr. 28:17; Ezra 1:9–10). Many articles for the tabernacle were made of silver, including trumpets (Num. 10:2), lampstands (1 Chr. 28:15), and sockets (Ex. 26:19).

Steel. Steel was not known during Bible times until the 1st century A.D. The Hebrew word for copper and bronze is incorrectly translated "steel" in the KJV (2 Sam. 22:35; Job 20:24; Ps. 18:34; Jer. 15:12).

Tin. A soft, bluish-white metal smelted from cassiterite, its principal ore. Tin was used chiefly as an alloy with copper to produce bronze, a much harder material than either copper or tin. The Hebrew word for tin means "a substitute or alloy."

Phoenicia supplied the ancient Mediterranean world with tin obtained from Spain, its chief colony. Some scholars believe the Phoenicians sailed the Atlantic to Cornwall, England, the principal supplier of tin. Tyre received tin from Tarshish (Ezek. 27:12). Some think Persia and Armenia exported tin also.

Tin was among the spoils the Israelites took from the Midianites (Num. 31:22). The prophet Ezekiel pictured Jerusalem being smelted as tin cast in a furnace (Ezek. 22:18–20; copper, REB; bronze, NASB, NRSV).

Vermilion. A red pigment obtained from cinnabar, the same mineral ore from which mercury or quicksilver is derived. Pure vermilion is a brilliant red, but it is brownish red when impurities such as clay, iron oxides, and bitumen are mixed with it. This ore is usually distributed in areas of volcanic rocks.

The prophet Jeremiah pronounced judgment on Shallum (Jehoahaz) for beautifying his own house with vermilion—decorating it in red (Jer. 22:14, NASB, NIV)—while neglecting the poor and needy. Ezekiel saw the images of the Chaldeans painted in vermilion on the walls (Ezek. 23:14).

MITHRAISM [MYTH rah iz em] — a Persian religious cult that flourished in the late Roman Empire. In the 2nd century A.D. it was stronger than Christianity in the Roman Empire. But it declined rapidly in the 3rd century. Mithras was considered the god of light and wisdom and the guardian against evil by the Persians.

MOABITE STONE — a black basalt memorial stone discovered in Moab by a German missionary in 1868. Nearly 4 feet high, it contained about 34 lines in an alphabet similar to Hebrew. The stone was probably erected about 850 B.C. by the Moabite king Mesha.

King Mesha's story written on the stone celebrated his overthrow of the nation of Israel. This event apparently is recorded in 2 Kings 3:4–27, although the biblical account makes it clear that Israel was victorious in the battle. The passage shows that Mesha honors his god Chemosh in terms similar to the Old Testament reverence for the Lord. The inhabitants of entire cities were apparently slaughtered to appease this deity, recalling the similar practices of the Israelites, especially as described in the book of Joshua. Besides telling of his violent conquests, Mesha boasted on the stone of the building of cities (with Israelite forced labor) and the construction of cisterns, walls, gates, towers, a king's palace, and even a highway.

The Moabite stone has profound biblical relevance. Historically, it confirms Old Testament accounts. It has a theological parallel to Israel's worship of one god. It is also valuable geographically because it mentions no less than 15 sites listed in the Old Testament. The writing on the stone also resembles Hebrew, the language in which most of the Old Testament was originally written.

Some pieces of the stone are now housed in the Louvre Museum in Paris.

MONEY OF THE BIBLE. As soon as ancient people stopped living the lives of wandering hunters and began an agricultural system, a medium of exchange became necessary. A system of barter, or trading of property, preceded the creation of any formal currency that can be called money.

In Old Testament times, land itself became an immediate asset. It was a possession that could be traded. But produce, and especially livestock, was more convenient, because it was so movable. The pharaoh of Egypt supplied Abraham with oxen, sheep, camels, and female donkeys (Gen. 12:16). King Mesha of Moab exacted a tribute of 100,000 sheep and 100,000 rams (2 Kin. 3:4). The ritual sacrifice of animals underscored their value as a standard of barter—and thus encouraged commerce near the temple area.

Grain, oil, and wine were also used in bartering, as when King Solomon traded wheat and olive oil for the cypress trees needed to build the temple (1 Kin. 5:11), or when the Israelites were taxed in the amount of one-tenth of their grain or wine (1 Sam. 8:15), or when the tribe of Levi (Levites) was directed by God to serve as priests in exchange for grain and wine (Num. 18:25–32). Spices were also an item of barter. These were offered by the queen of Sheba to Solomon (1 Kin. 10:2).

Gradually, as communities became more organized, tradesmen traveled between these settlements. Products circulated from one region to another. Soon metals began to replace goods and services as items of exchange. Copper or bronze was in demand for weapons (2 Sam. 21:16), for farming tools, and for offerings (Ex. 35:5). The early Egyptians, Semites, and Hittites shaped gold and silver into rings, bars, or rounded nodules for easier trading. The children of Jacob used "bundles of money" (Gen. 42:35), which may have been metal rings tied together with strings.

Silver generally was used in real estate transactions. Omri purchased the village and hill of Samaria for two talents of silver (1 Kin. 16:24). Gold was sometimes used, along with sil-ver, in the payment of tribute, such as Hezekiah's payment to Sennacherib of Assyria (2 Kin. 18:14). Abraham bought the cave of Machpelah for 400 shekels of silver (Gen. 23:15–16). David bought the threshing floor of Araunah for 50 shekels of silver (2 Sam. 24:24). Solomon purchased chariots and horses with silver (1 Kin. 10:28–29). Judas was paid for his betrayal of Jesus with 30 pieces of silver (Matt. 26:15). Silver was so commonly used as money that the Hebrew word for "silver" came to mean "money" (Gen. 17:13).

Gold, the most valuable of metals, was also used for major transactions. King Hiram of Tyre paid 120 talents of gold to Solomon for several cities near his land (1 Kin. 9:13–14). Later, Hezekiah paid Sennacherib 300 talents of silver and 30 talents of gold to obtain peace (2 Kin. 18:14). Copper was also used for barter but was considered less valuable (Ex. 35:5; 2 Sam. 21:16; Is. 60:17). Later, these same three metals were used to mint the nation's first coins.

In their early use as money, metals were probably in their raw form or in varying stages of refinement. However, in that form it was difficult to transport them and to determine their true value. Thus the metals were soon refined into the form of a wedge or a bar (Josh. 7:21) or various forms of jewelry.

Abraham's servant gave Rebekah a golden nose ring weigh-ing half a shekel and two gold bracelets weighing ten shekels (Gen. 24:22). The spoil of the Midianites included many arti-cles of jewelry (Num. 31:50). Gold and silver were also kept as ingots, vessels, dust, or small fragments that could be melted and used immediately. These small pieces of metal were often carried in leather pouches that could be easily hidden (Gen. 42:35).

The Bible frequently refers to "pieces" of silver or gold. The confusing term "shekel" did not denote any one value or weight at first, although it later became the name of a Jewish coin. For instance, there were heavy and light silver shekels (Phoenician), and heavy and light gold shekels (Babylonian). Fifteen heavy Phoenician shekels of silver equaled one heavy Babylonian gold shekel. Abraham paid pieces of silver, or shekels, for the cave of Machpelah (Gen. 23:16). David paid gold shekels to Ornan the Jebusite (1 Chr. 21:22–25).

Fractions of the shekel are mentioned in the Old Testament as well: the half-shekel, or bekah (Ex. 38:26); the third part of a shekel as a covenant obligation (Neh. 10:32); the fourth part of a shekel, or rebah, proposed to Saul by the servant as a gift to the prophet Samuel (1 Sam. 9:8); and the 20th part of a shekel, or a gerah (Lev. 27:25). The pin was two-thirds of a shekel (1 Sam. 13:21). These pieces were probably fragments of gold or silver bars.

The talent was the largest unit of silver, shaped in slabs, pellets, or rings, with approximately the value of one ox.

Before coins with stamped values were introduced, the pieces of precious metal for transactions had to be weighed on a scale. Abraham measured the shekels given to Ephron (Gen. 23:16). Such a system was certainly haphazard. Dishonest practices of weighing were banned (Deut. 25:13) in favor of a "perfect and just weight" (v. 15), because "a false balance is an abomination to the LORD" (Prov. 11:1).

Eventually pieces of metal were standardized, then stamped to designate their weight and value. Coins still had to be weighed, however, since their edges might have been trimmed or filed. Ancient coins often show other marks, indicating they may have been probed to assure their silver content.

Among the earliest coins were those struck in Lydia by King Croesus (561–546 B.C.), whose legendary Anatolian mines and stream beds supplied gold and silver. He was conquered by Cyrus the Great, who may have carried the idea of coined money back to Persia.

The Persian Darius the Great (522–486 B.C.) minted coins of gold. The coin known as a daric, which bore his name, was common with the Israelites during the captivity. It was similar to a U.S. five-dollar gold piece. Ten thousand darics were paid to craftsmen for their work on the temple built by Solomon (1 Chr. 29:7).

The Greeks soon adapted the Persian and Babylonian coinage, portraying animals, natural objects, and Greek gods on the coins—which were called drachmas (Greek for "handful"). The tetradrachma, or shekel of Tyre, was about the size of an American half-dollar. It probably circulated among the Israelites. Archaeologists have uncovered coins of Greek design marked "YHD" (Judah), probably minted by the Persians for use by the Jews. However, these particular coins are not mentioned in the Bible.

Alexander the Great of Greece conquered the Persian Empire. In the period between the Old and New Testaments, Greek coins (especially the tetradrachma) began pouring into Palestine. After Alexander's death, his successors known as the Ptolemies added mints at Gaza, Jaffa, and Tyre for making coins.

The Seleucids seized Palestine (about 200 B.C.), forcing Greek culture upon the Jews until they rebelled against Antiochus IV around 167 B.C. The right to mint coins was an issue, but the Jewish revolt led by Simon Maccabeus was thwarted. Later, Antiochus VII established a mint that struck coins bearing his name. But the Seleucids' domination lapsed as the Hasmonaeans gained their freedom and began minting their own small bronze coins (one-half, one-third, and one-fourth shekel in weight). These were inscribed to a certain high priest of that time and "the community of Jews." Still the Seleucids issued official gold and silver coins. This brief phase of freedom for the Jews ended when the Romans annexed Palestine in 63 B.C.

Roman coins common in New Testament times showed a profound Greek influence, including those issued by Herod the Great (37–4 B.C.) and his sons. But because of the Second Commandment, which prohibited graven images, the coins displayed only traditional, stylized pictures. However, they did include the date of issue.

The basic unit of Roman coinage was the silver denarius, probably equal to a laborer's daily wage, as in the parable of the vineyard workers (Matt. 20:9–10, 13). It was also used for paying tribute, or taxes, to the Roman emperor, whose image it carried. Jesus was shown a denarius, in a ploy by the Pharisees to trick him into opposing the Roman taxation authority. But he replied, "Render therefore to Caesar the things that are Caesar's, and to God the things that are God's" (Matt. 22:15–22).

The golden aureus was worth about 25 denarii. The "copper coin" (assarion, equal to one-sixteenth of a silver denarius) was mentioned by Jesus as being worth no more than two sparrows, in his counsel about God's concern for the smallest creatures as well as the most powerful (Matt. 10:29; Luke 12:6). The "penny" (quadrans or kodrantes) was equal to one-fourth of the copper assarion. It was also mentioned by Jesus (Matt. 5:26).

Greek coins generally bore religious symbols. They may have been minted at pagan temples, which served as business centers for granting loans and receiving estates. The cult of Astarte may have had a strong influence on the production of coins. Silver for Greek coins was supplied by the rich mines of Laurium. Gold coins were less popular among the Greeks.

The basic Greek coin was the drachma, roughly equivalent to a Roman denarius, or one day's wages. Probably the drachma is the "lost coin" of Jesus' parable (Luke 15:8–10). The apostle Paul, when he practiced tent making at Corinth, probably exchanged his work for the Corinthian coins that pictured the winged horse Pegasus. (Corinth had minted coins as early as 650 B.C.) Paul later preached in Athens, Greece, where one archaeologist has excavated 80,000 coins.

The Greek didrachma (two-drachma piece) was used by the Jews for their half-shekel temple tax (Matt. 17:24). The silver stater, or tetradrachma, was a four-drachma piece, used to pay the temple tax (Matt. 17:27). The mina, equaling 100 drachmas, illustrated Jesus' parable about the wise use of resources (Luke 19:11–27).

The only Jewish coin mentioned in the New Testament is the "widow's mite" or lepton, called a mite by the NKJV. These were very small copper coins worth only a fraction of a penny by today's standards. Yet Jesus commended the poor widow who gave two mites to the temple treasury, because "she out of her poverty put in all that she had, her whole livelihood" (Mark 12:44).

MONTH — one of the 12 divisions of a year, measured by the completed cycle in the changing of the moon. Solomon had 12 governors over all Israel, who provided food for the king and his household; each made provision for one month of the year (1 Kin. 4:7). The military divisions of Israel were also 12 in number, one for each month of the year, each division consisting of 14,000 men (1 Chr. 27:1–15).

MORNING — the first part of the day, extending from sunrise to noon (Gen. 1:5; Ps. 30:5; Matt. 16:3). Christ is called "the Bright and Morning Star" (Rev. 22:16) who brought a new day of hope and promise for the world.

MYSTERY RELIGIONS — secret religions that flourished in Syria, Persia, Anatolia, Egypt, Greece, Rome, and other nations several centuries before and after the time of Christ. The mystery religions were quite popular in the 1st century A.D. and thus provided strong religious competition for Christianity.

They were called mysteries because their initiation and other rituals were kept secret. These religions included the cults of Eleusis, Dionysus, Isis and Osiris, Mithra, Cybele (the Magna Mater, or Great Mother), the Dead Syria, and many local deities, all of which promised purification and immortality.

By means of the secret rituals of these religions—which might involve ceremonial washings, blood sprinkling, drunkenness, sacramental meals, passion plays, or even sexual relations with a priest or priestess—their followers became one with their god and believed that they participated in the life of that god.

Because of his contact with the Greek world, the apostle Paul was probably familiar with these mystery religions. But there is no evidence that his theological ideas were influenced by these pagan ideas and practices. Paul preached the gospel of salvation through Jesus Christ.

NABATEA [nab uh TEE ah] — an Arabic territory situated between the Dead Sea and the Gulf of Aqaba. Nebajoth, son of Ishmael and brother-in-law of Edom (Gen. 25:13; 28:9), may have been the ancestor of the Nabateans. Some time during the 6th century B.C. these peoples invaded the territory of the Edomites and Moabites. Their name first occurred in 646 B.C. when a people called the Nabaiate revolted against Ashurbanipal, king of Assyria. It took the Assyrians 7 years to subdue these people.

In 312 B.C. Antigonus, one of the successors of Alexander the Great, sent an expedition against the Nabatean capital of Petra. This rose-red city was situated more than 80 kilometers (50 miles) south of the Dead Sea in the wilderness and surrounded by mountains. Petra had only one entrance, a narrow passageway sometimes as little as 8 feet wide, between cliffs rising 60 to 90 meters (200 to 300 feet) above the road. The Greek army was unable to take the city.

At a later time the Nabateans took advantage of the turmoil of the Seleucid kingdom and extended their territory all the way to Damascus. During the 1st century B.C. they engaged in a war with the Maccabean king Alexander Jannaeus. An officer of the Nabatean king Aretas IV attempted to detain the apostle

Paul at Damascus (2 Cor. 11:32). Eventually the Romans, under Trajan, annexed Nabatea, and it became the province of Arabia in A.D. 106.

The Nabateans controlled the desert highways south of the Dead Sea, demanding outrageous fees from caravans before they allowed them to pass. They developed an advanced civilization in the middle of the desert wilderness. Out of the red sandstone cliffs they carved beautiful obelisks, facades, and high places, or altars, at which they worshiped pagan gods. They also developed a beautiful, thin pottery that was decorated with floral designs. With the rise of Palmyra, the trade that formerly passed through Petra was diverted, and the Nabateans were absorbed into the surrounding Arab population.

NAPHTALI, TRIBE OF [NAF tuh lie] — the tribe that sprang from Naphtali and the territory it inhabited (Num. 1:15, 42–43). The tribe's four great families were descendants of Naphtali's four sons: Jahzeel, Guni, Jezer, and Shillem or Shallum (Num. 26:48–49). The first wilderness census numbered the tribe of Naphtali at 53,000 fighting men (Num. 2:29–30); the second census put it at 45,400 (Num. 26:50).

Along with Asher, Naphtali was the northernmost tribe of Israel, occupying a long, narrow piece of land—about 80 kilometers (50 miles) north to south and 16 to 24 kilometers (10 to 15 miles) from east to west. Naphtali was mountainous (Josh. 20:7) and very fertile. Fortified cities within the tribe's boundaries included Ramah, Hazor, Kedesh, Iron, and Beth Anath (Josh. 19:36–38). The three cities given to the Levites in Naphtali were Kedesh (a city of refuge), Hammoth Dor, and Kartan (Josh. 21:32).

The tribe of Naphtali did not drive out all the Canaanites, but it did receive tribute from them. Members of the tribe of Naphtali fought bravely under Deborah and Barak (Judg. 4:6, 10; 5:18) and responded to Gideon's call (Judg. 6:35; 7:23). When

Saul's son Ishbosheth challenged David for the throne, 37,000 fighting men of Naphtali, led by 1,000 captains, joined David (1 Chr. 12:34).

A part of the Northern Kingdom after the Israelites divided into two kingdoms, Naphtali was ravaged by the Syrian king Ben-Hadad (1 Kin. 15:20). The Assyrian king Tiglath-Pileser III carried many from Naphtali into captivity (2 Kin. 15:29). Isaiah prophesied that one day the land of Naphtali, "in Galilee of the Gentiles," would see a great light (Is. 9:1–7).

Indeed, Jesus made the cities of Chorazin, Capernaum, and Tiberias—all situated within the former territory of Naphtali—a focal point of His ministry. "And leaving Nazareth, He came and dwelt in Capernaum, which is by the sea, in the regions of Zebulun and Naphtali" (Matt. 4:12–16).

NATIONS — countries other than the nation of Israel. In the Bible the word "nations" means the Gentiles, in contrast to the Jews. God promised that He would make Abraham and his descendants a great nation. Thus, God's elect people were kept clearly distinct and separate from all other nations. The nations were regarded by the Hebrew people as godless and corrupt. Yet God intended ultimately to bless the nations through His people Israel: "And in you all the families of the earth shall be blessed" (Gen. 12:3). Israel was thus meant to be "a light to the Gentiles" (Is. 42:6; 49:6).

The prophecy that "the Gentiles shall come to your light" (Is. 60:3) was fulfilled in the Gentile response to Christ in the New Testament. The Great Commission refers to "all the nations" (Matt. 28:19); Cornelius, the first Gentile convert, was brought to faith through the preaching of Peter (Acts 10). The apostle Paul repeatedly quoted the Old Testament to justify the preaching of the gospel to the nations (Rom. 15:9–12; Gal. 3:8).

NAVY — KJV word for "fleet of ships" (1 Kin. 9:26–27). Solomon built a merchant fleet to sail from Ezion Geber, a port on the Red Sea. The Hebrews disliked the sea, so some of the crew members of Solomon's fleet were Phoenician sailors (1 Kin. 9:27). These ships sailed at times with King Hiram's Phoenician fleet (1 Kin. 10:22).

NEBUCHADNEZZAR [neb you kad NEZ ur] (*O god Nabu, protect my son*) — the king of the Neo-Babylonian Empire (ruled 605–562 B.C.) who captured Jerusalem, destroyed the temple, and carried the people of Judah into captivity in Babylonia. He plays a prominent role in the books of Jeremiah (21–52) and Daniel (1:1–5:18) and also appears in 2 Kings (24:1–25:22), Ezra (1:7–6:5), and Ezekiel (26:7–30:10).

Nebuchadnezzar II was the oldest son of Nabopolassar, the founder of the Neo-Babylonian, or Chaldean, dynasty of Babylon. Nabopolassar apparently was a general appointed by the Assyrian king. But in the later years of Assyria he rebelled and established himself as king of Babylon in 626 B.C. Nebuchadnezzar succeeded his father as king in 605 B.C., continuing his policies of conquest of surrounding nations.

In about 602 B.C., after being Nebuchadnezzar's vassal for three years, King Jehoiakim of the nation of Judah rebelled against the Babylonians. Nebuchadnezzar then "came up against him and bound him in bronze fetters to carry him off to Babylon" (2 Chr. 36:6). Apparently, however, Nebuchadnezzar's intention of carrying him to Babylon was abandoned; according to Jeremiah, Jehoiakim was "dragged and cast out beyond the gates of Jerusalem" and "buried with the burial of a donkey" (Jer. 22:19). After reigning for 11 years, Jehoiakim was succeeded by his son Jehoiachin.

Jehoiachin was only 8 years old when he became king, and he reigned in Jerusalem about 3 months (2 Chr. 36:9). At that time Nebuchadnezzar took Jehoiachin captive to Babylon along with the prophet Ezekiel and "costly articles from the house of the Lord" (2 Chr. 36:10). He made Mattaniah, Jehoiachin's uncle (2 Kin. 24:17), king over Judah and Jerusalem, changing his name to Zedekiah.

For about 8 years Zedekiah endured the Babylonian yoke and paid tribute to Nebuchadnezzar. In 589 B.C., however, in the 9th year of his reign, Zedekiah rebelled against the king of Babylon, perhaps trusting in the Egyptian promises of military aid. Nebuchadnezzar and his army came against Jerusalem and besieged the city for about 2 years (2 Kin. 25:2). The siege may have been temporarily lifted with the approach of the Egyptian army (Jer. 37:5).

In 586 B.C. Jerusalem fell to the army of Nebuchadnezzar. Under cover of darkness, Zedekiah and many of his men fled through a break in the city wall. But they were overtaken by the Chaldeans in the plains of Jericho and brought captive to Riblah, a city in the land of Hamath where Nebuchadnezzar was camped. Nebuchadnezzar ordered that the sons of Zedekiah be killed before his eyes. Then Zedekiah was bound and taken captive to Babylon, along with the leading citizens of Jerusalem (2 Kin. 25:1–7).

Nebuchadnezzar's policy of resettling conquered peoples and transporting them to other provinces of his empire provided him with slave labor for conducting his extensive building projects. He rebuilt many sanctuaries, including the temple of Nebo at Borsippa and the great temple of Marduk at Babylon. He accomplished an immense fortification of Babylon, including the building of its great wall.

Although the famous "hanging gardens" cannot be identified among the impressive ruins of Babylon, this fabulous construction project—one of the "seven wonders of the ancient world"—was built by Nebuchadnezzar on the plains of Babylon to cheer his wife, who was homesick for her native Median hills. Nebuchadnezzar also built a huge reservoir near Sippar, providing interconnecting canals in an elaborate irrigation system.

Nebuchadnezzar made an arrogant boast about all that he achieved (Dan. 4:30). But he was stricken at the height of his power and pride by God's judgment. Nebuchadnezzar was temporarily driven out of office, living with the beasts of the field and eating grass like an ox (Dan. 4:32). Later, he was succeeded as king by his son Evil-Merodach.

NEW AGE — a future time when Jesus Christ will rule over the earth. The term "new age" does not appear in either the NKJV or KJV. However, Jeremiah prophesied of a new covenant (Jer. 31:31). Jesus Himself spoke of the regeneration when He would rule in His future kingdom (Matt. 19:28). The apostle Paul referred to this time as a "new creation" (2 Cor. 5:17). In recent years, the term "new age" has been appropriated by various pagan groups who engage in occult practices such as seances, spiritism, and "channeling." They are strongly influenced by oriental monistic religions.

NEW YEAR — a solemn occasion that occurred in the month of Tishri or Ethanim (1 Kin. 8:2), the first month in the Hebrew year. The law of Moses directed that this holiday should be observed by "blowing the trumpets" (Num. 29:1). Thus, this festival is also known as the feast of trumpets. Today this event is known as Rosh Hashanah (literally, beginning of the year), a Jewish high holy day that marks the beginning of the Jewish new year.

NICOLAITANS [nick oh LAY ih tuns] — an early Christian heretical sect made up of followers of Nicolas, who was possibly the deacon of Acts 6:5. The group is mentioned explicitly only in Rev. 2:6, 14–15, where it is equated with a group holding "the doctrine of Balaam," who taught Israel "to eat things sacrificed to idols, and to commit sexual immorality."

Balaam probably was responsible for the cohabitation of the men of Israel with the women of Moab (Num. 25:1–2; 31:16). Therefore, the error of this group was moral rather than doctrinal. If the "Jezebel" of Revelation 2:20–23 was a teacher of this sect, as many believe, their sexual laxity was indeed strong. Most likely, they were a group of anti-law practitioners who supported a freedom that became self-indulgence. It may have been the same heresy condemned in 2 Peter 2:15 and Jude 11. Some early church leaders believed the Nicolaitans later became a Gnostic sect.

NILE [nile] — the great river of Egypt that flows more than 5,700 kilometers (3,500 miles) from central Africa north through the desert to a rich delta area on the Mediterranean Sea. The source of the Nile is derived from two rivers: the Blue Nile from Ethiopia and the White Nile from Lake Victoria in central Africa.

The Blue Nile provides about twice as much water as the White Nile during the rainy season. This flood water, with the soil that it eroded, provided fertile topsoil for the agriculture of northern Egypt. Low flood levels usually meant a famine year, while a high flood level would result in a year of plenty. The Aswan Dam and the High Dam now enable the modern nation of Egypt to control these floods and provide a more constant flow of water.

Because the Nile was so essential to the life and prosperity of Egypt, it was personified as a god called Hapi. Egyptians had religious celebrations at the beginning of the annual flooding of the Nile. One text discovered by archaeologists contains praises in adoration of the Nile for the blessings that it provides.

The river was also one of the chief methods of transportation for the Egyptians. The Nile delta produced papyrus, which the Egyptians wove together to make household mats, baskets, sails for their boats, and paper. The Nile supported a fishing industry as well, and ancient drawings show the pharaohs hunting wild game in the thick undergrowth of the Nile Valley.

The river in Pharaoh's dream (Gen. 41:1–36) was the Nile. The seven fat cows that pastured in the lush grass by the Nile represented seven years when the Nile would flood and there would be plenty of food. The seven thin cows represented years when there would be little grass because of low floodwaters.

Later when the Israelites were slaves under persecution by a pharaoh who did not know Joseph, the king ordered that all male children born to the Israelites must be thrown into the Nile (Ex. 1:22). In an attempt to save her child, Moses' mother put him in a waterproofed papyrus basket and placed him among the papyrus reeds near where Pharaoh's daughter came to bathe (Ex. 2:1–5). When she saw the child, she had compassion on him; thus Moses was not killed.

Eighty years later Moses, returned to Egypt to deliver the Israelites from slavery. In order that the children of Israel might believe that God had sent Moses, God gave him three signs to perform; the last was to pour water from the Nile on dry ground and have it turn to blood (Ex. 4:9). After hearing God's word and seeing these signs, the people believed God and worshiped Him (Ex. 4:29–31).

Because Pharaoh refused to let the Israelites leave Egypt, God sent ten plagues. Moses met Pharaoh at the Nile (Ex. 7:15) and turned the Nile to blood to prove to him that the Nile was not a god, but that Moses' God was the true God (Ex. 7:17–21; Ps. 78:44). Some believe the water was turned to a reddish-brown color from the eroded red soil in the floodwater and that bacteria from the polluted water may have killed the fish. This naturalistic interpretation does not explain the intensity of the plague or the ability of Moses to start and conclude the plague on command. Since Pharaoh's magicians were able to reproduce a somewhat similar phenomenon, Pharaoh's heart was not moved to release the Israelites (Ex. 7:22–25).

The prosperity that the river provided and the annual flooding of the Nile were spoken of symbolically in the prophetic writings (Is. 23:10; Jer. 46:7–8). The judgment on Egypt was often described in terms of the drying up of the Nile (Ezek. 29:10; 30:12; Zech. 10:11), because the Nile will fail, the papyrus will wither, the grain will wilt, and the fishermen will mourn (Is. 19:5–8). Yet in spite of this judgment, the day will come when some from Egypt will turn to God and become His people (Is. 19:18–25).

NINEVEH [NIN eh vuh] — ancient capital city of the Assyrian Empire, a place associated with the ministry of the prophet Jonah. The residents of this pagan city repented and turned to God after Jonah's preaching of a clear message of God's judgment (Jon. 3:5–10).

Founded by Nimrod (Gen. 10:8–10), Nineveh was the capital of the great Assyrian Empire for many years. Its fortunes rose and fell as Babylonia and Assyria struggled with each other for the dominant position in the ancient world. During some periods Babylonia was stronger, while the Assyrians gained the upper hand at other times.

In 612 B.C. Nineveh was destroyed, as prophesied by the Hebrew prophets, especially Nahum. Many scholars questioned the existence of Nineveh until its discovery by A. H. Layard and H. Rassam in 1845–1854. The site has now been excavated thoroughly. Occupational levels on the site go back to prehistoric times, before 3100 B.C. Some of the pottery indicates the city may have originated with the Sumerians.

One of the exciting discoveries in this excavation was the great palace of the Assyrian king Sargon. Along with this find was a library of cuneiform documents and many striking wall ornamentations. This clear evidence of Sargon's existence verifies the accuracy of the book of Isaiah in the prophet's mention of this pagan king (Is. 20:1).

The wall around the city indicated that Nineveh was about 2 kilometers (3 miles) long and less than half that distance wide. The Hebrews, however, perhaps like other foreigners, included other cities under the name of Nineveh.

At the time of the greatest prosperity of Nineveh as described by Jonah, the city was surrounded by a circuit wall almost 13 kilometers (8 miles) long. This "great city" (Jon. 1:2) would have had an area sufficient to contain a population of 120,000, as indicated by Jonah 4:11 and 3:2. Evidence for this is provided by Calah to the south, where 69,754 persons lived in a city half the size of Nineveh. As a result, it would have required a "three days' journey" to go around the city, and a "day's journey" would have been needed to reach the city center from the outlying suburbs, just as the book of Jonah reports (Jon. 3:4).

Several centuries before Jonah's preaching mission to the city, Nineveh became one of the royal residences of Assyrian kings. Sennacherib (705–681 B.C.) made it the capital of the Assyrian Empire to offset the rival capital of Dur-Sharrukin (Khorsabad), built by his father Sargon II (722–705 B.C.). He greatly beautified and adorned Nineveh. The splendid temples, palaces, and fortifications made it the chief city of the empire (2 Kin. 19:36).

In Sennacherib's day the wall around Nineveh was 40 to 50 feet high. It extended for 4 kilometers (2½ miles) along the Tigris River and for 13 kilometers (8 miles) around the inner city. The city wall had 15 main gates, 5 of which have been excavated. Each of the gates was guarded by stone bull statues. Both inside and outside the walls, Sennacherib created parks, a botanical garden, and a zoo. He built a water system containing the oldest aqueduct in history at Jerwan, across the Gomel River. To bring new water supplies to the city, he cut channels for 20 kilometers

(30 miles) from the Gomel River at Bavian and built a dam at Ajeila to control the flooding of the Khosr river.

In the years 1849–1851 archaeologist A. Layard unearthed the 71-room palace of Sennacherib. The mound also yielded the royal palace and library of Ashurbanipal, which housed 22,000 inscribed clay tablets. These tablets included Assyrian creation and flood accounts that furnished Old Testament scholars with valuable information for background studies on the book of Genesis.

It was to Nineveh that Sennacherib brought the tribute he exacted from King Hezekiah of Judah (2 Kin. 18:15). He also returned here after his campaign against Jerusalem and Judah in 701 B.C. In 681 B.C. he was assassinated in the temple of Nisroch, which must have been situated within the city walls.

Esarhaddon, the younger son and successor to Sennacherib, recaptured Nineveh from rebels in 680 B.C. Here he built a palace for himself, although he spent much time in his other residence in Calah. One of his twin sons, Ashurbanipal, returned to live mainly at Nineveh where he had been crown prince during his school days. It was during his last days and the years of his sons Ahsur-etil-ilani and Sin-shar-ishkun that Assyria's vassals revolted.

At the same time the Medes, with the help of the Babylonians, sacked Ashur and Calah in 614 B.C. Two years later Nineveh fell to these combined forces. Nineveh was left in ruins (Nah. 2:10, 13) and grazed by sheep (Zeph. 2:13–15), just as the Hebrew prophets of the Old Testament had predicted.

Nineveh is such a large site that it will probably never be fully excavated. A modern village covers one of its larger palaces. A nearby mound, named "Mound of the Prophet Jonah," contains the palace of Esarhaddon. The popular tradition is that Jonah is buried beneath the mosque at Nebi Yunas.

NO, NO AMON [noe, NO a mahn] — the royal city of southern Egypt at modern Luxor, about 565 kilometers (350 miles) south of Cairo. Some modern versions translate Thebes (NASB, NIV, NRSV).

Thebes (or No) was of major importance from the time of Abraham about 2000 B.C. until it was sacked by the Assyrians in 663 B.C. Thebes not only was the capital of Egypt, it also served as the center of worship of the great Egyptian god Amon (Jer. 46:25) and as the place where many kings and queens were buried.

On the east bank of the Nile the huge temple complexes at Karnak and Luxor where the Egyptians worshiped their gods can still be seen. On the west bank are temples that contain the tombs of pharaohs, queens, and noblemen. The most magnificent of all discoveries in this Valley of the Kings was the tomb of Tutankhamun (King Tut), a pharaoh who flourished about 1358 B.C.

Nahum prophesied that Nineveh, the capital of Assyria, would be destroyed by God, just as No Amon was pillaged by the Assyrians in 663 B.C. (Nah. 3:8). Later, Jeremiah (46:25) and Ezekiel (30:14–16) predicted that Nebuchadnezzar, king of Babylon, would punish the king of Egypt, destroy the gods of Egypt, and bring further desolation to Thebes. This was proof that God had power over all nations and that their gods were powerless.

OPHEL [OH fell] (*knoll*) — the northeast part of the triangular hill in ancient Jerusalem on which the City of David stood. Situated south of the temple area, the hill was the site of the original city of the Jebusites. Surrounded on three sides by deep valleys, the ancient city was so strongly fortified that it was considered unconquerable. But David captured this center of Canaanite power and made it his new capital city (2 Sam. 5:6–9).

Usually the name Ophel is given to the entire hill. But it is more accurate to identify the hill of Ophel with the fortifications built on the eastern ridge of the hill that overlooks the Kidron Valley. Jotham, king of Judah (750–732 B.C.), built extensively on the wall of Ophel (2 Chr. 27:3). Manasseh, king of Judah (696–642 B.C.), built a high wall outside the City of David, and it enclosed Ophel (2 Chr. 33:14). The Nethinim, or temple servants, lived in Ophel after the captivity (Neh. 3:26–27; 11:21).

P

PALESTINE [PAL ess tyne] — the land promised by God to Abraham and his descendants and eventually the region where the Hebrew people lived.

Palestine (or Palestina) is a tiny land bridge between the continents of Asia, Africa, and Europe. The word itself originally identified the region as "the land of the Philistines," a warlike tribe that inhabited much of the region alongside the Hebrew people. But the older name for Palestine was Canaan, the term most frequently used in the Old Testament. The Amarna letters of the 14th century B.C. referred to "the land of Canaan," applying the term to the coastal region inhabited by the Phoenicians. After the Israelites took the land from the Canaanites, the entire country became known as the "land of Israel" (1 Sam. 13:19; Matt. 2:20) and the "land of promise" (Heb. 11:9).

The term "Palestine" as a name for the entire land of Canaan, beyond the coastal plains of the Phoenicians, was first used by the 5th-century B.C. historian Herodotus. After the Jewish revolt of A.D. 135, the Romans replaced the Latin name Judea with the Latin *Palaestinaas*, their name for this province. Although the prophet Zechariah referred to this region as the "Holy Land" (Zech. 2:12), it was not until the Middle Ages that this land became popularly known as the Holy Land.

Location. The medieval concept that Palestine was the center of the earth (see Ezek. 5:5) is not as far-fetched as one might expect. This tiny strip of land not only unites the peoples and lands of Asia, Africa, and Europe but also the five seas known as the Mediterranean Sea, the Black Sea, the Caspian Sea, the Red Sea, and the Persian Gulf. Palestine was sandwiched in between two dominant cultures of the ancient world—Egypt to the south and Babylon-Assyria-Persia between the Tigris and Euphrates rivers to the northeast.

Palestine is also the focal point of the three great world religions: Judaism, Christianity, and Islam. It has been the land corridor for most of the world's armies and, according to the book of Revelation, will be the scene of the final great conflict of history, the Battle of Armageddon (Rev. 16:16).

The boundaries of Palestine were not clearly defined in ancient times—a problem that plagues the area even today. Generally, the Israelites occupied the land bordered on the south by the Wadi el-'Arish and Kadesh Barnea and on the north by the foothills of Mount Hermon. The Mediterranean Sea formed a natural western boundary and the Jordan River a natural eastern boundary, except that two and a half of the Israelite tribes occupied the region known as Transjordan, the land east of the Jordan River.

At certain times in Israel's history, the territory they occupied was much larger. During the days of the United Monarchy under David and Solomon, Israel controlled Hamath, Damascus, and the region beyond as far as the Euphrates River. They also held dominion over Ammon, Moab, and Edom, stretching the nation's borders from the mountains of Lebanon to the waters of the Red Sea.

The boundaries of the promised land defined in Numbers 34, as promised to Moses, were much more extensive than the region in which the Hebrews eventually settled. The southern boundary was placed at Kadesh Barnea and the northern boundary at "the entrance of Hamath" (Num. 34:8; Lebo Hamath, NIV), which may either be the entrance to the Biqa Valley between the Lebanon and Anti-Lebanon Mountains or farther north near modern Lebweh, some 23 kilometers (14 miles) north of historic Baalbek.

It is also clear that the land promised to Abraham and his descendants for an everlasting possession included an area similar to that seen by Moses and greater than that area actually inhabited by the Israelites. This covenant promise to Abraham is the basis for the modern Israeli claim to Palestine (Gen. 12:7; 28:4; 48:4).

Size. To the jet-age traveler Palestine seems quite small. The expression "from Dan to Beersheba" (1 Sam. 3:20) refers to a north-south distance of only about 240 kilometers (150 miles). The width of the region is even less impressive. In the north, from Acco on the coast to the Sea of Galilee is a distance of only 45 kilometers (28 miles). In the broader south, from Gaza on the coast to the Dead Sea is a distance of only 88 kilometers (54 miles). The distance between Jaffa and Jericho is only 72 kilometers (45 miles); Nazareth to Jerusalem is only 98 kilometers (60 miles).

The land area from Dan to Beersheba in Cisjordan (the region west of the Jordan River) is approximately 6,000 square miles—a region smaller than Hawaii. If the area east of the Jordan River (Transjordan) is included, the maximum total area of Palestine amounts to only 10,000 square miles—an area smaller than the state of Maryland.

People. The history of Palestine is complicated by the many different cultures and civilizations that have flourished in the region. The first historical reference to the inhabitants of Canaan occurs in Genesis 10. Canaan, the son of Ham and the grandson of Noah (Gen. 10:6; 5:32), is said to have fathered most of the inhabitants of the land. These include Sidon (the Phoenicians), Heth (the Hittites), and the Jebusites (who lived near Jerusalem), the Amorites (in the hill country), the Girgashites (unknown), the Hivites (peasants from the northern hills), the Arkites (from Arka in Phoenicia), the Sinites (from the northern coast of Lebanon), the Arvadites (from the island of Arvad), the Zemarites (from Simura), and the Hamathites (from Hamath; Gen. 10:15–18).

The native inhabitants of Canaan were tall, giant-like, and stalwart races known as the Anakim (Josh. 11:21–22), the Rephaim (Gen. 14:5), and the Horites (Deut. 2:12). They lived in the hill country, and traces of their primitive population continued as late as the days of the United Monarchy under David and Solomon (2 Sam. 21:16–22). When Abraham arrived in the promised land it was almost entirely inhabited by the Canaanites, with a mixture of Amorites, Edomites, Ammonites, and Moabites.

History. The history of Palestine gains its significance for the Bible student with the beginning of the biblical period. But the region was inhabited by other cultures long before Abraham and his family arrived.

Prebiblical Period (Tower of Babel — 2000 B.C.) — As the human race was scattered over the earth, a number of cultures emerged. Small city-states began to be organized in Mesopotamia, the land between the Tigris and Euphrates rivers. A Sumerian civilization (about 2800–2360 B.C.) was one of the earliest classical civilizations of the world. The Akkadians as well built their cities in the Tigris-Euphrates plain. Almost at the same time Egypt emerged as a unified nation. In the 29th century B.C. the kingdoms of Upper and Lower Egypt were united, and a world power was born. Palestine witnessed the same urban development and population increases during this period. The cities of Jericho, Megiddo, Beth Shan, Ai, Shechem, Gezer, Lachish, and others were all in existence at this time.

Old Testament Period (Abraham — 2000 B.C. and after) — About 2000 B.C. the patriarch Abraham arrived in Canaan from Ur of the Chaldees and found the land controlled by Amorites and Canaanites. Abraham lived for a while in Egypt, where he was exposed to this great culture of the ancient world. He saw the great pyramids of Egypt and eventually returned to Palestine, where the wealth and influence of his family and his descendants expanded through the land.

For 430 years the descendants of Abraham were in Egyptian bondage, but God raised up a champion in Moses to lead them back to the land of promise (Exodus 3). God strengthened the new leader of Israel, Joshua (Josh. 1:1–9), and he led the people in successful campaigns to win control of Palestine (Josh. 11:16–23). The period of the judges that followed indicated the continuous struggle that Israel had with the peoples of the land (Judg. 2:16–23).

With the rise of the United Monarchy under David (2 Sam. 8:1–18) and Solomon (1 Kin. 9:15–11:13), people of Israel extended their influence over more of Palestine than ever before. But about 920 B.C. Israel was divided into two segments, the northern kingdom of Israel, and the southern kingdom of Judah. These were turbulent times in the history of Israel. The Old Testament period came to an end with the fall of Samaria, the capital of Israel, in 722 B.C. The Assyrians took Israel into captivity and this nation ceased to exist (2 Kin. 17:1–6).

Babylonian Period (605–539 B.C.) — The influence of the Babylonians in the land of Palestine was swift and deadly. In 605 B.C. Nebuchadnezzar, king of Babylon, annihilated the Egyptian army, effectively controlling all of Palestine to the Egyptian border. In 597 B.C. Jerusalem was attacked by the Babylonians. Jehoiachin the king was carried into captivity. Eleven years later the city of Jerusalem was destroyed and nearly all the Jewish inhabitants of Palestine were carried away as captives to Babylon (2 Kin. 25:1–21).

Persian Period (539–332 B.C.) — When Cyrus, the king of Persia, conquered Babylon, he allowed the Jews to return to Jerusalem. In 538 B.C. the first group of Jews returned to Jerusalem under Sheshbazzar (Ezra 1:1–11). As a Persian province, the region was governed by regional rulers under Persian authority.

Greek Period (332–167 B.C.) — During this period Alexander the Great conquered Palestine. Upon his death the land fell to the Ptolemies of Egypt and the Seleucids of Syria. In 167 B.C. the Seleucid king Antiochus IV (Antiochus Epiphanes) polluted the Jewish temple by offering pigs on the altar and putting up a statue of a pagan god.

Maccabean Period (167–63 B.C.) — Under the leadership of the aged priest Mattathias and his sons, the Jewish people revolted against the Seleucids and enjoyed nearly 100 years of independence.

Roman Period (63 B.C.–A.D. 330) — In 63 B.C. Pompey conquered Palestine for Rome. From 37 B.C. until 4 B.C. Herod the Great ruled the land under the Caesars. During the reign of this Herod, Jesus was born in Bethlehem. During Roman rule also, Christianity was born. In A.D. 70 Jerusalem was destroyed by the Roman general Titus as he crushed a revolt by the Jewish people.

Pre-Modern Period (A.D. 330–1917) — During these years, Palestine was under the successive rules of the Byzantines (330–634), the Arabs (634–1099), the Crusaders (1099–1263), the Mamelukes (1263–1517), and the Turks (1517–1917).

The most important historical events during this period were Saladin's consolidation of his control of Egypt, Syria, Mesopotamia, and most of Palestine in A.D. 1187 by his victory over the crusader kingdom of Jerusalem and the establishment of the Turkish Ottoman Empire in A.D. 1517.

Modern Period (1917–Present) — In 1917 the Balfour Declaration liberated Palestine from Turkish rule and placed the land under the control of Great Britain. On May 14, 1948, the modern State of Israel was established, and the British withdrew. Almost immediately the Jews and Arabs began their struggle for control of the land of Palestine. The borders of Palestine have been in a state of flux ever since.

The Geography of Palestine. The geography of Palestine falls naturally into five regions: the coastal plain, the central highlands, the Rift Valley, the Transjordan plateau, and the Negev.

The coastal plain — The coastal lowlands run along the western border of Palestine at the Mediterranean Sea. The plain varies in width from less than 5 kilometers (3 miles) to more than 40 kilometers (25 miles), but it forms an almost straight line for more than 320 kilometers (200 miles) north to south.

At the famous Ladder of Tyre in Upper Galilee, the hills reach the coast and divide the Plain of Phoenicia from the Plain of Acco. The Plain of Acco is about 13 kilometers (8 miles) wide and 40 kilometers (25 miles) long. It was the region allotted to the tribe of Asher (Josh. 19:24–31). At the foot of Mount Carmel the coastal plain is only a few hundred feet wide, but it quickly widens into the Plain of Dor and, at the Crocodile River (the Wadi Zerqa), into the marshy Plain of Sharon. The Plain of Sharon is some 64–80 kilometers (40–50 miles) in length and 13–16 kilometers (8–10 miles) wide. A fertile region, it was once covered with oak forests. Through it flow five streams, including the river Kanah, which in ancient Israel divided the territories of Ephraim and Manasseh. South of the Plain of Sharon is the triangle known as the Philistine Plain where the five lords of the Philistines built their great cities: Ekron, Gath, Ashdod, Ashkelon, and Gaza (1 Sam. 6:17).

One problem with this coastal plain is that it did not have a natural harbor. Joppa was a precarious harbor formed by offshore reefs (2 Chr. 2:16; Acts 9:36). Caesarea was built by Herod the Great, who created an artificial harbor. This territory was of little value to the ancient Israelites, a fact that may have contributed to Philistine dominance of the coastal plains long after the Israelites conquered Canaan.

The central highlands — Between the coastal plain and the hill country of Judea and Samaria runs a series of foothills known as the Shephelah. These hills were the scene of many battles between the Philistines and the Israelites. It is divided by three valleys: the Valley of Aijalon on the north, the Valley of Sorek in the middle, and the Valley of Elah on the south. At Aijalon Joshua commanded the sun to stand still (Josh. 10:12–14). And in Elah young David killed the giant Goliath (1 Sam. 17:2, 19; 21:9).

The central highlands are a mountain range running north to south the length of Palestine. In Lebanon the range rises to over 2,740 meters (9,000 feet) above sea level at Mount Hermon. The highest peak in Palestine itself is Jebel Jermaq, 1,200 meters (3,960 feet), in Upper Galilee.

The highlands consist of several distinct regions. The northernmost region is Galilee, customarily divided into Upper and Lower Galilee. Upper Galilee is almost double the altitude of its lower counterpart with corresponding differences in climate and vegetation. Lower Galilee has outcrops of chalk and marl that give the region a rugged beauty. Even today it is populated with small villages, many of which are mentioned in the New Testament. To the east lies the Sea of Galilee, separated from Lower Galilee by a series of hills and valleys.

South of Galilee is the Plain of Jezreel or Esdraelon. This plain is actually a low plateau of the hill country stretching from Mount Carmel on the west to Mount Gilboa on the east. This was an important corridor between the Via Maris, one of the main roads through Palestine, and the road to Damascus to the north. Many notable battles have been fought here (Josh. 17:16; 2 Chr. 35:22). Here too will be fought the Battle of Armageddon (Rev. 16:16; 19:11–21).

South of the central highlands is the hill country of Ephraim. This broad limestone upland consists of fertile valleys, tree-laden hills, and north-south, east-west highways.

This easy access to Samaria explains this region's greater receptivity to foreign influences in religion and politics than that of Galilee to the north or Judea to the south. The highest of these Samaritan hills are Mount Ebal (940 meters; 3,084 feet) and Mount Gerizim (881 meters; 2,890 feet).

Unlike the broken terrain of Samaria, the Judean highlands present a solid barrier that practically shuts off east-to-west traffic. Judea is subdivided into the Shephelah, the central hills, and the eastern wilderness. The terrain of these three divisions reflects quite a contrast, just like the annual rainfall (16–32 inches in the foothills, 32 inches in the highlands, and 12 inches or less in the wilderness).

Most of the towns in this region are built on a series of hills, just as Jerusalem is. All the land to the south is "down," although the central highlands continue to climb until they reach the area of Hebron, Judea's highest town (927 meters; 3,040 feet). As one continues south in these highlands, however, the elevation begins to drop. Thus at Beersheba, a few miles south, the region becomes a triangular depression between the hills of Judea and the hills of the Negev.

The central highlands are the most important natural region in Palestine, boasting such towns as Nazareth, Shechem, Samaria, Bethel, Jerusalem, Bethlehem, Hebron, and Beersheba. This region is known as the heartland of Palestine.

The Rift Valley — Between the western hills of Israel and the plateau east of the Jordan River lies the world's deepest depression, known as the Rift Valley. Beginning in the valley between the Lebanon and Anti-Lebanon Mountains and running south through Palestine, through the Arabah, through the Gulf of Aqaba and the Red Sea and on south through eastern Africa, this is the deepest geological fault on earth. The contrast in elevation is striking. Mount Hermon is a majestic 2,814 meters (9,232 feet) above sea level, while the Sea of Galilee just below it is 212 meters (695 feet) below sea level. The name of the

Jordan River, which flows from the foothills of Hermon to the Sea of Galilee and then on south to the Dead Sea, means "the descender." In one 9-mile stretch the Jordan plunges 284 meters (850 feet). North of the Sea of Galilee the river drops an average of 12 meters (40 feet) per mile. The Jordan is unique in that it is the world's only major river that runs below sea level along most of its course.

The distance between the Sea of Galilee and the Dead Sea is approximately 105 kilometers (65 miles). In the Rift Valley, or the Jordan Valley, the river has carved a narrow channel called the Zor. A haven for wildlife, this appears as a snakelike path of green vegetation when viewed from the air.

In the southern extremity of the Rift Valley, between the Dead Sea and the Red Sea, is the Arabah. This valley, from 3 to 9 miles wide but 169 kilometers (105 miles) in length, features terrain varying from salt flats to badlands. It is watered only by the flowing of seasonal streams in the rainy season.

From the Gulf of Aqaba the floor of this valley rises to 230 meters (755 feet) on a steep ridge. From there it drops dramatically, over 152 meters (500 feet) in 2 miles, toward the Dead Sea.

The Transjordan plateau — The beautiful hills of the Transjordan tableland are cut by four rivers as they wind their way to the Rift Valley. They are the Yarmuk, Jabbok, Arnon, and Zered rivers. These rivers provide natural boundaries for five discernible regions of Transjordan.

North of the Yarmuk River is Bashan, a plateau rising from 213 meters (700 feet) in the west to 914 meters (3,000 feet) in the east. South of the Yarmuk to the Jabbok is Gilead. This is the most fertile region of Transjordan. The rainfall of 28 to 32 inches a year provides sufficient water for rich agricultural land and pasture land.

This is where the Greco-Roman cities of the region known as the Decapolis were located. Here, too, the famous "balm of Gilead" was found. South of the deep Jabbok gorge to the southern tip of the Dead Sea lay the kingdoms of Ammon and Moab. Located here were the capital of the Ammonite kingdom, Rabbah, and Mount Nebo (802 meters; 2,631 feet), the commanding site from which Moses viewed the promised land (Deut. 34:1). The Arnon River was the approximate border between Ammon and Moab, with the Zered River to the south serving as the border between Moab and Edom.

Edom stretches for a hundred miles above the Arabah. In the mountains of Edom the reddish sandstones may have given rise to the biblical name, which means "red." In a basin secluded in these mountains is Petra, the famous capital of the Nabatean kingdom. The conquest of Edom for a brief time during the days of David and Solomon enabled Solomon to build the port of Ezion Geber on the Red Sea (1 Kin. 9:26–28).

The Negev — Directly south of Palestine lies the Negev, a barren wilderness. Shaped like a triangle with its apex pointing toward the Gulf of Aqaba, the steppe of the Negev is situated immediately south of the Valley of Beersheba. It encompasses over 12,500 square miles, more than all of Palestine itself. The inhabitable sector of the area is a small strip about 49 kilometers (30 miles) wide from north to south, centered at Beersheba. The rest of the Negev is a desert.

Because of its long desert frontier, the Negev has been inhabited mostly by tribal herdsmen known as the Bedouin, including the Amalekites (Num. 13:29; 1 Sam. 30:1). In the Old Testament this area was known as the Wilderness of Zin and the Wilderness of Paran. Occasionally permanent settlements would be found here in the days of Abraham and especially in the days of the Nabatean kingdom.

The Negev is crisscrossed with caravan routes. The important route to Egypt, known as "the way of Shur" (Gen. 16:7), went southwest from Beersheba through this area.

Geological Formations. Palestine has a wide variety of geological formations for a small 10,000-square-mile area.

A band of Nubian or Petra sandstone, red and soft, stretches along the eastern coast of the Dead Sea. Above this band is the most important geological formation in Palestine, the limestone, which makes up most of the tableland on both sides of the Jordan River. This limestone is particularly evident at Jerusalem; reservoirs, sepulchers, and cellars abound under the city.

The Philistine country north of Mount Carmel consists of sandstone. Between this sandstone and the sand dunes of the seacoast is a sedimentary bed. Along both sides of the Rift Valley, from Mount Hermon to south of the Sea of Galilee, is volcanic rock, called basalt, frequently found in other parts of the land. Another notable feature of the region is the blowing sand from Egypt and the Sinai deserts, which frequently invades the cultivated sections of Palestine.

On the west shore of Galilee as well as along both shores of the Dead Sea are hot springs. At the hot springs of Callirrhoe on the eastern shore of the Dead Sea, Herod the Great sought relief from his illness. Earthquakes also played a vital role in Palestinian life. David interpreted an earthquake as a sign of the anger of the Lord (Ps. 18:7). Jonathan's attack at Michmash was accompanied by an earthquake (1 Sam. 14:15). A memorable quake occurred during the days of Uzziah in the 8th century B.C. (Amos 1:1; Zech. 14:5). An earthquake also accompanied the crucifixion of Jesus in Jerusalem (Matt. 27:51–54).

The presence of these phenomena—plus volcanic activity, basalt, sulphur, petroleum, salt, bromide, phosphate, potash, and other chemicals in and around the Dead Sea—make Palestine a geologist's paradise. It is indeed one of the unique regions of the world.

The Climate and Vegetation of Palestine. The latitude of Palestine is approximately the same as southern California or Georgia. It is therefore marginally subtropical. Situated between the cool winds of the eastern Mediterranean and the hot winds of the desert, Palestine has a variety of weather patterns.

Temperature — The sea breeze has a moderating effect on the coastal plain. The average temperature at Haifa in January is 56 degrees F. and in August 83 degrees. However, the elevation at Jerusalem (777 meters, or 2,550 feet, above sea level), brings cooler temperatures, a 48-degree average in January and a 75-degree average in August.

In contrast, the temperatures in the Rift Valley are much hotter throughout the year. This makes the region comfortably warm in winter but unbearably hot in summer. Jericho has an average winter temperature of 76 degrees F., but the temperature consistently climbs well over 100 in the summer. Such temperature extremes are noted in the Bible. The midday sun caused the death of a lad in Elisha's day (2 Kin. 4:18–20), but King Jehoiakim sat in his winter house with a fire on the hearth (Jer. 36:22).

Precipitation — Two seasons characterize Palestine: winter, which is moist, rainy, and mild (November to April), and summer, which is hot with no rain (May to October). The exact time when the rainy season begins each year is not predictable. It usually begins about mid-October and includes our winter months plus some additional weeks (Song 2:11). Rainfall usually occurs three to four days in a row, alternating with three to four days of chilling winds from the desert.

The Bible frequently refers to "the early rains and the latter rains" (Deut. 11:14). This designation does not indicate the period of greatest rainfall, which was frequently in January and February (Lev. 26:4; Ezra 10:9, 13), but the period of the most important rainfall for agriculture. The initial autumn rains soften the hard Palestinian soil, making plowing and sowing an easier task. The latter rains fall in March and April when rain is needed to make the fruit and grain luscious and healthy (Hos. 6:3; Zech. 10:1).

The greatest amount of precipitation falls on the region of Galilee (28–40 inches a year). Average rainfall for other areas of Palestine are: Haifa (24 inches); Tiberias (17 inches); Beth Shean (12 inches); Jerusalem (25 inches); and Jericho (4 inches or less). In the summer the humidity is twice as intense as during other times of the year. Thus Jericho, with high temperatures and humidity and little rainfall, is almost unbearable in summer. However, the summer humidity condenses as the ground cools during the night. The result is a heavy dew each morning in Palestine.

Gideon was able to collect a bowl of water from dew on a fleece (Judg. 6:38). Dew was essential for the growing of grapes during the summer (Zech. 8:12). Without dew a devastating drought would occur (2 Sam. 1:21; Hag. 1:10). Frequently God's grace is compared to the dew (Gen. 27:28; Hos. 14:5).

Occasionally Palestine would be the victim of violent precipitation in the form of hail. Such hail would flatten the standing grain and destroy the tender vines (Ps. 78:47; Ezek. 13:11, 13). Sometimes hailstones big enough to kill a man would fall (Josh. 10:11). Occasionally the higher elevations of Palestine are covered with a light snow during the winter. In David's time Benaiah slew a lion on a day when snow fell (2 Sam. 23:20).

Vegetation — In areas with adequate precipitation, the abundance of sunshine and fertile soil make Palestine a garden paradise. More than 3,000 varieties of flowering plants exist in the region—a large number for such a small country. So plentiful were flowers in Bible times that floral patterns adorned the branches of the golden lampstand (Ex. 25:31–34) and the walls and doors of the temple (1 Kin. 6:18, 29, 32). The rim of the huge laver in the temple was shaped like the flower of a lily (1 Kin. 7:26; 2 Chr. 4:5).

Trees grow in abundance in Palestine. Grains and other crops are also plentiful. The land also produces fruits and vegetables of all kinds, spices, herbs, aromatics, perfumes, and preservatives. Although it was the scene of many fierce and bloody battles, and yet will be, still Palestine is a special place: the Holy Land.

PARTHIANS [PAHR thih uhns] — a tribal group from Parthia, a region southeast of the Caspian Sea in ancient Persia (Iran). Parthians are mentioned in Acts 2:9 as one of the many national and language groups gathered in Jerusalem for the Feast of Pentecost.

Parthia was one of the original Persian administrative districts established by Darius I (Dan. 6:1). Late in the 4th century B.C., the Persian Empire fell to Alexander the Great and his successors, the Macedonian emperors known as the Seleucids. In the middle of the 3rd century B.C., the Parthians revolted from the Seleucids under the leadership of King Arsaces. The kings who followed Arsaces gradually built a great empire; it extended from the Euphrates River in Mesopotamia to the Indus River in (modern) Pakistan. Fierce warriors, the Parthians were formidable in battle; their archers fought while mounted on horseback. Even the Roman armies were largely unsuccessful against the Parthians.

The Babylonians settled some citizens of the nation of Judah in Parthia after their deportation from Judah in 586 B.C. (2 Chr. 36:20). The Jewish historian Josephus reported that some of the Jews who settled in Parthia continued to practice the Israelite faith, apparently without harassment from the natives. Thus the "Parthians" in Jerusalem on Pentecost (Acts 2:9) may have included remnants of these deported Jewish people as well as converts to Judaism from among native Parthians.

PERSEPOLIS [purr SEP oh liss] (Persian city) — the ceremonial capital of the Persian Empire under Darius the Great (522–486 B.C.), his son Xerxes (486–465 B.C.), and their successors. The city was second in importance to Shushan (or

Susa), the administrative capital. Persepolis was destroyed in 330 B.C. by Alexander the Great. Its ruins are situated about 49 kilometers (30 miles) northeast of the modern city of Shiraz in southwestern Iran. Although Persepolis is not mentioned in the Bible, it appears in 2 Maccabees (9:1–2).

PERSIA [PURR zyah] — an ancient world empire that flourished from 539–331 B.C. The Babylonian Empire fell to the Persians, setting the stage for the return of the Jews to Jerusalem in 538 B.C., following their long period of captivity by the Babylonians.

The Old Testament contains many references to the nation of Persia and its representatives. Ezra 9:9 refers to the "kings of Persia." Ezra 6:14 cites "Cyrus, Darius, and Artaxerxes king of Persia." Daniel 8:20 speaks of the "kings of Media and Persia." Daniel 10:13 mentions the "prince of the kingdom of Persia." The book of Esther refers to the "powers of Persia and Media" (1:3), the "seven princes of Persia and Media" (1:14), and the "ladies of Persia and Media" (1:18). Daniel 5:28 prophesied that Belshazzar's kingdom would be "given to the Medes and Persians."

The Persians apparently sprang from a people from the hills of Russia known as Indo-Aryans. As early as 2000 B.C., they began to settle in Iran and along the Black Sea coast. Two of these Indo-European tribes settled on the Elamite border and to the east of the Zagros mountain range. The first references to them are made in the inscriptions of Shalmaneser III (858–824 B.C.). They are noted as the Parsua (Persians) and Madai (Medes).

The first mention of a Persian chieftain refers to his role as an ally aligned against Sennacherib of Assyria. His son was called "King, Great King, King of the City of Anshan." His grandson fathered Cyrus II, also known as Cyrus the Great, who was one of the most celebrated kings of history. He is called by the prophet Isaiah "My shepherd" (Is. 44:28). In another passage he is referred to as "His [the Lord's] Anointed" (Is. 45:1), a term used in the Old Testament of the Messiah. He is the only pagan king to be so designated in the Old Testament.

Cyrus II, founder of the mighty Persian Empire, ascended the throne in Anshan in 559 B.C. He conquered the Median King Astyages. Then he defeated Lydia (about 546 B.C.) and Babylon (539 B.C.), finally establishing the Persian Empire. This last conquest is referred to in Daniel 5. Cyrus's rule was a result of the sovereignty of God. Cyrus was the Persian king who issued the decree restoring the Jews to their homeland, following their long period of captivity by the Babylonians (2 Chr. 36:22–23; Ezra 1:1–4).

Cyrus was the founder of the system under which each province, or satrapy, was governed by an official who answered to the great king. However, he allowed a remarkable degree of freedom of religion and customs for the vassal states, including Palestine. He developed roads, cities, postal systems, and legal codes, and treated the subject nations kindly and humanely. The Bible refers to Cyrus in favorable terms (Is. 44:28–45:3).

Cambyses II (530–522 B.C.), the son of Cyrus, reigned after his father. During his reign, Egypt was added to the list of nations conquered by Persia. According to the Greek historian Herodotus, Cambyses accidentally wounded himself with his own sword in 522 B.C.

The next Persian king, Darius I (521–486 B.C.), was not a direct descendant of Cyrus but was of royal, Achaemenid blood. He defeated 9 kings to claim all 23 Persian satrapies. This was recorded on the famous Behistun Inscription, which was written in the Akkadian, Elamite, and Old Persian languages.

Darius I further unified the Persian Empire by using an efficient gold coinage, state highways, and a more efficient postal system. He was defeated by the Greeks at the Battle of Marathon in 490 B.C. This is the same Darius who, in his second year, ordered the Jewish temple at Jerusalem to be rebuilt after work on it had been discontinued for 16 years (Ezra 4:24; 6:1). He also gave a generous subsidy that made it possible to complete the temple. The extent of the Persian Empire under Darius is reflected in Esther 1:1 and 10:1. The vast territory was nearly 4,900 kilometers (3,000 miles) long and 800–2,400 kilometers (500 to 1,500 miles) wide.

Xerxes ruled Persia from 486 to 465 B.C. He was the Ahasuerus of the book of Esther. Esther did not become queen until the seventh year of his reign, which would be about 479 B.C. This was shortly after his devastating defeat at Salamis (480 B.C.), which ended Persia's last hope for conquering Greece.

Another Persian king, Artaxerxes I Longimanus (464–424 B.C.), illustrates one of the ironies of history. This minor Persian king was of major importance because of his connection with the Jewish people. Apparently two of the three returns of the Jews from captivity in Babylon occurred during his reign.

The second return was under Ezra in 458 B.C. (Ezra 7:7). This was made possible because of the generosity of Artaxerxes. The third return occurred in 445 B.C. (Neh. 1:1).

Among the kingdoms of the ancient world, Persia is remembered because it built many important cities. Persepolis was a showpiece of Persian power. Pasargadae was the ancestral capital rapidly supplanted in importance. Ecbatana served as the capital of the Median Empire and became a resort area for the Persians. Susa (the Shushan of Esther) was the former capital of the Elamite Empire.

The religion of the Persians centered around a reformation of the old Iranian religions developed by Zoroaster. He believed in a dualism in which Ahura Mazda (or Ormazd) headed the gods of goodness (Amesha Spentas) and Angra Mainyu (or Ahriman) headed the gods of evil (daevas). Some of this is revealed in the Jewish apocryphal literature, which developed from the fifth century B.C. to the time of Christ.

PETRA [PET ruh] (*rock*) — the capital of Nabatea, situated about 275 kilometers (170 miles) southwest of modern Amman and about 80 kilometers (50 miles) south of the Dead Sea. Petra is not mentioned by name in the Bible, but many scholars believe it was the same place as Sela (Judg. 1:36; 2 Kin. 14:7).

Petra is one of the most spectacular archaeological ruins in the Near East and is a popular attraction on Holy Land tours. Most of the buildings and tombs of Petra are cut into the rose-red rock cliffs of the area.

Petra's ruins consist of about 750 monuments, most of them dating from the second half of the 1st century B.C. to the 2nd century after Christ. In A.D. 131 the Roman emperor Hadrian (ruled A.D. 117–138) visited the city and ordered construction to begin on the so-called treasury, which has been called "Petra's gem"—a temple to Isis.

Many ruins of Roman construction may be seen at Petra: a triumphal arch; an amphitheater; remains of baths, temples, tombs; and sections of a road. Above the city is the great high place, containing sacrificial altars hewn from the solid rock. Such open-air sanctuaries have thrown light on the high places mentioned in the Old Testament.

Petra is reached from the west by ascending the Wadi Musa and passing through a narrow, high-walled gorge, known as the Siq. Over a mile in length, this gorge provided Petra with excellent defense. The city is situated in a basin that is about 900 meters (3,000 feet) wide and about 1,600 meters (1 mile) long. The city is surrounded by massive sandstone cliffs of a dark red color.

PHARISEES [FARE uh sees] (*separated ones*) — a religious and political party in Palestine in New Testament times. The Pharisees were known for insisting that the law of God be observed as the scribes interpreted it and for their special commitment to keeping the laws of tithing and ritual purity.

The Pharisees had their roots in the group of faithful Jews known as the Hasidim (or Chasidim). The Hasidim arose in the 2nd century B.C. when the influence of Hellenism on the Jews was particularly strong and many Jews lived little differently than their Gentile neighbors. But the Hasidim insisted on strict observance of Jewish ritual laws.

When the Syrian king Antiochus IV tried to do away with the Jewish religion, the Hasidim took part in the revolt of the Maccabees against him. Apparently from this movement of faithful Hasidim came both the Essenes—who later broke off from other Jews and formed their own communities—and the Pharisees, who remained an active part of Jewish life. Indeed, during the period of independence that followed the revolt, some of the Greek rulers who controlled Palestine favored the Pharisaic party.

As a result of this favoritism, Pharisees came to be represented on the Sanhedrin, the supreme court and legislative body of the Jews. At times, the Pharisees even dominated the assembly. In New Testament times, Pharisees, though probably in the minority, were still an effective part of the Sanhedrin.

One distinctive feature of the Pharisees was their strong commitment to observing the law of God as it was interpreted and applied by the scribes. Although the priests had been responsible for teaching and interpreting the law (Lev. 10:8–11; Deut. 33:8–10) in Old Testament times, many people had lost all respect for the priests because of the corruption in the Jerusalem priesthood. They looked to the scribes instead to interpret the law for them. Some scribes were priests; many were not. Still, they lived pious, disciplined lives, and they had been trained to become experts in the law. It was natural, then, for people to follow their leading rather than that of the priests.

The way in which the Pharisees spelled out the meaning of the Mosaic law, the ways in which they adapted that law to suit the needs of their day, the time-honored customs they endorsed—all these became a part of the "tradition of the elders" (Mark 7:3). Although these traditions were not put into writing, they were passed on from one scribe to another and from the scribes to the people. From this tradition, they claimed, the Jewish people could know the way God's law should be observed. The Pharisees agreed, and they were known for supporting and keeping the "tradition of the elders."

The Pharisees also believed it was important to observe all the laws of God, which they taught were 613 in all. But they were especially known for their commitment to keep the laws of tithing and ritual purity.

According to the New Testament, the Pharisees were concerned about strictly interpreting and keeping the law on all matters (Acts 26:5), including the Sabbath (Mark 2:24), divorce (Mark 10:2), oaths (Matt. 23:16–22), the wearing of phylacteries and fringes (Matt. 23:5), and so on. But they showed special zeal in insisting that laws of tithing and ritual purity be kept (Matt. 23:23–26; Mark 7:1–13; Luke 11:37–42; 18:12).

Since Pharisees found that other Jews were not careful enough about keeping those laws, they felt it was necessary to place limits on their contacts with other Jews as well as with Gentiles. For example, they could not eat in the home of a non-Pharisee, since they could not be sure that the food had been properly tithed and kept ritually pure.

Unlike the Sadducees, the Pharisees did believe in the resurrection of the dead. On this point, they were on common ground with the early Christians (Acts 23:6–9). The scribe in Mark 12:28 who thought that Jesus had answered the Sadducees well concerning the resurrection was probably a Pharisee.

The Pharisees and their scribes enjoyed a good deal of popular support. In one way this is surprising, since the Pharisees kept apart from other Jews. They always seemed to be ready to criticize others for not keeping the laws, and they often looked down on "sinners" who showed no interest in God's law (Mark 2:16; Luke 7:39; 15:2; 18:11).

Still, unlike the Sadducees, who were mostly rich landowners and powerful priests, many Pharisees were ordinary people. And even though other Jews could not be bothered with observing all the details of the law, they respected the Pharisees for making the effort. Even Paul credited unbelieving Jews with having a "zeal for God" (Rom. 10:2)—even though it was misguided. He probably was thinking primarily of the Pharisees when he wrote these words.

In the New Testament, the Pharisees appear frequently in the accounts of Jesus' ministry and the history of the early church. In these passages a number of the typical failings of the Pharisees are evident. Of course, not all Pharisees failed in all these points—and the same failings can be found among religious people of any age.

Pharisees observed the law carefully as far as appearances went, but their hearts were far from God. Their motives were wrong because they wanted human praise (Matt. 6:2, 5, 16; 23:5–7). They also had evil desires that were hidden by their pious show (Matt. 23:25–28). That is why Pharisees are often called hypocrites: their hearts did not match their outward appearance.

The Pharisees thought they could match God's standards by keeping all the outward rules. Luke 18:9 says they "trusted in themselves that they were righteous." This can easily happen when people think God's will is the same thing as their list of what they can and cannot do. Their desire to keep all of God's laws was commendable, but sometimes they put the emphasis on the wrong places. Minor details became a major preoccupation, and they forgot the more important things (Matt. 23:23).

Finally, because Pharisees thought they were doing their best to keep God's laws while others were not, they often looked down on such "sinners"—especially people like tax collectors and prostitutes. Religious people need to remember that they, too, are sinners in God's eyes, and that Christ died for everyone.

PHILISTIA [fih LIS tih uh] — the land of the Philistines, as used in the poetry of the book of Psalms (60:8; 108:9). This land lay between Joppa and Gaza on the coastal plain of Palestine.

PHILISTINES [fih LIS teens] — an aggressive nation that occupied part of southwest Palestine from about 1200 to 600 B.C. The name Philistine was used first among the Egyptians to describe the sea people defeated by Rameses III in a naval battle about 1188 B.C. Among the Assyrians the group was known as Pilisti or Palastu. The Hebrew word *pelishti* is the basis of the name Palestine, a later name for Canaan, the country occupied by God's Covenant People.

Little is known about the origins of the Philistines except what is contained in the Bible—that they came from Caphtor (Gen. 10:14), generally identified with the island of Crete in the Mediterranean Sea. Crete also was supposed to be the home of the Cherethites, who were sometimes associated with the Philistines (Ezek. 25:16). Philistine territory was considered Cherethite in 1 Samuel 30:14, suggesting that both peoples were part of the invading group defeated earlier by Rameses III of Egypt.

Liberal scholars have assumed that references to the Philistines during Abraham's time are incorrect historically and that the Philistine occupation actually occurred in the 12th century B.C. More careful examination indicates there were two Philistine settlements in Canaan, one early and another later.

Both these settlements were marked by significant cultural differences.

The Philistines of Gerar, with whom Abraham dealt (Genesis 20–21), evidently were a colony of the early settlement located southeast of Gaza in southern Canaan. This colony was situated outside the area occupied by the five Philistine cities after 1188 B.C. Gerar was also a separate city-state governed by a king who bore the name or title of Abimelech.

That Abimelech's colony was the chief one in the area seems probable from his title, "king of the Philistines" (Gen. 26:1, 8). This is different from a later period when the Philistines were governed by five lords. Unlike the later Philistines who were Israel's chief foes in the settlement and monarchy periods, the Gerar Philistines were peaceful. They encouraged the friendship of Abraham and Isaac. Finally, Gerar was not included among the chief cities of Philistia (Josh. 13:3). It was not mentioned as one of the places conquered by the Israelites. It is best, therefore, to regard the Genesis traditions as genuine historical records.

The early Philistine settlements in Canaan took on a new appearance when five cities—Ashkelon, Ashdod, Ekron, Gath, and Gaza—and the areas around them were occupied by the Philistines in the 12th century B.C. Probably all of these except Ekron were already in existence when the sea peoples conquered them. These five Philistine cities formed a united political unit. Archaeological discoveries in the area have illustrated how they expanded to the south and east. Broken bits of Philistine pottery were found at archaeological sites in those areas.

The Philistines possessed superior weapons of iron when they began to attack the Israelites in the 11th century B.C. The tribe of Dan moved northward to escape these Philistine attacks, and Judah also came under increasing pressure (Judges 14–18). In Samuel's time the Philistines captured the ark of the covenant in battle. Although the ark was recovered later, the

Philistines continued to occupy Israelite settlements (1 Sam. 10:5).

The threat of the Philistines prompted Israel's demands for a king. But even under Saul the united nation was still menaced by the Philistines—a threat that ultimately resulted in Saul's death (1 Samuel 31). David's slaying of Goliath, a giant from Gath, was a key factor in his rise to fame. By this time the Philistines had moved deep into Israelite territory. Archaeological evidence shows they had occupied Tell Beit Mirsim, Beth Zur, Gibeah, Megiddo, and Beth Shean. Yet by the end of David's reign their power had begun to decline significantly. By the time Jehoshaphat was made king of Judah (873–848 B.C.), the Philistines were paying tribute (2 Chr. 17:11), although they tried to become independent under Jehoshaphat's son, Jehoram (2 Chr. 21:16–17).

When the Assyrians began to raid Palestine in later years, the Philistines faced additional opposition. The Assyrian Adad-Nirari III (about 810–783 B.C.) placed the Philistine cities under heavy tribute early in his reign, while Uzziah of Judah (791–740 B.C.) demolished the defenses of several Philistine strongholds, including Gath. When he became king, Ahaz of Judah (732–715 B.C.) was attacked by Philistine forces, and cities in the Negev and the Judean lowlands were occupied. The Assyrian king Tiglath-Pileser III responded by conquering the chief Philistine cities.

In 713 B.C. Sargon II, king of Assyria, invaded Philistia and conquered Ashdod. The following year he launched another campaign against other Philistine cities. Hezekiah of Judah (716–686 B.C.) attacked Gaza (2 Kin. 18:8), supported by the people of Ekron and Ashkelon, but in 701 B.C. Sennacherib brought Philistine territory under his control to prevent any Egyptian interference. When Nebuchadnezzar came to power in Babylon, the Philistines formed an alliance with Egypt, but when the Jews were exiled to Babylonia between 597 and 586 B.C., the Philistines, too, were deported.

No Philistine literature has survived, making it difficult to reconstruct their religious beliefs or rituals. Old Testament records indicate they worshiped three gods, Ashtoreth, Dagon, and Baal-Zebub—each of which had shrines in various cities (Judg. 16:23; 1 Sam. 5:1–7; 2 Kin. 1:2). Philistine soldiers apparently carried images of their gods into battle, perhaps as standards (2 Sam. 5:21). Like other Near Eastern peoples, the Philistines were superstitious. They respected the power of Israel's ark of the covenant (1 Sam. 5:1–12).

As depicted on Egyptian reliefs, Philistine soldiers wore short tunics, were clean-shaven, had crested or decorated helmets, carried round shields, and fought with spears and swords.

In the days before David's reign, the Philistine cities were governed by a representative from each city. These authorities exercised complete power in both peace and war. This centralized control made the Philistines strong, in contrast to the loosely organized Israelites.

The Philistines were important culturally because they adopted the manufacture and distribution of iron implements and weapons from the Hittites. Goliath's equipment was obviously of Philistine manufacture. The golden objects that were offered to Israel's God (1 Sam. 6:4–5) show that the Philistines were skilled goldsmiths as well.

The remains of Philistine furnaces have been uncovered at Tell Jemmeh and Ashdod. The area around Ashdod has produced some examples of typical Philistine pottery. This pottery reflected Greek as well as Egyptian and Canaanite styles.

The Philistines loved beer. Large beer mugs decorated with red and black geometric designs were some of their important pottery products, along with large cups, beakers, and bowls. Some Philistine burial places discovered at Tell Far'ah reveal bodies encased in clay coffins shaped to match the human body. The coffin lid was decorated with crude figures of the head and clasped arms of the deceased.

PHOENICIA [foe KNEE shih uh] — the land north of Palestine on the eastern shore of the Mediterranean Sea, between the Litani and Arvad rivers. Phoenicia is a Greek word that means "land of purple." The area was famous from early times for its purple dyes, produced from shellfish. In the KJV, Phoenicia is spelled Phenicia.

Phoenicia was a long, narrow country on the seacoast covering much of the territory that today is called Lebanon and southern Latakia (coastal Syria). Like Israel, much of it is mountainous, with only a narrow coastal plain. The low hills and plain are very fertile. Phoenicia was famous in biblical times for its lush plant life, which included fruit, flowers, and trees (Hos. 14:5–7). "They shall be revived like grain, and grow like the vine. Their scent shall be like the wine of Lebanon" (v. 7).

The cedars of Phoenicia were cut and shipped as far away as Egypt and eastern Mesopotamia, because most other nations in this part of the world had very few trees suitable for timber. Many direct land and sea routes connected Phoenicia to northern Israel. The Phoenicians had many contacts with the Israelites. During their long history, the Hebrew people often fell into paganism and idolatry because of the influence of Phoenician religion.

PHOENICIANS [foe KNEE shih uns] — inhabitants of Phoenicia, the ancient nation along the Mediterranean Sea north of Palestine. The Phoenicians were known for their trade and commerce and their skill as a seafaring people. There were three major reasons why Phoenicia became a major trading power.

First, the Phoenicians lived on a narrow strip of coastland. Thus hemmed in, they took to the sea in order to expand their economy, eventually becoming one of the most distinguished seafaring peoples in history.

Second, the mountains that approach the Phoenician coast made travel by land unusually difficult; travel by sea was the logical alternative.

Finally, the plentiful supply of pine, cypress, and cedar trees in Phoenicia made shipbuilding an ideal pursuit for the Phoenician people. The men of Byblos were noted shipbuilders (Ezek. 27:9), and the people of the Phoenician city of Sidon were experts at felling trees (1 Kin. 5:6).

Phoenicia's two major ports, Tyre and Sidon, were semi-independent city-states. Besides these two, several other Phoenician cities grew in influence as the merchant fleets brought wealth into the country. By its "golden age" (about 1050–850 B.C.) the Phoenicians achieved their height of prosperity and influence. Phoenicia founded many colonies along shipping routes, so that Phoenicians lived in Crete, Cyprus, Sardinia, Sicily, North Africa (especially the important colony of Carthage), and even Spain.

In the course of their travels, Phoenician merchants developed many skills that had a lasting influence on world culture. They are usually given credit for originating the alphabet and for pioneering the skills of glass making and the dyeing of cloth. Scholars believe Solomon's temple and many of its furnishings were based on a Phoenician design.

Some archaeologists believe that the Phoenicians were extremely skilled in working with gold, iron, and copper, and that they were skilled jewelers. Also, Phoenician designs possibly inspired much of Greek, Assyrian, and Etruscan architecture.

As the Assyrians began to dominate the ancient world in the 8th century B.C., Phoenicia's influence declined. Phoenicia was progressively weakened in wars with Assyria during the 7th century B.C. In 585 B.C. the Babylonians, who had conquered Assyria only two decades earlier, laid siege to Tyre—the last remaining independent Phoenician city.

After 13 years of siege (585–572 B.C.), the mainland city of Tyre was captured. There was also an island city of Tyre, which did not fall until 332 B.C. when Alexander the Great built a causeway over half a mile long in order to reach it. Alexander destroyed the city, but Tyre was later rebuilt. The city was an important outpost in the Greek and Roman period.

Like its neighbor Israel, Phoenicia finally ceased to be an independent nation. It was dominated in turn by the Persians, Greeks, Seleucids, and Romans.

Phoenician Religion. Phoenician gods were male and female representations of nature. Their primary god was called Baal. He combined the attributes of several other Phoenician deities, including Hadad, the storm god; Shamash, the sun god; and Resheph, god of the earth and the netherworld. The Phoenician goddess honored as the "great mother" was called Ashtoreth. Additionally, Eshmun, the god of healing, was especially honored in Sidon.

Connections with the Old Testament. When David completed the conquest of the promised land and made Israel the strongest power in the area, the Phoenicians under Hiram of Tyre (981–947 B.C.) became involved commercially with the Israelites (2 Sam. 5:11). The Phoenicians of Tyre helped supply materials and laborers for the building of Solomon's temple (1 Kin. 5:1–12). In later years, Solomon bought Hiram's help by transferring ownership of large tracts of real estate in Galilee from Israel to Tyre (1 Kin. 9:11).

The Phoenicians also helped the Israelites in Solomon's kingdom to learn the shipping trade and to construct a merchant fleet that brought wealth to Israel (1 Kin. 9:26–28). Regrettably, Solomon fell under the influence of foreign religions later in his life.

These problems included worship of the Phoenician idol Ashtoreth, the supreme goddess of the Sidonians (1 Kin. 11:1–8). His turning from the Lord to the beliefs of people such as the

Phoenicians resulted in the division of the nation—an act of judgment by God (1 Kin. 11:9–13).

Phoenician religious influence in Israel was given a dramatic boost by King Ahab, who married the Phoenician princess Jezebel, the daughter of the king of the Sidonians. Ahab gave Jezebel the freedom to put prophets of Baal on the government payroll in Israel (1 Kin. 18:19) and to try to convert the nation to idolatry.

Although the Bible mentions Phoenicia rarely, it often refers to the major Phoenician cities of Tyre and Sidon. Isaiah (23:1–18), Jeremiah (25:22; 47:4), Ezekiel (26:2–28:23), and other Old Testament prophets predicted the judgment of God on Tyre and Sidon. This judgment came in large measure when the Babylonians captured these cities along with the rest of Phoenicia in the early 6th century B.C.

Connections with the New Testament. Phoenicians were among those who came to hear Jesus teach about the kingdom of God (Luke 6:17). After the death of Stephen, some Christians escaped persecution by going to Phoenicia, where they preached the gospel (Acts 11:19). The apostle Paul traveled through Phoenicia on more than one occasion (Acts 15:3; 21:2–3).

PLAGUES OF EGYPT — the series of ten afflictions used by God to break the will of Pharaoh and to bring about the release of the Hebrew people from slavery in Egypt.

After the Hebrews had been in Egypt for about 400 years, "there arose a new king over Egypt, who did not know Joseph" (Ex. 1:8). This new king enslaved the Hebrews and forced them to labor in his extensive building projects, "You shall no longer give the people straw to make brick. Let them go and gather straw" (Ex. 5:7–19). When the Hebrews cried out for deliverance, God sent Moses to lead them from bondage. The pharaoh resisted the release of the Hebrew people. The plagues of Egypt occurred as God's action to change the mind of the pharaoh, thus bringing the Hebrews' freedom.

Scholars generally agree that the first 9 plagues were regular, natural occurrences in Egypt. They were remarkable only in their intensity and in the timing with which they happened. But this does not mean that they were purely natural phenomena. They were miraculous in that God used natural forces to achieve His purpose. A sovereign God can use whatever methods He chooses to bring about a miracle. The method does not diminish the miraculous nature of the occurrence.

The 10th plague, the death of the firstborn of Egypt, was altogether supernatural. There is no known natural phenomenon closely related to this highly selective plague.

The sequence of the plagues has been studied and compared with the observations of travelers to Egypt. Many scholars point out that the first 9 plagues are logical consequences of an unusually high flooding of the Nile River. Such flooding usually occurred in July, August, and September. Based on the best estimates that can be made from the biblical account, the plagues probably occurred over a period of about 7 to 9 months, beginning in July or August and continuing until around April or May.

The plagues may be viewed as God's intervention to seek the release of the Hebrew people. They also represented God's challenge to the Egyptian religious system. To the Egyptians, the Nile River was a god. From it came the power and life of the Egyptian culture. They worshiped the Nile and the abundance of resources that it provided. Since the first 9 plagues seem to be a natural progression of God's attack on the Nile River, all of these plagues relate to God's challenge to the Egyptian religious system.

Following are the 10 plagues, as recorded in Exodus 7:14–12:30:

1. *The Water of the Nile Turned into Blood* (Ex. 7:14–25). This first plague probably was the pollution of the Nile River

by large quantities of fine, red earth, brought down from the Sudan and Ethiopia by abnormal flooding. The pollution of the water provided a favorable environment for the growth of microorganisms and parasitic bacteria. Their presence could have led to the death of the fish in the river (Ex. 7:21).

In addition to depriving Egypt of water and fish—an important part of their diet—the plague also had a religious effect. The Nile River, god of the Egyptians, had been confronted by the power of the Redeemer God of the Hebrew people.

2. *Frogs Cover the Land* (Ex. 8:1–15). Seven days after the first plague, frogs came out of the river and infested the land. The frogs would have been driven from the Nile and its canals and pools by the polluted water. When Moses prayed to God, the frogs died in the houses, courtyards, and fields. The frogs were symbols of the Egyptian goddess Heqt, who was supposed to help women in childbirth. This plague was another demonstration of the superior power of God over the gods of Egypt.

3. *Lice Throughout the Land* (Ex. 8:16–19). Insects of various kinds are common in Egypt. It is not easy to identify the exact pests involved in the third plague. Various translations have lice (KJV, NKJV), gnats (NASB, NRSV, NIV), and maggots (REB).

4. *Swarms of Flies* (Ex. 8:20–32). Many kinds of flies are common in Egypt. The mounds of decaying frogs would have provided an ideal breeding ground for these pests. Some scholars suggest that the swarms mentioned here were a species known as the stable fly, a blood feeder that bites people as well as cattle. This fly is a carrier of skin anthrax, which is probably the disease brought on by the 6th plague.

5. *Pestilence of Livestock* (Ex. 9:1–7). Either the frogs or the insects may have been the carriers of this infection. The livestock of the Israelites were miraculously protected (Ex. 9:6–7). This was the second time God had made a distinction between the Israelites and the Egyptians in the plagues He sent (Ex. 8:22–23).

6. *Boils on Man and Beast* (Ex. 9:8–12). This infection was probably skin anthrax, carried by the flies of the 4th plague. The festering boils broke into blisters and running sores.

7. *Heavy Hail, with Thunder and Lightning* (Ex. 9:13–35). Egypt was essentially an agricultural country. By destroying the crops, this plague and the next struck at the heart of Egypt's economy. Moses' warning gave the Egyptians a chance to save their remaining livestock, and some acted upon it (Ex. 9:19–20). The severe storm caused great destruction (Ex. 9:24–25). The flax and barley were ruined, but not the wheat because it had not yet been planted (Ex. 9:31–32). This would suggest early February as the time of this plague. Again the Israelites received special protection. There was no hail in the land of Goshen, where the Hebrews lived (Ex. 9:26).

8. *Swarms of Locusts* (Ex. 10:1–20). The destruction from the previous plague was fresh in the minds of Pharaoh's advisors (Ex. 10:7). The 8th plague must have followed the hail very closely. Heavy rainfall in July–September would have produced conditions favorable for locusts in March. These locusts, swarms of foliage-eating grasshoppers, probably were driven into the Egyptian delta by strong winds. They wiped out the vegetation that had survived the earlier destruction. Again, as after the 7th plague, Pharaoh confessed "I have sinned" (Ex. 10:16). But again, after the plague was withdrawn, Pharaoh hardened his heart and would not let the people of Israel go (Ex. 10:20).

9. *Three Days of Darkness* (Ex. 10:21–29). This darkness could have been caused by a severe dust storm. For 3 days darkness covered the land (Ex. 10:23). This storm would have been intensified by fine earth deposited over the land by previous flooding. This plague probably occurred in March. Again, the Israelites were spared the effects (Ex. 10:23). By showing God's power over the light of the sun—represented by one of

Egypt's chief deities, the sun-god Ra—this plague was a further judgment on the idolatry of the Egyptians.

10. *Death of Egyptian Firstborn* (Ex. 11:1–12:30). The 10th plague was the most devastating of all—the death of the first-born males in Egyptian families. The Hebrews were spared because they followed God's command to sprinkle the blood of a lamb on the doorposts of their houses. The death angel "passed over" the houses where the blood was sprinkled—hence, the name Passover for this religious observance among the Jewish people. Only a supernatural explanation can account for the selective slaughter of the 10th plague.

Some people might wonder if such a massive slaughter was really necessary. But Pharaoh had been given ample warning (Ex. 4:23). He had seen many demonstrations of God's real-ity and power, and yet he had refused to acknowledge Him. Although Pharaoh wavered at times and promised to release the Israelites (Ex. 8:8, 28; 9:28), once the danger passed he changed his mind (Ex. 8:15, 32; 9:34–35). Because he rejected the power of God, Pharaoh was forced to face one final, terrible manifes-tation of God's power. The deliverance of the Hebrews from slavery in Egypt was one of the most memorable occasions in Hebrew history. The Passover Feast was observed annually as a celebration of God's deliverance of His people from bondage.

PLANTS OF THE BIBLE — The land that God promised to Abraham and his descendants was extremely fertile. Because of its diverse climate, the world of the Bible contained many varieties of plants. Botanists have identified 3,500 species of plant life in Palestine and Syria. Plants or plant products are mentioned in almost every book of the Bible.

The flora of the Bible have been the subject of much discus-sion and research. Accurately identifying many of these plants has taken many years of scientific research. The Bible writers were not botanists, and they seldom bothered to describe or identify the plants they mentioned.

In the 16th century Levinus Lemmens wrote the first book on the plants of Scripture. It was not until the middle of the 18th century, however, that a botanist traveled to Palestine for firsthand knowledge of its vegetation. Since then much valuable information has been learned about the plants of the Bible.

Many of the Bible writers often used general terms to refer to plants. Sometimes a reference is no more specific than "tree," "grass," or "grain." Even if an individual grain such as "corn" or "wheat" is named, it is referring to all grains in general.

Although many types of flowers grow in Palestine and other Bible lands, very few are mentioned by name in the Bible. Some of the flowers found in the Holy Land are irises, roses, anemones, lilies, tulips, hyacinths, and narcissus.

Some of the other general terms referring to plant life include bush, herb, grass, cockle, fruit, and verdure.

The Hebrew people were certain that God provided the promised land for their use, but they were not careful to take good care of it. The land was cultivated continuously for thousands of years without rest until much of the soil was depleted and many areas became devastated wastelands. The great forests of Lebanon and Hermon were eventually destroyed and the soil was eroded. The people of that time did not know how to manage their environment intelligently. Eventually the land that once flowed with "milk and honey" became barren of much of its vegetation. Today many of these barren regions of the Holy Land are being turned again into fertile farmland. Effort is being made to restore the richness of the land as God intended it to be.

The following specific plants are mentioned in the Bible. This listing is keyed to the NKJV.

Acacia. A large thorny tree with rough gnarled bark. The orange-brown wood was hard grained, and it repelled insects.

It bore long locust-like pods with seeds inside and produced round, fragrant clusters of yellow blossoms. Many species of acacia grew in the desert of Sinai, in southern Canaan, and in Egypt.

Acacia wood was used to build the ark of the covenant and the first tabernacle (Ex. 36:20; 37:1). The acacia is called shittim and shittah in the KJV (Ex. 25:5, 10; Is. 41:19).

Algum, Almug. A large leguminous tree native to India and Ceylon. While its identity is uncertain, many consider it to be the red sandalwood. Its blossoms were pea-like, and its wood was close grained, dark outside, and red inside. It was highly scented, making it resistant to insects. Most authorities believe that algum and almug are two names for the same wood.

Solomon ordered the algum wood from Ophir and Lebanon (1 Kin. 10:11–12; 2 Chr. 9:10–11). The wood was well suited for making musical instruments, cabinet work, and pillars for the temple.

Almond. A large tree resembling the peach tree in both size and fruit. The almond was chiefly valued for the nuts it produced, which were used for making oil used in the home and as medicine. The Hebrew word for almond means "awakening," an allusion to the almond blossom, which is first to bloom in the spring. The almond's pinkish-white blossoms always appear before its leaves.

The almond played an important role in the history of Israel. Jacob included almond nuts in his gifts to Joseph in Egypt (Gen. 43:11). The decorations on the lampstands were modeled after the almond blossom (Ex. 25:33), and Aaron's rod was an almond twig (Num. 17:8). The almond also symbolized the dependability of God (Jer. 1:11–12). Many scholars think the hazel of Genesis 30:37 (KJV) is the almond tree.

Aloes. Two plants, one a tree and the other a flower.

1. The aloes mentioned in Psalm 45:8; Proverbs 7:17; and Song of Solomon 4:14 came from a large tree known as "eaglewood,"

a plant native to India. The wood of the aloe tree is fragrant and highly valued for perfume and incense. Many authorities believe the lign aloe to be the same tree (Num. 24:6, KJV).

2. The aloes brought by Nicodemus to wrap the body of Jesus (John 19:39) were probably the true aloes of the lily family. The aloin derived from the pulp of the aloe leaf was an expensive product used in embalming.

Amaranth. A large family of plants that includes weeds and garden plants. Goodspeed translates the amaranth, also called the "rolling thing," of Isaiah 7:13 as the tumbleweed. It is also called the "resurrection plant" and the "rose of Jericho." The Greek word for amaranth means "unfading." This meaning is used symbolically in 1 Peter 1:4 and 5:4, where the inheritance of the faithful is described as unfading. Thus, the amaranth became a symbol of immortality.

Anise. An annual herb that bears yellow flowers and fragrant seeds. The anise mentioned in the Bible is generally thought to be dill. Anise (dill) was used as medicine and for cooking. Jesus used the anise as an illustration when He scolded the Pharisees for keeping part of the law in detail while ignoring the rest (Matt. 23:23; also Deut. 14:22).

Apple. A tree that grows about 9 meters (30 feet) high and has rough bark and pink blossoms. Many authorities believe the apple of Scripture actually is the apricot, a native of Armenia. Other authorities suggest the quince, peach, citron, orange, or some other fruit; some believe it was in fact the apple.

The apple was described as sweet and fragrant (Song 7:8, REB), golden (Prov. 25:11), and suitable for shade (Song 2:3). This fruit was used figuratively to show how precious we are to God, and how extremely sensitive He is to our needs. The phrase "apple of (the Lord's) eye" (Deut. 32:10; Ps. 17:8; Zech. 2:8) refers to the pupil of the eye, which is its most precious part.

Balsam. A thorny tree growing 3 to 5 meters (10–15 feet) tall with clusters of green flowers, also known as the Jericho balsam. Some think the lentisk or mastic tree, a shrubby evergreen growing 1 to 3 meters (3–10 feet) tall, is meant.

Balsam was highly valued during Bible times (Gen. 37:25; 43:11; Jer. 8:22; 46:11; 51:8; Ezek. 27:17). It produced a fragrant, resinous gum called balm.

This was an article of export (Gen. 37:25) and was given as a gift by Jacob (Gen. 43:11). Balm was used as a symbol in Jeremiah 8:22 to refer to spiritual healing.

Barley. A grain known since early times. It was well adapted to varied climates, ripening quickly and resistant to heat; it usually was harvested before wheat. Because barley was considered a food for slaves and the very poor, however, it was held in low esteem as a grain.

In the Bible barley was first associated with Egypt (Ex. 9:31). It was used as an offering of jealousy (Num. 5:15), for fodder (1 Kin. 4:28), and for food (Judg. 7:13; John 6:5, 13).

Bay Tree. The laurel, a tree native to Canaan. The laurel grew to heights of 12 to 18 meters (40–60 feet) and produced small greenish-white flowers and black berries. Parts of the tree were used in medicine, while its leaves were used as seasoning. The Hebrew word means "a tree in its native soil"; this was a fitting way for David to describe the natural prosperity of the wicked (Ps. 37:35, KJV; native green tree, NKJV).

Bean. A hardy plant about 1 meter (3 feet) tall with pea-shaped fragrant blooms, large pods, and black or brown beans, which were eaten alone or cooked with meat. Beans have always been an important part of the Hebrew diet, especially among the poor, and they have been known since ancient times. When beans were threshed and cleaned, they were often mixed with grains for bread (Ezek. 4:9).

Box Tree. A tree of very hard wood and glossy leaves, which grew to a height of about 6 meters (20 feet). A native of northern Canaan and the Lebanon mountains, the box tree was well suited to beautify the temple (Is. 60:13). The box tree was used since Roman times for wood engravings and musical instruments. Isaiah symbolically used the box tree, along with other trees, to remind Israel of God's perpetual presence (Is. 41:17–20).

Some scholars have suggested that the box tree of Scripture may instead be the cypress or plane.

Broom. A dense, twiggy bush, almost leafless, which grew to about 3.6 meters (12 feet). It has small, white blooms. Common in the desert regions of Palestine, Arabia, and Egypt, it was used as charcoal (Ps. 120:4) and provided shade for the prophet Elijah (1 Kin. 19:4–5). The roots that Job ate were not from the broom, which was not edible, but may have been an edible parasite that infested the bush (Job 30:4). The broom is sometimes referred to as juniper in the NKJV, KJV, and NASB. Many scholars believe this to be the shrub or heath referred to in Jeremiah 17:6 and 48:6.

Calamus. A fragrant, reed-like grass growing along streams and river banks (Song 4:14), also referred to as sweet cane (Is. 43:24; Jer. 6:20). Calamus leaves are fragrant and ginger-flavored when crushed. It is named with other aromatic substances (Ezek. 27:19) and as one ingredient for the anointing oil (Ex. 30:23). It is believed to be a plant native to India (Jer. 6:20).

Caperberry. A plant with large, white, berry-producing flowers, which grows in clefts of rocks and on walls. Only the REB and NASB refer to the caper. Other versions translate the Hebrew word as "desire" (Eccl. 12:5).

Cassia. A plant with a flavor and aroma similar to cinnamon, but considered inferior. Some believe it could be the Indian perfume called orris. Moses included cassia in the anointing oil (Ex. 30:24). It was also an article of trade (Ezek. 27:19).

Cedar. An evergreen tree that sometimes grows more than 30 meters (100 feet) tall with a trunk circumference of 12 to 15 meters (40–50 feet). It grows in western Asia, the Himalayas, and Cyprus as well as Lebanon.

The cedar's fragrant wood was rot resistant and knot free, making it ideal for building purposes (2 Sam. 5:11; 1 Kin. 6:9), shipbuilding (Ezek. 27:5), and fashioning idols (Is. 44:14). The reference to cedar in Leviticus 14:4 and Numbers 19:6 is generally understood to be the juniper, which grew in the Sinai.

Chestnut. A tree of Syria and Lebanon thought by many scholars to be the plane tree. It grew to a height of about 21 to 27 meters (70–90 feet) and had a massive trunk. This tree is translated "chestnut" in the NKJV and KJV, but is translated "plane" by the NRSV, NIV, REB, and NASB.

Cinnamon. A member of the laurel family, the cinnamon tree grew to be more than 9 meters (30 feet) tall with white flowers and wide-spreading branches. A native of Ceylon, the cinnamon tree produced bark and oil that was used for the anointing oil (Ex. 30:23) and as perfume (Prov. 7:17; Rev. 18:13).

Citron. A fragrant wood from the sandarac tree. Citron is sometimes referred to as "sweet" or "scented" wood. The sandarac tree grew to a height of no more than about 9 meters (30 feet) tall. Citron is translated as "thyine" by the KJV (Rev. 18:12).

Coriander. An annual herb, growing from one-half to 1 meter (2 to 3 feet) tall, which produced grayish seeds used to flavor foods, for confections, and in medicine. The dried leaves of coriander were also used to flavor foods.

Cucumber. A climbing vine that produces vegetables. The cucumber was one of the vegetables the Israelites longed for after leaving Egypt (Num. 11:5).

Cummin. An annual seed-producing herb with pinkish-white blooms. Cummin is native to the eastern Mediterranean lands. When harvested, cummin was threshed with sticks (Is. 28:25, 27), a method still used today. Cummin was used to flavor foods and in medicine. It was subject to the tithe (Matt. 23:23).

The NKJV also mentions black cummin, which is translated dill (RSV, NEB, NASB), caraway (NIV), fitches (KJV), and holm tree (NRSV).

Cypress. A tall evergreen tree of hard and durable wood. Cypress wood was suitable for building, and was used to fashion idols (Is. 44:14). The word rendered "gopherwood" by the NKJV, KJV, RSV, and NASB in Genesis 6:14 is thought to be cypress. This was the wood that Noah used to build the ark. The word for cypress is also rendered as camel-thorn (Is. 55:13) and ilex (Is. 44:14) by the REB.

Dove Droppings/Dove's Dung. A bulbous plant which was edible after being boiled or roasted. Dove's dung was mentioned as food eaten during the siege of Samaria (2 Kin. 6:25). Some believe this was excrement from pigeons and doves, while others interpret it as an edible plant (seed pods, NIV; locust-beans, REB).

Ebony. A large tree that produces edible fruit. The hard, black wood from the inner portion of the tree is quite valuable and is used for fine furniture. It is also known to have been inlaid with ivory. Idols were sometimes carved from ebony.

Fig. A fruit-producing plant that could be either a tall tree or a low-spreading shrub. The size of the tree depended on its location and soil. The blooms of the fig tree always appear before the leaves in spring. When Jesus saw leaves on a fig tree, He expected the fruit (Mark 11:12–14, 20–21). There were usually two crops of figs a year.

Figs were eaten fresh (2 Kin. 18:31), pressed into cakes (1 Sam. 25:18), and used as a poultice (Is. 38:21). Jeremiah used the fig tree as a symbol of desolation (Jer. 8:13). It also signified security and hope for Adam and Eve (Gen. 3:7), the 12 spies (Num. 13:23), and the poets and prophets. Sycamore figs were similar to the fig but were smaller and of poorer quality (Amos 7:14). They were eaten by poor people who could not afford the better variety.

Fir. An evergreen tree of uncertain identity. Although this tree is mentioned several times in Scripture, biblical authorities question whether this was the true fir or some other evergreen of Palestine. Many suggest the Aleppo pine would fit this description, while others think the cypress, juniper, or cedar could be meant.

The Israelites valued the timber of the fir tree for building the temple (1 Kin. 6:15, KJV), for shipbuilding (Ezek. 27:5), and for making musical instruments (2 Sam. 6:5). The fir is used symbolically to describe the blessings of God for His people (Is. 41:19; 55:13, KJV).

Fitches. Two different plants mentioned in the KJV:

1. An annual herb one-half meter (1 to 2 feet) tall with finely cut leaves and blue flowers, which produces black poppy seeds used in curries and sprinkled on breads. It is translated black cummin in the NKJV (Is. 28:25, 27).

2. A plant mislabeled by the KJV in Ezekiel 4:9. The correct identification is spelt.

Flax. A plant growing 1 meter (3 feet) tall with pale blue flowers, and used for making linen. When mature, the entire flax plant was pulled and placed in water to separate the fibers from the stems. It was then laid on housetops to dry (Josh. 2:6), and later woven into linen. Twisted flax was also used as wicks for lamps in Bible times (Is. 42:3).

Frankincense. An aromatic gum resin obtained from the Boswellia tree. These trees are large with small, white, star-shaped flowers and leaves resembling the mountain ash. The gum is obtained by cutting into the bark and collecting the resin from the tree. When this substance hardens, it is gathered and used as incense.

Frankincense was part of the sacred anointing oil (Ex. 30:34). It was used in sacrificial offering (Lev. 2:1), as a fumigant during animal sacrifices (Ex. 30:7), and as perfume (Song 3:6). It was a gift to the baby Jesus (Matt. 2:11).

The trees are native to India, Arabia, and Africa. Palestine probably obtained this product through foreign trade. "The dromedaries of Midian and Ephah; all those from Sheba shall come" (Is. 60:6).

Galbanum. The gum from an herb that grew 1 to 1 and one-half meters (3 to 5 feet) high and had greenish-white flowers. Galbanum was the milky substance extracted from the stems that quickly hardened. It was used in perfume and anointing oil (Ex. 30:34).

Gall. A bitter, poisonous herb. This may have been the poppy or some other wild poisonous plant. Gall is used figuratively to mean a bitter punishment (Jer. 8:14; 9:15; 23:15) or any bitter experience (Acts 8:23). Gall and vinegar were offered to Jesus on the cross (Matt. 27:34), but He refused the drink.

Garlic. A strong-flavored herb, resembling the onion. Garlic was eaten with bread and used to flavor food and is still highly favored today. Garlic was highly esteemed in Egypt and was believed to have been used as wages for the workers who built the pyramids. The Hebrews yearned for garlic after leaving Egypt (Num. 1:5).

Gourd. A fast-growing shrub that grew to a height of 3 to 4 meters (10–12 feet). One of Elisha's servants put the fruit of the gourd into a pot of stew (2 Kin. 4:39).

The gourd (Jon. 4:6–10, KJV, REB; vine, NIV) is identified as the plant under which Jonah found shade. Some biblical scholars suggest this may have been pumpkin, squash, or ivy.

Many types of wild gourds also flourished in the Mediterranean region. Some of these were poisonous. The decorations used on the temple called ornamental buds (1 Kin. 6:18; 7:24) are thought to be a type of wild gourd.

Grapes. A luscious fruit cultivated on vines. Large clusters of grapes weighing about 5 kilograms (12 pounds) each (Num. 13:23) have been reported in Palestine.

Grapes were used in a variety of ways. They were eaten fresh or dried and were made into wine or vinegar. Dried grapes were called raisins. The first suggestion of grapes in Scripture was in connection with Noah's vineyard (Gen. 9:20).

The soil and climate of Palestine was well suited for vineyards, where grapes were grown. They were cultivated here long before the Israelites occupied the land (Gen. 14:18). The vineyards of Palestine produced immense clusters of grapes (Num. 13:20, 23–24).

Vineyards were hedged or fenced as protection from wild animals (Song 2:15). In each vineyard a tower was erected and a guard placed to protect the vines from robbers (Matt. 21:33).

Vinedressers were hired to care for the vines and prune them yearly (Lev. 25:3; Is. 61:5). The grapes were gathered in baskets in September and October with much festivity (Judg. 9:27; Is. 16:10). Provision was made for the poor to glean the fields (Lev. 19:10; Deut. 24:21). The choicest grapes were dried or eaten fresh and the rest were placed in presses to extract the juice (Is. 61:5; Hos. 9:2–4). This was drunk fresh or fermented.

Jesus alluded to His relationship with His followers by referring to Himself as the vine and to them as the branches (John 15:5). The fruit of the vine symbolized Jesus' shed blood (Matt. 26:27–29). He also used the vineyard in many of His parables (Matt. 9:17; 20:1–6; 21:28–32; Luke 13:6–9).

Hemlock. A poisonous plant that grows to about 2 meters (5 feet) tall and has small white flowers. Hemlock is referred to only once in the NKJV (Hos. 10:4). Other translations use the more general term "weeds."

Henna. A plant used to produce a valuable orange-red dye. It was 2 to 3 meters (7 to 10 feet) tall and bore fragrant white flowers. Solomon compared his beloved to a cluster of henna (Song 1:14; 4:13; camphire, KJV).

Hyssop. A species of marjoram and a member of the mint family. Hyssop was an aromatic shrub under 1 meter (3 feet) tall with clusters of yellow flowers. It grew in rocky crevices and was cultivated on terraced walls. "From the cedar tree of Lebanon even to the hyssop that springs out of the wall" (1 Kin. 4:33). Bunches of hyssop were used to sprinkle blood on the doorposts in Egypt (Ex. 12:22), and in purification ceremonies (Lev. 14:4, 6, 51–52). David mentioned it as an instrument of inner cleansing (Ps. 51:7). It was used at the crucifixion to relieve Jesus' thirst (John 19:29).

Leek. A bulbous vegetable resembling the onion that grows 15 centimeters (about 6 inches) high. The stems and bulbs of leeks were eaten raw and used to flavor foods. Named with garlic and onions, the leek was a food the Hebrew people ate in Egypt (Num. 11:5).

Lentil. A small annual plant with white, violet-striped flowers. The seeds of lentils grew in pods similar to the pea. During Bible times lentil was threshed like wheat and boiled into a reddish-brown pottage. This was the dish Esau purchased with his birthright (Gen. 25:34). Lentils could also be used as an ingredient for bread (Ezek. 4:9).

Lily. A flower with white or rosy-purple blooms measuring up to 30 centimeters (12 inches) across. Many scholars think the lily is sometimes a term applied to flowers in general. Others believe specific types such as the Turks Cap, the Madonna, or the lotus is referred to.

The lily was used as an ornament for the temple (1 Kin. 7:22). The Beloved and the Shulammite used lilies to describe their love (Song 2:1, 16; 4:5; 5:13; 6:3).

Locust. An evergreen tree growing about 6 to 9 meters (20–30 feet) tall and having small, glossy leaves. A native of Syria and Palestine, it bears long pods known as carob or locust beans (Luke 15:16; husks, KJV). These may have been used for food in dire circumstances (2 Kin. 6:25; locust beans, REB).

Mallow. A shrub growing 1 and one-half to 3 meters (5 to 10 feet) high and having thick, succulent leaves and small, purple flowers. The Hebrew word for mallow means "salt plant." It thrived in dry, salty regions especially around the Dead Sea. Although the leaves were sour and had little nutritive value, they were boiled and eaten by the poor in dire circumstances.

Mentioned only once in the Bible (Job 30:4), mallow is also translated as salt herbs in the NIV and saltwort in the REB.

Mandrake. A fruit-producing plant with dark green leaves and small, bluish-purple flowers. The mandrake grew abundantly throughout Palestine and the Mediterranean region.

The yellow fruit of the mandrake was small, sweet tasting, and fragrant. It had narcotic qualities and may have been used medicinally. The fruit of the mandrake was also referred to as the "love apple." It was considered a love potion (Gen. 30:16).

Melon. A type of gourd that bears sweet fruit. Both cantaloupes and watermelons may have grown along the banks of the Nile River in Egypt. Melons were used as food and medicine. An intoxicating drink was made from their juice.

The Hebrews had become accustomed to eating melons and other tasty foods in Egypt. They looked back on these fondly while in the wilderness (Num. 1:5; watermelon, REB).

Millet. An annual grain-producing grass that was under 1 meter (3 feet) high and produced many seeds. The seeds of millet were smaller than other cereal grains. Millet has been known since ancient times in Palestine and Egypt. It was used for bread (Ezek. 4:9) and eaten raw, especially by the poor.

Millet is referred to in several different ways in Ezekiel 27:17 (pannag, KJV; confections, NIV; meal, REB; cakes, NASB).

Mint. A sweet-smelling herb that grew to a height of 1 meter (3 feet) and produced spikes of lilac flowers. Mint was used in medicine and to flavor foods.

Mulberry. A tree that grew to a height of about 8 to 10 meters (25–30 feet) and produced red berries. A refreshing drink was prepared from the fruit. Jesus used the mulberry tree as an illustration when teaching about faith (Luke 17:6). It is called sycamine in the KJV and NRSV, and mulberry in the REB. The mulberry trees mentioned in 2 Samuel 5:23–24 and 1 Chronicles 14:14–15 are believed to be a species of poplar.

Mustard. A plant that grew wild along roadsides and in fields, reaching a height of about 4.6 meters (15 feet). The black mustard of Palestine seems to be the species to which Jesus referred (Matt. 13:31–32; Mark 4:31–32; Luke 13:19). It was culti-vated for its seeds, which were used as a condiment and for oil.

The mustard seed was the smallest seed known in Jesus' day (Matt. 13:32). Nevertheless, Jesus said that if one has faith like a mustard seed, he can move mountains (Matt. 17:20) or trans-plant a mulberry tree in the sea (Luke 17:6).

Myrrh. An extract from a stiff-branched tree with white flowers and plum-like fruit. After myrrh was extracted from the wood, it soon hardened and was valued as an article of trade. It was an ingredient used in anointing oil (Ex. 30:23), and was used as perfume (Ps. 45:8; Prov. 7:17; Song 3:6), in purification rites for women (Esth. 2:12), as a gift for the infant Jesus (Matt. 2:11), and in embalming (John 19:39). According to the Gospel of Mark (15:23), the drink offered to Jesus before His crucifixion was "wine mingled with myrrh."

The reference to myrrh in Genesis 37:25 and 43:11 is thought to be ladanum, sometimes called onycha, from a species of rockrose and not the true myrrh.

Myrtle. An evergreen tree with dark, glossy leaves and white flowers. The leaves, flowers, and berries of the myrtle were used for perfume and as seasoning for food. The myrtle tree had a religious significance for the Jews (Zech. 1:8–11) and was a sym-bol of peace and joy. Queen Esther's Hebrew name, Hadassah (Esth. 2:7), meant "myrtle."

Nettle. Two different plants referred to in the Bible:

1. The nettles mentioned in Isaiah 34:13 and Hosea 9:6 are believed to be the true nettle. It is a spiny-leaf plant sometimes growing to a height of about 2 meters (6 feet).

2. The nettles referred to in Job 30:7 and Proverbs 24:31 are considered by some to be the acanthus, a stinging plant common in Palestine.

The nettles of Zephaniah 2:9 (KJV) are translated weeds by the NKJV.

Oak. A large tree with a massive trunk that grew abundantly in Palestine and the surrounding countries. Many Hebrew words refer to the oak. Some scholars think these words could have referred to any large tree such as the terebinth or elm.

The oak tree was an important historical landmark to the Hebrews. Some specific oak trees are mentioned in the Bible. These include the oaks of Bashan (Is. 2:13; Zech. 11:2), the oak of Bethel (Gen. 35:8, KJV; terebinth tree, NKJV), and the oaks of Mamre (Gen. 13:18, NRSV; terebinth trees, NKJV).

Oak wood was also used in shipbuilding (Ezek. 27:6), and for fashioning idols (Is. 44:14).

Oil Tree. A tree of uncertain identity. Many oil-producing trees mentioned in the Bible could be identified as the oil tree. Many authorities believe the oleaster or wild olive is the tree meant. It grew to a height of about 4.5 to 6 meters (15–20 feet) and produced small, bitter fruit resembling an olive. The oleaster yielded an inferior oil that was used medicinally.

The oil tree of Isaiah 41:19 is translated "the olive" in the NRSV, NIV; "wild olive," REB; and "the olive tree" in NASB.

Olive. A fruit-bearing tree about 6 meters (20 feet) tall with a gnarled, twisted trunk, white flowers, and berries that ripen to a black color. The olive tree grew slowly and continued to bear fruit after reaching a great age. Before it died, new branches sprouted from its roots.

The fruit was harvested by beating the boughs of the olive tree with a stick (Deut. 24:20), or by shaking the tree (Is. 17:6). The ripe fruit was enjoyed fresh, and the green fruit was often pickled or made into a relish.

The best oil was obtained from the green olive fruit. It was used as fuel for lamps (Ex. 27:20), as anointing oil (Lev. 2:1), as an article of commerce (1 Kin. 5:11), and for dressing wounds (Luke 10:34).

Olive trees were cultivated in groves or orchards (Ex. 23:11; Josh. 24:13). The most famous olive garden mentioned in the Bible is Gethsemane, meaning "oil press" (Matt. 26:36).

Onion. A plant with a large, edible bulb. The onion was one of the foods the Hebrews longed for in the wilderness (Num. 11:5). The onion was known in Egypt from ancient times and is pictured on the walls of Egyptian tombs.

Onycha. A dark brown gum resin obtained from the stem and leaves of a species of the rockrose, also known as ladanum. Onycha was used as an ingredient in the holy anointing oil (Ex. 30:34). It was highly valued for its fragrance and medicinal qualities.

The rockrose was a bush growing to a height of about 1 meter (3 feet) and having large, white flowers measuring 8 centimeters (3 inches) across. Some scholars believe the substance referred to as myrrh in Genesis 37:25 and 43:11 was onycha.

Palm. A tree that grew to a height of about 18 to 30 meters (60–100 feet) and had long, feathery leaves (branches, Neh. 8:15; John 12:13; Rev. 7:9). These branches were about 2 to 3 meters (6 to 8 feet) long and grew from the top of the trunk. Also called the date palm, this tree lives to be 100 to 200 years old.

Palm branches were considered a symbol of victory (John 12:13; Rev. 7:9). Many places in the Bible were identified by the abundance of palm trees (Ex. 15:27; Deut. 34:3; Judg. 1:16).

One of the Hebrew words for palm, *tamar,* was often used as a woman's name (Gen. 38:6; 2 Sam. 13:1).

Pine. An evergreen tree of uncertain identity. Biblical scholars believe pine refers to either the Brutian or the Aleppo pine (Is. 41:19; 60:13). The Brutian pine grew to a height of about 9 to 11 meters (30–35 feet). It is smaller and has longer needles than the Aleppo pine, which grew to a height of about 27 meters (90 feet). Both trees grew in Lebanon and in Palestine.

Bible scholars are not agreed on the identity of the many evergreens mentioned in the Bible. Other trees suggested for these references are the ash, fir, cypress, cedar, or juniper.

Pistachio Nut. A product of the pistacia tree, which was about 9 meters (30 feet) tall with wide, spreading branches. The pistachio nut is about 2.5 centimeters (1 inch) long and has a thin, hard outer shell. The smooth husk or skin that shields the green kernel is red. These nuts were sweet and considered a luxury. Jacob included them in the gifts sent to Egypt. "Take some of the best fruits of the land in your vessels and carry down a present for the man" (Gen. 43:11).

Pomegranate. A round, sweet fruit about 10 centimeters (4 inches) across with a hard rind. It is green when young and turns red when ripe. There are numerous edible seeds inside the pomegranate.

The pomegranate tree has been cultivated in Palestine and Egypt since ancient times (Num. 13:23; Deut. 8:8). It grew as a bush or small tree, sometimes reaching a height of about 9 meters (30 feet) with small, lance-shaped leaves. The blossoms were bright red. The fruit usually ripened in August or September.

The hem of Aaron's robe was decorated with blue, purple, and red pomegranates (Ex. 28:33–34; 39:24–26). It was listed among the pleasant fruits of Egypt (Num. 20:5). Solomon decorated the temple with the likeness of the pomegranate (1 Kin. 7:18, 20). A spiced wine was made from the juice (Song 8:2).

Poplar. A tree that grew to a height of about 9 to 18 meters (30–60 feet) and had wide, spreading branches. The leaves were green with white undersides. Jacob stripped the bark from poplar branches to reveal the white wood. This was supposed to control the color of his cattle. "Now Jacob ... exposed the white which was in the rods" (Gen. 30:37).

Hosea refers to the Israelites worshiping idols in the shade of poplar trees. This brought God's condemnation for their sin (Hos. 4:13).

Reed/Rush. Gigantic hollow-stemmed grasses that grew along riverbanks and in moist areas of Egypt and Palestine. Many different Hebrew words refer to the marsh plants of the Bible. They form a large order of plants, such as flax, flags, bulrush, cane, calamus, and papyrus.

Reeds and rushes grew anywhere from 1 to 6 meters (3–20 feet) high and had long, narrow leaves. A cluster of white flowers formed at the top of each stem.

The reeds were used in various ways, including walking sticks, fishing poles, musical instruments, and pens. People also used them for weaving baskets, mats, and for other domestic purposes. Moses' basket was woven from reeds. Papyrus, a particular reed, was used to make paper.

Reeds were a symbol of weakness (Is. 36:6). Jesus refers to them as shaking in the wind (Matt. 11:7). A reed was placed in Jesus' hand as He was mocked by the Roman soldiers (Matt. 27:29).

Rose. The name of two different plants:

1. Most authorities think that the rose referred to in Song of Solomon 2:1 and Isaiah 35:1 is not what we know as the rose today, but a low-growing bulbous plant producing from 2 to 4 yellow flowers on each stalk. This flower is noted for its fragrance. Other scholars have suggested the mountain tulip, anemone, saffron, or crocus as the flower in question. All of these flowers grew wild in Palestine. This particular flower is translated crocus by the NRSV, NIV, and NASB (Is. 35:1) and asphodel by the REB (Song 2:1; Is. 35:2). The flower we call the "Rose of Sharon" is a native of China and is not the one mentioned by Solomon (Song 2:1).

2. The rose of Ecclesiasticus 24:14; 39:13 (REB) is thought to be the oleander. This shrub grows to a height of about 3.6 meters (12 feet) and has pink or white flowers.

Rue. A garden herb growing one-half to 1 meter (2 to 3 feet) high with gray-green foliage and clusters of small, yellow flowers. Rue had a strong odor. It was valued for its antiseptic and disinfectant qualities. It was also used to flavor foods.

Saffron. The product of many varieties of crocus, a flower that grew from a bulb and produced light-blue flowers.

Crocus blooms were gathered, dried, and pressed into cakes of saffron. Saffron was used as a coloring for curries and stews. It was also used as a perfume for the floors of theaters and for weddings. Solomon was the only Bible writer to refer to saffron (Song 4:14).

Spelt. An inferior kind of wheat. Although the bread made from this grain was of a poorer quality than that made from wheat, spelt was preferred over barley by many in the ancient world. The KJV translates this word as rye in Exodus 9:32 and Isaiah 28:25, and as fitches in Ezekiel 4:9. Spelt was sown later than wheat. It thrived in poor soil and under adverse conditions.

Spikenard. A costly oil derived from the dried roots and stems of the nard, an herb of Asia. This oil was used as a liquid or made into an ointment. Solomon praised the fragrance of spikenard (Song 1:12; 4:13–14).

Spikenard was imported from India in alabaster boxes. These were stored and used only for special occasions. When household guests arrived, they were usually anointed with this oil. Jesus was anointed on two occasions as an honored guest (Mark 14:3; John 12:3).

Many spikes grew from a single nard root that produced clusters of pink flowers. The stems were covered with hair, giving them a woolly appearance. Some translations of the Bible refer to spikenard as nard.

Stacte. A resin believed to be an extract of the stems and branches of the storax tree. Stacte was highly prized as perfume and as incense. It was one of the ingredients of anointing oil (Ex. 30:34).

The storax was a small, stiff shrub growing to a height of about 3 to 6 meters (10–20 feet), which grew abundantly in Lebanon and throughout Palestine. Its leaves were dark with grayish-white undersides. In spring the storax flowered profusely with highly fragrant white blooms that resembled the orange blossom.

Straw. The dried stalks of various grains such as spelt, barley, millet, or many kinds of wheat. Straw could also include stalks of wild grasses. Straw was mixed with grain and used as fodder (Gen. 24:25; Judg. 19:19; 1 Kin. 4:28). The Egyptians mixed straw with clay for stronger bricks (Ex. 5:7).

Sycamore. A huge evergreen tree growing to a height of about 12 to 15 meters (40–50 feet) with a trunk circumference of over 6.5 meters (20 feet). The trunk forked near the ground, and the branches grew outward.

The leaves of the sycamore, sometimes called the sycamore fig, were heart-shaped, resembling mulberry leaves. The fruit was similar to the true fig but was inferior in quality (Amos 7:14). These yellow figs grew in clusters close to the branches.

Sycamores were trees of the plains (1 Kin. 10:27) and could not tolerate colder climates (Ps. 78:47). The sycamore was the tree Zacchaeus climbed to gain a better view of Jesus (Luke 19:4).

Tamarisk. A small tree with thick foliage and spikes of pink blooms. It provided ample shade for desert travelers (1 Sam. 22:6). The word for tamarisk is translated tree, grove, or oak by the KJV.

Tares. A poisonous grass resembling wheat, but with smaller seeds. The tares were usually left in the fields until harvest time, then separated from the wheat during winnowing. Jesus used tares growing with wheat as a parable to illustrate evil in the world (Matt. 13:25–30, 36–40). Tares is translated weeds in the NRSV and NIV, and darnel in the REB.

Terebinth. A large, spreading tree that grew to a height of about 6 to 8 meters (20–26 feet) with reddish-green leaves and red berries in clusters. The terebinth is mentioned several times in the Bible. It is sometimes translated as teil (Is. 6:13), elm (Hos. 4:13), or oak (Gen. 35:4) by the KJV.

Thistles/Thorns. General terms for any spiny plant. Such plants are characteristic of arid and desert regions. Some of these were brambles, briers, thorny bushes, small trees, weeds, and prickly herbs. They grew abundantly in Palestine and other Bible lands.

The most noted use of thorns in the Bible was the crown of thorns placed on the head of Jesus on the cross. "When they had twisted a crown of thorns, they put it on His head" (Matt. 27:29).

Some of the thorns and thistles were annuals, scattering their seed in autumn. The industrious farmer would destroy the plants before he seeded (Matt. 13:7). Many of them were used as fuel for ovens (Ps. 58:9; Eccl. 7:6; Is. 33:12).

Thorny shrubs were used as hedges to guard fields and vineyards (Prov. 15:19; Mark 12:1). The prophet Micah declared that even the most upright person is "sharper [more destructive] than a thorn hedge" (Mic. 7:4).

Wheat. The most important cereal grass mentioned in the Bible. It was cultivated in Bible lands from early times, "Now Reuben went in the days of wheat harvest" (Gen. 30:14). Egyptian wheat was the many-eared variety called "mummy wheat." This was the wheat of Pharaoh's dream (Gen. 41:5–57). It was also depicted on Egyptian monuments.

Wheat was sown after barley in November or December. It was usually broadcast and then either plowed or trodden into the soil by oxen or other animals (Is. 32:20). This grain was used for bread (Ex. 29:32), and was also eaten parched (Lev. 23:14; Ruth 2:14). It was used in ceremonial offerings (Lev. 2:1; 24:5–7) and as an article of commerce (Ezek. 27:17; Acts 27:38).

When corn is mentioned in the Bible, it refers to wheat, as corn was not known in Bible times (Ps. 72:16; Matt. 12:1; Mark 4:28). Jesus compared His death to a grain of wheat that must die to produce fruit (John 12:24).

Willow. A tree that grew to about 9 to 12 meters (30–40 feet) and had reddish-brown bark; narrow, pointed leaves; and flowers or catkins that hung downward. Willow branches were used to construct the booths for the Feast of Tabernacles (Lev. 23:40). The Jews hung their harps on willows while in Babylon.

Some biblical scholars think the willow mentioned in the Bible was actually the poplar or Euphrates aspen. The word for willow is consistently translated as poplar by the NIV. In Isaiah 44:4 it is translated willow by the REB and poplar by the NASB.

Wormwood. A woody shrub covered with small, green leaves, with greenish-yellow flowers growing in clusters. Wormwood grows in the desert regions of Palestine and Syria. This plant is mentioned many times in the Bible. It had a bitter taste and a strong aroma (Jer. 9:15).

Wormwood was used symbolically to refer to any calamity or bitter experience (Deut. 29:18; Prov. 5:4; Amos 5:7; Rev. 8:10–11). An intoxicating drink could also be made from this plant (Lam. 3:15). Wormwood is sometimes translated as bitter weeds or hemlock (Amos 6:12, KJV).

PRAETORIUM, PRAETORIAN GUARD — a special group of Roman soldiers in New Testament times, established to guard the emperor of the Roman Empire. Originally, they were restricted to the city of Rome, but later they were sent to the Roman provinces as well. This guard was an elite corps of soldiers whose salaries, privileges, and terms of service were better than the other soldiers of the Roman Empire.

In the NKJV, Praetorium is mentioned with reference to a place (Matt. 27:27; Mark 15:16; John 18:28, 33; 19:9). The implication from the Gospels is that the Praetorium was part of Herod's palace or the governor's residence in Jerusalem. Paul, when he was in prison in Caesarea, was "kept in Herod's Praetorium" (Acts 23:35).

Philippians 1:13 refers to the "imperial guard" (NRSV) or to the "whole palace guard" (NKJV). Commentators are not sure whether this reference is limited to the guard or whether it may refer to the imperial high court as well.

The Praetorium guard was discontinued in the 3rd century A.D. because they had become too powerful, threatening the authority of the Roman emperor himself.

PREPARATION DAY — the day immediately before the Sabbath and other Jewish festivals. Preparation Day always fell on Friday among the Jewish people, because all religious festivals began on the Sabbath, or Saturday (Matt. 27:62; John 19:14, 31).

With a week of holidays ahead, the Preparation Day for the Passover was especially busy. The details for preparing the Passover supper had to be completed by afternoon. Preparations included baking the unleavened bread, gathering festive garments to wear for the occasion, and taking a ceremonial bath.

But above all, the paschal lamb had to be slain. Slaughtering began an hour or more earlier than for the usual daily evening sacrifice. At the temple, the priests slaughtered thousands of lambs brought in by the people. Their blood was poured at the foot of the altar. Then the lambs were roasted whole in preparation for the Passover meal in each home that evening.

PURIM [**POOR im**] (*lots*) — a Jewish holiday observed on the 14th and 15th of the month of Adar, a month before Passover, in commemoration of the deliverance of the Jews, by Esther and Mordecai, from a massacre plotted by Haman (Esth. 3:7; 9:24–32).

R

RAMESES, RAAMSES [RAM uh seez, RAM seez] (*the god Ra has fathered a son*) — the royal city of the Egyptian kings of the 19th and 20th dynasties (about 1300–1100 B.C.) situated in the northeastern section of the Nile delta. While the people of Israel were slaves in Egypt, they were forced to work on at least two of Pharaoh's vast construction projects—building the supply cities of Pithom and Raamses (Ex. 1:11, KJV, NASB, NKJV; Rameses, NIV, NRSV, REB).

The reference to "the land of Rameses" (Gen. 47:11) in the story of Joseph, well before Pharaoh Ramses II lived, suggests that the author of Genesis used the "modern" name (Rameses)— the name that was common in his day and not the earlier name of the city, which was used during the time of Joseph. This may also be true of the use of Rameses in the account of the Exodus, because the Hebrews apparently left Egypt around 1446 B.C., well before the time of King Ramses.

"The land of Rameses" (Gen. 47:11) was "the best of the land"—the most fertile district of Egypt. This almost certainly refers to the land of Goshen, in the northeastern Nile delta.

RED SEA — a narrow body of water that stretches in a southeasterly direction from Suez to the Gulf of Aden for about 2,100 kilometers (1,300 miles). It is an important section of a large volcanic split in the earth that goes southward into east Africa and continues north along the Jordan Valley to the Lebanon mountain range.

The Red Sea separates two large portions of land. On the east are Yemen and Saudi Arabia. On the west are Egypt, the Sudan, and Ethiopia. From ancient times the Red Sea has been an impressive sea covering some 169,000 square miles. It measures about 310 kilometers (190 miles) at its widest part and almost 2,900 meters (about 9,500 feet) at its greatest depth. The Red Sea branches at its northern end into two distinct channels, the northeasterly one being the Gulf of Aqaba and the northwesterly one named the Gulf of Suez. The Suez branch is fairly shallow and has broad plains on either side. By contrast, the Gulf of Aqaba is deep and clear, with a narrow shoreline.

The Red Sea is usually bright turquoise, but periodically algae grow in the water. When they die, the sea becomes reddish-brown, thus giving it the name the Red Sea. This body of water has the reputation of being one of the hottest and saltiest on earth. The reason for this is the presence of volcanic slits in the ocean floor that have become filled with salt deposits and other minerals. The sea is heavily traveled because the Suez Canal links it with the Mediterranean. But navigation is difficult at the southern end because of outcroppings of coral reefs that force ships into a narrow channel of water. No large rivers flow into the Red Sea, and there is little rainfall in the area it crosses.

The name "Red Sea" has found its way into the Bible as a translation of the Hebrew *yam suph*, which means "sea of reeds" and not "Red Sea." The term *suph* comes from the Egyptian *twf*, meaning "papyrus." This confusion is unfortunate because papyrus reeds and similar vegetation do not grow in the Red Sea or in the Gulf of Suez. This fact excludes them as the area that witnessed the deliverance of the Hebrew captives at the time of the Exodus. The term *yam suph*, however, seems to have been applied from the time of Solomon onward to some area near to, or identical with, the Gulf of Aqaba. In 1 Kings 9:26 Ezion Geber, Solomon's port in the gulf, is described as being on the shore of the *yam suph* in the land of Edom. A further possible reference to the Gulf of Aqaba is in Jeremiah 49:21. In this prophecy dealing with Edom, Jeremiah spoke of their desolation being heard as far as the *yam suph*.

Perhaps the place-name Suph in Deuteronomy 1:1, where Moses spoke God's words to the Israelites, was either a short-ened form of *yam suph*, indicating the Gulf of Aqaba, or some settlement in that area. Just before Korah, Dathan, and Abiram met their end as the result of an earthquake, the Israelites had been instructed to go into the wilderness by way of the *yam suph* (Deut. 1:40). At a later stage, after the death of Aaron, the Hebrews left Mount Hor by a route near the *yam suph* to go around hostile Edomite territory (Num. 21:4). Such a jour-ney would have brought them to the northeast of the Gulf of Aqaba, which might suggest that this body of water was being described by the term *yam suph*.

There is a strong argument against identifying the Gulf of Aqaba with the *yam suph*, or "Red Sea," that the fleeing Israelites crossed under the leadership of Moses. A crossing of the Gulf of Aqaba would have taken the Israelites much too far from the Goshen area. To reach the gulf they would have had to skirt the western edge of the Wilderness of Shur and make a direct southeast journey through the rugged central Sinai region and the Wilderness of Paran. Having crossed this *yam suph*, the Israelites would then have had to go north and then return to the Sinai Peninsula to meet with God at Mount Horeb.

An alternative suggestion is to regard the term *yam suph* not merely as describing a specific body of water, but as a general title that could be applied to any marshy area where reeds and papyri grew. The Egyptians used such terms in a wide sense.

In the 15th century B.C. they spoke of both the Mediterranean and the Red Sea as the "Great Green Sea." Since there were several marshes in the Nile delta, *yam suph* could apply to any one of them. It is even possible that the *yam suph* of Numbers 33:10–11 referred to the Gulf of Suez but that the Israelite visit there occurred after the Exodus. The view that the Gulf of Suez extended much further northward into the area of the Bitter Lakes during the time of the Exodus cannot be supported by archaeological evidence or other studies.

The best understanding of *yam suph* is that it does not refer to the Red Sea or any of its branches. Instead, it probably refers to water bordered by papyrus reeds and located somewhere between the southern edge of Lake Menzaleh and the lakes close to the head of the Gulf of Suez that were drained when the Suez Canal was constructed. Such a location for the Exodus would be directly opposite the Wilderness of Shur, which was the first encampment of the Israelites after crossing the *yam suph* (Ex. 15:22).

RELEASE, YEAR OF — a term applied to the Year of Jubilee, the end of a cycle of seven sabbatical years. To safeguard against a small group gaining control of much land and people falling into poverty because of high interest, the Year of Jubilee was established (Lev. 25:8–17, 23–55). It occurred every 50 years.

During this year, land that had been sold during the past 50 years was returned to its original owner, and Israelite slaves were released. The principle behind this custom was the belief that land does not belong to Israel but to God, who permits its use (Lev. 25:23). Another principle was that human beings are not to be in lifelong service to other people, but to God, who freed all Israel from slavery in Egypt (Lev. 25:38, 55).

REUBEN, TRIBE OF — the tribe whose ancestor was Reuben (Num. 1:5). During 430 years in Egypt, the descendants of Reuben increased from 4 sons to 46,500 men of war (Num. 1:20–21). In the wilderness the tribe of Reuben was represented in a conspiracy against Moses. As representatives of the tribe, Dathan and Abiram tried to assert their legal rights as descendants of Jacob's oldest son to a role of leadership in Israel (Num. 16:1–3), but their efforts failed.

The Reubenites were a pastoral people. The tribe requested an early inheritance east of the Jordan River where the land was suitable for cattle (Num. 32:1–33). They helped the other tribes claim their land, however, and Joshua commended them for their efforts (Josh. 22:9–10). The tribe also built an altar—along with the tribe of Gad and the half-tribe of Manasseh—in the Jordan Valley as a witness to their unity with the tribes west of the Jordan (Josh. 22:11–34).

Later, members of the tribe of Reuben refused to assist Deborah and Barak in fighting the Canaanite Sisera (Judg. 5:16), although the tribe apparently assisted the other tribes in their war against Benjamin (Judg. 20:11). During Saul's reign, Reuben joined Gad and Manasseh in fighting the Hagrites (1 Chr. 5:18–22). When the kingdom divided under Rehoboam, Reuben joined the Northern Kingdom under Jeroboam.

While never prominent, the tribe of Reuben was never forgotten. Ezekiel remembered Reuben in his description of Israel (Ezek. 48:6). The tribe is also represented in the 144,000 sealed—12,000 from each of the twelve tribes of Israel (Rev. 7:5).

ROMAN EMPIRE — the powerful pagan empire that controlled most of the known world during New Testament times.

Rome was founded in 753 B.C. by Romulus, who became its first king. The little kingdom grew in size and importance, absorbing its immediate neighbors through the reign of 7 kings, until the tyranny of Tarquinius Superbus drove the people to revolt and to take the government into their own hands. A republic was established, and Roman citizens had a voice in governmental affairs. During the period of the republic, Rome extended her borders throughout all of Italy and the known world.

In 63 B.C., Judea became formally subject to Rome and this was the case during the entire New Testament period.

The republic was subject to internal strife that eventually led to the decline of a people-oriented government. The emperor Octavian, who was also known as Augustus, became emperor in 27 B.C. He was still reigning at the time of Jesus' birth.

Roman Religion. The religion that was native to Rome was basically primitive in nature. The Romans believed that impersonal spirits or supernatural powers inhabited such natural objects as trees, streams, and earth. They believed that these spirits affected one's personal life for good or evil.

But the most striking feature of Roman religion was its ability to merge the best features of several religions. As the empire expanded, it imported and assimilated many religious ideas and pagan gods from Greece and the Orient. Roman gods were fused and identified with the gods of the Greeks. Buildings, temples, and monuments to these gods were erected. Astrological beliefs and magical practices flourished.

An "imperial ruler cult" developed in the 1st century B.C. when the Roman senate voted to deify Julius Caesar and to dedicate a temple in his honor. Among all the emperors, only Julius Caesar, Augustus, and Claudius were deified. This phenomenon apparently had more political than religious meaning.

Throughout the entire New Testament period, various emperors ruled over the Roman Empire. During the reign of Augustus, Christ was born. His crucifixion occurred during the reign of the succeeding emperor Tiberius. The martyrdom of James, the brother of John, took place in the reign of the emperor Claudius (Acts 11:28; 12:1–2). It was to the emperor Nero that Paul appealed (Acts 25:11). The destruction of Jerusalem prophesied by Jesus (Matthew 24; Mark 13; Luke 19:41–44) was accomplished in the year A.D. 70 by Titus, who later became emperor. Thus, all of the New Testament story unfolded under the reign of Roman emperors.

The Roman Empire reached the height of its power from about A.D. 100 to 175. By the end of the 2nd century, however, the Romans and their power had begun to decline. Because of the vast expanse of its territory, the empire grew increasingly difficult to administer. High taxation and political infighting also took their toll.

Morally, Rome was also a sick society; its life of sin and debauchery served to hasten its collapse from within, even as barbaric tribes moved in to challenge the Romans' military rule. By A.D. 450 the Roman Empire was only a skeleton of its former self, reduced to a third-rate power among the nations of the ancient world.

The Jews Within the Empire. Contact between Rome and the Jews took place when some of the Jews were scattered to various parts of the Mediterranean world and when Rome moved into Palestine as a part of its eastern expansion. Technically, however, contact between the Romans and the Jews began in 63 B.C., when Pompey marched into the land of Palestine.

From the time of the captivity in Babylon—or perhaps even earlier—many Jews made their homes outside Palestine. While some of them did this for economic reasons, others had been deported as prisoners of war to such places as Assyria and Babylon. The prophet Jeremiah indicated that some Jews had settled in Egypt during his time (Jer. 44:1).

Under Roman rule the Jews were given a special status with certain legal rights. They were permitted to practice their own religion and to build their synagogues. They also were exempt from military service and were not required to appear in court on the Sabbath.

Relationships between the Jews and the Romans were mostly positive. But a few major disturbances did occur. The emperor Caligula alienated the Jews by opposing their belief in one God and forcibly erecting a statue of himself in their synagogues. Also, in A.D. 19, the emperor Tiberius expelled some Jews from Italy. This edict was renewed under Claudius in A.D. 49 (Acts 18:2). Apparently this edict did not last long, because Jews were living in Rome when Paul arrived there about A.D. 62.

The situation of the Jews varied considerably under the different Roman rulers. Basically, the Romans treated the Jews fairly. Herod the Great began to rebuild the temple in 20 B.C., and Herod Agrippa sought Jewish favor by persecuting the Christians (Acts 12:1–3). Archelaus, on the other hand, was a cruel and tyrannical ruler who massacred many Jews (Matt. 2:22).

Resentful of the presence of these foreign oppressors, the Jews refused to recognize anyone but God as sovereign. Revolutionary activities of Jewish nationalists such as the Zealots increased and threatened the peace in Palestine. By A.D. 66, Rome was forced to subdue a Jewish revolt in Judea. And in A.D. 70, Titus, a Roman general who later became emperor, marched on the city of Jerusalem to destroy Jewish resistance. Many Jews lost their lives by crucifixion and other violent means. A small group of freedom fighters held out at Masada, but they took their own lives just before the Roman soldiers broke into their fortress.

The destruction of Jerusalem did not wipe out the Jewish state or religion. In some ways, it made the Jews more determined to resist. During the next 60 years Rome and the Jews clashed on a number of occasions. From A.D. 132–135 a second rebellion was led by a self-proclaimed messiah, Simon Bar Koseba. Hadrian, emperor at the time, issued an edict that virtually destroyed Judaism. Jerusalem was rebuilt as a Roman colony, complete with a pagan Roman temple, erected on the site of the Jewish temple. The province of Judea was replaced by Syria Palestine. In this rebellion, some 500,000 Jews were killed and many others were sold into slavery. Those who survived were scattered beyond this new province.

Christianity Within the Empire. The birth and development of Christianity took place within the borders of the Roman Empire. The New Testament contains several references to Romans who were ruling at this time. Among them were Augustus (Luke 2:1), Quirinius (Luke 2:2), and Tiberius (Luke 3:1; 20:22). Other minor officials ruled on behalf of Rome, particularly those of the Herodian dynasty.

The book of Acts shows how Christianity spread throughout the Roman Empire. Under Paul, the great missionary to the Gentiles, the gospel may have been preached as far west as Spain (Rom. 15:28). A Christian church existed in Rome as early as A.D. 50 (Acts 18:2–3). By the time Paul wrote his epistle to the Romans (A.D. 58), a large Christian community existed in the imperial city.

Paul's appearance in Rome was ironic, because he came as a prisoner and not as a missionary (Acts 25:12; 27:1; 28:19–31). Here he was held in confinement awaiting a trial that apparently never took place. According to tradition, Paul lost his life under Nero's persecution about A.D. 64.

In its early stages, Christianity was regarded by Rome as a sect of Judaism. This is why it was ignored during its early years. On several occasions, Roman authorities viewed conflicts between Jews and Christians as an internal matter, not worthy of their attention (Acts 18:12–17). When Christians were accused by the Jews of breaking the law, they were acquitted (Acts 16:35–39). Rome even protected Christians from Jewish fanatics (Acts 19:28–41; 22:22–30; 23:23–24) and assured Paul the right of a proper trial (Acts 23:26; 28:31).

Most Christians had a positive and respectful attitude toward Roman authority. They were careful not to promote any revolutionary or treasonous acts. Jesus spoke about paying taxes (Mark 12:17). Paul reminded his readers to respect, pray for, and honor governing authorities (Rom. 13:1–7; 1 Tim. 2:1–2; Titus 3:1). Peter admonished the churches: "Honor all people. Love the brotherhood. Fear God. Honor the king" (1 Pet. 2:17).

The first known persecution of Christians by the Roman authorities took place under Nero. But this was an isolated case and not a general policy. Many Christians, including Paul, lost their lives at this time. Tacitus, a Roman historian, refers to vast multitudes of Christians who were arrested, tortured, crucified, and burned.

Hardships came to Christians in parts of Asia while Domitian was emperor. Later, under Trajan, there were further problems, especially in Bithynia, where Pliny was governor (A.D. 112). Ignatius, bishop of Antioch, was martyred during this persecution. Rome may have feared that Christians could become a political threat because they would not acknowledge Caesar as lord.

Marcus Aurelius took official action against Christianity. As emperor, he was responsible for the death of Justin Martyr (A.D. 165). Celsius (A.D. 249–251) launched attacks against Christians and, like Nero, used them as scapegoats for his own failures.

Under Diocletian, intense persecution of the church took place for 3 years (A.D. 303–305). Many churches were destroyed. Bibles were burned, and Christians were martyred. With the coming of Constantine, however, this policy of persecution was reversed. His Edict of Milan in A.D. 313 made Christianity the official religion of the Roman Empire.

ROMAN LAW — the unique laws and judicial codes by which the Roman Empire governed itself and the various nations and foreign provinces under its control.

Judicial authority ranged from the absolute power of the emperor to the function of the senate and the imperial civil service (governors, procurators, prefects, magistrates, etc.). Judicial procedure in Rome generally included appearance before a magistrate, a trial, and the selection of a judge who would then render judgment on a case.

In the provinces, Roman law was administered by Roman officials. Pontius Pilate, for example, was the Roman governor involved in the trial of Jesus. The gospel accounts of this episode give considerable insight into the judicial procedure of the Romans and how they related to local Jewish officials (Matthew 27; Mark 15; Luke 23; John 18–19).

The apostle Paul's Roman citizenship granted him certain privileges as well as protection from Jewish and Roman fanaticism (Acts 16:35–39; 22:22–29). His imprisonment in Caesarea and defense before Felix, Festus, and King Agrippa (Acts 23:26–26:32), as well as his specific appeal to plead his case before Caesar (25:10–12), are good examples of Roman civil and legal law.

Christianity began in Roman territory and expanded into additional areas controlled by Rome. Christians were expected to observe Roman law and not to get involved in any disorderly, suspicious, or treasonous activity.

The book of Acts shows that the early Christians were protected and acquitted by the Roman authorities. They recognized Christianity as a legal and valid religion with the right to exist. Paul affirmed that he had not broken any Jewish, religious, or Roman law (Acts 25:8).

ROME, CITY OF — capital city of the ancient Roman Empire and present capital of modern Italy.

Founded in 753 B.C., Rome was situated 24 kilometers (15 miles) from where the Tiber River flows into the Mediterranean Sea. From its initial settlement on the Palatine Hill near the river, the city gradually grew and embraced the surrounding area. Ultimately, the city was situated on 7 hills: Capital, Palatine, Aventine, Caelian, Esquiline, Viminal, and Quirinal.

As capital of the Roman Empire, the city was the seat of Roman government. During its long history, Roman government went through the forms of a monarchy, a republic, and an empire.

The monarchy lasted from 753 to 510 B.C. when Rome was ruled by kings. After Romulus, the first king (ruled 753–714 B.C.), Rome was ruled by six other princes until the decline of the monarchical form of government in 510 B.C.

As a republic, Rome was governed by elected consuls who in turn presided over the senate. Under the republic, Rome expanded its borders and engaged in major internal reforms. The period of the republic lasted until 31 B.C. when Caesar Augustus became the first emperor. He developed Rome into a beautiful and stately city.

During the reign of Augustus as emperor in Rome, Jesus was born in Bethlehem of Judea. At that time and during the entire New Testament period, Judea was under Roman rule. Roman influence penetrated the entire Jewish community and continued to be felt in the life and mission of the New Testament church. During the reign of Tiberius, successor to Augustus, Jesus' public ministry occurred. The great missionary endeavors of the apostle Paul took place during the reign of Claudius. Under Nero, the city of Rome was burned, Christians were persecuted, and the apostle Paul was martyred.

The book of Acts describes the thrilling story of the early church as it shared the gospel, beginning at Jerusalem and finally reaching Rome.

The apostle Paul's first known connection with Rome was when he met Aquila and Priscilla at Corinth (Acts 18:2). They had left Rome when Claudius expelled all the Jews from the city. Some few years after meeting Aquila and Priscilla, Paul decided that he "must also see Rome" (Acts 19:21). When he wrote his letter to the Christians at Rome, his plan was to visit friends in the city on his way to Spain (Rom. 15:24).

However, Paul actually went to Rome under very different conditions than he had originally planned. To keep from being killed by hostile Jews in Jerusalem, Paul appealed to Caesar. The binding effect of that appeal ultimately brought him to the capital city as a prisoner. Here he waited for his trial. The book of Acts closes at this point, and one must rely on secular history and references in the Pastoral Epistles for the rest of the story. Tradition holds that Paul was ultimately martyred by Nero during the emperor's persecution of Christians.

The city to which Paul came was very similar to a modern city. The public buildings and other structures were lavishly constructed. A new senate house and a temple to honor Caesar had been constructed in A.D. 29. In A.D. 28 the senate had authorized Augustus to rebuild or restore some 82 temples in need of repair. In the process, he built a great temple to Apollo near his palace on the Palatine Hill. Other buildings included the Colosseum, where Roman games occurred.

The houses of the wealthy people of Rome were elaborately constructed and situated on the various hills, but most of the people lived in tenements. These crowded apartment dwellings were multistoried buildings that engulfed the city. Over a million people lived in these tenements, which were surrounded by narrow and noisy streets with a steady flow of traffic day and night.

The people of Rome were provided with food and entertainment by the state. Wine was also plentiful and cheap. Admission to the games was free. Large crowds attended these games, which included chariot racing, gladiatorial contests, and theatrical performances.

Like Babylon, the city of Rome became a symbol of paganism and idolatry in the New Testament. The book of Revelation contains several disguised references to the pagan city. Most scholars agree that Revelation 17–18 should be interpreted as predictions of the fall of Rome.

S

SABBATH [SAB bahth] — the practice of observing 1 day in 7 as a time for rest and worship. This practice apparently originated in creation, because God created the universe in 6 days and rested on the 7th (Genesis 1). By this act, God ordained a pattern for living—that people should work 6 days each week at subduing and ruling the creation and should rest 1 day a week. This is the understanding of the creation set forth by Moses in Exodus 20:3–11, when he wrote the Ten Commandments at God's direction.

History of the Sabbath. The practice of the weekly Sabbath is suggested at several places in the Bible, long before the Ten Commandments were given at Mount Sinai. In Genesis, for example, starting with Seth (Gen. 4:26), people began to call upon the name of the Lord in acts of worship. Thus, periods of 7 days play a prominent role at crucial points throughout Genesis (7:4, 10; 8:10, 12). The mention of a 7-day week and a 7-year cycle in the life practice of Laban, Abraham's relative, is striking.

The formal institution of the Sabbath is a basic part of the Mosaic law system. Each division of the law contains specific sections relating to the practice of the Sabbath: the moral law (the Ten Commandments), the civil law (Ex. 31:14), and the ceremonial law (Lev. 23:3). The keeping of the Sabbath was a sign that God truly ruled Israel. To break His Sabbath law was to rebel against Him—an action meriting death (Ex. 21:14). Society was not to seek advancement outside of submission to God. Therefore, all work except acts of mercy, necessity, and worship were forbidden on the Sabbath (Is. 58:13; Matt. 12:1–13).

The Old Testament prophets recounted God's blessings upon those who properly observed the Sabbath (Is. 58:13). They called upon the people to observe the Sabbath (Neh. 10:31; 13:15–22), while soundly condemning those who made much of external observance and ignored the heart and moral issues to which the Sabbath bound them (Is. 1:13; Hos. 2:11; Amos 8:5).

During the period between the Old and New Testaments, Jewish religious leaders added greatly to the details of Sabbath legislation. They sought to ensure proper and careful observance by making certain that people did not even come close to violating it. This substituted human law for divine law (Matt. 15:9), made the law a burden rather than a rest and delight (Luke 11:46), and reduced the Sabbath to little more than an external observance (Matt. 12:8). Jesus, like the Old Testament prophets, kept the Sabbath Himself (Luke 4:16) and urged others to observe the day (Mark 2:28). But He condemned the pharisaical attitude that missed the deep spiritual truth behind Sabbath observance (Matt 12:14; Mark 2:23; Luke 6:1–11; John 5:1–18).

The Christian Sabbath. Many Christians feel that God still expects His people to set aside 1 day in 7 to Him. They argue that such an observance is a creation ordinance that is binding until this creation comes to an end and our ultimate rest as Christians is realized in heaven (Hebrews 4). They also believe that as part of the moral system known as the Ten Commandments, the Sabbath is morally binding upon all people for all time.

Historically, Christians of this persuasion usually observe Sunday, the first day of the week, as the Christian Sabbath. They note that Christ arose on the first day of the week (Matt.

28:1) and, thereafter, the New Testament church regularly worshiped on Sunday (Acts 20:7; 1 Cor. 16:2; Rev. 1:10). This day on which Jesus arose was called the Lord's Day (Rev. 1:10). A few Christian groups, however, deny that observance of the 7th day as the Sabbath was ever abolished. Among them are Seventh-Day Adventists and Seventh-Day Baptists.

Meaning of the Sabbath. The Sabbath is a means by which our living pattern imitates God's (Ex. 20:3–11). Work is followed by rest. This idea is expressed by the Hebrew word for Sabbath, which means "cessation."

Sabbath rest is also a time for God's people to think about and enjoy what God has accomplished. Another Hebrew word meaning "rest" embodies this idea, "But the seventh day is the Sabbath of the LORD your God. In it you shall not do any work" (Deut. 5:14). God's people are directed to keep the Sabbath because God delivered and redeemed His people from the bondage in Egypt. Thus, the Sabbath is an ordinance that relates redemption directly to history.

Sabbath rest also holds promise of the ultimate salvation that God will accomplish for His people. As certainly as He delivered them from Egypt through Moses, so will He deliver His people from sin at the end of the age through the Great Redeemer (Gen. 3:15; Hebrews 4).

Finally, the Sabbath includes the idea and practice of celebrating rest, or salvation. To this end, God declared that His Sabbath was a day for public convocation (Lev. 23:3; Ex. 31:13; Ezek. 20:12).

The concept of celebration also presents the Sabbath as a delight (Ps. 92; Is. 58:13; Hos. 2:11). The sabbatical holy days (holidays) prescribed rest from work for everyone (Ex. 23:21; Num. 15:32). To this end the daily morning and evening sacrifices were doubled on the weekly Sabbath day (Num. 28:9; Ps. 92).

On the Sabbath the showbread was to be renewed (Lev. 24:8). The people were to meet together to praise God and to be instructed in His law (Lev. 10:11; Deut. 14:29; 33:10).

SABBATICAL YEAR — a year of rest and redemption that occurred every 7 years in the Hebrew nation. By God's prescription, Israel was to set apart every 7th year by letting the land go uncultivated (Lev. 25:4–5). The crops and harvest that were reaped during this year were considered the common possession of all people and animals (Ex. 23:11; Deut. 15:1–18). None of this harvest was to be stored for future use.

During a sabbatical year, Israelites were to cancel all debts owed to them by their fellow Israelites (Deut. 15:1–5). At the least, a period of grace was to be set aside in which payment was not required. The people of Israel were also to free their Hebrew slaves, remembering that they were also slaves in the land of Egypt at one time and that God had redeemed them by His goodness.

God's anger fell on Israel because the sabbatical year was not observed from the time of Solomon (Jer. 34:14–22). This was one reason why Israel spent 70 years in bondage at the hands of the Babylonians.

SADDUCEES [SAJ uh seez] — members of a Jewish faction that opposed Jesus during His ministry. Known for their denial of the bodily resurrection, the Sadducees came from the leading families of the nation—the priests, merchants, and aristocrats. The high priests and the most powerful members of the priesthood were mainly Sadducees (Acts 5:17).

Some scholars believe the name "Sadducees" came from Zadok, the high priest in the days of David (2 Sam. 15:24) and Solomon (1 Kin. 1:34–45). Many wealthy laypeople were also Sadducees. This may be the reason why the Sadducees gave the impression of wanting to preserve things as they were. They enjoyed privileged positions in society and managed to get along well under Roman rule. Any movement that might upset order and authority was bound to appear dangerous in their eyes.

The Sadducees rejected "the tradition of the elders," that body of oral and written commentary that interpreted the law of Moses. This automatically placed them in direct conflict with another Jewish group, the Pharisees, who had made the traditions surrounding the law almost as important as the law itself. The Sadducees insisted that only the laws that were written in the law of Moses (the Pentateuch, the first five books of the Old Testament) were really binding. The Sadducees thought this way because of religious practices that had taken place for several centuries.

For many years the priests were in charge of teaching the law of God to the Israelites; they were the authorities to go to for interpretation or application of the law (Deut. 17:8–13). Unfortunately, the leading priests lost the respect of the people by becoming corrupt. When this happened, many Jews began to respond to the scribes, people who had become experts in God's law and who usually lived pious, disciplined lives, although many of them were not priests. People began to follow the teaching of the scribes and to let the scribes interpret the law of God for them. The "tradition of the elders" that followed was made up of customs, rulings, and interpretations that the scribes passed on as the authoritative way in which God's law should be applied.

The Sadducees rejected this approach to authority in favor of the written law of Moses. They felt the original law alone could be trusted. Naturally, they felt Sadducean priests should be the ones to serve as the law's interpreters.

The Sadducees did not believe in the resurrection of the dead or the immortality of the soul, since these doctrines are not mentioned in the law of Moses. Neither did they believe in rewards or punishments handed out after death, as in the doctrines of heaven and hell. Acts 23:8 indicates that they did not believe in angels or spirits, either. They believed in free will—that people are responsible for their own prosperity or misfortune. They interpreted the law literally and tended to support strict justice as opposed to mercy toward the offender.

Only a few references are made to the Sadducees in the New Testament. They opposed the early church (Acts 4:1–3; 5:17–18), much more so than even the Pharisees (Acts 5:34–39; 15:5; 23:6–9). Since the chief priests usually came from among the Sadducees, it is clear that they played a major role in the arrest of Jesus and the preliminary hearing against Him (Mark 14:60–64), and that they urged Pilate to crucify Him (Mark 15:1, 3, 10–11). Jesus warned His disciples about the "leaven"— the "doctrine" or teaching—of the Sadducees (Matt. 16:1–12). John the Baptist was suspicious of their supposed "repentance" (Matt. 3:7–12).

One incident when Jesus clashed with the Sadducees is recorded in all 3 of the Synoptic Gospels (Matt. 22:23–33; Mark 12:18–27; Luke 20:27–40). Apparently one of the favorite sports of the Sadducees was to make fun of their opponents by showing how their beliefs led to ridiculous conclusions. They approached Jesus with a "what if" question, designed to show the absurd consequences that can arise from believing in the resurrection of the dead. "Suppose," they asked, "a woman had seven husbands in this life, and each of them died without leaving children? Whose wife would she be in the world to come?"

Jesus replied with a two-part answer. First, He said that they were wrong to suggest that earthly relationships, such as marriage, will continue after the resurrection. Second, Jesus pointed out that they were wrong in not believing in the resurrection at all: "Have you not read what was spoken to you by God, saying, 'I am the God of Abraham, the God of Isaac, and the God of

Jacob'? God is not the God of the dead, but of the living" (Matt. 22:31–32; also Ex. 3:6, 15–16).

Jesus' argument was that God told Moses that He was the God of Abraham, Isaac, and Jacob. Of course, these 3 men had died long before the time of Moses. Yet, if they were not "alive" at the time of Moses (that is, if they did not live on after their deaths), then God would not have called Himself their God, for "God is not the God of the dead, but of the living." Abraham, Isaac, and Jacob must live on if God is still their God; therefore, it is wrong to deny life after death and the resurrection of the dead.

After posing His reasons, Jesus stated that the Sadducees were "greatly mistaken" in their beliefs (Mark 12:27). The multitude who heard Jesus' argument were "astonished at His teaching" (Matt. 22:33) and the Sadducees were "silenced" (Matt. 22:34).

S AMARIA, REGION OF [suh MAR ih uh] — a territory in the uplands of central Canaan that corresponded roughly with the lands allotted to the tribe of Ephraim and the western portion of Manasseh. Samaria consisted of about 1,400 square miles of attractive, fertile land, bounded by Bethel on the south and Mount Carmel on the north. Its rich alluvial soil produced valuable grain crops, olives, and grapes. This productivity was made all the more important by the presence of two north-south and three east-west roads. Samaria was able to engage in commerce with neighboring Phoenicia as well as the more distant nations of Syria and Egypt.

Because Samaritan soil was considerably more fertile than the soil in Judah, the Northern Kingdom was always more prosperous. But the very attractiveness of the territory brought invaders, while trade with such pagan nations exposed the people to corrupt foreign religions. The prophets strongly condemned the wickedness of Samaria—its idolatry, immorality, idle luxury, and oppression of the poor (Hos. 7:1; 8:5–7).

In the time of Jesus, Palestine west of the Jordan River was divided into the three provinces of Galilee, Samaria, and Judea. Because of their intermarriage with foreigners, the people of Samaria were shunned by orthodox Jews. Situated between Galilee and Judea, Samaria was the natural route for traveling between those two provinces. But the pure-blooded Jews had no dealings with the Samaritans (John 4:9). They would travel east, cross the Jordan River, and detour around Samaria.

SAMARITANS [suh MAR ih tuhns] — natives or inhabitants of Samaria, a distinct territory or region in central Canaan.

Until the rise of Assyrian power in the ancient Near East, Samaria was occupied by the tribes of Ephraim and the western portion of the tribe of Manasseh. Many of the sites in Samaria held important places in Israelite history. Mount Gerizim and Mount Ebal were the scene of the covenant-renewal ceremony in Joshua's time (Josh. 8:30–35). Shechem, situated near Mount Gerizim, was an ancient Canaanite town that regained its earlier prosperity during the monarchy. It became capital of the northern kingdom of Israel briefly under Jeroboam I (about 931–910 B.C.; 1 Kin. 12:25), but it was replaced by Penuel and then Tirzah.

Construction on the city of Samaria was begun by Omri about 880 B.C. and completed by his son Ahab (about 874–853 B.C.). Samaria became the new capital of Israel, and successive kings added to it and rebuilt sections to make it a well-fortified capital. But the city fell to the Assyrians in 722–721 B.C. Most of the leading citizens of the Northern Kingdom were deported to places in Syria, Assyria, and Babylonia.

Sargon replaced the deported Israelites with foreign colonists (2 Kin. 17:24). These newcomers intermarried among the Israelites who remained in Samaria. Later, their numbers were increased when Esarhaddon and Ashurbanipal (the biblical Osnapper; Ezra 4:10) sent more Assyrian colonists to the district of Samaria. These people took the name "Samaritans" from the territory and attempted to settle the land. However, "they did not fear the Lord, and the Lord sent lions among them, which killed some of them" (2 Kin. 17:25). In despair they sent to Assyria for "one of the priests" who would "teach them the rituals of the God of the land" (2 Kin. 17:27). Thereafter the Samaritans worshiped the God of Israel. But they also continued their idolatry, worshiping the pagan gods imported from foreign lands (2 Kin. 17:29).

So the Samaritans were a "mixed race" contaminated by foreign blood and false worship. The Jewish historian Josephus indicates that the Samaritans were also opportunists. When the Jews enjoyed prosperity, the Samaritans were quick to acknowledge their blood relationship. But when the Jews suffered hard times, the Samaritans disowned any such kinship, declaring that they were descendants of Assyrian immigrants. When a group of Jews, led by Zerubbabel, returned from the Babylonian captivity, the Samaritans offered to help Zerubbabel rebuild the temple. When their offer was rejected, they tried to prevent the Jews from finishing their project (Ezra 4:1–10). When Nehemiah attempted to rebuild the wall of Jerusalem, he was opposed by Arab and Samaritan groups (Neh. 2:10–6:14). The breach between the Samaritans and the Jews widened even further when Ezra, in his zeal for racial purity, pressured all Israelite men who married during the captivity to divorce their pagan wives (Ezra 10:18–44).

The final break between the two groups occurred when the Samaritans built a rival temple on Mount Gerizim, claiming Shechem rather than Zion (Jerusalem) as the true "Bethel" (house of God), the site traditionally chosen and blessed by the Lord.

Present-day Samaritans trace their beginnings to the time of Eli, who established the sanctuary for worship of God in Shiloh. They also believe their religion is distinctive because they base their beliefs and practices on the Torah, or the Law—the first five books of the Old Testament. They recognize no other Hebrew Scriptures as authoritative.

At what stage the pagan elements of Mesopotamian religion were removed from Samaritan belief is impossible to determine. But probably by the time of Nehemiah (about 450 B.C.), the Samaritans considered themselves orthodox. The Samaritans also claimed that Ezra changed the Hebrew text to favor Jerusalem over Mount Gerizim as the site for the second temple. But the Samaritans themselves may also be guilty of changing the wording of the Law to reflect favorably on their traditions.

In the Roman period the Samaritans appeared to prosper. Their religion was made legal in the empire, being practiced in synagogues in Italy and Africa. Suffering persecution from Christians, they finally revolted in the 5th and 6th centuries. The Roman emperor Justinian (ruled A.D. 527–565) suppressed the Samaritans and brought them almost to extinction, a condition from which they never recovered. But two small units of Samaritans survive until the present time—one group in Nablus (ancient Shechem) and a second group near Tel Aviv.

The pride of the modern Samaritan community at Nablus is a large scroll of the books of the Law, inscribed in an angular script much as Hebrew was written long before the time of Christ.

The Samaritans retained their belief in God as the unique Creator and Sustainer of all things. They also worshiped Him in the three feasts prescribed in the books of the Law—Passover, Pentecost, and Booths (or Tabernacles)—and the solemn Day of Atonement. But their faith was influenced in later periods by Islamic and other beliefs, unlike the orthodox Jewish community. To this day they sacrifice one or more lambs on Mount Gerizim during the Feast of Passover.

SANHEDRIN [SAN hee drun] (*council* or *assembly*) — the highest ruling body and court of justice among the Jewish people in the time of Jesus. Headed by the high priest of Israel, the Sanhedrin was granted limited authority over certain religious, civil, and criminal matters by the foreign nations that dominated the land of Israel at various times in its history. The Sanhedrin was exercising this limited power when it charged Jesus with the crime of blasphemy but then sent him to Pilate, the Roman official, for a formal trial and sentencing.

The word *Sanhedrin* is not found in the NKJV; instead the word *council* is used. Usually the assembly itself is meant, although the word may also refer to the assembly meeting (John 11:47) or to the place where the assembly met (Luke 22:66; Acts 4:15). The same word is also used for smaller, local courts of justice (Matt. 10:17; Mark 13:9). The Sanhedrin is also implied in Bible passages that mention a meeting of the various groups that made up the council: the chief priests, the elders, and the scribes (Mark 14:53–55). Sometimes some of the members of the Sanhedrin are simply called rulers (Luke 24:20; Acts 4:5).

The Sanhedrin had 71 members. The New Testament mentions some of them by name: Joseph of Arimathea (Mark 15:43), Gamaliel (Acts 5:34), Nicodemus (John 3:1; 7:50), the high priests Annas and Caiaphas (Luke 3:2) and Ananias (Acts 23:2). The high priest was always president of the Sanhedrin. Some scholars suggest that the apostle Paul was a member of the Sanhedrin before his conversion to Christianity, but this is not known for sure.

The Sanhedrin grew out of the council of advisors for the high priest when the Jewish people lived under the domination of the Persian and Greek empires. In the beginning, the council was made up of the leading priests and the most distinguished aristocrats among the laypeople. Later, however, as the influence of the scribes grew, they were also given some positions on the Sanhedrin. In this way, the Sanhedrin came to include both Sadducees—or "chief priests" and "elders"—and Pharisees or scribes. These were the two main groups within Judaism, and the Sanhedrin usually tried to maintain a balance of power between them. But Acts 23:1–10 shows that the Sanhedrin would sometimes divide along party lines. As he stood before the Sanhedrin, the apostle Paul was shrewd enough to pit the Pharisees against the Sadducees to his own advantage.

After A.D. 6 the official authority of the Sanhedrin extended only to the province of Judea in southern Palestine. Still, Jews living elsewhere respected the Sanhedrin highly and would often be guided by its decisions. Within the province of Judea, which included the city of Jerusalem, the Romans left most of the business of governing the Jews to the Sanhedrin. The Sanhedrin even had its own police force, or temple police, so it could make arrests on its own. This is the force that arrested Jesus in the Garden of Gethsemane (Mark 14:43; Acts 4:1–3).

The Sanhedrin also served as the supreme court of the Jews. This does not mean that people who were dissatisfied with the verdict of the lower court could appeal to the Sanhedrin for a different decision. But matters of special importance and other matters that lower courts were unable to resolve were brought to the Sanhedrin. The Roman rulers did, however, reserve the right to interfere with what the Sanhedrin was doing, as happened in the case of Paul (Acts 23:10; 24:7), but this probably happened very seldom. The Romans denied the power of capital punishment to the Sanhedrin. This is why the Jews said to Pilate after they had tried Jesus, "It is not lawful for us to put anyone to death" (John 18:31).

In the New Testament the Sanhedrin was involved in hearings against Jesus (Matt. 26:59; Mark 14:55), Peter and John and the other apostles (Acts 4:1–23; 5:17–41), Stephen (Acts 6–7), and Paul (Acts 22–24). Jesus probably was not officially tried by the Sanhedrin. It is more likely that He was given a preliminary hearing to establish the charges against Him and then taken to Pilate. It is also not clear whether Stephen was officially condemned and executed by the Sanhedrin or simply was stoned by an angry mob without due process of law (Acts 7:54–60).

SCIENCE — the systematic organization of knowledge about the laws that govern the world and the universe. The word *science* occurs twice in the KJV (Dan. 1:4; 1 Tim. 6:20), but in both cases the NKJV renders the word as "knowledge." All truth, whether revealed in Scripture or gained from experimentation and observation of God's creation, is God's truth. Ultimate knowledge comes from God and His Word.

SCYTHIANS [SITH ee uhns] — a barbaric race who lived in Scythia, an ancient region of southeastern Europe and southwestern Asia, now generally identified as Russia. In biblical times, the Scythians were a tribe of nomadic raiders notorious for their cruelty and barbarism.

Originally from western Siberia, the Scythians migrated to southern Russia about 2000 B.C. Several centuries later they moved into northern Persia. Eventually they became allies of the Assyrians and oppressed western Persia for almost three decades. After the Medes became a world power, they finally drove the Scythians back to southern Russia.

Famous as raiders, the Scythians carried out a major campaign of plunder against Syria and Palestine in the late 7th century B.C. The prophets Zephaniah and Jeremiah may have referred to this raid. Jeremiah spoke of waters that would rise out of the north and eventually become "an overflowing flood" of God's judgment against the nations of that region of the world (Jer. 47:2).

SECOND COMING — Christ's future return to the earth at the end of the present age. Although the Bible explicitly speaks of Christ's appearance as a "second time," the phrase "second coming" occurs nowhere in the New Testament. Many passages, however, speak of His return. In fact, in the New Testament alone it is referred to over 300 times.

The night before His crucifixion, Jesus told His apostles that He would return (John 14:3). When Jesus ascended into heaven, two angels appeared to His followers, saying that He would return in the same manner as they had seen Him go (Acts 1:11). The New Testament is filled with expectancy of His coming, even as Christians should be today.

Various opinions exist about what is meant by the Second Coming. Some regard it as the coming of the Holy Spirit on the day of Pentecost. Others regard it as the coming of Christ into the heart at conversion. Christ's coming for the believer at the time of death is still another view. Careful examination of the New Testament, however, makes it clear that the Second Coming will be a climactic historical event. The Lord will return in the same manner in which He left. His coming will be personal, bodily, and visible.

The time of the Second Coming is unknown. In fact, Jesus stated that only the Father knew the time. Therefore, the return of the Lord should be a matter of constant expectancy. As He came the first time, in the "fullness of time" (Gal. 4:4), so will the Second Coming be. The believer's task is not to try to determine the time of the Second Coming. We should share the gospel message diligently until He returns (Acts 1:8–11).

SHEBAT [SHEE bat] — the fifth month of the civil year in the Hebrew calendar (Zech. 1:7; Sebat, KJV).

SIDON [SIGH dun] — an ancient Phoenician city on the Mediterranean coast in northern Palestine. Sidon dominated the coastal plain in the area of the Lebanon Mountains. Built on a hill across several small islands, it was connected by bridges.

Sidon was the oldest of the Phoenician cities. Founded by the son of Canaan (Gen. 10:15), it became a principal Canaanite stronghold (Gen. 10:19; 1 Chr. 1:13; Zidon, KJV). So dominant was Sidon originally that "Sidonian" and "Phoenician" became interchangeable terms. Even after the city of Tyre on the coast to the south assumed a position of dominance, Ethbaal, king of Tyre, was called king of the Sidonians (1 Kin. 16:31).

After the Israelites settled the land of Canaan, Sidon was near the territory of Zebulun (Gen. 49:13) and Asher (Josh. 19:28). But the tribe of Asher failed to drive out the inhabitants of Sidon (Judg. 1:31). This indicates something of the strength of the city. Sidon, however, frequently was destroyed by foreign invaders during the next several centuries. But it was rebuilt following each defeat and restored to a position of prominence.

By the time of Alexander the Great in the 4th century B.C., Sidon was still a major Phoenician city. Alexander was received by the Sidonians as a deliverer, and they assisted Alexander as he besieged their neighboring city of Tyre. Later, under Roman rule, Sidon was given the privilege of self-government, which it enjoyed during New Testament times.

Not only did the city of Sidon resist the efforts of the tribe of Asher to inhabit that region but it also oppressed Israel during the period of the judges (Judg. 10:12). Once they were settled in the land, the Israelites began to worship the gods of Sidon, including their chief god Baal (1 Kin. 16:31) but especially Ashtoreth, the goddess of fertility (2 Kin. 23:13). Ethbaal, the king of Sidon, was the father of Jezebel (1 Kin. 16:31), who was mainly responsible for introducing the worship of pagan gods into Israel.

The people of Sidon came to Galilee to hear the preaching of Christ and to be healed by His touch (Mark 3:8; Luke 6:17). Jesus even went to the borders of Tyre and Sidon (Matt.

15:21–28; Mark 7:24–31), where He healed the Syro-Phoenician woman's daughter. Herod Agrippa I was displeased by the people of Tyre and Sidon, but they won over his servant Blastus and begged for peace "because their country was supplied with food by the king's country" (Acts 12:20).

The apostle Paul stopped briefly at Sidon on his way to Rome, meeting with Christian friends there (Acts 27:3). In early Christian history, the city became an important Christian center, sending a bishop to the Council of Nicea in A.D. 325.

Frequently Sidon was the subject of prophecies of judgment. Isaiah predicted that Sidon would pass into the control of Cyprus (Is. 23:12). Jeremiah predicted its defeat by Nebuchadnezzar, king of Babylon (Jer. 27:3, 6). Ezekiel denounced Sidon (Ezek. 28:20–24) because her inhabitants had been "a pricking brier [and] a painful thorn for the house of Israel" (Ezek. 28:24). Joel denounced Sidon for helping to plunder Jerusalem (Joel 3:4–6).

In the 8th century B.C. Sidon was noted for its artistic metalwork and skilled tradesmen who made objects of silver and gold. Like the citizens of Tyre, the Sidonians were also known for their purple dye. The art of glass blowing was in evidence in the 1st century B.C. at Sidon. In the 1st century learned Sidonians were also noted for their study in the sciences of astronomy and arithmetic. Sidon also had a law school that was famed throughout the ancient world.

SIEGE — a prolonged military blockade of a city or fortress to force it to surrender. The purpose of a siege was to take away the advantage of the city's massive defensive walls by cutting off its supplies and contacts from the outside. Without supplies, the defending city would be forced to surrender or to attack the besieging army.

The attacking army would sometimes press the siege by trying to scale the walls with ladders or ramps. Other techniques included battering down the walls or tunneling under them.

But attack was dangerous because the city's defenders were well protected and could carry on the battle from a superior position.

A siege might continue for several months. To shorten a siege, the attacking army usually tried to capture a city's water supplies. These were usually situated outside the city walls.

Much of the warfare described in the Old Testament is siege warfare. For instance, Joab laid siege to Rabbah (2 Sam. 12:26–31) and Sennacherib besieged Jerusalem and all the fortified cities of Judah (Is. 36:1). In the New Testament Jesus predicted the Roman siege of Jerusalem (Luke 19:43–44).

SILOAM [sigh LOW um] (*sent*) — a storage pool and water tunnel that provided a water supply for early residents of the city of Jerusalem. The pool and tunnel drew water from the Gihon spring outside the city wall.

Under the peril of an impending invasion by the armies of Sennacherib, king of Assyria (reigned about 705–681 B.C.), King Hezekiah of Judah "made a pool and a tunnel [or conduit] and brought water into the city" (2 Kin. 20:20). The parallel account in 2 Chronicles says he "stopped the water outlet of Upper Gihon, and brought the water by tunnel to the west side of the City of David" (2 Chr. 32:30).

Hezekiah's tunnel was discovered accidentally in 1838 and was explored by the American traveler Edward Robinson and his missionary friend Eli Smith. They found the Siloam tunnel to be about 518 meters (1,750 feet) long, although the straight line distance between the storage pool and the Gihon spring is only 332 meters (1,090 feet). The course has numerous twists and turns. Some scholars have suggested that by following such a crooked course, the tunnel builders were trying to avoid the royal tombs cut into the same area through which the conduit was cut. But it is just as possible that more accurate surveying methods were unavailable to Hezekiah's technicians.

By any standards, however, Hezekiah's tunnel was a notable achievement.

The tunnel was explored in 1867, but it was not until 1880 that an important Hebrew inscription was discovered near the entrance to the reservoir. It gave a graphic description of how the tunnel was built. Two work crews cut the tunnel through solid rock, working from opposite ends until they met in the middle.

It may have been through another tunnel or gap such as this that David's warriors entered the ancient city of Jerusalem about 1000 B.C. The city was known as Jebus at that time. David captured it and turned it into the capital city of his kingdom.

The Bible does contain some puzzling references to a more ancient pool. The prophet Isaiah, for instance, speaks of Hezekiah's "reservoir between the two walls for the water of the old pool" (Is. 22:11). Perhaps Hezekiah and his craftsmen used an existing reservoir and linked it to his tunnel and pool.

SIMEON, TRIBE OF — One of the 12 tribes of Israel, descended from Simeon No. 1 (Rev. 7:7). Simeon had 6 sons—Jemuel (Nemuel), Jamin, Ohad, Jachin (Jerib), Zohar (Zerah), and Shaul—and all but Ohad founded tribal families (Ex. 6:15).

The tribe of Simeon numbered 59,300 fighting men at the first census in the wilderness (Num. 1:23; 2:13) and 22,200 at the second (Num. 26:12–14). This tribe was omitted in Moses' blessing of the nation of Israel (Deuteronomy 33). A comparison of the cities assigned to Simeon with those assigned to Judah (Josh. 15:20–63; 19:1–9; 1 Chr. 4:28–33) makes it appear that the tribe of Simeon had been assimilated into the tribe of Judah, thus fulfilling Jacob's prophecy (Gen. 49:5–7).

When the land of Canaan was divided, the second lot fell to Simeon. The tribe received land in the extreme southern part of Canaan, in the middle of Judah's territory (Josh. 19:1–9).

Simeon united with Judah in fighting the Canaanites (Judg. 1:1, 3, 17). Among the Simeonite cities were Beersheba, Hormah, and Ziklag (Josh. 19:1–9). Although the descendants of Simeon disappeared as a tribe, Ezekiel mentions it in his prophecies about a future land of Canaan (Ezek. 48:24–25, 33). The book of Revelation mentions 12,000 of the tribe of Simeon who were sealed (Rev. 7:7).

SIVAN [sih VAN] — the third month of the sacred Hebrew year (Esth. 8:9). Sivan went from the new moon of May to the new moon of June.

STOICISM [STOW uh siz em] — the doctrine of the Stoics, a Greek school of philosophy that taught that human beings should be free from passion, unmoved by joy or grief, and submissive to natural law, calmly accepting all things as the result of divine will.

Stoicism was one of the most influential Greek schools of philosophy in the New Testament period. It took its name from the Stoa Poikile, the portico or lecture place in Athens where its founder, Zeno, taught.

The Stoics believed that people are part of the universe, which itself is dominated by reason. God is identified with the world-soul and so inhabits everything. Therefore, one's goal is to identify oneself with this universal reason that determines destiny, to find one's proper place in the natural order of things. Since people cannot change this grand design, it is best for them to cooperate and to take their part in the world order. Moreover, they must live above any emotional involvement with life, exemplifying a detached virtue in serving others. Above all, they must be self-sufficient, living life with dignity and pride.

The apostle Paul used the word *self-sufficient* in a radically different sense in Philippians 4:11. Here Paul spoke of the believer's self-sufficiency in God. Paul's speech on the Areopagus, or Mars Hill (Acts 17:16–34), interacts with Stoic ideas, arguing that the highest good is not internal (in our union with nature) but external (in a right relationship with God).

In his address, Paul quoted one of the Stoic poets (Aratus), who said, "For we are also His offspring" (Acts 17:28). Some of these philosophers ridiculed Paul, but others invited him to address them again about the Christ in whom he believed so strongly (Acts 17:32).

SUMER [SOO mehr] — the southern division of ancient Babylonia, consisting primarily of the fertile plain between the Tigris and Euphrates rivers. This area is now the southern part of modern Iraq.

In the Old Testament Sumer is the territory referred to as "Shinar" (Gen. 10:10; Is. 11:11; Zech. 5:11) or Chaldea (Jer. 50:10; Ezek. 16:29). The term "Shinar" is also used to describe the land of the great tyrant and empire builder Nimrod, who founded his kingdom in Babel, Erech (Sumerian Uruk), Accad (Akkad or Agade), and Calneh, "in the land of Shinar" (Gen. 10:10). The Tower of Babel was also built "in the land of Shinar" (Gen. 11:2), or Sumer.

Archaeologists believe the inhabitants of ancient Sumer, or the Sumerians, developed the first high civilization in the history of mankind, before 3000 B.C. The Sumerians were the first people to develop writing, consisting of a form of cuneiform-script. Major cities of ancient Sumer included the biblical Ur (Gen. 11:28, 31; 15:7), the city from which Abraham migrated.

Before 2100 B.C. Sumer was conquered by invading tribesmen from the west and north. A mighty warrior named Sargon (later known as Sargon I, Sargon the Great, and Sargon of Akkad) conquered this area and extended his empire from the Persian Gulf to the Mediterranean Sea. He founded a new capital city, Agade, which was, for more than half a century, the richest and most powerful capital in the world. This magnificent capital was destroyed during the reign of Naram–Sin, Sargon's grandson, by the Guti, semibarbaric mountain tribes.

Sumer enjoyed a brief revival at Ur (about 2050 B.C.), only to decline before the rise of the Elamites, a people to their east. Finally, in about 1720 B.C., Hammurapi of Babylon united Sumer (the southern division of ancient Babylon) and Akkad (the northern division of ancient Babylon) into one empire. This conquest by Hammurapi marked the end of ancient Sumer. But the cultural and intellectual impact of the Sumerians continued until after the Persians became the dominant force in this part of the ancient world.

SYNAGOGUE — a congregation of Jews for worship or religious study. The word *synagogue* comes from the Greek *synagoge* (literally, "a leading or bringing together"), which refers to any assembly or gathering of people for secular or religious purposes. Eventually the term came to refer exclusively to an assembly of Jewish people.

The synagogue was a place where local groups of Jews in cities and villages anywhere could gather for the reading and explanation of the Jewish sacred Scriptures and for prayer. The original emphasis was not on preaching but instruction in the law of Moses.

Function. A distinction must be made between synagogue worship and tabernacle or temple worship. The tabernacle of Moses' day was enclosed by a fence of curtains. None but the priests dared enter this area. The people brought their animals for sacrifice to the gate of the court but could go no further. The later temples of Solomon, Zerubbabel, and Herod (the temple of Jesus' day) did have courts or porches where the people could pray or have discussions (Matt. 26:55; Luke 2:46; Acts 2:46), but the temple precincts proper were for the priests only.

In synagogues, on the other hand, the people took part in worship, reading of the Scriptures, and prayer. By New Testament times synagogues were very numerous and popular. They became centers of community activity, playing a number of roles.

Sometimes they were local courts of justice that could sentence the offender as well as inflict the punishment of scourging (Matt. 10:17; 23:34). The synagogue was also an elementary school for teaching children to read. It was, no doubt, a center of social life for the Jewish community.

Origin. The Jewish captives in Babylon did not have a temple or an altar, but they longed for communion with God. This longing is clearly reflected in Psalm 137 and Daniel 9. It was only natural for them to meet in local groups for prayer and the reading of the Scriptures.

When the Jews returned to their land, Ezra the scribe promoted the reading of the Law and prayer (Nehemiah 8). But Zerubbabel had rebuilt the temple, giving the Palestinian Jews a worship center. Many Jews, however, lived in Persia and others had fled to many countries. By about 300 B.C. a large community of Jews lived in Alexandria, Egypt. A marble slab found near Alexandria bears an inscription dedicating a synagogue to Ptolemy III (Euergetes), who ruled Egypt from 246–221 B.C., and his queen Berenice. This is the first solid evidence of a true synagogue. Within Palestine one of the oldest known synagogues is the one uncovered on Masada near the Dead Sea, built in the 1st century B.C.

In Jesus' day synagogues were common even in the villages. They must have been well established with the customary officials and order of worship (Luke 4:14–30; 8:41). Paul found synagogues in cities throughout the Roman Empire (Acts 9:2, Damascus; 13:5, Salamis; 13:14, Antioch in Pisidia; 14:1, Iconium; 17:1, Thessalonica; 17:10, Berea; 17:16–17, Athens; 19:1,

8, Ephesus). This shows that the synagogue had existed for a long time.

The Building. Three types of synagogue architecture developed. The earliest was the basilica. This was a rectangular building with one of the narrower ends facing Jerusalem. The door on this side was a triple door with elaborate stone carvings above the doors. Inside were two rows of three or four pillars each. This made a large central seating area with two smaller areas, one on each side, beyond the pillars.

Along the side walls were some stone benches, but not enough to seat the congregation. Probably the people sat cross-legged on the floor as they still do in Eastern mosques. At the far end of the room was a platform that held the Torah Ark, a cabinet or chest that contained the scrolls of the sacred Scriptures, wrapped in linen. Here too were the lamps and the lectern on which the scrolls were laid to be read in the service. Arranged in front were the "best seats" of the elders (Matt. 23:6).

The basilica had an awkward problem. Prayer and the reading of Scripture had to be done facing Jerusalem, but the entrance door was toward Jerusalem; therefore, the Torah Ark had to be carried or wheeled to the other end of the building. The congregation had to stand up and turn around during the reading and prayer.

The broadhouse solved this problem by making the long side of the building face Jerusalem. This created room on each side of the door for a platform for the Torah Ark and the bema or lectern. Most broadhouses did not have pillars.

The apsidal synagogue was arranged like a modern church or synagogue. On the side toward Jerusalem was a platform with a niche or alcove back of it for the Torah Ark. The main door was at the rear.

The Officials. A synagogue could not be formed unless there were at least ten Jewish men in the community. Some synagogues paid ten unemployed men a small sum to be present at

every service to be sure this rule was met. The following officials served in a synagogue.

Elders — A board of elders made up of devout and respected
men of the community regulated the policies of the synagogue.

Ruler of the synagogue — There could be one or more rulers.
They were appointed by the elders. Their duty was to attend
to matters concerning the building and the planning of the
services.

Minister — The minister (chazzan) had several duties. He
had charge of the sacred scrolls that were kept in the Ark; he
attended to the lamps; and he kept the building clean. If an
offender was found guilty by the council of elders, the chazzan
administered the number of lashes prescribed for the scourging. During the week the chazzan taught elementary children
how to read.

Delegate of the congregation — This was not a permanent
office. Before each service the ruler chose a capable person to
read the Scripture lesson, to lead in prayer, and to preach or
comment on the Scripture. Jesus was selected for this office in
the synagogue in Nazareth (Luke 4:16–20).

Interpreter — The Scriptures were written in ancient Hebrew.
By Jesus' day the people spoke Aramaic, a language related to
Hebrew but different enough to call for an interpreter.

Almoners — These were two or three persons who received
money or other necessities for the poor.

Order of Worship. The customary seating order placed the
elders in the chief seats at the platform. Jesus rebuked some of
those who loved the best seats merely for the praise and honor
they conferred (Matt. 23:6). The front seats in the congregation
were for the older spiritual leaders. The younger people and
other individuals sat to the rear. A special section was reserved
for lepers.

The service began with the recitation of the Shema by the
people. Shema ("Hear") is the first Hebrew word in the passage

in Deuteronomy 6:4–9: "Hear, O Israel: The LORD our God, the LORD is one!" The Shema includes Numbers 15:37–41 and Deuteronomy 6:4–9; 11:13–21.

The speaker for the day then led the congregation in prayer as they stood facing Jerusalem with hands extended. At the close of the prayer the people said "Amen."

Before the service the minister took from the Torah Ark the scrolls containing the lesson for the day and placed them on the lectern. The chosen speaker stood and read the lesson from the Law of Moses and the interpreter translated it verse by verse into Aramaic. Then the passage from the Prophets was read and translated.

For the commentary or sermon the speaker usually sat down (Luke 4:20). After the sermon, a priest, if one was present, pronounced a benediction and the people said "Amen." If no priest was present, a closing prayer was offered.

Influence. Synagogue worship has influenced both Christian and Muslim worship. The earliest Christians were Jews. Therefore, church worship followed the synagogue pattern with Scripture reading, prayer, and a sermon. In the 7th century A.D. Muhammad learned much from Jewish customs and also spent some time at Bosora or Bostra in the desert east of Gilead where a Christian bishopric was located. Hence, the mosques of Islam reflect worship patterns from both Jewish and Christian services.

SYRIA [SIHR ih uh] — a major nation northeast of Palestine that served as a political threat to the nations of Judah and Israel during much of their history. The name "Syria" comes from the Greek language. The Hebrew language of the Old Testament uses the word *Aram* for the region. Almost 2 percent of the Old Testament was originally written in the Aramaic language.

The boundaries of Syria changed often in biblical times. Often a particular group of Syrians such as those of Damascus or Zobah or else some combination of cities or regions are referred to as "Syria" or "the Syrians" in the Old Testament. Most of these references designate the region that makes up the southeastern part of the modern nation of Syria.

The Syrians (Arameans) were part of the massive migrations of population groups that occurred from about 3000 to 2100 B.C. They eventually settled in several parts of the ancient world, including much of northern Mesopotamia. One group, probably seminomads from the Arabian desert fringes, settled in force in the area north and east of Canaan. It is this group that the Israelites had most contact with during the time of the Israelite kings.

Gradually, these settlements produced the Aramean states known as Hamath, Zobah, and Damascus, each of which was an independent city-state. At times, all of these states were allied together against a common threat, such as that posed by the Assyrians. One or another of these "states" was often at war with Israel, until the Assyrians, under one of their kings, Tiglath-Pileser III (745–727 B.C.), defeated Syria and annexed it to the Assyrian Empire.

After this conquest, many Syrians were exiled to various parts of the Assyrian Empire, just as many citizens of the northern kingdom of Israel were carried away (2 Kin. 17:23). Some Syrians were even forced to settle in Samaria (2 Kin. 17:24). Thereafter Syria was ruled as a province by Babylonia, Persia, the Seleucids, and Rome in successive conquests by these ancient world powers.

In New Testament times Syria was a Roman province, linked with Cilicia. Syrians were among those who first responded to Jesus' preaching and healing ministry (Matt. 4:23–24). The gospel spread rapidly in Syria. Many of the places mentioned in the book of Acts (Damascus, Antioch, Seleucia, Caesarea Philippi) were located in Syria.

Saul of Tarsus (the apostle Paul) was converted in Syria, while he was on the road to Damascus (Acts 9:3). His first missionary journey began from the great church at Antioch of Syria (Acts 13:1–3), and he traveled through Syria on several occasions (Acts 15:41; 18:18; Gal. 1:21).

SYRIANS [SIHR ih uns] — inhabitants or citizens of Syria, the ancient nation northeast of Palestine. The Hebrew people had many contacts with these people during their history. Jacob was a Syrian (Deut. 26:5).

During the period of the Judges, one of the foreign oppressors of the Israelites was a Syrian (Aramean), Cushan-Rishathaim. He was king of Aram-Naharaim, a kingdom of Syrians in Mesopotamia. The NKJV and the KJV translate the term simply as Mesopotamia (Judg. 3:8, 10). The "gods of Syria" (Judg. 10:6) are mentioned among the various idols the Israelites began to worship at this time, as their faithfulness to the Lord faltered and they were influenced by the Syrians living in Canaan (Josh. 13:13).

David (1010–971 B.C.) fought against and either conquered or subdued several of the Syrian states, including Zoba, Rehob, Tob, Maacah, and Abel of Beth Maachah (2 Sam. 10:8; 20:15). Eventually David made even Damascus a part of his kingdom (2 Sam. 8:5), and he had influence over Toi, king of Hamath (2 Sam. 8:9–10). In fact, David's victories over the Syrians were probably his most famous military achievements. He killed 18,000 Syrians in the Valley of Salt (2 Sam. 8:13).

Solomon (970–931 B.C.) won a military victory against Hamath Zobah, which some scholars interpret as the allied Syrian city-states of Hamath and Zobah (2 Chr. 8:3–4). He used the area of Hamath as a place to build storage cities—something he would not have done if he did not have military control of the area. Some time later in Solomon's reign, however, a Syrian named Rezon seized power in Damascus and became an enemy of Solomon (1 Kin. 11:23–25; Rezon is probably to be identified with Hezion, the grandfather of Ben-Hadad, 1 Kin. 15:18).

The Bible says that Rezon "reigned over Syria" (1 Kin. 11:25). This can only mean that Solomon's power began to wane so that he lost control of Syria. God caused Israel's kingdom to weaken in order to punish Solomon and Israel for their idolatry (1 Kin. 11:14–40), and the Syrians were part of this process.

Once Rezon (or Hezion) had come to power, most of Syria, except for the area around Hamath, was under the control of Damascus. His son, Tabrimmon, and his grandson, Ben-Hadad I, succeeded him as kings over Syria, reigning in succession through the middle of the 9th century B.C. (1 Kin. 15:18). Ben-Hadad fought major wars with Israel, but was defeated by Ahab (ruled 874–853 B.C.) each time (1 Kin. 20:1–34).

Later in Ahab's reign, however, Israel and Syria put aside their differences long enough to join a coalition in battle against the Assyrians at Qarqar (853 B.C.), on the Orontes River—a battle that kept the Asyrians from adding Syria and Palestine to the Assyrian Empire. But Ahab's unwillingness to crush Ben-Hadad I and the Syrians brought on the wrath of God (1 Kin. 20:35–43).

After Hazael (843–796 B.C.) became king of Syria in Damascus by assassinating Ben-Hadad (2 Kin. 8:7–15), the Syrians again were at war with Israel (2 Kin. 8:28) and gained more and more against Israel as God planned (2 Kin. 10:32–33). King Joash of Judah had to pay tribute to Hazael to keep him from destroying Jerusalem (2 Kin. 12:17–18). God had caused the Syrians to turn the tables on Israel (2 Kin. 13:13).

In His mercy, however, God delivered Israel (2 Kin. 13:4) when Jehoahaz (ruled 814–798 B.C.) was king, probably by causing the Assyrians to attack the Syrians, thus relieving Israel. King Joash, or Jehoash (ruled 798–782 B.C.) of Israel was successful in battle against Ben-Hadad II of Syria, as the prophet Elisha had prophesied on his deathbed (2 Kin. 13:14–19, 25). Thereafter, Israel ruled over Syria once again (2 Kin. 14:28) under the powerful Israelite King Jeroboam II (ruled 793–753 B.C.).

When Rezin became king in Damascus, he threw off Israelite control. Then, in alliance with Pekah (740–732 B.C.), king of Israel, he attacked Judah, because King Ahaz (735–715 B.C.) of Judah refused to join a group of allies in rebelling against the control of the Assyrians. The war that followed is called the Syro-Ephraimite War (734–732 B.C.). Ahaz turned directly to the Assyrians for help. The Assyrians captured and annexed Syria (and most of Israel), thus ending the threat to Judah and ending Syria's existence as an independent nation (2 Kin. 16:9).

T

TABERNACLE [TAB ur nack el] — the tent that served as a place of worship for the nation of Israel during their early history.

On Mount Sinai, after the Lord had given the commandments, judgments, and ordinances to Moses, He instructed Moses to construct the tabernacle. This was to be a center for worship and a place where the people could focus upon the presence of the Lord. This tabernacle was to replace the temporary tent that had been pitched outside the camp (Ex. 33:7–11). God began the description of this building by giving His people the opportunity to participate in its construction. They did this by giving an offering of the needed materials, including a combination of rare and beautiful fabrics and precious metals, along with supplies easily available in the wilderness.

After describing the offering (Ex. 25:1–9), the Lord proceeded to specify in minute detail the pattern for the tabernacle. He began by giving a description of the holiest item in the entire structure: the ark of the covenant (Ex. 25:10–22). Other items in the tabernacle for which the Lord gave minute construction details included the seven-branched lampstand (Ex. 25:31–39); the intricate curtains of the tabernacle (Ex. 26:1–25); the veils and the screen (Ex. 26:1–37); the large bronze altar of burnt offering (Ex. 27:1–8); and the hangings for the courtyard (Ex. 27:9–19).

A brief recipe for the oil to be used in worship is given in Exodus 27:20–21, followed by a description of the priests' garments and consecration (Exodus 28–29). Directions for making the golden incense altar are given in Exodus 30:1–10. After a brief statement about a tax assessment (Ex. 30:11–16), the Lord told Moses to build a bronze laver (Ex. 30:17–21).

Mixed in with these instructions about specific items of the tabernacle are plans for the architecture and design of the building. The tabernacle was in the form of a tent 10 cubits wide and 30 cubits long. It was to be set up with its only entrance toward the east. The tent consisted of a wooden framework made of 46 identical planks 10 cubits long and 1 and one-half cubits wide; there were 20 planks each on the north and south sides. Six of the planks were on the west end, along with 2 additional planks that were one-half cubit wide. All of these planks were acacia wood plated with gold.

Over this framework were 4 separate coverings that made up the roof of the structure. The first covering was made of fine-twined linen of blue, scarlet, and purple with intricately portrayed cherubim. The second covering was of pure white goats' hair. The third was of rams' skins dyed red. The topmost covering was of material referred to in the NKJV as badger skins. Other English translations suggest that this should be translated porpoise skins, skins of sea cows, or possibly leather.

The tent constructed in this manner was then divided into 2 rooms divided by an intricate veil of blue, scarlet, and purple linen embroidered with cherubim.

The inner, western room was called the Holy of Holies. It was 10 cubits square, and it contained only 1 piece of furniture—the holiest item in the tabernacle, the ark of the covenant. The ark was a chest made of acacia wood covered with gold, 2 and one-half cubits long and 1 one-half cubits in width and height. In addition, a gold border extended above the top of the ark to keep the lid stationary. The ark also had golden rings on each side so it could be transported with poles that were placed through the rings. The lid of the ark was called the Mercy Seat. Upon it were 2 gold cherubim that faced each other. The ark contained a copy of the stone tablets with the Ten Commandments, a gold pot filled with manna, and Aaron's rod that budded.

The outer, eastern room was called the Holy Place. Ten cubits wide and 20 cubits long, it was entered through the blue, scarlet, and purple linen curtains that served as a door. This door was always aligned toward the east. It contained 3 items. On its western side, next to the veil, was the altar of incense, or golden altar, 1 cubit square and 2 cubits high. Upon this altar, made of acacia wood overlaid with gold, the morning and evening incense was burned.

On the southern side of the Holy Place was the 7-branched golden lampstand, or candlestick, comprising a pedestal, a shaft, and 3 branches extending to both sides of the shaft. This lampstand was made of a talent of fine gold. On the northern side of the Holy Place was the table for the showbread, or bread of the Presence. This table was made of gold-covered acacia wood 2 cubits long, 1 cubit wide, and 1 and one-half cubits high.

Surrounding the main building of the tabernacle was a spacious courtyard 100 cubits long in its east-west direction and 50 cubits wide from north to south. This courtyard was surrounded by a fence 5 cubits high, formed of bronze pillars with silverwork, resting in bronze sockets, placed 5 cubits apart, and hung with fine linen. In the western half of this courtyard the tabernacle itself was to be pitched, and in the eastern half stood two items—the altar of burnt offering or the great bronze altar, and the laver.

The description of the actual building of the tabernacle is recorded in Exodus 35–40. The workers were first enlisted. Then the building of each item of the tabernacle is described in Exodus 36–39. The record of the tabernacle's construction occurs in Exodus 40. Up to this time, the nation of Israel had used a temporary tent called the tabernacle of the congregation; it is mentioned in Exodus 33:7–11. The tabernacle continued to be called the tabernacle of the congregation, among other names, after its construction. When the Israelites pitched camp in the wilderness, the tabernacle was to be placed in the center, with the Levites camping next to it (Num. 1:53). Then the tribes were to be arrayed in specific order on the 4 sides of the tabernacle (Numbers 2).

Responsibilities for the care and moving of the tabernacle were delegated to various families of the tribe of Levi (Num. 1:50–52; 3–4). The Levitical family of Kohath was to disassemble the structure and cover the tabernacle furnishings with the badger skins. The tapestries were the responsibility of the family of Gershon. Merari's family had charge of the boards, pillars, foundations, pins, and cords. All these Levitical families were commissioned to care for the sanctuary.

The first day of tabernacle worship is described in Numbers 7–9. The guiding pillar of cloud and fire rested upon the tabernacle when the people were encamped. When the people were on the march, with the pillar serving as their guide, the tribes that camped on the east of the tabernacle were first in marching order. These were Judah, Issachar, and Zebulun. The tabernacle was carried by the assigned family members of Gershon and Merari.

The next group in the marching order were the tribes that camped on the south of the tabernacle. These were Reuben, Simeon, and Gad. Following these, the family of Kohath carried the holy objects of the tabernacle.

Then came the tribes that camped on the west of the tabernacle. These were Ephraim, Manasseh, and Benjamin.

The rear guard of the march comprised the tribes that camped on the north of the tabernacle. These were Dan, Asher, and Naphtali.

When the tribes were camped, 2 silver trumpets were used to summon the tribes to gather at the tabernacle. The tabernacle was also the place where the 70 elders advised and counseled the people (Num. 11:16). It was also the place of specific judgments (Num. 12:4) and appointments (Deut. 31:14).

During the conquest of the land of Canaan by the Israelites, the tabernacle remained at Gilgal, while the ark of the covenant was evidently carried from place to place with the armies of Israel. The ark was reported at the crossing of the Jordan (Josh. 3:6), at Gilgal (Josh. 4:11), at the conquest of Jericho (Josh. 6:4), at the campaigns against Ai (Josh. 7:6), and at Mount Ebal (Josh. 8:33).

The tabernacle was finally placed on the site it was to occupy during the duration of the period of conquest and judges, at Shiloh (Josh. 18:1). Here the tribes were assigned their territorial allotments.

As the years passed, certain other structures were added to the tabernacle while it remained at Shiloh. These included living quarters for the priests and Levites who served at the tabernacle. By the end of the period of the judges, during the administration of Eli, at least some of the attendants lived on the premises (1 Sam. 3:3).

During the Israelites' battle against the Philistines at Aphek, the ark of the covenant was removed from the tabernacle and taken into battle. Lost to the Philistines, it finally came to rest at Kirjath Jearim (1 Sam. 4:1–7:1). It remained here until the time of David's reign.

With the departure of the ark, the tabernacle lost some of its esteem in the eyes of the Hebrew people (Ps. 78:60). During the reign of Saul, the tabernacle was at Nob (1 Sam. 21:1). From the latter part of David's reign throughout the fourth year of

Solomon's reign, the tabernacle was at the high place of Gibeon (1 Chr. 16:39; 21:29). When the temple was completed, Solomon had the Levites bring the tabernacle to Jerusalem (1 Kin. 8:4; 2 Chr. 5:5), presumably to be stored in the temple area.

The New Testament uses some terminology and concepts drawn directly from the tabernacle. The supreme event of all the ages is the existence of God's son in human form. The Bible declares that the Word became flesh and "tabernacled" (Greek word rendered as "dwelt" in the NKJV) among us (John 1:14). In his final speech, Stephen accepted the Old Testament account of the tabernacle as historical (Acts 7:44). In Romans 3:25, Paul used the word *propitiation*, which might also be translated "mercy seat." Titus 3:5 probably refers to the laver. Revelation 8:3–5 speaks of the golden incense altar. In Revelation 13:6 and 15:5, reference is made to the heavenly tabernacle. Practically every feature of the tabernacle is found in the book of Hebrews.

TAX, TAXES — a compulsory fee or financial contribution for the maintenance of government. Taxes may have originated with the custom of giving presents for protection from harm (Gen. 32:13–21; 33:10; 43:11). When Joseph revealed to the Pharaoh in Egypt that there would be 7 years of famine after 7 years of abundance, Pharaoh put him in charge of raising revenues. During the time of famine as well as plenty, he collected a 20 percent tax to store up food and then to buy land for Pharaoh (Gen. 47:20–26).

During the time of the Exodus, Moses asked for voluntary revenues for the construction of the tabernacle (Ex. 25:2; 35:5, 21). The Mosaic law prescribed that every male over the age of 20 was to give half a shekel for the service of the tabernacle (Ex. 30:11–16).

With the establishment of the United Kingdom under David and Solomon, several avenues of taxation were established: a 10 percent tax on the produce of land and livestock (1 Sam.

8:15, 17); compulsory military service for one month each year (1 Chr. 27:1); and import duties (1 Kin. 10:15). Tribute was also paid by subject peoples (2 Sam. 8:6; 2 Kin. 3:4). The oppressive taxation by Solomon was one of the causes of the split of the kingdom after his death (1 Kin. 12:4).

When the Persians came into power and ruled over Palestine, they set up a new system of taxation. Instead of paying tribute to a foreign master, each province in the Persian Empire was required to collect its own taxes. Each Persian satrap was to collect for his own province. The decree of Darius Hystaspis states that the satraps paid a fixed amount into the royal treasury. The revenue collected was derived from tribute, custom, and toll (Ezra 4:13). Priests and others involved in religious service were exempted from these taxes (Ezra 7:24). Beyond the central government's tax, a tax was also collected for the maintenance of the governor's household. The taxes were so heavy that many people were forced to mortgage their fields and vineyards. Some even sold their own sons and daughters into slavery (Neh. 5:1–5).

During the period between the Old and New Testament, the Jews were first under the Egyptian Ptolemaic rule (301–198 B.C.) and later under the Syrian Seleucid rule (198–63 B.C.). Under the Ptolemies taxes were not collected by an Egyptian representative. Instead, taxing privileges were farmed out to the highest bidders. From the various provinces people would come to Alexandria to bid for the privilege of collecting taxes from their own people. The bidder who won the contract would tax the people up to double the amount required by law in order to make a handsome profit. These contracted tax collectors were given military assistance to enable them to enforce their demands.

This same type of taxation system probably continued in Palestine under Syrian rule. A poll tax, a salt tax, and a crown tax were enforced during this time. The Syrians taxed as much as one-third of the grain, one-half of the fruit, and a portion of the tithes the Jews paid to support the temple.

When the Romans under Pompey captured Jerusalem in 63 B.C., a tax of 10,000 talents was temporarily imposed on the Jews. The tax-contracting system was reformed by Julius Caesar, who reduced the taxes and levied no tax in the sabbatic years. But soon after the Herods came to power in Palestine, they demanded heavy taxes.

The Herods instituted a poll tax and a tax on fishing rights in the rivers and lakes. Customs were collected on trade routes by men like Levi, who collected in Capernaum (Matt. 9:9; Mark 2:14; Luke 5:27). This city may have also been a place for port duties and fishing tolls. Some items sold for 1,000 percent above their original prices because of all the taxes. There may have been sales tax on slaves, oil, clothes, hides, and furs. Over and above these taxes were the religious dues. These were generally between 10 and 20 percent of a person's income before government tax.

During Jesus' time, the Jews were probably paying from 30 to 40 percent of their income on taxes and religious dues.

TEMPLE — a building in which a god (or gods) is worshiped. The Old Testament describes temples as some of the oldest buildings ever constructed. The Tower of Babel (Gen. 11:4) is the first recorded example of a structure that implies the existence of a temple, although this tower was not a temple itself. A temple was thought of as the building where the god manifested his presence, so the place the temple occupied was holy or sacred. Because the god was thought to dwell in the temple, the Old Testament had no specific word for temple. It refers instead to the "house" of a deity.

Abraham was from Mesopotamia, where each city had a temple for its patron god. The Mesopotamians believed that the god owned their land, that the king was the vassal of the god, and that the land had to be blessed by the god in order to be fruitful. Their religious practices were, in part, designed to win the god's favor.

Several Canaanite temples are mentioned in the Old Testament. They include the temples of the god Berith in Shechem (Judg. 9:46) as well as Dagon in Ashdod (Judg. 16:23–30; 1 Sam. 5:2–5; 1 Chr. 10:10) and in Beth Shean (1 Sam. 31:12).

Because they were wandering herdsmen, the patriarchs such as Abraham and Jacob did not build temples. However, they did have shrines and altars in places where God had revealed Himself to them, such as by the oak of Moreh (Gen. 12:6–7; 33:20), at Bethel (Gen. 12:8; 28:18–22), and at Beersheba (Gen. 21:33; 26:23–25).

Even after Solomon's temple was completed, rival sanctuaries at Bethel and Dan (1 Kin. 12:28–33) competed with it. Later the Samaritans had a temple on Mount Gerizim (John 4:20). A Judeo-Aramaic colony founded a temple at Elephantine in Upper Egypt. According to the Jewish historian Josephus, Ptolemy VI Philometor (181–145 B.C.) granted Jewish refugees in Egypt the use of an ancient temple in the delta region.

Solomon's Temple. Once the land was fully conquered and all the tribes were properly settled, it was important that the worship of God be centralized. Because he was a man of war, David was not allowed to build the temple, but he was allowed to gather the materials for it and to organize the project (1 Chr. 22:1–19). The actual work began "in the four hundred and eightieth year after the children of Israel had come out of the land of Egypt, in the fourth year of Solomon's reign over Israel" (1 Kin. 6:1). Solomon began to reign about 970 B.C., so his fourth year would have been about 966 B.C. The temple was completed about 7 years later (1 Kin. 6:37–38).

In biblical times three temples were built on the same site: Solomon's, Zerubbabel's, and Herod's. Solomon built the temple on the east side of Jerusalem on Mount Moriah, "where the

Lord had appeared to his father David, at the place that David had prepared on the threshing floor of Ornan the Jebusite" (1 Chr. 21:28; 2 Chr. 3:1). The highest part of Mount Moriah is perhaps now the site of the Dome of the Rock in Jerusalem.

Solomon contacted Hiram, king of Tyre, to supply workmen and materials to help construct the temple (2 Chr. 2:3). First Kings 5:6 calls those workmen Sidonians. Additionally, Solomon "raised up a labor force out of all Israel" of 30,000 men to assist Hiram in the forests of Lebanon (1 Kin. 5:13). According to 1 Kings 5:15, "Solomon had seventy thousand who carried burdens, and eighty thousand who quarried stone in the mountains." The Gebalites also helped to quarry stones (1 Kin. 5:18). Those who quarried stones were overseen by 3,300 of Solomon's deputies (1 Kin. 5:16).

Solomon's temple is described, though incompletely, in 1 Kings 6–7 and in 2 Chronicles 3–4. The description of Ezekiel's temple (Ezek. 40–43), an elaborate version of Solomon's, may supplement those accounts. Solomon's temple was in the shape of a rectangle that ran east and west. Like Ezekiel's temple (Ezek. 41:8), it may have stood on a platform. The accounts in Kings and Chronicles suggest that there was an inner and an outer courtyard.

Three main objects were situated in the inner courtyard. The bronze altar that was used for burnt offerings (1 Kin. 8:22, 64; 9:25) measured 20 cubits square and 10 cubits high (2 Chr. 4:1). Between that and the porch of the temple stood the bronze laver, or molten sea, that held water for the ritual washings (1 Kin. 7:23–26). It was completely round, 5 cubits high, 10 cubits in diameter, and 30 cubits around its circumference (1 Kin. 7:23). Twelve bronze oxen, in 4 groups of 3, faced outward toward the 4 points of the compass, with the bronze laver resting on their backs (1 Kin. 7:25; Ahaz removed the bronze laver from the oxen; 2 Kin. 16:17).

Finally, at the dedication of the temple, Solomon is said to have stood on a "bronze platform five cubits long, five cubits wide, and three cubits high" that stood in the middle of the courtyard (2 Chr. 6:12–13).

The interior dimensions of the temple were 60 cubits long, 20 cubits wide, and 30 cubits high (1 Kin. 6:2). The 10 steps to the porch of the temple were flanked by 2 bronze columns, Jachin and Boaz, each 25 cubits high (including the capitals) and 12 cubits in circumference (1 Kin. 7:15–16; 2 Chr. 3:15). The porch was 10 cubits long, 20 cubits wide, and, supposedly, 120 cubits high (2 Chr. 3:4). But since the rest of the building was only 30 cubits high, some scholars question this figure of 120 cubits.

To the west of the porch was the Holy Place, a room 40 cubits long, 20 cubits wide, and 30 cubits high where ordinary rituals took place. Windows near the ceiling provided light. In the Holy Place were the golden incense altar, the table for the showbread, 5 pairs of lampstands, and the utensils used for sacrifice. Double doors, probably opened once a year for the high priest on the Day of Atonement, led from the west end of the Holy Place to the Holy of Holies, a 20-cubit cube. In that room 2 wooden cherubim, each 10 feet tall, stood with outstretched wings. Two of the wings met above the ark of the covenant and 2 of them touched the north and south walls of the room (1 Kin. 6:27). God's presence was manifested in the Holy of Holies as a cloud (1 Kin. 8:10–11).

The outside of the temple building, excluding the porch area, consisted of side chambers, or galleries, that rose 3 stories high (1 Kin. 6:5). The rooms of the temple were paneled with cedar, the floor was cypress, and the ornately carved doors and walls were overlaid with gold (1 Kin. 6:20–22). Not a stone could be seen.

Shishak, king of Egypt, took away the temple treasures during the reign of Rehoboam, Solomon's son (1 Kin. 14:26). Asa used the temple treasure to buy an ally (1 Kin. 15:18) and to buy off an invader (2 Kin. 16:8). Manasseh placed Canaanite altars and a carved image of Asherah, a Canaanite goddess, in the temple (2 Kin. 21:4, 7). Ahaz introduced an altar patterned after one he saw in Damascus (2 Kin. 16:10–16). By about 630 B.C., Josiah had to repair the temple (2 Kin. 22:3–7). After robbing the temple of its treasures and gold during his first attack (2 Kin. 24:13), in 586 B.C. the Babylonian king Nebuchadnezzar looted, sacked, and burned the temple (2 Kin. 25:9, 13–17), but people still came to the site to offer sacrifice (Jer. 41:5).

Ezekiel's Temple. Ezekiel's vision of a future temple (Ezekiel 40–43) comforted the Jewish captives in Babylon (Psalm 137) who remembered the glory of Solomon's temple and its destruction by the Babylonians. The temple in Ezekiel's vision differs in its physical configuration and dimensions from Solomon's.

The Second Temple. Cyrus, king of Persia, authorized the return of the Jewish captives, the return of the temple vessels Nebuchadnezzar had looted, and the reconstruction of the temple (about 538 B.C.), which was finished about 515 B.C. The completed temple was smaller than and inferior to Solomon's (Ezra 3:12). The ark of the covenant was never recovered, and so the second temple (and Herod's temple) had no ark. Neither were Solomon's ten lampstands recovered. One 7-branched lampstand, the table of showbread, and the incense altar stood in the Holy Place of the second temple (as they did in Herod's temple), but these were taken by Antiochus IV Epiphanes (about 175–163 B.C.), who defiled the altar in 167 B.C. The Maccabees cleansed the temple, restored its furnishings (164 B.C.; 1 Macc. 4:36–59), and later turned it into a fortress.

Herod's Temple. King Herod, an Idumean, sought to appease his Jewish subjects by constructing an enormous, ornate, cream-colored temple of stone and gold that began in 19 B.C. The main building was finished by 9 B.C., but the entire structure was not completed until A.D. 64. The Romans destroyed it in A.D. 70.

The gold-and-white stone shone so brightly in the sun that it was difficult to look directly at the temple.

The temple building occupied an area that measured about 446 meters (490 yards) from north to south and 296 meters (325 yards) from east to west. The entire temple complex was enclosed by a massive stone wall, the southeast corner of which stood about 45 meters (50 yards) above the floor of the Kidron ravine. The parapet above this corner may have been the "pinnacle of the temple" referred to in the Gospels (Matt. 4:5). There was 1 gate in the north wall, 1 in the east wall, 2 in the south wall, and 4 in the west wall facing the city.

The Fortress of Antonia, the Jerusalem residence of the Roman procurators, stood at the northwest corner of the complex. The fortress housed a Roman garrison (Acts 21:31) and, as a symbol of submission, the robes of the High Priest.

Double porticoes, 30 cubits wide and supported by shining marble columns 25 cubits high, were constructed along the inside of the main walls, surrounding the outer court of the temple, the Court of the Gentiles. Including the Tower of Antonia, these porticoes were about 11,800 meters (3,600 feet) in circumference. The Royal Porch, along the south wall, had 4 rows of columns. Solomon's Porch, located along the east wall, had 2 rows of columns (John 10:23; Acts 3:11; 5:12). This was the place where the scribes had their debates (Mark 11:27; Luke 2:46; 19:47) and where the merchants and moneychangers transacted business (Luke 19:45–46; John 2:14–16).

Inside of and slightly higher than the outer court (the Court of the Gentiles) was a smaller enclosure surrounded by a balustrade 3 cubits high. This enclosure was posted with recurring notices in Greek and Latin that any Gentile who entered the inner area was subject to death. After passing through 1 of several openings in the balustrade, 14 steps led up to the inner area, which was surrounded by a wall 25 cubits high. This wall was separated from the steps by a terrace 10 cubits wide. Flights of 5 steps led from the terrace to 8 gates in the wall, 4 on the north and 4 on the south side.

The inner area of Herod's temple contained 3 courts. The easternmost court was the Court of Women, and it contained the temple treasury where people donated their money (Mark 12:41–44). Three gates led into this court, 1 on the north, 1 on the south, and a third on the east. This third gate was probably the "Beautiful Gate" (Acts 3:2, 10). A 4th, larger, more massive and ornate gate led from the Court of the Women west into the Court of Israel (for male Jews), which was elevated 15 steps above the Court of the Women.

Inside the Court of Israel was the innermost court, the Court of the Priests. During the Feast of Tabernacles, men could enter the Priest's Court to walk around the altar. The Court of the Priests immediately surrounds the temple building itself (the Holy Place and the Holy of Holies) and the altar of burnt offering.

The layout of Herod's temple was patterned after Solomon's. The 2-story temple building was in the shape of a "T." The porch of the building (the cross member of the "T") was a vestibule 100 cubits long and 100 cubits high, with an opening 70 cubits high and 25 cubits wide. In front of the porch at the foot of the steps, surrounded by a cubit-high stone barrier, was the altar of burnt offering (15 cubits high and 50 cubits square). At the back of the vestibule were the main double doors (16 cubits wide and 55 cubits high) that led into the Holy Place.

The Holy Place was 40 cubits long, 20 cubits wide, and 60 cubits high. It contained the table of showbread, the 7-branched lampstand, and the altar of incense. The Holy Place was divided from the Holy of Holies by a curtain that stretched from floor to ceiling (Matt. 27:51; Mark 15:38; 2 Cor. 3:14). The Holy of Holies was 20 cubits by 20 cubits by 60 cubits high. It contained no furniture. The temple was surrounded on the north, south, and west sides by 3 stories of rooms that rose 60 cubits.

Temple in the New Testament. The New Testament uses 2 words for temple. One of these words refers to the collection of buildings that made up the temple in Jerusalem, while the other usually refers to the sanctuary of the temple.

Jesus related to the temple in four distinct ways. First, as a pious Jew who was zealous for the Lord, Jesus showed respect for the temple. He referred to it as "the house of God" (Matt. 12:4) and "My Father's house" (John 2:16). He taught that everything in it was holy because of the sanctifying presence of God (Matt. 23:17, 21).

Second, Jesus' zeal led Him to purge the temple of the moneychangers (Mark 11:15–17; John 2:16) and to weep over it as He reflected on its coming destruction (Mark 13:1; Luke 19:41–44). Because Malachi 3:1 prophesied the cleansing of the temple as something the Lord and His Messenger would do, Jesus' act implied His deity and messiahship. Consequently, the hard-hearted scribes and chief priests "sought how they might destroy Him" (Mark 11:18; Luke 19:47).

Third, because He was the Son of God incarnate, Jesus taught that He was greater than the temple (Matt. 12:6). Jesus' teaching that if the temple of His body was destroyed in three days He would raise it up (John 2:19) likewise affirms His superiority to the temple building. That saying of Jesus may have provided the basis for the claim of the two false witnesses at His trial who stated that Jesus said, "I am able to destroy the temple of God and to build it in three days" (Matt. 26:60–61; 27:40; Mark 14:57–58; 15:29).

Finally, Jesus taught that the church (Matt. 16:18) is the new, eschatological temple (Matt. 18:19–20; John 14:23).

At Jesus' death, the curtain of the temple was torn from top to bottom (Matt. 27:51; Mark 15:38; Luke 23:45). By His death, Jesus opened a new way into the presence of God. A new order replaced the old. No longer was the temple in Jerusalem to be the place where people worshiped God. From now on they would worship Him "in spirit and truth" (John 4:21–24).

The first Christians were converted Jews. They continued to worship at the temple as Jesus had (Luke 24:52; Acts 2:46; 3:1; 5:12, 20–21, 42). As they began to understand the meaning and significance of Jesus' person, work, and teaching, they realized they were the new people of God, infused by God's Spirit. As such, they were a new, living temple. A new order had replaced the old. Stephen, a Christian of Gentile background (Acts 6:1–5), was the first person to understand that the church had replaced the temple as the place where God's presence was manifested in a special way among His people.

In Acts 15:13–18 Stephen's insight was carried forward by James, who identified the church with Amos's prophecy about the "tabernacle of David, which has fallen" (v. 16). According to James's application of Amos's prophecy about the end times, the restoration of David's tabernacle, the temple, would serve as the rallying point for Gentiles who wished to come to the Lord (Amos 9:11–12). James understood the church as the new temple that fulfilled that prophecy.

According to the apostle Paul, "All the promises of God" are "Yes, and ... Amen" in Christ (2 Cor. 1:20). Ezekiel and other prophets had prophesied a new temple (Ezekiel 40–43), and Paul understood the church as the fulfillment of those prophecies. Individually the Christian's body is "the temple of the Holy Spirit" (1 Cor. 6:19). Corporately the church is "the temple of God" where the Spirit of God dwells (1 Cor. 3:16; 2 Cor. 6:16). Christians are growing "into a holy temple in the Lord ... a dwelling place of God in the Spirit" (Eph. 2:21–22). Because we are God's new temple where the Holy Spirit dwells, Christians are to be holy (1 Cor. 6:18–20; 2 Cor. 7:1).

Because God dwells in us, Christians are holy to God, and He will destroy anyone who defiles us (1 Cor. 3:16–17). Because there is only one new temple and all Christians—regardless of race or religious background—are members of it, all Christians have equal access to God (Eph. 2:19–22). Paul understood the church, then, as the eschatological temple to which God is gathering Israel and the other nations of the world (Is. 2:2–4; Mic. 4:1–5).

Paul used the metaphor of the temple to express the unity of the new people of God that God is bringing about through the preaching of the gospel. The members of this new race are Jews and Gentiles who formerly were separated by the "middle wall of separation" and the "ordinances" that forbade them to mix (Eph. 2:14–15). Christ's sacrificial death on the cross ushered in a new age in God's relationship with mankind and abolished the enmity between Jew and Gentile by abolishing the validity of the ordinances that gave expression to it (v. 15). He abolished those ordinances in order to create "one new man," a new race composed of Jewish and Gentile Christians at peace with one another (vv. 15, 17). This "new man" is a living temple (v. 21) that is based on the teaching of the New Testament apostles and prophets and on the teaching, work, and person of Christ (v. 20).

Jesus Himself is the chief cornerstone of the building and so gives it shape and character (v. 20). The building is holy because it is growing "in the Lord" (v. 21) and because God dwells there in the Spirit (v. 22). "Lord," "God," and "Spirit" define this new temple in a trinitarian fashion. The metaphors of God's new people being a temple ("building") and being a body ("growing") are blended in verse 21.

In a similar way, Peter used the word *house* to describe Christians as members of a new, spiritual temple (1 Pet. 2:4–10). Christ is the chief cornerstone (v. 6). He is "a stone of stumbling and a rock of offense" (v. 8), a "living stone, rejected ... by men, but chosen by God and precious" (v. 4). Like Christ, Christians are "living stones" who are being built into a "spiritual house," or temple (v. 5). The metaphor of the "spiritual house" is combined with that of the "holy priesthood" that offers "spiritual sacrifices" (v. 5). And this "royal priesthood" of believers is a "holy nation," God's new people who proclaim His praises (vv. 9–10), the New Israel (Ex. 19:6).

In addition to understanding the church as the new, spiritual temple of God on earth that replaced the temple in Jerusalem, the New Testament alludes to a heavenly temple in whose life the church participates. John (John 1:51; 14:2) and Paul (Gal. 4:26; Phil. 3:20) both allude to the heavenly temple, but the idea is most developed in Hebrews and Revelation.

The author of Hebrews was concerned to demonstrate that the new covenant is better than the old. Among other things, Christians have a better covenant, a better sacrifice, a better high priest, and a better temple. The temple in Jerusalem was only a "copy and shadow," a type, of the true temple, which is in heaven (Heb. 8:5). Therefore the true, heavenly sanctuary into which Christ has entered on our behalf is better than its earthly copy (9:24). Because Christ our High Priest dwells in this heavenly sanctuary (9:24; 10:12; 19–22), we can enter the heavenly Holy of Holies and participate in the worship of the heavenly temple (10:19–22; 12:18–24). The author appears to define the heavenly temple as "the general assembly and church of the firstborn" (12:23).

According to John, the author of Revelation, there is a celestial Mount Zion (14:1; 21:10), a heavenly Jerusalem (3:12; 21:2), and a heavenly temple (11:19; 15:5–16:1). Christians who overcome temptation and trials are made pillars in the heavenly temple of God (3:12). As in Ephesians, then, the heavenly temple grows.

From this heavenly temple God will issue His judgments on the nations during the Tribulation (11:19; 14:14–20; 15:5–16:1). The martyrs of the Tribulation will serve God "day and night in His [heavenly] temple" (7:15). The temple in Jerusalem will be measured and judged during that time (11:1–2).

In the New Jerusalem there will not be a temple because "the Lord God Almighty and the Lamb are its temple" (Rev. 21:22). In that city nothing will come between God and His people, and we "shall see His face" (22:4). In the new heaven and earth "the tabernacle of God" will be "with men, and He will dwell with them, and they shall be His people. God Himself will be with them and be their God" (21:3).

Paul identified the new temple with the church, but John and the author of Hebrews identified it with the heavenly realm where Christ dwells. Furthermore, just as there was no temple before the Fall, so John anticipated a new heaven and earth without a temple. These different ways of understanding the relation of the temple to the new people of God are complementary, not contradictory.

TIBERIAS [tigh BEER ee uhs] — the name of a city and a lake in the New Testament:

1. A city on the western shore of the Sea of Galilee. Tiberias stands on a rocky cliff about 19 kilometers (12 miles) south of where the Jordan River flows into the Sea of Galilee. Still, Tiberias is 208 meters (682 feet) below the level of the nearby Mediterranean Sea, and it has a semitropical climate that is mild in winter but humid in summer.

The city was founded by Herod Antipas (about A.D. 20) and named after the emperor Tiberius Caesar. It was said to have occupied the site of Rakkath, an old town of Naphtali (Josh. 19:35), and to have been built over a graveyard. Because of this, it was declared unclean by the Jews, who would not enter the city. Although Tiberias was an important city in the days of Christ, there is no record that He ever visited it. In fact, it is only mentioned once in the New Testament (John 6:23).

The city enjoyed a commanding view of the lake. Because of the numerous hot springs just south of the city, it was a popular resort for the Romans. Pliny the Elder mentions the healthful nature of the springs. Today the city contains a number of health spas.

Although the Jews would not enter the ancient Roman town, after the fall of Jerusalem in A.D. 135, Tiberias ironically became the center of rabbinic learning. Here the Mishna was completed about A.D. 200 and the Jerusalem (or Palestinian) Talmud was finished about A.D. 400. The pointing system later used by the Masoretes to add vowels to the Hebrew text was first developed in Tiberias.

2. A lake in northern Galilee (John 6:1; 21:1), the same lake as the Sea of Galilee.

TIME — a measurable period during which an action or condition exists or continues. Among the Hebrew people, units of time were measured in hours, days, weeks, months, and years. The more abstract concept of time is also mentioned in the Bible.

Present Time. The Bible speaks of God who exists eternally, as well as people who live in a time-space framework. A key passage for the present time is Ecclesiastes 3:1–11, which declares, "There is ... a time for every purpose under heaven." This passage goes on to note that there is a time for birth and death, mourning and dancing, keeping and throwing away, silence and speaking, and war and peace. People do not know their times (Eccl. 9:12), and their times are in the Lord's hands (Ps. 31:15). We are warned not to plan our times as if they belonged to us, but to do what the Lord wills in our lives (James 4:13–17).

The accepted time of salvation is now (2 Cor. 6:2). We are to seek (Hos. 10:12) and trust the Lord at all times (Ps. 62:8) and practice righteousness during our lives on earth (Ps. 106:3). Since the days are evil, Christians are to make the most of their opportunities (Eph. 5:16). God is honored in these things. Scripture bears testimony that God is working out His purposes in people's time. He promised Abraham that he and

Sarah would have a child (Gen. 18:10, 14), and the promise was fulfilled (Gen. 21:1–4). God also told the wicked Pharaoh of a plague that would come to him the next day (Ex. 9:18). God is working in our present time-space world; therefore, the present time is to be used for God's purposes and glory.

Fulfillment of Time. The fulfillment of time is an important concept because it shows God's sovereign control of time in order to bring His promises to pass. Only the Lord knows the times and seasons for fulfillment (Acts 1:7; 1 Thess. 5:1). God has indicated that what He promised long ago would be fulfilled (Is. 37:26; Titus 1:3). God warned that Jerusalem would be destroyed if His people continued in disobedience. The prophet Jeremiah lamented after their downfall that their time was fulfilled (Lam. 2:17).

In the New Testament Jesus announced that the promised kingdom of God was at hand (Matt. 4:17). Jesus continually stated that His hour, or time, had not yet come (John 2:4; 7:6, 8, 30; 8:20); it was to be fulfilled when He was crucified (John 12:23; 13:1; 17:1). In fact, when Jesus came into Jerusalem in His triumphal entry, He stated that Israel should have known the time of the visitation of the Messiah (Luke 19:44). Jesus' death was prophesied in the Old Testament and the fulfillment of this was seen in His death at the appointed time (Rom. 5:6; Gal. 4:4; 1 Tim. 2:6).

The Future and the End Times. The future and the end times are in God's control. Many references to future time are related to judgment. Daniel's prophecy outlines the succession of world empires, and this prophecy involved judgments (Dan. 2:28–29). The nations will face a time of doom in the future (Ezek. 30:3; Dan. 8:17, 19). Israel will also suffer in "the time of Jacob's trouble" (Jer. 30:7). During that time many will fall (Matt. 24:10). Nations as well as individuals will face the future time of judgment (Ps. 81:15; Jer. 10:15). In fact, the demons realize that they will face a time of torment in the future (Matt. 8:29).

However, the future will not be all doom, because in that time Israel will be a restored kingdom (Joel 3:1; Zeph. 3:20). Messiah will endure forever (Dan. 2:44). The future of the unbeliever will be judgment (Rev. 11:18), while the believer will be exalted by God (1 Pet. 5:6). Believers eagerly await the time of the Second Coming (Heb. 9:28), which is nearer than when they first believed (Rom. 13:11). The future is in God's hands. This means the future is filled with hope and certainty for the believer.

Eternity. The Bible portrays God as existing eternally (Ex. 3:14; Ps. 90:2; Rev. 1:4; 15:7). This is also true for Christ, His Son (Is. 9:6; John 1:1–3, 18; Heb. 13:8). The unbelievers will face an eternity of punishment (Matt. 25:41; Rev. 14:11; 20:10–15). The eternal life of believers begins the moment they believe (John 3:16, 36; 5:24; 1 John 5:11). After this present time the believers will live eternally with God and His kingdom (Dan. 7:18, 27; Rev. 22:5).

Although people now live within a time-space framework, they will live eternally. God who exists eternally will remove time and space, and people will relate to God in an eternal relationship.

TISHRI [TISH rih] — the 7th month of the religious year in the Jewish calendar, also called Ethanim (1 Kin. 8:2).

TOOLS OF THE BIBLE — Tools in Bible times were used to form, shape, cut, measure, move, or fasten materials. Various types of knives, saws, hammers, drills, and other tools were common in the ancient world.

In the earliest times—long before Abraham—people used stone tools fixed to wooden handles. Many of these were naturally shaped stones. Others were shaped by people for specific purposes. Flint, a very hard stone that can be shaped into sharp-edged blades by hammering or pressing it with another stone, was in use from the earliest days.

By about 3200 B.C., techniques for smelting copper had been discovered, and metalworking tools made their first appearance in Palestine. Copper is relatively soft and does not hold an edge well. It was soon replaced by bronze, an alloy of copper and tin that was much harder and more efficient. The older versions of the Bible use the term "brass" to refer to this alloy. But true brass, an alloy of copper and zinc, was not in use in Bible times.

Bronze tools and weapons were used by the Hebrews right down to the time of the judges and Saul (about 1050 B.C.). By then the secrets of smelting iron had been learned from the Philistines, and iron farm implements were available in Israel.

The Philistines tried to keep the secrets of the technology from the Israelites who had no iron spears or swords (1 Sam. 13:19–22). But with David's victory over the Philistines, iron became readily available to the Israelites (1 Kin. 6:7).

Many specific tools—from general and household tools to those used by specialists such as metalsmiths—are mentioned in the Bible. The following alphabetical list is keyed to the NKJV.

Anvil. A large iron block on which metal was hammered and shaped. The only use of this word in the Bible occurs in Isaiah 41:7 where the word usually translated "foot" or "foundation" is translated as "anvil." Metalsmiths, whether working in delicate jewelry making or in heavy construction work, used anvils as bases on which to shape metal.

Awl. Awls were used by carpenters and leatherworkers to punch holes. The only biblical references to awls are in regard to the ceremony by which a slave had an earlobe pierced as a sign of his willingness to serve his master all his life (Ex. 21:6; Deut. 15:17). Archaeologists have found many samples of such tools. They are usually about 15 centimeters (6 inches) long, made of iron or bronze, and come to a sharp conical point.

Ax. A cutting and chopping tool. Eight different Hebrew words and 1 Greek word are translated "ax" in English versions of the Bible. Several of these axes were tools designed for specific jobs. One type of ax was a sort of pruning tool (Jer. 10:3) with a curved blade that could also be used by a blacksmith to pick up hot metal (tongs, Is. 44:12).

Iron axes were used to clear forests and cut wood (Deut. 19:5; Is. 10:15; Matt. 3:10). Sometimes the iron head would separate from the wooden handle and either be lost, as in the miracle of the floating ax head (2 Kin. 6:5–6), or possibly injure someone standing nearby. Deuteronomy 19:5 provides for this sort of accident. First Samuel 13:20–21 records the prices the Philistines charged for sharpening iron axes and agricultural tools.

Battle axes of various sorts are also mentioned in the Bible. They were used either as weapons or as tools to destroy captured cities (Ps. 74:5–6; Jer. 46:22; Ezek. 26:9). Some versions translate this tool as hatchet.

Another special type of ax was used by stonecutters to break out the large sawn blocks from a quarry or to shape the stone after it was quarried.

One other Hebrew word, translated ax (NKJV) in 2 Chronicles 34:6 (mattock, KJV) and Ezekiel 26:9, is more properly a weapon, either a large sword (Gen. 3:24; 1 Sam. 17:51) or a smaller dagger (Judg. 3:16). This word suggests a sturdy blade that could be used to cut down enemies as an ax cuts a tree.

Bellows. A device that provided a gust of air when squeezed. These small blowing instruments were made of leather and pottery and were operated by either hand or foot. To raise the temperature in the furnace high enough to work bronze or iron, it was necessary to get a good supply of air into the fire. The earliest furnaces were built so the prevailing wind blew through, increasing the draft. Later, in order to make it possible to work without the wind, bellows were used to force the air into the fire. The only biblical reference to this tool is in Jeremiah 6:29.

Chisel. A chisel has a sharp metal blade and is commonly used for cutting and shaping wood or stone. Examples of chisels with bronze or iron blades from biblical times have been found. The only reference to a chisel in the Bible is as a stonecutter's tool (1 Kin. 6:7). The NIV uses "chisel" in Isaiah 44:13 for a word translated "plane" by the NKJV and other translations.

Compass. A device for drawing circles or parts of circles. The only mention of a compass in the Bible is in Isaiah 44:13. A primitive compass can be made by using a length of cord fixed at one end to a nail or pin and a marking instrument at the other. More accurate wooden or metal holders for the marking tool were also used.

Fan. The fan mentioned in the Old Testament was probably a type of long-handled fork used to toss the threshed grain into the air. The wind blew the chaff away, allowing the heavier grain to fall into a separate pile (Is. 30:24; Jer. 15:7). Some versions translate this tool as fork or winnowing fork.

John the Baptist's description of the Messiah as one who would separate good from evil in the last days uses this illustration (Matt. 3:12; Luke 3:17).

File. The file was probably some sort of stone used to sharpen the edge of metal blades. This word appears only in the KJV (1 Sam. 13:21).

Furnace. Many tradesmen needed the fiery heat provided by the furnace to perfect their goods. Furnaces made of stone or brick were used mostly by potters and metalsmiths. The word used for household furnaces or stoves in Bible times is usually translated as oven.

Clay pots and jars were of limited use unless they had been "fired" by being raised to a very high temperature. The heat changed the chemical makeup of the clay, leaving it very strong but brittle. By carefully controlling the amount of fuel and the air supply, the proper temperature was reached and maintained until the clay was cured.

Special furnaces were also necessary for smelting metal ores. Finely ground ores were mixed with charcoal and fluxes of limestone or crushed seashells, and placed into the fire. Bellows kept the fire hot enough to melt the ore. As it melted, the liquid metal sank to the bottom of the furnace, allowing the waste slag to float to the top. This waste was removed through a small pipe. The metal was allowed to cool and then remelted in a crucible for purification. It was then cast into molds to be shaped into many useful items.

Large furnaces big enough for several people to walk into were used in Babylon to make bricks. This is probably the "burning fiery furnace" of Daniel 3:15–30.

Goad. A sharpened metal point on the end of a long pole. Goads were used by farmers to prod animals to keep them moving, but they could also be dangerous weapons (Judg. 3:31). Ecclesiastes 12:11 notes that the wise instruction of a good teacher acts like a goad (also see Acts 26:14).

Hammer. Hammers and mauls were very useful to the people of the Bible. Four different Hebrew words are translated by these two English words. One refers to the small hammer used by stonecutters or carpenters to drive nails or shape stones (1 Kin. 6:7; Jer. 10:4). This same word is used in Judges 4:21 of the hammer that Jael used to kill the Syrian general Sisera. When the incident is related in Judges 5, the NRSV translates this word as hammer.

Another word translated as hammer is what would be known today as a sledgehammer. This tool was used to break up rocks (Jer. 23:29) or shape iron (Is. 41:7).

Harrow. A toothed bar, dragged by oxen, which was used to level plowed ground for planting. The harrow is not mentioned in the NKJV, but it does appear in the KJV (2 Sam. 12:31) and other translations (Job 39:10, NRSV, REB; Is. 28:24, NIV,

NASB). No examples of this tool have been identified from the ancient world.

Knife. Three Hebrew words are sometimes translated as knife. The first describes either flint blades used for ritual circumcision or self-mutilation (Josh. 5:2–3; 1 Kin. 18:28), or short metal swords or daggers used in battle (Gen. 3:24; 34:25–26). The second word describes a knife used for the slaughter of animals for food or sacrifice (Gen. 22:6, 10; Judg. 19:29; Prov. 30:14). The third word occurs only in Proverbs 23:2. This tool was apparently similar to the second type of knife.

Knives were usually bronze or iron blades with the handle and the blade consisting of one piece of metal. Sometimes the blade was fastened to a wooden or bone handle with rivets.

Marking Tool. Isaiah 44:13 describes a carpenter marking out divisions on a piece of wood. The Hebrew word occurs only here in the Bible, so the exact nature of the tool is not certain. It appears to be some sort of sharp-pointed instrument that was used to scratch marks in wood.

Mattock. A mattock was similar to a hoe. It was a flat iron head fastened to a wooden handle, used to weed the terraced gardens and fields. Mattock appears in only one passage in the NKJV (1 Sam. 13:20–21). The KJV translates two other Hebrew words as mattock (axes, 2 Chr. 34:6; hoe, Is. 7:25).

Measuring Tools. Both builders and surveyors used measuring tools. These were of two types: a solid rule, rod, or straight edge, up to 3 meters (10 feet) long; and a flexible rope, cord, or line that could be used to measure longer distances or irregularly shaped objects.

The prophet Ezekiel mentioned a measuring rod that was "six cubits long" (Ezek. 40:5). The ordinary cubit was about 45 centimeters (18 inches) long and the "long" cubit about 55 centimeters (22 inches), so Ezekiel's rod was about 3.3 meters (11 feet) long.

Measuring lines were probably much longer. No definite length is mentioned, although 1 Kings 7:23 suggests at least 30 cubits, or 13.5 meters (45 feet), or more. According to Ezekiel 40:3, these lines were made of flax or linen, although other fibers were probably also used. The measuring line was used as a symbol of God's judgment on evil (Lam. 2:8) or as a sign of His blessing and restoration (Jer. 31:39).

Mill. Mills and millstones were tools used to grind grain. The most common household mills of Bible times were flat stones on which grain was placed and crushed as other stones rolled over the grain.

Commercial mills were of different construction and considerably larger. One type was made of 2 round flat stones. A wooden peg was firmly fastened in the center of the bottom stone. The upper stone, which had a funnel-shaped hole through the center, was placed over the peg. Grain was poured between the stones and around the peg through the hole. The upper stone was turned by a peg handle placed near the outside edge, crushing the grain. Some of these larger mills required 2 operators.

A second type of commercial mill was similar in operation but of a different shape. The lower stone was in the shape of an upside-down cone. The upper stone, with a cone-shaped hollow cut into the bottom side, was placed over the lower stone. Grain was poured through a hole in the top. The upper stone was turned either by animals hitched to wooden arms attached to the stone or by slaves or prisoners (Judg. 16:21).

A third type of mill consisted of a large circular stone set on its edge and rolled around in a trough in the lower stone. This was also operated by animals or slaves.

The sound of grinding was heard constantly in the villages and towns. Its absence was a prophetic sign of famine and death (Jer. 25:10; Rev. 18:22). The loss of a millstone could mean disaster for a family (Deut. 24:6).

Mirror. Many examples of small, bronze mirrors on decorated handles are known from ancient times. It was impossible
to get a perfectly flat surface on these metal mirrors, so the
reflection was always somewhat distorted, like the mirrors in
a fun house. Paul's comment in 1 Corinthians 13:12 recognized
this problem.

Since glass mirrors were not made until after the time of
the New Testament, the KJV references in 1 Corinthians 13:12,
James 1:23, and Isaiah 3:23 are mistranslations.

Mortar and Pestle. A mortar was a cup, usually made of
stone, in which various materials were ground to powder or
mixed together. A pestle was a small stick with a knob on the
end that did the actual grinding (Prov. 27:22).

Nail. Metal nails of either bronze or iron were commonly
used by carpenters and cabinet makers. They were usually
hand-forged and about the same size as our modern cut nails.
First Chronicles 22:3 and 2 Chronicles 3:9 describe the large
quantities of iron and bronze nails gathered by David for use in
constructing the temple in Jerusalem. Jeremiah 10:4 describes
fancy work done by craftsmen and goldsmiths, and the use of
nails for decoration by these people. Archaeologists have found
many samples of decorative nails with gold or silver heads.

A different word than the one for nail described the large
iron spikes used in the crucifixion of Jesus (John 20:25). Another
word, translated nail in the KJV, is translated peg by the NKJV
and other translations (Ex. 35:18; Judg. 4:21–22; Zech. 10:4).

Needle. The Old Testament has many references to nee-
dlework or embroidery, particularly the woven linen used in
the tabernacle hangings (Ex. 26:1–13) and the fine clothes of
wealthy Israelites (Ezek. 16:10–18; 27:7, 16, 24). Needles must
have been used also for sewing and repairing family clothing
(Gen. 3:7; Job 16:15; Eccl. 3:7; Ezek. 13:18). Samples of needles
found in numerous archaeological excavations are made of
bone, bronze, or iron. They are of various sizes, from very fine

to the size of large darning needles. Their shape is similar to the common needles of today.

Jesus' words in Matthew 19:24 (also Mark 10:25; Luke 18:25), that it is easier for a rich man to enter heaven than "for a camel to go through the eye of a needle," reflect an idea found in early rabbinic writing. There is no archaeological or historical support for the common idea that the "needle's eye" was a small pedestrian gate through the city wall. The statement simply means that humanly speaking, this is an impossible thing. Only a divine miracle can make it possible.

Oven. Cooking was usually done in small clay or stone ovens (Lev. 2:4; 26:26; Hos. 7:4). The word translated oven by the NKJV is translated in the KJV as furnace in Genesis 15:17 and Nehemiah 3:11 and 12:38. The REB translates Genesis 15:17 as brazier, while the NRSV and NIV use fire pot.

Ovens were either rectangular or circular, about 60 centimeters (2 feet) in diameter and about 30 centimeters (1 foot) high, with the top flattened and slightly hollow. The food was cooked on the flat top, with the fire inside the oven or stove. The usual fuel was animal dung or wood, but straw was used to make a quick fire and to rekindle the embers.

Malachi 4:1 describes the day of judgment when the evildoers will be destroyed in a day "burning like an oven." Nehemiah 3:11 and 12:28 mention the "Tower of the Ovens" on the city wall. This may have been a section of the city where commercial baking was carried on, but more likely it is a reference to either potters' or brickmakers' kilns or to metal smelters.

Pick. An iron tool of uncertain use. It is listed, along with saws and axes, as a tool used by the people of Rabbah (2 Sam. 12:31; 1 Chr. 20:3).

Plane. The word *plane* occurs only in Isaiah 44:13. The exact nature of ancient Hebrew planes is not certain, but they were used to shape wood by scraping or shaving motions. The NIV translates this word as chisel.

Plow/Plowshare. The earliest plows were probably simple wooden sticks used to scratch furrows in the ground for planting seeds. Eventually, larger forked branches drawn by animals were used. These "single-handed" plows were light enough for one man to lift around obstructions. They had the advantage of leaving one hand free for the farmer to guide the animals.

By the time of Saul (about 1050 B.C.), iron tips were commonly fastened to the wooden plows. This made it easier to cultivate the stony soil of Israel. The Philistines were concerned that the Israelites not learn the secrets of iron smelting (1 Sam. 13:19–22). They apparently recognized it would be easy to make "plowshares into swords" for warfare (Joel 3:10). On the other hand, the age of the Messiah, the "Prince of Peace," was to be a time when "they shall beat their swords into plowshares" (Is. 2:4; Mic. 4:3).

Plumb Line/Plummet. A small, heavy weight on the end of a long cord, used to make sure a wall is standing vertically (2 Kin. 21:13; level, Is. 28:17, NASB). In a vision, the prophet Amos saw the Lord measuring the nation of Israel with a plumb line. The people were not considered true and straight in their devotion to God because they had fallen into worship of false gods (Amos 7:7–8).

Press. A device used to crush fruits in order to make oil or juice. The cultivation of olives was an important part of the agricultural activity in Israel, since olive oil was a major item of trade and export. To extract the oil from the fruit, olives were placed in large shallow presses hewn out of rock and crushed with a large stone roller operated by 2 people. The oil was collected in a container, then strained to remove impurities before being bottled in clay pottery jars.

The New Testament name Gethsemane (Matt. 26:36; Mark 14:32) is a compound word meaning "oil press." Gethsemane was the place where the olives from the groves on the Mount of Olives were processed.

Wine presses were deep pits dug out of the rock. The grapes were put in and trampled by the workers with their bare feet (Amos 9:13). If the harvest was good, this was a joyous occasion and a time of singing and celebration (Is. 16:10; Jer. 25:30). The juice was channeled to another pit where it was allowed to settle before being put into skin bags or pottery jars for fermentation.

The description of Gideon threshing wheat in a winepress illustrates how carefully he had to hide the crop from the invading Midianites. Threshing such as this was normally done on the high ground to take advantage of the wind. But he was threshing in a pit in the valley (Judg. 6:11).

Pruninghook. A sickle-shaped knife used by the keepers of the vineyards to prune grapevines in the spring (Is. 18:5). This regular cutting was essential if the vines were to continue to produce good crops.

Razor. Razors of the ancient world were usually bronze or iron blades fastened to wooden handles. Those used by kings or for ritual purposes often had more elaborate bone or ivory handles. The prophet Isaiah predicted the Assyrians would conquer the northern kingdom of Israel, shaving Israel with a razor and bringing judgment on His people (Is. 7:20). The prophet Ezekiel (5:1–2) used a similar picture to illustrate the destruction of Jerusalem by the Babylonians.

Saw. Saws were metal blades with a toothed edge. They were used by ancient peoples to cut wood or stone. Prisoners of war were sometimes put to work in the quarries cutting stone with saws. Marks left by the stonecutter's saws can still be seen in many of the ancient quarries of Palestine.

Hebrews 11:37 describes the faithful Israelites who were killed for their faith. Some were "sawn in two," a common method of execution among the Greeks. It is traditionally believed that the prophet Isaiah was killed in this way.

Shovel. According to Isaiah 30:24, shovels were sometimes used in the winnowing process. This was in addition to winnowing fans. Shovels were usually wooden paddle-type implements with long handles. These were different from the metal shovels used in the tabernacle and temple to remove the ashes from the altar (Ex. 27:3; 1 Kin. 7:40).

Sickle. A small hand tool used for cutting stalks of grain. The oldest known examples have flint teeth set in wood or bone handles. Later, metal blades were used. The grain was held in one hand and cut off near the ground by the sickle. The final judgment is sometimes pictured in terms of reaping with a sickle (Joel 3:13; Rev. 14:14–19).

Sieve. Scholars are not certain what kind of tool a sieve was. Two unrelated words, used once each in the Old Testament, are translated as sieve (Is. 30:28; Amos 9:9). In both places the word for sieve is used with a verb meaning "to sift."

Threshing Sledge. The purpose of threshing was to separate usable grain from the waste straw or chaff. This was usually done by spreading the stalks of grain several inches deep on a smooth flat area that was on a high piece of ground open to the wind. Specially shod animals walked around on the stalks until the grain separated from the hulls.

Frequently threshing sledges (Is. 28:27) made of wood (2 Sam. 24:22) with stone or metal teeth embedded in the bottom side were dragged over the grain by these animals.

The city of Damascus was called under judgment because that nation "threshed Gilead with implements of iron" (Amos 1:3–5) or behaved with unnecessary cruelty against a conquered people. God promised to make His people into a "new threshing sledge" with sharp teeth and use them to bring judgment on those who oppress the godly (Is. 41:15).

Tongs. Tongs were a type of tool with a hook or a blade. They were used by blacksmiths to handle hot metal (Is. 44:12). These are called forges by the NIV and RSV. The same Hebrew word is translated ax in Jeremiah 10:3.

Wheel. The potter's wheel was a device used by potters to make their pottery even and symmetrical. Before its invention, pots and jars were built up of coils of clay smoothed and shaped by hand. The "slow wheel" was a small, flat disk on a spindle, with a larger stone disk on the other end. It was spun by hand as the potter alternated between keeping the wheel in motion and shaping the clay.

The "fast wheel" was really two wheels, one above the other, with an axle joining them. The potter sat on a bench and turned the lower wheel with his feet. This way, he could keep it going rapidly, yet still have both hands free to shape the clay on the upper wheel.

The most symbolic and descriptive use of a potter's wheel in the Bible appears in the book of Jeremiah. Jeremiah visited a potter at his wheel. He compared the potter who molds his clay to God who has the power to mold the nation of Israel (Jer. 18:2–8).

Yoke. A type of harness that connected a pair of animals to a plow or similar tool. Oxen were the most common animals used in working the land. A yoke of oxen was a pair (1 Sam. 11:7; Luke 14:19). Using a pair to pull a plow required a yoke to link them together so they could work efficiently. Yokes were usually made of a wooden beam shaped to fit over the necks of the two animals and held in place by wooden or leather fasteners.

The yoke was also used as a symbol of the burden or oppression of heavy responsibility, duty, sin, or punishment (1 Kin. 12:4–14; Jer. 27:8–12; Acts 15:10). In New Testament times the phrase "take the yoke of" was used by the Jewish rabbis to mean "become the pupil of" a certain teacher. Jesus gave a gentle invitation to His disciples: "Take My yoke upon you and learn from Me, for I am gentle and lowly in heart, and you will find rest for your souls. For My yoke is easy and My burden is light" (Matt. 11:29–30).

TRADE AND TRAVEL — commercial buying and selling in Bible times and the travel required to conduct these activities.

The nation of Israel had little in the way of natural resources. But its geographic situation made the nation a strategic corridor through which all military and economic traffic between Europe, Asia, and Africa had to pass. Important roads from Egypt crossed the southern wilderness to Kadesh-Barnea and Elath and then proceeded north along the edge of the desert through Moab, Heshbon, Ammon, and Ramoth-Gilead to Damascus. Numerous secondary roads ran along the mountain ridge from Beersheba and Hebron to Jerusalem, Dothan, and Beth-Shean, then along the Jordan Valley from Jericho to Galilee. Several east-west roads linked the coast with the inland towns and cities.

The major route through Canaan was the "Way of the Sea," an important highway that ran along the coast from Egypt through Gaza and Ashkelon to Joppa. Because of the swamps along the central coast, this road then swung inland to Aphek and up through the Aruna Pass through the Carmel mountains to Megiddo. At Megiddo the road divided, the western branch continuing along the coast to the Phoenician ports of Acco, Tyre, and Sidon. The eastern branch cut across the Esdraelon plain in Lower Galilee to Capernaum, Hazor, Dan, and Damascus, where it joined the highway coming up from Gilead.

The strategic military importance of this road meant that the nations struggled to control the key cities and passes at Megiddo and Hazor. Because of this constant ebb and flow of armies and traders, Israel was greatly influenced by neighboring nations. In turn, the nation became a major factor in international trade and commerce.

Israel's wealth was primarily agricultural. Grain, especially wheat and barley, grew abundantly in the shallow valleys along the foothills of Judah and Samaria. These were major export crops. Figs, grapes, and olives were plentiful in the hill country of Judah.

The land around Hebron produced magnificent grapes (Num. 13:23–24). Large quantities of raisins and wine were produced around Hebron for home consumption and export. Olives were used either as food or crushed for cooking oil. Olive oil was also used in lamps or as a body rub, making it a major item in the economy of the region.

Large herds of sheep and goats were raised in Palestine (1 Sam. 16:11; John 10:1–16). Wool and the cloth made from this product were important sources of revenue.

Fish were taken along the Mediterranean Sea coast and in the Sea of Galilee. The northern part of the Mediterranean coast was also the source of the murex shell, which was used to make a very valuable purple dye. Extensive textile industries, using both wool and the linen made from the flax grown in the coastal plain, produced the distinctive Tyrian purple cloth that was in great demand all around the Mediterranean. Lydia of Philippi and Thyatira was engaged in this business (Acts 16:14).

The southern end of the Jordan Valley and the Dead Sea area was the source of a large and profitable salt-mining industry. The city of Jericho appears to have been involved in this trade as early as 6000 B.C.

Asphalt or bitumen was easily obtained from the tar pits in the Dead Sea area (Gen. 11:3; 14:10). This substance was used as caulking in boats and rafts, as mortar in building, and for making monuments and jewelry. Timber from the Lebanon mountains was also a significant trade item.

Little pottery was exported from Israel, except for simple containers for wine and oil. Israelite pottery was more practical and less artistic than Philistine and Greek pottery.

Neither did Israel export a great deal of metals, except during the time of Solomon when the copper mines in Sinai and the iron mines in Syria were worked commercially.

One major industry was the manufacture of millstones from the high-quality basalt stone found in the volcanic hills of northern Galilee. These were shipped as far away as Spain, Italy, and North Africa.

During the early days of the United Kingdom under David and Solomon, Israel controlled all the major trade routes through the area. It was impossible to ship anything anywhere between Asia Minor, the Mesopotamian Valley, and Egypt without going through Israelite-controlled territory. Heavy excise taxes and import and export duties on all goods traveling through Israel produced huge sums of money. These revenues went into the construction of elaborate palaces and temples and extensive public works and military projects (1 Kin. 5–7; 1 Chr. 29:1–5; 2 Chr. 1:14–17).

Ezekiel 27:1–24 lists a number of products that were traded through the city of Tyre. Israel probably also traded in these items. Much of the material was carried by camel or donkey, but ox-drawn wagons were also extensively used (Gen. 37:25).

By New Testament times, travel was relatively simple and considerably safer than in the earlier periods. The establishment of Roman control over the Mediterranean Sea and the lands around it put an effective end to piracy and highway robbery in the empire. The Roman road system linked every part of the empire and made travel much easier.

For long distances, ship travel was common (Jonah 1; Acts 13:4; 27:1–44). Government officials and the wealthy frequently used various types of chariots (Acts 8:28) and portable chairs (Song 3:6–10). Horses were mostly used for military purposes (Acts 23:23–24). But for most people, the only way of traveling was on foot or donkey back. Foot travelers could average about 16 miles a day. Under normal circumstances Mary and Joseph's trip from Nazareth to Bethlehem (Luke 2:1–7) probably took at least five days. With Mary unable to travel easily because of her pregnancy, that trip could well have taken two weeks or more.

TRANSJORDAN [trans JORE dahn] — a large plateau east of the Jordan River, the Dead Sea, and the Arabah. The term "Transjordan" is not used in the NKJV, KJV, or NRSV, but the general area is often called "beyond the Jordan" (Gen. 50:10–11; Deut. 3:20; Judg. 5:17; Is. 9:1; Matt. 4:15; Mark 3:8). The King's Highway (Num. 20:17; 21:22) crossed the entire length of Transjordan from north to south.

Before the time of Joshua, Transjordan was made up of the kingdoms of Ammon, Bashan, Gilead, Moab, and Edom. After the conquest, this area was occupied by the tribes of Reuben and Gad and the half-tribe of Manasseh.

TRIBULATION, THE GREAT — a short but intense period of distress and suffering at the end of time. The exact phrase "the great tribulation" is found only once in the Bible (Rev. 7:14). The great tribulation is to be distinguished from the general tribulation a believer faces in the world (Matt. 13:21; John 16:33; Acts 14:22). It is also to be distinguished from God's specific wrath upon the unbelieving world at the end of the age (Mark 13:24; Rom. 2:5–10; 2 Thess. 1:6).

The great tribulation fulfills Daniel's prophecies (Daniel 7–12). It will be a time of evil from false christs and false prophets (Mark 13:22) when natural disasters will occur throughout the world.

TYRE [tire] (*rock*) — an ancient seaport city of the Phoenicians situated north of Israel. Tyre was the principal seaport of the Phoenician coast, about 40 kilometers (25 miles) south of Sidon and 56 kilometers (35 miles) north of Carmel. It consisted of 2 cities: a rocky coastal city on the mainland and a small island city. The island city was just off the shore. The mainland city was on a coastal plain, a strip only 24 kilometers (15 miles) long and 3 kilometers (2 miles) wide.

Behind the plain of Tyre stood the rocky mountains of Lebanon. Tyre was easily defended because it had the sea on the west, the mountains on the east, and several other rocky cliffs (one the famous "Ladder of Tyre") around it, making it difficult to invade.

History. Tyre was an ancient city. According to one tradition, it was founded about 2750 B.C. However, Sidon—Tyre's sister city—was probably older (Gen. 10:15), perhaps even the mother city (Is. 23:2, 12). The Greek poet Homer mentioned "Sidonian wares," without reference to Tyre. This seems to confirm that Sidon was older. About 1400 B.C. Sidon successfully besieged the city of Tyre and maintained supremacy over it. However, when sea raiders left Sidon in ruins about 1200 B.C., many people migrated to Tyre. The increasing greatness of Tyre over Sidon, and its closer location to Israel, caused the order of mentioning Tyre first and then Sidon to be established by biblical writers (Jer. 47:4; Mark 3:8).

The period from 1200 to 870 B.C. was largely one of independence for Phoenicia. This enabled Tyre to realize her expansionist dreams. Hiram I, the ruler of Tyre (980–947 B.C.), apparently began a colony at Tarshish in Spain. He fortified Tyre's 2 harbors, 1 on the north of the city and 1 on the south. Tyrian ships began to dominate Mediterranean commerce. Their merchants were princes, the honorable of the earth (Is. 23:8). In the 9th century B.C. a colony from Tyre founded the city of Carthage on the north coast of Africa.

The most celebrated product of Tyrian commerce was the famous purple dye made from mollusks found in the waters near Tyre. This dye became a source of great wealth for Tyrians. In addition they produced metal work and glassware, shipping their products to and buying wares from peoples in remote parts of the earth (1 Kin. 9:28).

Friendly relations existed between the Hebrews and the Tyrians. Hiram was on excellent terms with both David and

Solomon, aiding them with materials for the building of David's palace (1 Kin. 5:1; 1 Chr. 14:1), Solomon's temple, and other buildings (1 Kin. 4:1; 9:10–14; 2 Chr. 2:3, 11). Hiram and Solomon engaged in joint commercial ventures (1 Kin. 9:26–28).

The dynasty of Hiram came to an end early in the 9th century B.C. when a priest named Ethbaal revolted and assumed the throne. Still, cordial relations between the Tyrians and Israelites continued. Ethbaal's daughter Jezebel married Ahab of Israel (1 Kin. 16:31). From this union Baal worship and other idolatrous practices were introduced into Israel.

While the people of Tyre were mostly interested in sea voyages, colonization, manufacturing, and commerce, they were frequently forced into war. Phoenician independence ended with the reign of Ashurnasirpal II (883–859 B.C.) of Assyria. More than a century later Shalmaneser V laid siege to Tyre and it fell to his successor, Sargon II. With the decline of Assyria after the middle of the 7th century B.C. Tyre again prospered.

Tyre in Prophecy. Several prophets of the Old Testament prophesied against Tyre. They condemned the Tyrians for delivering Israelites to the Edomites (Amos 1:9) and for selling them as slaves to the Greeks (Joel 3:5–6). Jeremiah prophesied Tyre's defeat (Jer. 27:1–11). But the classic prophecy against Tyre was given by Ezekiel.

Ezekiel prophesied the destruction of Tyre (Ezek. 26:3–21). The first stage of this prophecy came true when Nebuchadnezzar, king of Babylon, besieged the mainland city of Tyre for 13 years (585–572 B.C.) and apparently destroyed it. However, Nebuchadnezzar had no navy, so he could not flatten the island city. But losing the mainland city was devastating to Tyre. This destroyed Tyre's influence in the world and reduced her commercial activities severely.

The second stage of Ezekiel's prophecy was fulfilled in 332 B.C., when Alexander the Great besieged the island city of Tyre for 7 months. He finally captured it when he built a causeway from the mainland to the island. Hauling cedars from the mountains of Lebanon, he drove them as piles into the floor of the sea between the mainland and the island. Then he used the debris and timber of the ruined mainland city as solid material for the causeway. Hence, the remarkable prophecy of Ezekiel was completely fulfilled.

Tyre in the New Testament. During the Roman period Tyre again was rebuilt, eventually achieving a degree of prosperity. A Roman colony was established at the city. Herod I rebuilt the main temple, which would have been standing when Jesus visited the coasts of Tyre and Sidon (Matt. 15:21–28; Mark 7:24–31). People of Tyre listened to Jesus as He taught (Mark 3:8; Luke 6:17). The Lord Jesus even cited Tyre as a heathen city that would bear less judgment than the Galilaean towns in which He had invested so much of His ministry (Matt. 11:21–22; Luke 10:13–14).

In the New Testament period a Christian community flourished at Tyre. At the close of Paul's third missionary journey he stopped at Tyre and stayed with the believers there for a week (Acts 21:1–7).

TYROPOEON VALLEY [tie ROW pih un] (*valley of the cheesemakers*) — a small valley in the city of Jerusalem that divides the hill of Ophel—site of the original City of David—from the site known as the Western Hill, or Upper City. This valley, not mentioned by name in the Bible, exists today only as a slight depression because it has been filled in by debris and waste throughout the centuries.

UR — Abraham's native city in southern Mesopotamia; an important metropolis of the ancient world situated on the Euphrates River. Strategically situated about halfway between the head of the Persian Gulf and Baghdad, in present-day Iraq, Ur was the capital of Sumer for 2 centuries until the Elamites captured the city. The city came to be known as "Ur of the Chaldeans" after the Chaldeans entered southern Babylonia after 1000 B.C. References to "Ur of the Chaldeans" in connection with Abraham are thus examples of later editorial updating.

Abraham lived in the city of Ur (Gen. 11:28, 31) at the height of its splendor. The city was a prosperous center of religion and industry. Thousands of recovered clay documents attest to thriving business activity. Excavations of the royal cemetery, which dates from about 2900 to 2500 B.C., have revealed a surprisingly advanced culture. Uncovered were beautiful jewelry and art treasures, including headwear, personal jewelry, and exquisite dishes and cups.

The Babylonians worshiped many gods, but the moon god Sin was supreme. Accordingly, the city of Ur was a kind of theocracy centered in the moon deity. Ur-Nammu, the founder of the strong Third Dynasty of Ur (around 2070–1960 B.C.), built the famous ziggurats, a system of terraced platforms on which temples were erected. The Tower of Babel (Gen. 11:3–4) was probably a ziggurat made of brick. It is a miracle of God's providence that Abraham resisted Ur's polluted atmosphere and set out on a journey of faith to Canaan that would bless all mankind.

Ur's glory was suddenly destroyed about 1900 B.C. Foreigners stormed down from the surrounding hills and captured the reigning king, reducing the city to ruins. So complete was the destruction that the city was buried in oblivion until it was excavated centuries later by archaeologists.

WADI [**WAH dih**] — a valley, ravine, or riverbed that usually remains dry except during the rainy season; a stream that flows through such a channel. While the word *wadi* does not occur in most translations, they are often called by other names, such as brook (Josh. 15:47; 2 Kin. 23:12) and torrent (Judg. 5:21).

At the conclusion of the Sermon on the Mount, Jesus probably had a wadi in mind when He told the parable of the 2 builders and the houses they built (Matt. 7:24–27; Luke 6:47–49). In Palestine the pleasant, bone-dry valley of summertime frequently becomes an angry, turbulent flood that demolishes everything in its path during the winter rains.

WAR, WARFARE — armed conflict with an opposing military force. From the perspective of the Hebrew people, a holy war was one that God Himself declared, led, and won. The concept was at its height during the period of the judges. By the time of the United Kingdom under David and Solomon, however, political concerns began to cloud the concept of holy war. The prophets saw war as God's judgment against Israel. Those looking for a violent end to human existence saw war as a sign of the end times, both in the Old and New Testaments.

Jesus emphasized peace instead of war, and the New Testament church saw war as a spiritual battle between good and evil.

The concept of holy war required that God declare the war (Ex. 17:16; Num. 31:3). Every warrior considered himself consecrated to God (Is. 13:3). Before and during a war, soldiers abstained from certain activities to sanctify themselves (Judg. 20:26; 2 Sam. 11:11). Those who fought under a divinely ordained leader (Judg. 6:34) had to be single-minded in their devotion to God. Those who were frightened, newly married, or beset by domestic or financial problems were asked to go home (Deut. 20:5–9). The ark of the covenant, the symbol of God's presence, went with Israel's army into battle (2 Sam. 11:11).

The Israelites determined the right moment to enter into battle and sought guidance in battle by casting the sacred lot or by heeding the words of a prophet (Judg. 1:1; 1 Sam. 23:2; 1 Kin. 22:5). King Ahab was killed when he failed to heed the warning of Micaiah, the Lord's prophet (2 Chronicles 18).

In Numbers 21:14, Moses mentioned a book that has remained a mystery to biblical scholars—"the Book of the Wars of the Lord." This was probably a collection of records or songs celebrating the victories of Israel over its enemies. The Old Testament contains many references to God's role in battle against Israel's foes (Ex. 15:3; Ps. 24:8). God struck Israel's enemies with terror, overtaking and killing all fugitives (Ex. 15:1–27; Josh. 10:10–11). The judge Deborah cursed those who did not come to the Lord's aid against mighty Sisera (Judg. 5:23). As Israel's king, David fought "the Lord's battles" (1 Sam. 18:17). Jeremiah cursed those who refused to fight the Lord's battles (Jer. 48:10).

According to 2 Samuel 11:1, wars were usually waged "in the spring of the year." In springtime, the land dries out after the winter rains and therefore does not impede the movement of troops and chariots. In addition, armies can live off the land as the early grain crops begin to ripen. The trumpet or ram's horn, symbolic of the voice of God, called Israel into battle (Judg. 3:27; 1 Sam. 13:3). The number of soldiers whom Israel mustered for battle made no difference, for God fought alongside them (Judges 7; 1 Sam. 14:6). Indeed, the Israelites were forced to wander 40 years in the wilderness because they did not believe God could help them win over the Canaanites, who outnumbered the Israelites in both manpower and equipment (Num. 14:1–12).

The tactics of war were simple. They included surprise, ambush, pretended flight, and surrounding the enemy (Gen. 14:15; Josh. 8:2–7; 2 Sam. 5:23). On occasion a representative of each army met in combat (1 Samuel 17).

According to Deuteronomy 20:10–20, 3 outcomes of a holy war were possible. If the besieged city surrendered, the occupants' lives were spared, but all were enslaved. If the city refused to agree to peace terms and had to be taken by force, all males were killed by the sword. An exception to both these policies occurred when the captured city lay within Israel's boundaries. Then all occupants and their possessions were utterly destroyed. Known as the ban, this custom was intended to keep Israel free of any heathen influence (Josh. 6:17; 1 Sam. 15:3).

Besieging a city required elaborate planning. If possible, the city's water supply was cut off. Often the towers and gates of the city were set on fire (Judg. 9:52). In order for armies to use their battering rams and catapults that propelled arrows or stones, ramps were built to raise the weapons to appropriate height. From the ramps, scaling ladders were laid against the wall so soldiers could get inside the city. All the while, the city's defenders were using their own similar weapons to kill the enemy and destroy their war machinery (2 Sam. 11:21, 24; 2 Chr. 26:15).

A famous battle using these techniques was the Roman siege of Masada, a rock fortress about 1.6 kilometers (1 mile) west of the Dead Sea. Masada had been considered impregnable. In fact, it took the Romans nearly 3 years to gain entry into

Masada, only to find its some 960 inhabitants dead as a result of a suicide pact.

By the time of Solomon, warfare was the result of national policy set by the ruling king who supposedly was acting at God's direction. Court prophets, when asked about the advisability of entering into war, rarely went against the king's wishes—although Micaiah the son of Imlah did so (1 Kin. 22:8–28; 2 Chr. 18:7–27). Israel entered into international treaties with the great earthly powers rather than relying on God's strength for security (1 Kin. 15:18–19; 2 Kin. 17:4). After the captivity, the concept of holy war was applied to any revolt against the current ruling power.

The early prophets accepted the holy war concept and even stirred up war. But the later prophets often condemned war, because they felt Israel's wars did not meet the qualifications for a holy war. Herod the Great, fearing revolt by the Jews, built several military strongholds in Palestine, such as this one, Machaerus, located in the Transjordan area.

WATCH — either a group of soldiers or others posted to keep guard (Neh. 4:9; 7:3; 12:25) or one of the units of time into which the night was divided (Ps. 63:6; Lam. 2:19; Luke 12:38).

Because of the mention of the "middle watch" (Judg. 7:19), there must have been 3 such units in the Old Testament period. The "beginning of the watches" (Lam. 2:19) was apparently the first of these and the "morning watch" was the third (Ex. 14:24; 1 Sam. 11:11). However, by the New Testament period the Roman system of four watches had been adopted (Matt. 14:25; Mark 6:48). These were apparently named as follows: evening, midnight, cockcrow (NRSV; the crowing of the rooster, NKJV), and morning (Mark 13:35).

WEEK

WEEK — any 7 consecutive days; the interval between 2 sabbaths (Lev. 12:5; Jer. 5:24; Luke 18:12). The Hebrew people observed the seventh day of the week, from Friday evening (beginning at sunset) to Saturday evening, as their Sabbath, or day of rest and worship (Ex. 16:23–27).

The early Christians, to commemorate the resurrection of Christ, worshiped not on the old Jewish Sabbath, but on the Lord's Day (the first day of the week, or Sunday), which became the new Christian "sabbath" (Mark 16:2, 9; Acts 20:7; 1 Cor. 16:2).

WEIGHTS AND MEASURES OF THE BIBLE

WEIGHTS AND MEASURES OF THE BIBLE — Early in the development of society, people learned to measure, weigh, and exchange commodities. At first this trade was simple barter, the exchange of one type of goods for another type. As society became more complex, the need for standardized trade values became apparent. Yet each city set up its own standards of weights and measures, thus creating great confusion in trade between different peoples and cultures.

Weighing (pounds) and measuring (volume, length, and area) are 2 distinct functions in the Bible. The various units by which these 2 functions were expressed in Bible times are discussed in this article under these 2 major divisions.

Weights. The balance was an early method of determining weight. The balance consisted of a beam supported in the middle with a pan suspended by cords on each end. A known quantity of weight would be placed in the pan on one side of the balance and the object to be weighed on the other side. By adding or removing known weights until each side was equal, the weight of the object could be determined.

Most of the weights in the ancient world were made of stone or metal. The weights appeared in many forms, such as cubes, spheres, cones, cylinders, domes, or animal shapes. Some of these weights were inscribed with the amount of their weight, but most were not. Since these weights varied from one place to the next, many people carried pouches which contained their own weights (Deut. 25:13; Prov. 16:11), so they could see if they were receiving just value.

These ancient weights were sometimes used as money. Instead of referring to a talent of gold or silver or a shekel of gold or silver, people would merely refer to a talent or a shekel (2 Kin. 7:1; Matt. 25:15–28).

In Canaan, both the Canaanites and the Israelites used the Mesopotamian weight system. Each level of weight had 4 separate standards—the common, the heavy (twice the common weight), the common royal (5 percent heavier than the common weight), and the heavy royal (5 percent heavier than the heavy weight). Several of these weights are mentioned in the Bible.

Talent — The heaviest unit of weight in the Hebrew system. The talent was used to weigh gold (2 Sam. 12:30), silver (1 Kin. 20:39), iron (1 Chr. 29:7), bronze (Ex. 38:29), and many other commodities. The common talent weighed about 3,000 shekels or the full weight that a man could carry (2 Kin. 5:23). In Revelation 16:21 giant heavenly hailstones are described as heavy as a talent.

Kesitah — A unit of unknown weight and value (Gen. 33:19, piece of money; Josh. 24:32, piece of silver). Since the root meaning of the word is "lamb," this particular weight may have been shaped like a lamb. Jacob paid Hamor of Shechem a hundred kesitah for a parcel of land (Gen. 33:19; sheep, REB). At the end of Job's encounter with God, his friends brought him a kesitah and a ring of gold (Job 42:11).

Mina — A weight equal to about 50 common shekels, similar to the Canaanite system (1 Kin. 10:17; Ezra 2:69; pound, KJV). Ezekiel 45:12 seeks to redefine the weight (maneh, KJV, NASB), to equal 60 shekels, as in the Mesopotamian system. In Daniel 5:25 the words *Mene, Mene, Tekel, Upharsin* may be interpreted as a play on monetary values of that day ("Mina,

mina, shekel, and half shekels"). The phrase, then, may refer to the Babylonian rulers Nebuchadnezzar, Nabonidus, and Belshazzar, implying that they were decreasing in importance.

The mina is used in Luke 19:13, 16 (pound, NRSV, NEB) to refer to approximately a pound of money. "So he called ten of his servants, delivered to them ten minas, and said to them, 'Do business till I come'" (v. 13).

Pound — A Roman weight of about 340 grams, or 12 ounces (John 12:3). This term is used in the NKJV to designate the pound of precious ointments used to anoint Christ. The same word is also used to describe the amount of myrrh and aloes used to anoint the body of Christ in John 19:39.

Shekel — The most common weight in the Hebrew system (Josh. 7:21; Ezek. 4:10). The shekel weighed about 11.4 grams, or less than half an ounce. Its use was so common that in Genesis 20:16, the Hebrew text states "a thousand pieces of silver" without even bothering to specify shekel.

The shekel of the sanctuary (Ex. 30:13; Ezek. 45:12) was said to weigh 20 gerahs, the same weight as the common shekel. It is possible that the standard for the common shekel was kept at the sanctuary and became known as the sanctuary shekel. There is no clear reference to the use of the heavy shekel in Israel, but the shekel of the king's standard (the royal shekel) is referred to in 2 Samuel 14:26.

Pim — A weight that apparently weighed about two-thirds of a shekel (1 Sam. 13:21). This verse is difficult to translate accurately, but it probably should read "and the charge ... was a pim for the ploughshares." This charge is not mentioned in the KJV.

Bekah — One-half shekel. The bekah was the weight in silver that was paid by each Israelite as a religious tax (Ex. 30:13; 38:26). The bekah, spelled beka in some translations, is named only once in English translations (Ex. 38:26), but is referred to more often (Gen. 24:22; Ex. 30:13, 15).

Gerah — The smallest of the Israelite weights. The Bible defines it as one-twentieth of a shekel (Ex. 30:13; Lev. 27:25).

Measures. Measurements recorded in the Bible are of 3 types: (1) measures of volume, which told the amount of dry commodity (for example, flour) or liquid (for example, oil) that could be contained in a vessel; (2) measures of length, for height, width, and depth of an object or person; and (3) measures of total area, which described the size of a building, field, or city.

Measures of Volume. Measurements of volume were originally made by estimated handfuls. Eventually containers (jars, baskets, etc.), which held an agreed upon number of handfuls, were used as the standard measure. The terms used for such measures were frequently taken from the name of the containers.

The Israelites adapted the Mesopotamian system of measure of volume from the Canaanites. Their system contained several major designations for measuring dry volume.

Homer — The standard unit for dry measure (Ezek. 45:11–14; Hos. 3:2). This unit contained about 220 liters (6 one-quarter bushels). It was a large measure weighing the equivalent of the normal load a donkey could carry (the Hebrew word for "donkey" is *hamor*). In Leviticus 27:16, a homer of barley is worth 50 shekels of silver. In Numbers 11:32 God provided quail so generously for his people that they could gather 10 homers of them. Isaiah's prophecy of only an ephah of wheat from a homer of seed was a sign of God's judgment (Is. 5:10).

Kor — The same size as the homer (Ezek. 45:14, cor; measure, KJV). The kor was used to measure flour (1 Kin. 4:22), wheat, and barley (2 Chr. 2:10; 27:5).

Ephah — a unit equal to one-tenth of a homer (Ex. 29:40; deal, KJV; Is. 5:10).

Seah — a unit of uncertain capacity, but one-third of an ephah is probably correct (1 Sam. 25:18; 1 Kin. 7:1; measure, KJV, NRSV, REB, NASB).

Omer — a unit equal to one-tenth of an ephah (Ex. 16:36). The Hebrew word, *issaron*, "one-tenth of an ephah" (Ex. 29:40; Lev. 14:10; Num. 15:4), was a dry measure of similar size to the omer.

Kab — a unit containing about 1.2 liters or 1.16 quarts. The kab is mentioned only once in the Bible (2 Kin. 6:25). During the Syrian siege of Samaria, prices were inflated so badly that one-fourth of a kab of dove's dung was sold for 5 pieces of silver.

The New Testament contains 4 major designations for measuring dry capacity. These Greek words are not mentioned in the English translations of the New Testament.

Koros — (Luke 16:7; measure, NKJV, KJV, NRSV, NASB; bushel, REB, NIV) was a measure of wheat equal to about 453 liters (13 bushels).

Modios — (Matt. 5:15; Mark 4:21; Luke 11:33; basket, NKJV; bushel, KJV, NRSV) contained about 9 liters (one-quarter bushel).

Saton — (Matt. 13:33; Luke 13:21; measure, NKJV, KJV, NRSV; bushel, REB; peck, NASB; large amount, NIV) contained about 13 liters (three-eighths bushel).

Choinix — (Rev. 6:6; quart, NKJV; measure, KJV) contained about 1.1 liters (1 quart).

The Old Testament contained 5 major designations for liquid measure. The homer (Ezek. 45:11–14), containing 10 baths, was the largest liquid measure. The kor was the same size as the homer (Ezek. 45:14). The bath was the equivalent in liquid measure to the ephah in dry measure (Ezek. 45:11, 14). It was the standard liquid measure, equaling about 22 liters (5.83 gallons). It was used to measure water (1 Kin. 7:26), wine (Is. 5:10), and oil (2 Chr. 2:10). The hin, equal to one-sixth of a bath, was used to measure water (Ezek. 4:11), oil (Ex. 29:40), and wine

(Lev. 23:13). One-sixth of a hin was considered the daily ration of water (Ezek. 4:11). The log, found only in Leviticus 14:10–24, was a measure of oil in the ceremony for the purification of a leper. The log was equal to one-twelfth of a hin.

The New Testament contains 3 major terms for liquid measure. These words appear in Greek manuscripts but are translated by different words in English versions of the Bible.

The largest of these measures was the metretes (John 2:6; gallon, NKJV; firkin, KJV; water-jar, REB). Batos (Luke 16:6; measures, NKJV, KJV; gallons, REB, NIV) was the next smaller measure. Xestes (Mark 7:4, 8; pitcher, NKJV; pot, KJV; copper pot, NASB; hundred jars, REB; kettles, NIV; bronze kettles, NRSV) was the smallest unit of liquid measure.

Measures of Length. Linear measure, as with other units of measure, was originally based upon parts of the body, such as the hand, arm, or foot. Sometimes the unit was named for the part of the body it represented (palm, finger, etc.). Early linear distances were also based upon common but difficult-to-define objects, such as the step, bowshot, or a day's journey. By New Testament times, the Greek and Roman influences had caused these measures to be defined quite clearly.

Lengths were measured by various devices, including the measuring line (Zech. 2:1), measuring rod or measuring reed (Ezek. 40:5), and the meteyard (Lev. 19:35, KJV).

Several units expressing measurements of length are mentioned in the Bible.

Cubit — The distance from the elbow to the fingertip— about 45 centimeters (18 inches). The cubit was the standard unit of length. It was the common designation of the height of a man (1 Sam. 17:4) or an object (Ezek. 40:5). There was more than one size cubit, for the bed of Og, king of Bashan, is described "according to the standard cubit" (Deut. 3:11), while Ezekiel's measuring rod extended "six cubits long, each being a cubit and a handbreadth" (Ezek. 40:5). The long cubit was probably 51.8 centimeters (20.4 inches). The cubit is mentioned several times in the New Testament (Luke 12:25; Rev. 21:17). In each case it probably refers to the common cubit.

Rod/Reed — Units of measure equal to 6 cubits. The rod (Ezek. 40:5) and the reed (Ezek. 29:6) appear to be interchangeable. (Ezekiel 40:5 specifies that this measure is according to the long cubit.)

Span — The distance between the extended thumb and the little finger (1 Sam. 17:4). The span was equivalent to one-half cubit.

Handbreadth — The width of the hand at the base of the four fingers (1 Kin. 7:26; 2 Chr. 4:5). The handbreadth was considered to be one-sixth of a cubit.

Finger — The smallest subdivision of the cubit, equal to one-fourth of a handbreadth (Jer. 52:21). The finger is also called the cubit.

Fathom — A Greek unit equal to the length of the outstretched arms, about 1.8 meters (6 feet), or 4 cubits (Acts 27:28).

Furlong — A distance equal to about 200 meters, or one-eighth of a mile (Rev. 14:20; two hundred miles, NRSV).

Mile — A Roman measurement of 1,000 paces (5 Roman feet to the pace), equaling about 1,477.5 meters, or 1,616 yards (Matt. 5:41).

Several less definite distances are expressed in the Bible. Before the Babylonian captivity, distance was expressed variously as "a bowshot" (Gen. 21:16), "the area plowed by a yoke (of oxen in a day)" (1 Sam. 14:14, footnote), "a day's journey" (Num. 11:31; 1 Kin. 19:4), "three days' journey" (Gen. 30:36; Ex. 3:18; 8:27; "a journey of three days" (Num. 10:33), "seven days' journey" (Gen. 31:23), or even "eleven days' journey" (Deut. 1:2). No one knows for sure the amount of these distances, but a "day's journey" has been estimated to be approximately 32 to 40 kilometers (20 to 25 miles).

The "Sabbath day's journey" (Acts 1:12) was the product of rabbinical exegesis of Exodus 16:29 and Numbers 35:5. The rabbis fixed the legal distance for travel on the Sabbath at 2,000 cubits.

Many modern English translations of the Bible often use modern measurements of length, such as feet and inches (Gen. 6:15–16, NIV), and yards (John 21:8, NASB, REB, NIV, NRSV).

Measures of Area. Measures of area are not well defined in the Bible. Sometimes an area was determined by the amount of land a pair of oxen could plow in a day (1 Sam. 14:14). According to the NKJV, this was considered to be about one-half of an acre. Another method of designating area was to estimate the space by the amount of seed required to sow it (Lev. 27:16).

WINTER — the season between autumn and spring. In Palestine winters usually were short and mild, but snow and hail sometimes occurred in higher elevations (Jer. 18:14). Winter is also known as the rainy season in Palestine (Song 2:11).

WINTER HOUSE — a section of the palace of King Jehoiakim exposed to the sun and used in wintertime because of its warmth (Jer. 36:22; winter apartments, REB, NIV).

YARMUK [YAHR muck] — a river, or wadi, on the eastern side of the Jordan River valley close to the southern end of the Sea of Galilee. The Yarmuk is not mentioned in the Bible, although numerous biblical events happened in its vicinity.

YEAR — the period of time required for the earth to complete a single revolution around the sun. The year of the Hebrew people consisted of 12 months (1 Kin. 4:7; 1 Chr. 27:1–5). These months were based on the changing cycles of the moon. Such a year would contain about 354 days. Periodically a 13th month had to be added to the Hebrew calendar to make up for this discrepancy of time.

YHWH — the Hebrew name of the God of Israel, probably originally pronounced Yahweh. Eventually the Jews gave up pronouncing it, considering the name too holy for human lips. Instead they said *Adonai* or "Lord." This oral tradition came to be reflected in the written Greek translation of the Old Testament as *kurios* or "Lord," and it is often so quoted in the New Testament (Mark 1:3; Rom. 4:8). English versions of the Old Testament also tend to translate this word as "LORD."

There is also a shorter form, YAH (Ps. 68:4; Is. 12:2; 26:4; 38:11). In Exodus 3:14–16 YHWH is linked with the verb *hayah*, "to be," probably referring to the presence of God with His people (Ex. 3:12).

Z

ZEALOT [ZELL uht] (*devoted supporter*) — a nickname given to Simon, one of Jesus' 12 apostles (Luke 6:15; Acts 1:13), perhaps to distinguish him from Simon Peter. Simon the Zealot is also called Simon the Canaanite (Matt. 10:4; Mark 3:18; Cananaean, NRSV; Simon the Zealot, REB). The Aramaic form of the name means "to be jealous" or "zealous."

Simon was given this name probably because he had been a member of a Jewish political party known as the Zealots. A Zealot was a member of a fanatical Jewish sect that militantly opposed the Roman domination of Palestine during the 1st century A.D. When the Jews rebelled against the Romans in A.D. 66 and tried to gain their independence, the "Zealots" were in the forefront of the revolt. They thought of themselves as following in the footsteps of men like Simeon and Levi (Gen. 34:1–31), Phinehas (Num. 25:1–13), and Elijah (1 Kin. 18:40; 19:10–14) who were devoted supporters of the Lord and His laws and who were ready to fight for them.

Like the Pharisees, the Zealots were devoted to the Jewish law and religion. But unlike most Pharisees, they thought it was treason against God to pay tribute to the Roman emperor, since God alone was Israel's king. They were willing to fight to the death for Jewish independence.

The Zealots eventually degenerated into a group of assassins known as Sicarii (Latin, daggermen). Their increasing fanaticism was one factor that provoked the Roman–Jewish war. The Zealots took control of Jerusalem in A.D. 66, a move that led to the siege of Jerusalem and its fall in A.D. 70. The last stronghold of the Zealots, the fortress of Masada, fell to the Romans in A.D. 73.

ZEBULUN, TRIBE OF — the tribe that sprang from Zebulun, son of Jacob (Num. 1:9; Deut. 27:13; Josh. 19:10, 16; Judg. 1:30). The tribe was divided into 3 great families headed by Zebulun's 3 sons (Num. 26:26–27). At the first census taken in the wilderness, the tribe numbered 57,400 fighting men (Num. 1:30–31). The second census included 60,500 members of the tribe of Zebulun (Num. 26:27).

Zebulun played an important role in Israel's history during the period of the Judges. Its fighting men were an important part of Barak's force against Sisera (Judg. 4:6–10; 5:14, 18) and of Gideon's army against the Midianites (Judg. 6:35). Elon the Zebulunite judged Israel for 10 years (Judg. 12:12). At Hebron, 50,000 Zebulunites joined the other tribes in proclaiming David king (1 Chr. 12:33, 40).

Although Zebulun suffered during the Assyrian wars, when Tiglath-Pileser carried away captives to Assyria (2 Kin. 15:29), Isaiah prophesied that in the future Zebulun would be greatly blessed: "The land of Zebulun and the land of Naphtali ... in Galilee of the Gentiles. The people who walked in darkness have seen a great light; those who dwelt in the land of the shadow of death, upon them a light has shined" (Is. 9:1–2). According to the Gospel of Matthew, this prophecy was fulfilled when Jesus began His Galilean ministry (Matt. 4:12–17). Nazareth, Jesus' hometown, and Cana, where He performed His first miracle, both lay in the territory of Zebulun.

ZIGGURAT [ZIG guh rat] — an ancient Mesopotamian temple tower consisting of a lofty pyramid-like structure built in successive stages with outside staircases and a shrine at the top.

The ziggurat was an architectural form common to the Sumerians, Babylonians, and Assyrians from about 2000 to 600 B.C. The ancient ziggurat at Uris typical of others built in this part of the world. It is a massive, solid structure with a mud-brick core and fired-brick shell. This tower originally stood to a height of about 21 meters (70 feet) above the plain, although only about 15 meters (50 feet) of the lowest platform now remains. At the summit was a shrine of Nannar, the moon god.

The ziggurat was thought to symbolize a mountain, with the temple on top bridging the gap that separates humanity from the gods. The Tower of Babel (Gen. 11:1–9) is thought by many scholars to be a ziggurat.

ZIV [zihv] — the eighth month of the civil year and the second month of the sacred year in the Hebrew calendar (1 Kin. 6:1, 37; Zif, KJV).

ZOROASTRIANISM [zoe roh ASS tree un ism] — the religious system founded in Persia by the prophet Zoroaster, or Zarathustra (6th century B.C.) and set forth in the Avesta, or Zend-Avesta, but with many additions. Zoroastrianism is characterized by worship of Ahura Mazda (also known as Ormazd or Ormuzd), the Supreme Being represented as a spirit of light, truth, and goodness.

Ahura Mazda is opposed by an archrival, Ahriman (or Angra Mainyu), a spirit of darkness, falsehood, and evil. Thus the human soul becomes a seat of war between the dualistic forces of good and evil. Ahura Mazda requires people's good deeds for help in this cosmic struggle against Ahriman. The struggle is desperate and bitter—the children of light against the children of darkness. Zoroaster taught, however, that eventually Ahura Mazda will defeat Ahriman and good will triumph over evil.

Zoroastrianism has barely survived in its homeland. Fewer than 10,000 persons in Iran (ancient Persia) practice the religion today. A larger group has survived in India under the name Parseeism. The present-day Parsees of India are descendants of Persians who moved there from Persia several centuries before the birth of Christ.